# MOON HANDBOOKS®
# BUENOS AIRES

Colonial Cabildo, Plaza de Mayo, Monserrat

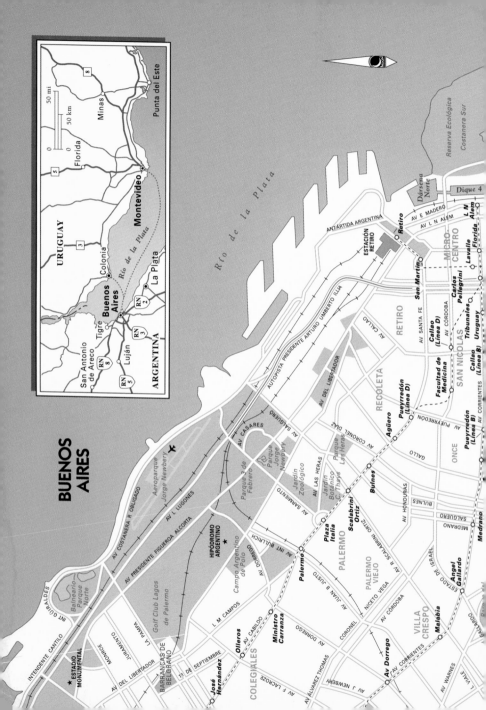

Cabildo Rose Garden and Basílica de Luján, Buenos Aires province

# MOON HANDBOOKS®
# BUENOS AIRES

### FIRST EDITION

## WAYNE BERNHARDSON

**AVALON
TRAVEL**

# MAPS

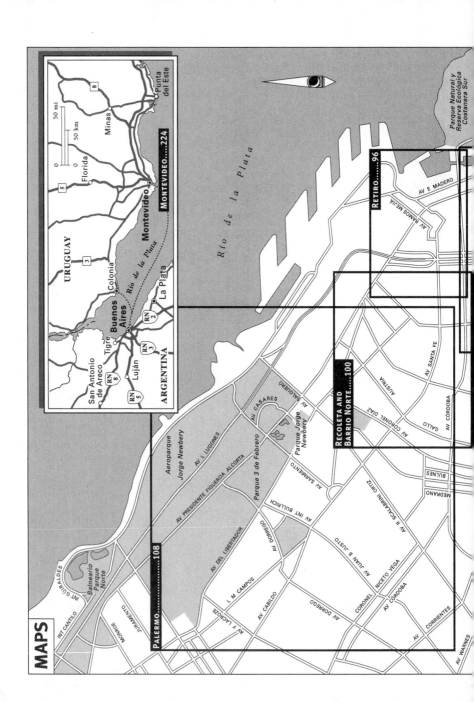

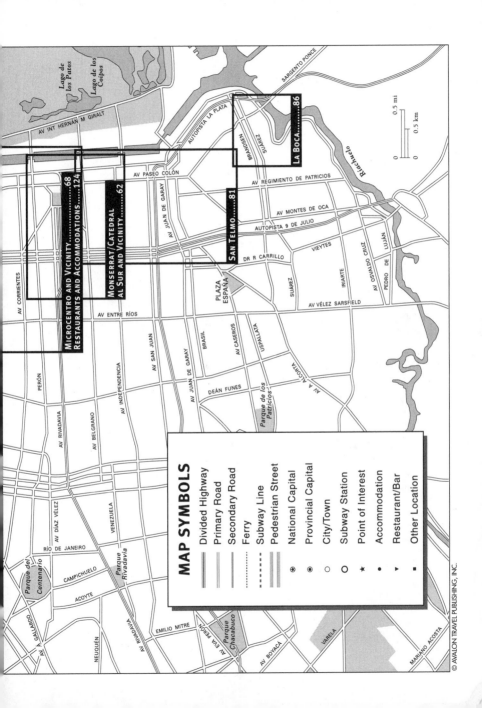

MICROCENTRO AND VICINITY............68
RESTAURANTS AND ACCOMMODATIONS....124

MONSERRAT/CATEDRAL
AL SUR AND VICINITY......62

SAN TELMO......81

LA BOCA......86

## MAP SYMBOLS

| | |
|---|---|
| ▬▬▬ | Divided Highway |
| ▬▬ | Primary Road |
| ▬ | Secondary Road |
| ⋯⋯ | Ferry |
| ▬▬▬ | Subway Line |
| ▬▬▬ | Pedestrian Street |
| ⊛ | National Capital |
| ◉ | Provincial Capital |
| ○ | City/Town |
| ◯ | Subway Station |
| ★ | Point of Interest |
| • | Accommodation |
| ▶ | Restaurant/Bar |
| ■ | Other Location |

# Contents

© WAYNE BERNHARDSON

## Introduction ..........................................................1

*A New World city to rival the capitals of the Old World, this "Paris of the South" features broad avenues, colossal monuments, and mansard-capped mansions. Through spectacular growth as well as economic misfortune, the* porteños' *zest for life has helped their city retain its identity and cosmopolitan flavor.*

## Travel Basics ..........................................................24

*Need the lowdown on getting there, getting around, what to bring, and what the devaluation of the peso really means for travelers? It's all here.*

# Sights

*Like New York City, this is a city of neighborhoods—48 in all. Colorful streetlife abounds, with plentiful murals, open-air markets, and innumerable museums. Explore the tango bars and antique shops of San Telmo, experience the prime dining and nightlife in Recoleta, and relax in Palermo's parks.*

Monserrat/Catedral al Sur and Vicinity; Microcentro and Vicinity; Puerto Madero; San Telmo and Vicinity; La Boca; Once and the Abasto (Balvanera); Caballito and Vicinity; Retiro; Recoleta and Barrio Norte; Palermo; Belgrano; Outer Barrios

# Accommodations

*Hostels,* hospedajes, casas de huéspedes, *internationally recognized hotels—from simple to luxurious, Buenos Aires offers places for every traveler and every budget.*

Camping; Hostels; Budget Accommodations; Mid-Range Accommodations; High-End Accommodations

# Food and Drink

*The Spanish and Italian traditions have long influenced Argentine cuisine, and many other once-exotic world cuisines continue to crop up on menus throughout the city. Be sure to try Argentina's great wines, and partake in the ritual drinking of yerba mate.*

Where to Eat; What to Eat and Drink; Restaurants

# Arts and Entertainment

*Music, literature, art, and architecture have strong traditions here, thriving even as the economy suffers. A lively rock music scene, innovative galleries, theaters, and tango venues delight visitors, day or night.*

**FINE ARTS**
Literature; Visual Arts; Architecture; Music and Dance; Cinema; Theater; Arts and Crafts

# Sports and Recreation ...................................... 184

*Sports also thrive here: Check out the rugged Argentine style of polo or the traditional gaucho game,* pato. *And what better place to catch a* fútbol *match than soccer-mad Buenos Aires?*

# Shopping ...................................................... 191

*The city is known for its antiques, silver, and leather goods ... this chapter is where you'll find the best selections in bargain, upscale, and trendy stores.*

# Excursions from Buenos Aires ...................... 201

*Porteños escape city life by heading to gaucho country, the forested channels of Tigre, or across the river to Uruguay's capital, Montevideo, and the beaches of Punta del Este. Here's your chance to join them.*

# Resources

# ABOUT THE AUTHOR
# Wayne Bernhardson

© WAYNE BERNHARDSON

Wayne Bernhardson first traveled to Buenos Aires in 1981 during a military dictatorship. He has stuck with the Argentine capital through good times and bad, returning repeatedly to broaden and deepen his knowledge of and appreciation for both the city and the country in general. He has been successful enough that *porteños* constantly stop him in the street to ask directions. Wayne owns an apartment near the botanical gardens in Palermo.

Having authored best-selling guides to Chile, Argentina, Buenos Aires, Santiago de Chile, and Baja California, Wayne earned a Ph.D. in geography at the University of California, Berkeley before forsaking academia for a life on the road that many university faculty envy. This is his third Moon Handbook, following *Moon Handbooks Guatemala* (2001) and *Moon Handbooks Chile* (2002).

Wayne has also written for magazines and newspapers including *Trips,* the *San Francisco Chronicle,* the American Geographical Society's *Focus, Travel Holiday,* and *National Geographic Traveler,* and he often gives slide lectures on destinations he covers in his books.

When not in Buenos Aires, he resides in Oakland, California with his wife María Laura Massolo, their daughter Clio Bernhardson-Massolo, their Alaskan malamute Gardel, named for the famous Argentine tango singer (Gardel barks better every day!), and their recently adopted Japanese Akita Sandro (named for a contemporary Argentine pop singer). Wayne can be reached directly by email at knoblauch @earthlink.net or through www.guidebookwriters.com.

# Introduction

Cosmopolitan Buenos Aires, the first Latin American city to have a million inhabitants, may still be South America's most interesting city. Since its origin as a Spanish imperial backwater, it has experienced extraordinary transformations: massive post-independence immigration and increasing prosperity changed Argentina's capital from an intimate *Gran Aldea* (Great Village) into "The Paris of the South," with its broad avenues, colossal monuments, and mansard-capped mansions.

For much of the 20th century, though, Buenos Aires underwent a steady decline, interrupted by spectacular growth spurts and even more spectacular economic and political misfortunes. Yet somehow, like its melancholy traditional music

and dance—the tango—it has retained its identity and mystique.

Despite Buenos Aires's cosmopolitan outlook, many of its inhabitants, known as *porteños* (port residents), still identify strongly with their own *barrios* (neighborhoods) in the Gran Aldea. Like New Yorkers, they are often assertive to the point of brashness, and have a characteristic accent that sets them apart from the people of Argentina's other provinces.

Every *Baires* neighborhood has a distinctive personality. The compact, densely built "Microcentro" boasts the major shopping and theater districts, as well as the capital's version of Wall Street—"La City." Immediately to the south, in

The Argentine flag flies between the Casa Rosada (presidential palace, right) and Edificio Libertador (army headquarters, left).

the barrio of Monserrat, the Avenida de Mayo is the city's civic axis—the site of spectacle and debacle in Argentina's tumultuous 20th-century politics; Monserrat gives way to the cobbled colonial streets of San Telmo, with its tango bars and famous flea market at Plaza Dorrego. Farther south is the working-class outpost of La Boca, also an artists' colony known for the Caminito, its colorful curving pedestrian mall.

Northern neighborhoods like Retiro and Recoleta are more elegant and even opulent— so much so that many affluent Argentines have elected to spend eternity at the Cementerio de la Recoleta, one of the world's most exclusive graveyards. Beyond Recoleta, the parks of Palermo were once the province of 19th-century despot Juan Manuel de Rosas, but much of the barrio itself has become a middle- to upper-middle-class area with some of the city's finest dining and wildest night life. North of Palermo, the woodsy barrio of Belgrano is a mostly residential area that fancies itself not just a suburb or a separate city, but a republic in itself—and it was in fact briefly Argentina's capital.

When *porteños* tire of the city, there are plenty of nearby escapes both within Buenos Aires province and beyond it. Built on a grid resembling that of Washington, D.C., the streets of the provincial capital of La Plata, only an hour to the southeast, feature imposing architecture and cultural resources (including theaters and museums) that many national capitals cannot match.

An hour west of Buenos Aires, the city of Luján, with its towering basilica, is a major pilgrimage destination and also boasts an impressive complex of historical museums. Another half-hour west, San Antonio de Areco is Argentina's symbolic gaucho capital.

Truly unique, though, are the intricate channels of the Río Paraná delta, easily reached by launch from the increasingly fashionable northern suburb of Tigre, itself easily reached by train. One of the highlights is the island of Martín García, a colonial fortress and onetime prison camp that offers nature trails and historic architecture.

For those wishing to go farther afield, daily ferries cross the Río de la Plata to the Uruguayan destinations of Carmelo (a riverside resort), Colonia (a UNESCO World Heritage Site), the capital city of Montevideo (a repository of colonial and art deco architecture), and the Atlantic beach resort of Punta del Este (a favored vacation spot for Argentines until the recent crisis).

All in all, despite Argentina's problems, the megalopolis of Buenos Aires and its hinterlands still have much to offer the adventurous urban explorer. Like New York, Buenos Aires never sleeps. For catering to diverse interests, it's one of the most underrated destinations on an underrated continent—notwithstanding the fact that, in the midst of the economic crisis of 2001–2002, *Travel & Leisure* named it the top tourist city in Latin America.

## The Land

Buenos Aires sits atop the coastal margin of the almost unrelentingly flat, fertile La Pampa region, whose beef and grain exports made Argentina a wealthy country throughout much of the 19th and 20th centuries. The city has little relief—its highest elevation is only about 25 meters—except along the original *barrancas* or riverbanks, which now lie well inland because of landfill along the muddy estuary of the Río de la Plata. The only other significant body of water is the heavily polluted Riachuelo, a tributary that forms part of the city's southern

boundary; the densely built city has covered all the smaller arroyos.

The Río de la Plata, misleadingly glossed into English as the River Plate (it literally means the River of Silver), is one of the world's great river systems. It is in a class with the Amazon, the Nile, and the Mississippi in terms of length, width, and flow. Originating in the heights of the Bolivian altiplano and draining an area of more than 3.1 million square kilometers, it is in reality an estuary at the confluence of the Río Paraná (length 3,945 km) and the Río Uruguay (length 1,650 km).

Its delta, northwest of Buenos Aires proper, is a series of islands in a maze of muddy channels whose sedimentary surface is largely covered by dense gallery forest. The combined waters of the Paraná and Uruguay carry sediments far out into the southern Atlantic Ocean.

## GEOGRAPHY

The Ciudad Autónoma de Buenos Aires is a compact, politically autonomous federal district surrounded by contiguous suburbs of Buenos Aires province. It occupies 192 square kilometers on the right bank of the Río de la Plata.

Together with the federal capital, the conurbation of Gran Buenos Aires (Greater Buenos Aires) includes 24 contiguous and surrounding *partidos* (roughly translatable as counties): Almirante Brown, Avellaneda, Berazategui, Estéban Echeverría, Ezeiza, Florencio Varela, General San Martín, Hurlingham, Ituzaingó, José C. Paz, La Matanza, Lanús, Lomas de Zamora, Malvinas Argentinas, Merlo, Moreno, Morón, Quilmes, San Fernando, San Isidro, San Miguel, Tigre, Tres de Febrero, and Vicente López.

> *Because it is in the southern hemisphere, Buenos Aires's seasons are reversed from those in the northern hemisphere. For most Argentines, the summer months are January and February, when schools are out of session and families take their holidays.*

## CLIMATE

Because it is in the southern hemisphere, Buenos Aires's seasons are reversed from those in the northern hemisphere: the summer solstice falls on December 21, the autumnal equinox on March 21, the winter solstice on June 21, and the vernal equinox on September 21. For most Argentines, the summer months are January and February, when schools are out of session and families take their holidays.

Thanks to its midlatitude setting (34° 37' S) and proximity to the Atlantic Ocean, Buenos Aires's climate is humid and temperate, with annual precipitation of about 1.2 meters distributed evenly throughout the year. It resembles southern parts of the eastern seaboard of the United States except in winter, when temperatures remain mild and frosts are rare. Summer can be uncomfortably hot and humid, as temperatures frequently exceed 30° C and thunderstorms are common. *Pamperos* (southwesterly cold fronts) and *sudestadas* (southeasterly cool high winds) are the most problematical climatic phenomena; snow is unheard of.

# Flora and Fauna

As one of the world's largest cities, Buenos Aires has no truly untouched natural habitat, but many birds, fish, and other wildlife survive among the gallery forests, channels, and oxbow lakes of the Río Paraná delta. Many of these plants and animals are opportunistic species that have colonized the former landfill east of Puerto Madero.

Like many other cities, the capital is home to unfortunately large numbers of stray dogs and even larger numbers of feral cats that infest areas like Palermo's *jardín botánico* (botanical garden). Because of their presence, the only bird species to survive in substantial numbers appears to be the pigeon.

## CONSERVATION ORGANIZATIONS

For information on protected areas, a few of which are in the vicinity of Buenos Aires, contact the Administración de Parques Nacionales, Avenida Santa Fe 680, Retiro, tel. 4312-0820, informes@parquesnacionales.gov.ar, www.parquesnacionales.gov.ar. Although its selection of brochures on national parks and other protected areas is improving, the staff is the best resource for information on the country's most high-profile destinations, such as Parque

Nacional Iguazú and Parque Nacional Los Glaciares. Hours are 10 A.M.–5 P.M. weekdays only.

The pro-wildlife advocacy organization Fundación Vida Silvestre Argentina is at Defensa 251, tel. 4331-4864, Monserrat, socios@vidasilvestre.org.ar, www.vidasilvestre.org.ar. Membership rates, including the newsletter *Otioso,* start around US$30 per annum; the US$90 membership also includes the foundation's magazine, *Revista Vida Silvestre.*

Bird-watchers will enjoy the Asociación Ornitológica del Plata at 25 de Mayo 749, 2nd floor, in the Microcentro, tel. 4312-8958, www.avesargentinas.org.ar, info@avesargentinas .org.ar; hours are 3–9 P.M. weekdays.

The Argentine branch of Greenpeace is at Mansilla 3046, Barrio Norte, tel. 4962-2291, www.greenpeace.org.ar.

# FLORA

The main trees of the Río Paraná delta gallery forest are medium-size species such the contorted *ceibo* (*Erythrina crytagalli*), whose blossom is Argentina's national flower; the *sauce criollo* (*Salix humboldtiana*), a native willow; and canelón (*Rapanea iaetevirens*).

Seasonally flooded areas along the river feature sizeable marshes of large herbaceous plants like rushes, totora reeds, cattails, and bunch grasses. There are also "floating islands" of aquatic vegetation in calm, protected areas of the delta.

# FAUNA

## Marine, Coastal, and Aquatic Fauna

In the murky, sediment-filled waters of the La Plata estuary, it can be difficult to spot any kind of aquatic fauna, but in the water hide oceangoing fish species like the yellow corvina (*Micropogonias furnieri*) and the black corvina (*Pogonias cromis*), as well as crustaceans such as crabs and shellfish such as mussels. The outstanding marine mammal is the La Plata river dolphin (*Pontoporia blainvillei*). The nutria, or La Plata river otter (*Lutra platensis*), is also present here and farther up the estuary.

## Terrestrial and Freshwater Fauna

In the upper reaches of the Plata estuary, as far as the confluence of the Paraná and the Uruguay, freshwater game fish like the *boga* (*Leporinus obtusidens*), *dorado* (*Salminus brasiliensis*), *sábalo* (*Prochilodus platensis*), *surubí* (*Pseudoplatystoma coruscans*), and *tararirá* (*Hoplias malabaricus*) mix with some of the oceanic species.

Marshes along the river provide habitat for mammals like the *carpincho* or capybara (*Hydrochoerus capybara*, a rottweiler-sized rodent) and the marsh deer *Blastocerus dichotomus.* The amphibian *rana criolla,* or Creole frog, (*Leptodactylus ocellatus*) is large (up to 130 mm in length), and meaty enough that it is occasionally eaten.

## Birds

In the gallery forests along the La Plata estuary, common birds include the *boyero negro* or black cacique, an oriole-like species that breeds in hanging nests; the rufous-capped antshrike (*Thamnophilus ruficapillus*); and *pava de monte* (*Penelope obscura*) or black guan. Typical aquatic species include coots, ducks, and swans.

Marshland species include the *junquero* or marsh wren (*Phleocryptes melanops*), the polychromatic *sietecolores* (literally, "seven colors," *Thraupis bonariensis*), and the striking *federal,* with black plumage crowned by a scarlet hood. There are also several species of rails and crakes.

## Invertebrates

In such a dense urban environment, of course, the most conspicuous invertebrates are usually cockroaches, flies, and mosquitoes, but Buenos Aires is free of contagious insect-borne diseases like malaria and dengue. Nonetheless, in well watered rural areas like the Paraná delta, mosquitoes can be a real plague, so a good repellent is imperative.

# The Cultural Landscape

In immediate pre-Columbian times, bands of nomadic Querandí hunter-gatherers peopled what is now Buenos Aires and its surrounding pampas. Living in smallish bands with no permanent settlements, they relied on wild game like the guanaco (a relative of the domestic llama) and the flightless ostrichlike *ñandú* (rhea), as well as fish for subsistence. What remains of their material culture is primarily lithic (arrowheads, spearpoints, and the rounded stone balls known as *boleadoras*) and ceramic.

## AGRICULTURE AND THE LANDSCAPE

The arrival of the Spaniards, of course, led to major transformations. Though their initial efforts at colonizing the pampas failed because of Querandí resistance and their own poor preparation, feral European livestock—cattle and horses—proliferated almost beyond belief on the nearly virgin grasslands. By the late 19th century, large rural estates known as *estancias* produced hides, beef, and then wool for export to Europe via Buenos Aires; in the 20th century, Argentine agriculture diversified with grain exports. The pattern of large rural landholdings persists in the province of Buenos Aires, but the capital has expanded onto lands that were only recently agricultural.

## SETTLEMENT LANDSCAPES

Cities, of course, differ greatly from the countryside. By royal decree, Spanish cities in the New World were organized according to a rectangular grid surrounding a central plaza where all the major public institutions—*cabildo* (town council), cathedral, and market—were located. Buenos Aires was no exception to the rule; though the transformation from colonial city to modern metropolis obliterated some of these landmarks, the essential grid pattern remains.

Traditionally, in colonial barrios such as San Telmo, houses fronted directly on the street or sidewalk, with interior patios or gardens exclusively for family use; houses set back from the street were almost unheard of. This pattern has largely continued to the present, though materials have changed from adobe to reinforced concrete and multistory apartment buildings have replaced traditionally low-slung structures.

Though it's rare to find houses with large yards or gardens of the North American suburban model in the capital city, they're common enough in the northern suburbs and a few other areas—often surrounded by high fences and state-of-the-art security.

## Environmental Issues

Like other global megacities, the Capital Federal and its suburbs suffer from environmental degradation, though not all indicators are negative.

### Air Pollution

Buenos Aires's aging diesel buses may be the primary culprit in the capital's declining air quality, but private vehicles (some of which still run on leaded gasoline) and taxis contribute more than their share. Superannuated factories, with their subsidized smokestacks, are another source.

One advantage that Buenos Aires has over some other cities is the frequency of rain and even thunderstorms that clear pollutants from the air. Storms, hovever, also ensure that airborne pollutants hit the ground and drain onto city streets and eventually into the waterways.

### Water Pollution

Buenos Aires may have potable drinking water, but the success of the hides and livestock industry, and then of heavy industry, has left a legacy of polluted waterways. The textbook example is the Riachuelo, in the working-class barrio of La Boca. Its water more closely resembles sludge than water; its bottom sediments, thanks to chemical runoff from factories in La Boca and in nearby Avellaneda, are an even greater toxic hazard. To give credit where it's due, there has been progress in removing rusting hulks from the Vuelta de Rocha, near the popular tourist area of Caminito, but that's the easy part.

### Noise Pollution

Just as motor vehicles cause most of the city's air pollution, they produce most of its noise pollution, due partly to inadequate mufflers. According to one study, vehicular noise accounts for 80 percent of levels that, at corners like Rivadavia and Callao, reach upwards of 80 decibels.

Aeroparque Jorge Newbery, the capital's domestic airport, rates highly for convenience and accessibility, but noisy jet takeoffs and landings are particularly bothersome to residents of Palermo and Belgrano. Interestingly enough, it's these upper-class barrios and not working-class neighborhoods, that have to put up with these high decibel levels. But plans to close Aeroparque are on the table.

### Solid Waste

Like other megacities, Buenos Aires produces prodigious amounts of garbage. In 2001, the total monthly amounts ranged from a minimum of 123,974 tons in February to 142,290 in March; for Gran Buenos Aires, the corresponding figures were 292,038 tons in September and 338,455 tons in January. The highest cumulative totals were 478,628 tons in January, the lowest 417,882 in September.

According to the daily *Página 12,* citing the municipal waste management agency Ceamse, *porteños* produce an average of 1.357 kg per day of solid waste; this February 2002 figure, however, was down from 1.735 kg per capita only four months earlier—apparently because of the severe economic recession. A partial explanation was that people were buying fewer items with expensive packaging, but also that 35,000 *cartoneros* or *cirujas* (the latter an ironic *lunfardo* (slang) term derived from the Spanish word for "surgeon," but meaning "street scavengers") were spontaneously recycling items left for streetside pickup.

Municipal authorities are attempting to do away with this practice, which often results in garbage-strewn streets and sidewalks, by creating a formal recycling program that would hire the scavengers to separate recyclables. They are also beginning to require city residents to separate these materials in the bags they place on the streets nightly.

There is a dark side to recycling, however. Some *cartoneros*—apparently in league with criminal elements—have absconded with valuable bronze and other precious metals that cover utility boxes and similar objects accessible from the street. Sold and melted into ingots, the stolen items are almost untraceable.

Another sort of solid waste is even more problematic. Greenpeace Argentina has protested an agreement with Australia to import that country's nuclear waste for reprocessing near Ezeiza. Argentina's constitution prohibits storage of nuclear waste, though Argentina has its own 357-megawatt Atucha I reactor near the town of Lima, northwest of the capital.

## Urban Forestry

Buenos Aires has some 375,000 street trees of more than 500 species. The *fresno* or European ash (*Fraxinus excelsior*) comprises nearly half the total, and the sycamore is the next most common. The distribution of trees, however, is uneven—the northern neighborhoods are woodsier—but even there, many specimens are in poor condition. Heavy thunderstorms often knock down branches and even entire trees.

Municipal authorities estimate that at least 110,000 additional trees would be desirable, but inadequate maintenance is working against the existing urban forests, and the economic crisis works against afforestation. A new law that permits private parties to plant their own street trees from a list of approved species could help close the gap.

## Energy

Argentina is self-sufficient in fossil fuels and has substantial hydroelectric resources in the subtropical north and along the Andean foothills, but Argentine governments have promoted nuclear power since the 1950s. Although the country has renounced any intention to build nuclear weapons, the 344-megawatt Atucha I reactor has powered the capital's electrical grid since 1974. For much of the time since then, it has operated at reduced capacity thanks partly to the availability of cheaper hydroelectricity, but also due to inadequate maintenance; the controling Comisión Nacional de Energía Atómica (CNEA, National Atomic Energy Commission) is not known for its transparency. Atucha I is due to close in 2014.

# History

Buenos Aires's origins are, in some ways, as murky as the muddy Río de la Plata. Everyone agrees that bands of Querandí hunter-gatherers roamed the southern banks of the river, but their encampments of *toldos* (tents of animal skins) shifted with the availability of game, fish, and other resources. No Querandí settlement could reasonably be called a city, a town, or even a village.

## THE FIRST BUENOS AIRES

Buenos Aires proper dates from January 1536, when the Spaniard Pedro de Mendoza, commanding a fleet of at least a dozen ships and perhaps as many as 2,500 men plus nearly 100 horses, landed on its shores. Mendoza came to establish a colony, but his summer arrival was too late for planting and the colonists suffered from food shortages during the cool, wet winter. Spanish demands for food and supplies provoked violent and effective Querandí opposition; within

five years, the insecure colonists abandoned their settlement.

Traditionally, Argentine histories place Mendoza's settlement on the *barrancas* (natural levees) of what is now Parque Lezama, in the barrio of San Telmo, and a monument to Mendoza is one of the park's highlights. Though it is now far inland, thanks to nearly five centuries of landfill, during Mendoza's time it directly fronted on the river.

*Porteño* author Federico Kirbus, however, has argued that Mendoza's expedition didn't land anywhere near Parque Lezama or even within the area that now comprises the Capital Federal. Instead, relying on historical accounts of the time complemented by field observations, he concludes that the first Buenos Aires may have been some distance up what is now the Paraná delta, closer to the provincial town of Escobar, before several centuries of sedimentary deposition would have filled in the river and complicated navigation for such a large fleet as Mendoza's. Although the evidence is circumstantial rather than definitive, it's an intriguing hypothesis.

## BUENOS AIRES BECOMES PERMANENT

While Mendoza's initial settlement failed, some members of his expedition sailed up the Paraná to found Asunción, capital of present-day Paraguay. Almost four decades later, in 1580, Juan de Garay led an expedition in the opposite direction to found Santa Fe; he also refounded Buenos Aires, settling 60 colonists in the vicinity of what is now the Plaza de Mayo. Garay fell victim to the Querandí within three years, but the settlement he established—peopled by *mancebos de la tierra* (offspring of Spaniards and native Guaraní)—survived.

On the muddy banks of the river, the location had little to recommend it as a port, but this was largely irrelevant—the new Buenos Aires was subordinate to Asunción, which was in turn subordinate to the Viceroyalty of Lima and the Spanish capital of Madrid via a long, indirect overland-and-maritime route. It took nearly two centuries for Buenos Aires, a backwater on the periphery of Spain's American empire, to match Lima's viceregal status.

## COLONIAL BUENOS AIRES

Barred from direct contact with Europe by Spain's mercantile bureaucracy, early colonial Buenos Aires had to survive on the resources of the sprawling pampas. The Querandí and other indigenous groups had subsisted on guanacos, rheas, and other game, in addition to edible fruits and plants they gathered, but these resources were inadequate and culturally inconceivable for the Spaniards.

The Mendoza expedition, however, had left behind horses that thrived on the lush but thinly populated pastures of the pampas, and the multiplication of escaped cattle from the Garay expedition soon transformed the Buenos Aires backcountry into a fenceless feral cattle ranch. The presence of horses and cattle, nearly free for the taking, resulted in the gaucho culture for which Argentina became famous. Hides were the primary product because they were durable; beef had little market value because it was perishable.

Buenos Aires had no easily accessible markets in which to sell their hides, though, because hides were too low-value a product to ship to Spain via Lima and Panama; consequently, there developed a vigorous contraband trade with British and Portuguese vessels in the secluded channels of the Paraná delta. As this trade grew, Spain acknowledged Buenos Aires's growing significance by making it capital of the newly created Virreinato del Río de la Plata (Viceroyalty of the River Plate) in 1776. Reflecting its significance and the need to curb a growing Portuguese influence in the region, the viceroyalty even included the bonanza silver district of Potosí in present-day Bolivia, then known as Alto Perú (Upper Peru).

The city's population, only about 500 in the early 17th century, grew slowly at first. By 1655, it was barely 4,000, and it took nearly a century to reach 10,000 in 1744. By the time of the new viceroyalty, though, the population exceeded 24,000, and nearly doubled again by the early 19th century. Open to European commerce as Madrid loosened its control, the livestock economy expanded with the development of *saladeros* or meat-salting plants, adding value to the beef that was almost worthless before.

Unlike the densely populated central Andean area, where the Spaniards established themselves atop an already hierarchical society and exploited the native population through tribute and forced labor, Buenos Aires did not have an abundant labor force. The improving economy and growing population—which consisted of peninsular

> *Unlike the densely populated central Andean area, where the Spaniards established themselves atop an already hierarchical society and exploited the native population through tribute and forced labor, Buenos Aires did not have an abundant labor force.*

Spaniards, *criollos* ("creoles," or American-born Spaniards), *indígenas* (indigenous people), and mestizos (the offspring of Spaniards and *indígenas*)—soon included African slaves. Increasing political autonomy and economic success quickly paved the way for the end of Spanish rule.

## The Dissolution of Colonial Argentina

Appointed by the Spanish crown, all major officials of the viceroyalty governed from Buenos Aires, and economic power was also concentrated there. Outside the capital and isolated by geographic barriers, provincial bosses created their own power bases. When Napoleon invaded Spain in the early 19th century, the glue that held together Spain's colonial possessions began to dissolve, leading to independence in several steps.

Contributing to the move toward independence was a changing sense of identity among the people of what is now Argentina. In the early generations, the Spanish settlers of course identified themselves as Spaniards, but over time *criollos* began to differentiate themselves from *peninsulares* (European-born Spaniards). It bears mention that while the mestizos and even the remaining indigenous population may have identified more closely with Argentina than with Spain, it was the criollo intelligentsia who found the Spanish yoke most oppressive, and to whom the notion of independence had the greatest appeal.

The South American independence movements commenced on the periphery, led by figures like Argentina's José de San Martín, Venezuela's Simón Bolívar, and Chile's Bernardo O'Higgins, but their heroism was built on a broad support base. In Buenos Aires, this base developed as opportunistic and unauthorized British forces took advantage of Spain's perceived weakness and occupied the city in 1806 and 1807.

As the shocked Viceroy Rafael de Sobremonte fled Buenos Aires for Córdoba, city residents organized a covert resistance that, under the leadership of the Frenchman Santiago de Liniers, dislodged the invaders. Based on the belief that Spain's legitimate government had fallen and as reflection of their confidence, the

*porteños* chose Liniers as viceroy in an open *cabildo*. The royalist Liniers, ironically enough, died at the hands of independence fighters during the Revolution of 1810.

Returning from Spain to Buenos Aires, San Martín led independence forces against royalist forces deployed from Peru, in what is now northwestern Argentina. In 1816, in the city of Tucumán, delegates of the Provincias Unidas del Río de la Plata (United Provinces of the River Plate) issued a formal declaration of independence. But this was only a loose confederation that glossed over differences between the "Federalist" *caudillos*—provincial landholders and warlords intent on preserving their fiefdoms—and the cosmopolitan "Unitarists" of Buenos Aires.

The struggle between Federalists and Unitarists was slow to resolve itself; in the words of historian James Scobie, "It took 70 years for Argentina to coalesce as a political unit." Even today, tensions between the provinces and the central government have not disappeared, but it took a Federalist to ensure the primacy of Buenos Aires.

## REPUBLICAN ARGENTINA AND BUENOS AIRES

After having achieved independence, the Provincias Unidas were less successful in creating institutions. Several attempts at agreeing upon a constitution failed, resulting in series of ministates that quarreled among themselves. In Buenos Aires, the largest of the provinces, Federalist caudillo Juan Manuel de Rosas took command and ruled from 1829 until his overthrow in 1852. The ruthless and shrewd Rosas did more than anyone else to ensure the primacy of the city which, nevertheless, did not become the country's capital until 1880.

By the time Rosas took power, Buenos Aires's population had grown to nearly 60,000; in 1855, only a few years after he left, it reached 99,000. In 1833, Charles Darwin (who admired the loyalty of Rosas's followers even as he questioned the dictator's ruthlessness) was impressed with the city's size and orderliness:

*Every street is at right angles to the one it crosses, and the parallel ones being equidistant, the houses are collected into solid squares of equal dimensions, which are called quadras. On the other hand the houses themselves are hollow squares; all the rooms opening into a neat little courtyard. They are generally only one story high, with flat roofs, which are fitted with seats, and are much frequented by the inhabitants in summer. In the centre of the town is the Plaza, where the public offices, fortress, cathedral, &c., stand. Here also, the old viceroys, before the revolution had their palaces. The general assemblage of buildings possesses considerable architectural beauty, although none individually can boast of any.*

In the early years of independence, Unitarist visionaries like Mariano Moreno and Bernardino Rivadavia had advocated an aggressive immigration policy to Europeanize the young republic, but Rosas's dictatorial rule, obstinate isolationism, and continual military adventures discouraged immigration. His defeat at the battle of Caseros in 1853 opened the country to immigration and accelerated the diversification of the economy from extensive *estancias* and *saladeros* to the more intensive production of wool and grains for export.

For the city, still a provincial rather than a national capital, this meant explosive growth—its population more than doubled to 230,000, by 1875. In 1880, when the other provinces forced the federalization of Buenos Aires, irate provincial authorities shifted their own capital to the new city of La Plata, but the newly designated federal capital continued to grow. By the early 20th century, it became the first Latin American city with more than a million inhabitants.

## THE PORTEÑOS GET A PORT

Unfortunately, for a fast-growing city of *porteños*, Buenos Aires was a poor natural port. Its muddy river banks and shallow waters made loading and unloading slow, laborious, expensive, and even hazardous, as freighters had to anchor in deep water and transfer their cargo to shallow-draft lighters. Before it could become a great commercial port, Buenos Aires would have to speed up a process that took months rather than weeks for the average steamship.

Everyone agreed port improvements were imperative, but there were different visions of how to accomplish them. Engineer Luis Huergo offered the simplest and most economical solution: to broaden, dredge, and straighten the Riachuelo to provide better access to existing port facilities at La Boca and Barracas, promoting development in the city's southern barrios. As so often happens in Argentina, though, political influence trumped practical expertise, as the congress approved wealthy downtown businessman Eduardo Madero's vague plan to transform the mudflats into a series of deep *diques* (basins) immediately east of the central Plaza de Mayo, even as work advanced on the Riachuelo option.

Approved in 1882, Puerto Madero took 16 years to complete, came in well over budget, caused a scandal because of shady land dealings in the vicinity of the port, and finally, even proved inadequate for the growing port traffic. Only improvements at La Boca and the 1926 opening of Retiro's Puerto Nuevo (New Port) finally resolved the problem, but port costs remained high.

## FROM GRAN ALDEA TO COSMOPOLITAN CAPITAL

Federalization gave the city a new mayor— Torcuato de Alvear, appointed by President Julio Argentino Roca—and Alvear immediately imposed his vision on the newly designated capital. Instead of the traditionally intimate *Gran Aldea*, Buenos Aires was to become a city of monuments; a cosmopolitan showpiece symbolizing Argentina's integration with the wider world. Where single-story houses once lined narrow colonial streets, broad boulevards like the Avenida de Mayo soon linked majestic public buildings such as the Casa Rosada presidential palace and the Congreso Nacional, the federal legislature.

Newly landscaped spaces like the Plaza de Mayo, Plaza del Congreso, and Plaza San Martín, not to mention the conversion of Rosas's former Palermo estate into parklands, reflected the aspirations—or pretensions—of an ambitious country. Some, though, castigated Alvear for favoring upper-class barrios such as Recoleta, Palermo, and Belgrano over struggling immigrant neighborhoods like San Telmo and La Boca.

As immigrants streamed into Buenos Aires from Spain, Italy, Britain, Russia, and other European countries, such differential treatment exacerbated growing social tensions. In 1913, Buenos Aires became the first South American city to open a subway system, beneath the Avenida de Mayo, but in poorer neighborhoods large families squeezed into *conventillos* (tenements) and struggled on subsistence wages. The gap between rich and poor frequently exploded into open conflict—in 1909, following police repression of a May Day demonstration, anarchist immigrant Simón Radowitzky killed police chief Ramón Falcón with a bomb, and in 1919, President Hipólito Yrigoyen ordered the army to crush a metalworkers' strike during what is now recalled as *La Semana Trágica* (The Tragic Week).

Ironically, Yrigoyen pardoned Radowitzky a decade later, and his was the first administration to suffer one of repeated military coups that plagued the country for most of the 20th century. The military dictatorship that followed him continued the policy of demolishing narrow colonial streets to create broad thoroughfares like Corrientes, Córdoba, and Santa Fe, all parallel to the Avenida de Mayo, and the crosstown boulevard Avenida 9 de Julio. The populist Perón regimes of the 1940s and 1950s, despite public deference to working-class interests, splurged on pharaonic works projects, heavy and heavily subsidized industry, and unsustainable social spending that squandered the country's post–World War II surpluses.

## THE DIRTY WAR AND ITS AFTERMATH

As Gran Buenos Aires grew, encompassing ever more distant suburbs, the capital and its vicinity became home to more than one-third of the country's population; by 1970, it had more than eight million inhabitants. Continued political instability, though, emerged into almost open warfare until 1976, when the military ousted President Isabel Perón (widow of Juan Perón, who died shortly after returning from exile in 1973) in a bloodless coup that introduced the most systematic and bloodiest reign of terror in Argentine history.

Under its euphemistically named Proceso de Reorganización Nacional (Process of National Reorganization), the military's *Guerra Sucia* (Dirty War) claimed the lives of as many as 30,000 Argentines, ranging from leftist urban and rural guerrillas to suspected sympathizers and large numbers of innocent bystanders whose links to armed opposition groups were tenuous at best. Many more were imprisoned and tortured, and more still were either sent or escaped into exile. Only a few courageous individuals and groups, such as Nobel Peace Prize winner Adolfo Pérez Esquivel and the equally famous Madres de la Plaza de Mayo, who marched around Buenos Aires's main plaza in quiet defiance, dared to risk public opposition.

One rationale for the military coup was the corruption of civilian politicians, but the military and their civilian collaborators were just as adept at diverting international loans to demolish vibrant but neglected neighborhoods and to create decadent monuments such as freeways that went nowhere. Much of the nation's money, of course, found its way into offshore bank accounts. The horror ended only after the military underestimated the response to the invasion of the British-ruled Falkland (Malvinas) Islands in 1982; after a decisive defeat, the military meekly ceded control to civilians. The main coup plotters and human-rights violators went to prison—an unprecedented occurrence in Latin America, even if they were later pardoned.

Following the return to constitutional government in 1983, Argentina underwent several years of hyperinflation in which the Radical government of President Raúl Alfonsín squandered an enormous amount of good will. The succeeding Peronist government of Carlos Menem overcame hyperinflation by pegging the Argentine peso at par with the U.S. dollar through a "currency basket" that ensured the country would print no more pesos than it had hard currency reserves to back.

Menem's strategy, the brainchild of Economy Minister Domingo Cavallo, brought a decade of economic stability during which foreign investment flowed into Argentina, and Buenos Aires was one of the main beneficiaries. Privatization of inefficient state-run monopolies, which had had thousands of so-called *ñoquis* (ghost employees) on the payroll, brought major improvements in telecommunications, transportation, and other sectors. The financial and service sectors flourished, and ambitious urban renewal projects like the transformation of Puerto Madero into a fashionable riverfront of lofts and restaurants, gave *porteños* a sense of optimism through most of the 1990s.

There was a dark side to the boom, however: "crony capitalism" in which associates of the president enriched themselves through favorable contracts for privatization. Governmental reform did not touch the provinces, which maintained large public payrolls for patronage, and even printed their own *bonos* (bonds), "funny money"

that further reduced the confidence of international investors.

Even before the partial debt default of late 2001, the economy contracted and *porteños* began to suffer. After the resignation of Menem's hapless successor Fernando De la Rúa in December, the country had a series of caretaker presidents before the *congreso* chose Peronist Eduardo Duhalde (whom De la Rúa had defeated two years earlier) to serve until 2003, when Néstor Kirchner was elected president. In a controversial move, Duhalde ended Cavallo's convertibility policy and devalued the peso, which lost nearly 75 percent of its value within a few months. At the same time, he continued the De la Rúa administration's *corralito* policy, which restricted bank withdrawals to maintain hard currency reserves, but also strangled the economy of the city and the country.

As the economy stagnated and unemployment rose, homelessness also rose and scavengers became a common sight even in prosperous barrios like Palermo and Belgrano. Strikes, strident pickets blocking bridges and highways, and frustration with politicians and institutions like the International Monetary Fund (IMF) contributed to the feeling of *bronca* (aggravation). Yet somehow the city continued to function, with its blend of neighborhood integrity, cosmopolitan sophistication, and rich cultural life.

## Government and Politics

Argentine politics is often contentious and includes little consensus, but since the end of the military dictatorship of 1976–83 it has been remarkably stable and peaceful, all things considered. The major exception, of course, was the storm of political and economic protest that led to the deaths of five demonstrators in the Plaza de Mayo on December 20, 2001, and brought the resignation of President Fernando De la Rúa, a former city mayor. The country had three provisional presidents in two weeks before Senator Eduardo Duhalde of Buenos Aires province, who had lost the 1999 presidential election to De la Rúa, assumed the office in a dubiously extra-constitutional vote of congress.

Argentines' lack of faith in institutions, however, has led to barrio activism through *asambleas populares* (popular assemblies) and less-constructive extra-constitutional practices such as *escrache*, in which groups of citizens loudly and publicly demonstrate against politicians, judges, bankers or representatives of other institutions at their homes or workplaces. *Escraches*, which often deteriorate into shouting matches, originated as a tactic to identify and publicize the whereabouts of alleged torturers and murderers from the military dictatorship after a series of pardons and other measures limited their prosecution.

Unlike the Argentina of the 1970s, however, the Argentina of the early 21st century is imploding rather than exploding, and the villains are not always so conspicuous as they were in previous years.

## ORGANIZATION

Buenos Aires is Argentina's capital, and also its economic powerhouse and cultural cornerstone. Like Washington, D.C., it is a geographically and administratively separate federal district; the 24 *partidos* (counties) of Gran Buenos Aires belong to Buenos Aires province, the most populous and important of the country's 23 provinces.

Superficially, Argentina's constitution resembles that of the United States. The popularly elected President leads the executive branch; a bicameral legislature consists of an upper house, the Senado (Senate), and a lower Cámara de Diputados (Chamber of Deputies); the Corte Suprema (Supreme Court) is the independent judiciary.

In practice, however, institutions are often weak and dysfunctional. The president dominates the system, often ruling by decree when an opposition legislature obstructs his programs. The Corte Suprema is notoriously vulnerable to political pressure. Much depends on individuals, as institutions are weak. The charismatic President Carlos Menem (1989–1999), for instance, exercised unquestionable power despite (or perhaps because of) his ethical shortcomings, while successors like Fernando De la Rúa (1999–2001) and Eduardo Duhalde (appointed in 2001 to serve until 2003) have proved ineffectual even with legislators of their own parties.

Politically, the Capital Federal holds a special constitutional status as the Ciudad Autónoma de Buenos Aires (Autonomous City of Buenos Aires, which is similar to the District of Columbia in the US), with its own elected mayor and legislature. (Until reforms in 1996, the president appointed the mayor and legislature.) Unlike the largely disenfranchised voters of Washington, D.C., however, the voters of Buenos Aires enjoy voting representation in the Congreso Nacional (National Congress) as well.

## POLITICAL PARTIES

Although the Peronists, or Justicialists, are the largest political party in the country, the most important political force in the capital has been Alianza, an alliance of the rather misnamed Radical party (a middle-class institution that seems to function far better in opposition than in power) and the slightly left-of-center Frente del País Solidario (Frepaso, National Solidarity Front). The current mayor is the Alianza's Aníbal Ibarra.

In the current 63-member legislature, the Alianza holds 22 seats and the Peronists 16, while 14 other parties hold the remaining 25 seats. None of the latter holds more than four seats, and many of them hold only one.

The Peronists, Radicals, and similar entities, however, are barely parties in the European or North American sense—it might be more accurate to call them movements. Voters, for instance, cannot vote directly for candidates, but only for lists chosen by party bosses to reward loyalists.

More often than not, the major Argentine parties are patronage machines that, after mobilizing their most militant members for elections, reward them with well-paid public posts that may not actually involve working for their paychecks. Such "ghost employees" are called *ñoquis* after the inexpensive potato pasta traditionally served the 29th of each month in restaurants and cash-strapped households—the insinuation is that they start making their appearance in the office just in time to collect their salary on the first of the following month.

Historically, many officeholders have used their supporters for political intimidation instead of dialogue. In Argentina's present political chaos, however, political affiliations mean even less than it did in the past. Many Argentines have assumed a "plague on all your houses" attitude toward politicians in general, and ambitious individuals ranging from populist Elisa Carrió (a left-wing member of the Cámara de Diputados), to conservative businessman Mauricio Macri (president of the Boca Juniors soccer team) have consciously distanced themselves from traditional parties.

# ELECTIONS

On a national level, Argentina operates under an 1853 constitution, amended in 1994 to permit re-election of the president while reducing his or her term from six to four years; no president may serve more than two consecutive terms. Each of the 23 provinces, as well as the Buenos Aires federal district, chooses three senators; in the 257-member Cámara de Diputados, each province has a delegation proportionate to its population. The population and corresponding number of delegates is subject to revision with each new census. Senators serve six-year terms, deputies four-year terms.

*Porteño* voters choose the city's 63-member Poder Legislativo by proportional representation for four-year terms; half of the legislature is renewed every two years. Term limits prohibit both the mayor and legislators from serving more than two consecutive terms without a lapse of at least four years.

# BUREAUCRACY

The government institutions most travelers are likely to come into contact with are immigration, customs, and police. Immigration and customs generally treat foreigners fairly, but Argentine police are notoriously corrupt. The capital's Policía Federal are not quite so bad as the Buenos Aires provincial police, a "mafia with badges" who are particularly infamous for shaking down motorists for bribes after stopping them for minor equipment violations.

The politicized administrative bureaucracy remains one of Argentina's most intractable problems due to the continuing presence of *ñoquis* at the federal, provincial, and municipal levels. Abuses are not so extreme as they were in the past, when individuals often drew multiple paychecks without performing any work whatsoever, but bloated state payrolls are still cause for concern.

While the privatizations of the 1990s reduced federal sector employment by nearly two-thirds, they had little impact on the provinces. Provincial payrolls still include nearly 1.4 million Argentines—many in what might be more accurately

The extravagant facade of Retiro's Centro Naval reflects the military's traditional sense of privilege.

called positions rather than jobs. For the tourist, it may be gratifying to find a tiny obscure museum open 60 hours per week and staffed by three people, but the cumulative economic impact of such practices has been catastrophic.

In practical terms, lack of a professional civil service means a lack of continuity, as officials lose their jobs with every change of administration; continuing political influence in the bureaucracy means an abundance of uninterested and often ill-qualified officials who take their time dealing with any but the most routine matters. It also means nepotism and corruption—Transparency International consistently ranks Argentina among the worst countries in the world in its annual survey of perceived corruption. In 2002, Argentina was 70th of 102 countries surveyed; on the South American continent, only Ecuador and Bolivia (tied for 89th) and Paraguay (98th) ranked lower.

## THE MILITARY

Because of repeated coups in the 20th century and the particularly vicious dictatorship that brought the 1976–83 Dirty War, the Argentine military earned a reputation as one of the worst even on a continent infamous for armed repression. Its ignominious collapse in the 1982 Falkland Islands War, followed by public revelations of state terrorism and the conviction of the top generals and admirals responsible for kidnapping, torture, and murder, helped civilian authorities overcome the tradition of impunity.

Since the return to constitutional government in 1983, civilian governments have eliminated conscription, the military budget has declined to barely one percent of the GDP (less than half that of neighboring Chile), and Argentine forces have undertaken more strictly military operations such as peacekeeping missions in the Balkans. Although periods of political disorder such as 2001–2002 always bring coup rumors, the military appears to have little or no interest in taking the reins of government.

The size of the military services has also been reduced. As of 2001, for instance, the navy had only 27,000 personnel, though heavily weighted toward noncommissioned officers. It has about 50 ships, including three submarines.

Nevertheless, there remains an ugly reminder of military fanaticism in Colonel Mohamed Alí Seineldín, who mounted a rebellion against the constitutional government in 1989 and is presently serving a life term in a military prison. Seineldín, a fundamentalist Catholic, has taken to making bizarre public statements regarding oral and anal sex, and to asserting that the CIA and the Fuerzas Armadas Revolucionarias de Colombia (FARC, the Colombian guerrilla forces) are conspiring to destabilize Argentina—as if Argentines were incapable of doing so themselves.

Despite the country's reputation for dictatorial bellicosity, two Argentines have won Nobel Peace Prizes: foreign minister Carlos Saavedra Lamas (1936) for mediating a settlement to the Chaco War between Paraguay and Bolivia, and Adolfo Pérez Esquivel (1984) for publicizing the human rights abuses of the 1976–83 military dictatorship.

# Economy

The urban economy is mostly administrative, financial, and service-oriented. The capital remains the country's major port as well, but most industrial jobs are in Buenos Aires's provincial suburbs like Avellaneda. Along with northern Argentina's Iguazú falls and Patagonia's Moreno Glacier, the city is one of the country's principal tourist attractions.

To most foreign observers, Argentina's economy is an enigma. Rich in natural resources and having a well-educated populace and modern infrastructure, for most of seven decades it has lurched from crisis to crisis, with the notable exception of the stable, prosperous 1990s. In late 2001, it stunned the world and even many Argentines by defaulting on part of its US$141 billion foreign debt, triggering a political and

economic meltdown comparable to the Great Depression of the 1930s. In the first quarter of 2002, the economy shrank 16.3 percent, marking 14 consecutive quarters of contraction.

Argentina emerged from World War II in an enviable position, but the government of the charismatic general Juan Domingo Perón and its successors squandered enormous budget surpluses from agricultural exports by funding bloated state enterprises. Those enterprises, in collusion with corrupt labor leaders, became industrial dinosaurs impossible to reform. Then, during the 1970s and 1980s, large loans destined for massive public works projects filled the pockets—or Swiss bank accounts—of the nefarious generals and their civilian collaborators who ruled the country.

Corruption and deficit spending resulted in hyperinflation that reached levels of 30 percent or more *per month*. Shortly after taking power in 1989, the administration of President Carlos Menem became the first Argentine government in recent memory to tackle the inflation problem through Economy Minister Domingo Cavallo's "convertibility" policy; his "currency basket" fixed the value of the Argentine peso at par with the U.S. dollar, and required the government to back every peso printed with a dollar or other hard currency.

Selling off unprofitable state enterprises such as Aerolíneas Argentinas, the state telecommunications enterprise Entel, and most of the extensive railroad network made convertibility possible. Inflation dropped to zero and, after an initial glitch, there was steady economic growth. But the Mexican crisis of 1995 followed by a Brazilian devaluation that reduced Argentine competitiveness led to increasing unemployment and recession. After a brief recovery, convertibility proved to be an economic straitjacket that, by the second year of the De la Rúa administration, was unsustainable.

In a desperate move, De la Rúa reappointed Cavallo to the Economy Ministry, but a run on bank deposits brought severe restrictions on withdrawals, known collectively as the *corralito* (literally, "little fence"). The *corralito*'s unpopularity triggered Cavallo's resignation and De la Rúa's downfall. De la Rúa's successor, Eduardo Duhalde, made things even worse by eliminating convertibility, converting dollar-based savings accounts to peso-based accounts at a 1:1.4 rate, and floating the local currency (leaving it open to market forces to find its own level rather than intervening to control the market) so that those accounts soon lost most of their value. At the same time, in a classic case of Argentine "crony capitalism," the new president converted dollar debts to peso debts at a rate of 1:1, benefitting the large industrialists who were his political base.

With devaluation, according to the Economist Intelligence Unit, in less than a year Buenos Aires went from the 22nd most expensive city in the world (of 131 surveyed) to the 120th. As the peso plummeted from 1:1 to 1:3.5 in only a few months, citizens with the discipline to save saw their frozen wealth evaporate, and those who accumulated large debts saw their burdens reduced. Devaluation has also meant the return of inflation, though not on the nightmarish level of the 1980s because banking restrictions limited the cash in circulation.

In theory, a devalued peso should make Argentine exports more competitive, but this has not yet happened—partly because the new administration also slapped an export tax on all profits in excess of US$5 million. Banks have taken the brunt of criticism for not repaying their depositors, but even though some are solvent enough to do so, government restrictions prevent them from it.

Economic statistics from 2002 suggest that the Argentine economy will contract by 10–12 percent; the government's speculative inflation figure of 22 percent seems far too optimistic. Some economists, such as Arturo Porcezanski, believe the only way to stabilize prices is to adopt the dollar as Argentina's currency, as "Any effort to convince Argentines that the peso is worth anything are in vain. They only have faith in the dollar." In a similar sentiment, Cavallo remarked that "forcing Argentines to save in pesos would be as difficult as forcing them to learn to speak Chinese instead of Spanish."

This, of course, has long been the case—for many decades, Argentines have speculated on the dollar in times of crisis. In the 1970s, when Montoneros guerrillas headed by Rodolfo Galimberti kidnapped empresario Jorge Born, they demanded and got a ransom of US$60 million—at a time when that was *real* money. In an only-in-Argentina scenario, the pardoned Galimberti later became the business partner of the man he abducted.

## EMPLOYMENT, UNEMPLOYMENT, AND UNDEREMPLOYMENT

Through four years of recession, Argentine unemployment has risen dramatically—estimates as of mid-2003 are around 23 percent—and many people are underemployed as well. These figures are probably not quite so bad in Buenos Aires as in the provinces, but street, bus, and subway vendors are far more numerous than in the past, and the numbers of people rummaging through garbage for recyclables are shocking even to Argentines.

During the economic crisis of early 2002, many unemployed individuals spent the night in line to buy dollars at Banco de la Nación and private exchange houses, in hopes of selling their spot to those who did have sufficient pesos to purchase dollars. Similarly, individuals waited in lines outside the Italian consulate and other European missions to sell their places in line for passports and visas.

## AGRICULTURE

Since the 19th century, the Argentine pampas have developed from the meat locker and woolshed of the world to one of its main granaries, growing corn, wheat, oats, sorghum, and soybeans, among other crops. The country's agriculture has diversified, however, to include vegetables such as potatoes, onions, carrots, squash, beans, and tomatoes, and to fruit crops like apples, pears, and grapes—the latter of which help make Argentina the world's fifth-largest wine producer.

Other commercial crops include subtropical cultigens such as sugar cane, olives, tea, yerba mate, and tobacco, mostly in provinces to the north and west of the capital. Agriculture accounts for roughly six percent of GDP but about 40 percent of exports, which comprise about 26 billion pesos per year.

## INDUSTRY

Argentina's industrial heyday was the immediate post–World War II period, when President Juan Domingo Perón invested vast sums in manufacturing products such as steel, chemicals, and petrochemicals; the military controlled large parts of the economy, including its own weapons manufacture and support industries.

Despite the privatization of the 1990s, much of Argentine industry is still inefficient and unable to compete without state assistance—or cronyism. Accounting for about 32 percent of GDP, it also includes food processing, motor vehicles, consumer durables, textiles, printing, metallurgy, and steel. Much of this activity is concentrated in the southern suburbs of Avellaneda and Quilmes, across the Riachuelo.

## RICH AND POOR

Historically, the disparity between rich and poor in Argentina has been far less extreme than in other Latin American countries, but the meltdown of 2001–2002, with its devastating impact on the middle class, has resurrected the issue. As of mid-2002, nearly half of all Argentines were considered to fall beneath the poverty line, and six million (one-sixth of the population) were considered indigent.

Statistics can be misleading, though. According to World Bank figures from the calendar year 2000, with the Argentine peso at par with the U.S. dollar, the country's per capita income was US$7,460, while that of neighboring Paraguay was US$1,470. As the flailing Argentine peso sinks to nearly a quarter of its former value, these two figures would be roughly comparable in dollar terms; yet it would be difficult to argue that the Argentina's standard of living, no matter how dire the economy, is equivalent to that of impoverished Paraguay.

## EDUCATION

Literacy is formally high, nearly 97 percent, one of the highest in the Americas. Education is free through high school and compulsory to age 12, but the curriculum is rigid. Some public secondary schools, most notably the Colegio Nacional Buenos Aires, are even more prestigious than some of their private bilingual counterparts.

Public universities like the capital's Universidad de Buenos Aires and the Universidad Nacional de La Plata, in the provincial capital, are generally superior to private universities. Public university education is free of charge, but has generated a surplus of high-status degrees in fields like law, psychology, and sociology—and not enough in

# THE PORTEÑO PSYCHE

In May of 2002, the daily *Clarín* posed the online forum question "Do you think winning the World Cup would improve Argentines' self-esteem?," while an editorial bore the title "Chocolate is not an Antidepressant" and another piece argued the pros and cons of sofa-based psychoanalysis. Meanwhile, the *Buenos Aires Herald* was carrying classified ads for "post-modern psychotherapy with a family focus," and the 2002 Festival de Tango even included a session on *Tango de Autoayuda* (Self-Help Tango) by Mexico-based Argentine Liliana Felipe.

New Yorkers may talk about their therapists, but *porteños* can more than match them—in Buenos Aires, psychoanalysis and other therapies are not for the upper and upper middle classes alone. During registration at the Universidad de Buenos Aires medical school, a proliferation of flyers offers psychoanalysis and psychotherapy with UBA professionals—the first session free, for individuals, couples and groups.

To a degree, the current obsession with therapy may be a function of the economic crisis, and even the *corralito* banking restrictions have been interpreted in this context. According to an early 2002 interview by National Public Radio's Martin Kaste, a Freudian psychiatrist made the case that "Money has a certain symbolic equivalence to the penis. People put their money in the bank, but at the moment they want to withdraw it they lose their money, so this produces a castration anxiety."

Another commented that "sexual desire has also been caught in the *corralito*—men worry about lack of desire and premature ejaculation, and women are unable to have orgasms." In a different context, angry real estate brokers picketed the residence of caretaker president Eduardo Duhalde, himself a former realtor, but not necessarily in the hope that they would get any relief for a frozen real estate market. Rather, remarked one of the protestors, "This turned into our therapy, a place to set our anguish free."

Therapy, though, is not just a function of the times; it has a long history in Buenos Aires, beginning with the arrival of Jewish refugees from Europe in the 1930s. Mariano Ben Plotkin has chronicled this history in *Freud on the Pampas: the Emergence and Development of a Psychoanalytic Culture in Argentina* (Stanford University Press, 2001).

Many of Buenos Aires's 30,000 or so shrinks practice in Palermo's so-called Villa Freud, an area bounded by Avenida Santa Fe, Avenida Las Heras, Avenida Scalabrini Ortiz and Avenida Coronel Díaz. Many businesses in the area play on this reputation, including the Bar Sigi at Salguero and Charcas, and patients can top off their medications at the Farmacia Villa Freud at Paraguay and Medrano. One online magazine specializes in listings for professional office rentals. Even acting classes are often exercises in therapy.

Several institutions contribute to the capital's therapeutic ambiance. The Asociación Psicoanalítica Argentina, Rodríguez Peña 1674, tel. 4812-3518, apainfo@pccp.com.ar, www.apa.org.ar, organized a month-long exhibition on *Psychoanalysis, Culture and Crisis*, at the Microcentro's Centro Cultural Borges. Buenos Aires's Museo de Psicología, at Avenida Independencia 3063, 3rd floor, is open 9 A.M.–2 P.M. weekdays.

The locus of Villa Freud, though, is the bookstore Librería Paidós, in the Galería Las Heras at Avenida Las

Staying on your medication is easy at the Farmacia Villa Freud, Palermo.

© WAYNE BERNHARDSON

Heras 3741, tel. 4801-2860, www.libreriapaidos .com.ar, info@libreriapaidos.com. It now has a Barrio Norte branch at Avenida Santa Fe 1685, tel. 4812-6685.

If *porteños* and other Argentines continue to feel the need for therapy, their Chilean neighbors may have had the last word, though. In the midst of the 2002 crisis, a satirical Santiago newspaper published a short note under the headline "New Foundation, Argentines Anonymous, Created." According to the article, "A group whose members hope to rehabilitate themselves from

their nationality met yesterday for the first time. At the beginning, each one must announce his name and then continue, 'I am an Argentine.'"

Barrio Freud's Bar Sigi welcomes therapists and patients alike.

hands-on disciplines like engineering and computer science.

School teachers generally do not receive university degrees, but attend special teachers' colleges. There is vocational and techical training as well, but these skills enjoy little respect even when those jobs pay more than white-collar positions or office work.

Several Argentine scientists have won Nobel Prizes, including Bernardo Houssay (Medicine, 1946), Luis Federico Leloir (Chemistry, 1972), and César Milstein (Medicine, 1984). One continual concern is the "brain drain" of educated Argentines overseas; Milstein, for instance, spent his most productive years in England because political pressures at Argentine universities made research impossible. Many talented individuals, though, have left simply because the economy has failed them.

## TOURISM

For most overseas visitors, Buenos Aires is the gateway to globally famous attractions like the subtropical Iguazú falls in the northern province of Misiones and the Perito Moreno glacier in

Patagonia's Santa Cruz province. Still, the city is an attraction its own right—on the entire continent, probably only Rio de Janeiro has an international profile anywhere close to the Argentine capital.

Thanks partly to the tourist sector, Buenos Aires's economy remains relatively prosperous compared to the provinces. According to official statistics for 1999, the last year for which figures are currently available, the city received more than two million foreign visitors, who spent slightly more than US$2 billion. Approximately 185,000 of the visitors were from North America and 239,000 from Europe. Most of the remainder came from the neighboring countries of Uruguay, Brasil, Paraguay, Bolivia, and Chile.

Many other visitors to the city, of course, come from elsewhere in the country. In 1999, 7.2 million Argentines spent a total of US$2.7 billion on visits to the capital.

© WAYNE BERNHARDSON

# The People

According to the 2001 census, Argentina has 36,223,947 people. Of these, 2,768,772 reside in Buenos Aires, the Capital Federal; this is a decline of eight percent from the 1991 census, when its population was 2,965,403. Another 8,684,953 reside in the 24 counties of Gran Buenos Aires, for a total of 11,453,725.

## POPULATION GEOGRAPHY

Nearly a third of all Argentines live in the Capital Federal and Gran Buenos Aires. Most of the rest are also city dwellers, in population centers such as Rosario, Córdoba, Mar del Plata, Mendoza, Salta, and other provincial capital and cities. The southern Patagonian provinces of Chubut, Santa Cruz, and Tierra del Fuego are very thinly populated.

### Indigenous Peoples

Argentina has the smallest indigenous population of any South American country except Uruguay, but many Kollas (Quechuas) from northwestern Argentina and Mapuches from the southern Patagonian provinces reside in the capital. There is also a handful of Tobas, Matacos, and others from Chaco and Santa Fe.

### Ethnic Minorities

Argentina is a country of immigrants, both recent and not-so-recent, and the capital reflects that history. Spaniards, of course first colonized what is now Argentina, but a 19th-century tidal wave of Italians, Basques, English, Irish, Welsh, Ukrainians, and other nationalities made Buenos Aires a mosaic of immigrants; Italo-Argentines even came to outnumber Argentines of Spanish origin.

Some immigrant groups retain a high visibility, most notably a Jewish community that numbers at least 200,000 and is historically concentrated in the Once district of Balvanera. Since the onset of the economic crisis of 2001–2002, however, many have needed assistance from Jewish community organizations, and significant numbers of Argentine Jews have emigrated or considered emigrating to Israel despite the insecurity there. It's worth mentioning that still-unresolved terrorist incidents in Buenos Aires killed 29 people in the Israeli Embassy in Retiro in 1992, and 87 people in Once's Asociación Mutua Israelita Argentina (AMIA), a Jewish cultural center, in 1994; most Jewish community landmarks are well fortified.

Middle Eastern immigrants are less numerous, but have occupied high-profile positions in Argentine society—the most notable example of this is former president Carlos Menem, of Syrian descent. Palermo's new Islamic Center, funded by Saudi Arabia, is nevertheless disproportionately large compared to the capital's Muslim population. Argentines misleadingly refer to anyone of Middle Eastern descent as *turcos* (Turks), a legacy of the initial immigration from the region.

Asian faces have become more common in recent years. There has long been a community of about 30,000 Japanese-Argentines, concentrated in the capital and the Greater Buenos Aires suburb of Escobar, but Belgrano also has a modest Chinatown near the Barrancas. Many Koreans work in Once and live in the southern barrio of Nueva Pompeya.

Other South Americans, mostly Bolivians, Paraguayans, and Peruvians, flocked to Argentina during the early 1990s boom. They generally work at menial jobs, and many have returned home since the economic meltdown of 2001–2002. They are mostly concentrated in certain neighborhoods—Peruvians in Congreso, Paraguayans in Constitución, and Bolivians in Nueva Pompeya.

## RELIGION

Roman Catholicism remains Argentina's official and dominant religion, but evangelical Protestantism, with its street preachers and storefront churches, is growing even in sophisticated Buenos Aires, mostly but not exclusively among working-class people. Other religions have fewer adherents.

# THE AFRO-ARGENTINES AND THEIR "DEMISE"

In a country of immigrants, the heritage of many Argentines is often conspicuous. According to some accounts, there are even more Argentines with Italian surnames than *Gallegos* of Spanish ancestry. Anglo-Argentines are prominent and have their own daily newspaper, and German-Argentines still support a weekly. Buenos Aires has numerous Jewish community landmarks, and so-called *Turcos* of Middle Eastern descent, such as former President Carlos Menem, have made their mark in politics.

Yet an Afro-Argentine population that, by official statistics, once comprised nearly a third of Buenos Aires's population has been nearly invisible. When the revolutionary government of 1810 tentatively banned the slave trade three years later, nearly 10,000 of more than 32,000 *porteños* were of African origin. As late as 1838, the figure was nearly 15,000 of almost 63,000. Yet in 1887, the number had dropped to only 8,000 among more than 430,000 city residents.

After the turn of the century, Afro-Argentines virtually fell off the city map. In the 1970s, newspaper and magazine articles even puzzled over the disappearance of a community that fought honorably in the 19th-century civil and regional wars, supported a variety of social and charitable organizations, sponsored a lively local press, and made substantial contributions to the arts. How and why this could have happened was, seemingly, an enigma.

Two plausible hypotheses were widely accepted. One was that Afro-Argentines were front-line cannon fodder, particularly in the war with Paraguay, where they suffered disproportionate casualties. Another was that the 19th-century yellow fever epidemics in San Telmo, where many Afro-Argentines lived, decimated their numbers as wealthier *criollos* moved to higher, healthier ground in the northern suburbs.

Historian George Reid Andrews, though, challenged the orthodoxy by arguing that there was slim evidence for either hypothesis and, moreover, little for the disappearance of the community itself. What he did learn, through examination of archival materials and the capital's Afro-Argentine press, was that the community itself was unconcerned with demographic decline but clearly worried about its socioeconomic status.

As the slave trade ended by the mid-19th century and massive European immigration transformed the city a couple decades later, Afro-Argentines were clearly a declining *percentage* of the population, but that does not explain their plunging absolute numbers. Andrews, though, found that Argentine authorities and opinion-makers consciously excised the Afro-Argentine presence in an attempt to promote the country as a European outpost in the Americas.

Some of this, certainly, owed its origins to a racism that was present from early independence times. The political opponents of Bernardino Rivadavia, a presumed mulatto who served as president in 1826–27 before his forced resignation, stigmatized him with the epithet "Dr. Chocolate." Modern Argentine school children are taught proudly that the country was among the first to abolish slavery, in 1813, but these measures were so half-hearted that the institution lingered nearly another half-century.

More insidiously, though, census-takers systematically undercounted Afro-Argentines by equally half-hearted efforts that sometimes even avoided the neighborhoods in which they lived. When summarizing the data, they minimized the black presence by creating vague new racial categories such as *trigueño* (wheat-colored), and incorporating individuals with African background into them. Eventually, in Andrews's words, the Afro-Argentines of Buenos Aires were "forgotten, but not gone."

Even as more and more European immigrants streamed into Argentina, Afro-Argentines kept alive institutions such as the Shimmy Club, a social organization that held regular dances only half a block off Avenida Corrientes, into the 1970s. Here, at regular intervals, rhythmic drum-based *malambo*, *milonga* and *zamba* filled the hall and, on occasion, spilled out into the street.

Andrews thought that Argentine society was absorbing blacks and, indeed, defining them as whites in accordance with an unspoken ideology, even as their contributions to that society survived. In recent years, though, there has been a small but

*continued on next page*

## AFRO-ARGENTINES (cont'd)

complex revival of black culture in Buenos Aires that involves Afro-Argentines (now estimated at about 3,000) but also Afro-Uruguayans, Afro-Brazilians, Cape Verde Portuguese (perhaps 8,000), and Cubans and Africans. This has not always been convivial, as the remaining Afro-Argentines clearly distinguish themselves from the latecomers even as they share some cultural features.

Still, Argentine society's continued refusal to acknowledge their presence and its own African heritage may be their greatest adversary. Created in 1996, the Fundación Africa Vive (Africa Lives Foundation) claims there are more than two million Argentines of African descent; according to director María Magdalena Lamadrid, "A single drop of blood is enough" to define an Afro-Argentine.

Yet when, in 2002, Lamadrid herself attempted to fly to Panama to participate in a conference on the life of Dr. Martin Luther King Jr., immigration officials detained her on suspicion of carrying a false passport. One, allegedly, said that "she can't be black and Argentine."

---

Catholicism in particular has left the city with many of its greatest landmarks, ranging from the colonial churches of San Telmo and Recoleta to the dignity of the neoclassical Catedral. Immigrant Protestant communities are also responsible for ecclesiastical landmarks like the Danish and Swedish churches of San Telmo and the impressive Russian Orthodox dome opposite Parque Lezama, also in San Telmo.

### Roman Catholicism

Starting with the famous Dominican Bartolomé de las Casas in Mexico, factions in the Church have wrestled with the contradictions between its official mission of recruiting and saving souls and its duty to alleviate the misery of those who have experienced secular injustice and persecution. Argentina is no exception—figures such as the late Cardinal Antonio Quarracino were outright apologists for the vicious military dictatorship of 1976–83, but others lobbied against its excesses and for return to democracy. Some more militant clergy worked in the slums under the influence of "liberation theology," and some lost their lives in the aftermath of the 1976 coup.

Folk Catholicism, including spiritualist practices, often diverges from Church orthodoxy in the veneration of unofficial saints, like the Difunta Correa of San Juan province, and even historical figures like Juan and Evita Perón, tango legend Carlos Gardel, and healer Madre María, all of whose tombs are in Buenos Aires's landmark cemeteries at Recoleta and Chacarita. Novelist Tomás Eloy Martínez has sardonically labeled his countrymen as "cadaver cultists" for their devotion to those dead and gone.

### Protestantism

Anglicans were the original bearers of Protestantism in Argentina, but Scandinavian communities were numerous enough to justify construction of Danish and Swedish churches. More recent Protestant denominations are often shrill evangelicals; nearby Uruguay's capital city of Montevideo is one of the centers of Reverend Sun Myung Moon's cultish Unification Church (no relation to Moon Handbooks!).

### Other Religions

The Argentine constitution guarantees freedom of religion, and adherents of non-Christian faiths are not rare, if not exactly widespread or numerous. The largest and most conspicuous of these other religions is Judaism, as the capital's Jewish community is at least 200,000 strong (a planned community census may well reveal a larger number). The government of Saudi Arabia sponsored the construction of Palermo's Centro Islámico Rey Fahd, whose capacity is disproportionately large for the capital's relatively small community of observant Muslims.

## LANGUAGE

Spanish is Argentina's official language, but English is widely spoken in the tourist and business sectors of the economy. Foreign language use is also vigorous among ethnic communities such as Italo-Argentines, Anglo-Argentines, and German-Argentines. The Anglo-Argentine and business communities even support a daily tabloid, *The Buenos Aires Herald*, while the German-Argentine community has the weekly *Argentinisches Tageblatt*.

Buenos Aires also has its own distinctive street slang, known as *lunfardo*, which owes its origins to working-class immigrant communities. Many *lunfardo* words have worked their way into everyday Argentine speech even though they may be unintelligible at first to those who have learned Spanish elsewhere. Some are fairly obvious in context, such as *laburar* instead of *trabajar* for work or labor, but others are obscure.

While many of its idioms are crude by standards of formal Spanish, *lunfardo* has acquired a certain legitimacy among Argentine scholars. There is even an academy for the study of *porteño* slang, the Academia Porteña del Lunfardo at Estados Unidos 1379, Monserrat, tel. 4383-2393.

> *Buenos Aires also has its own street slang, **lunfardo**, which owes its origins to working-class immigrant communities. Many **lunfardo** words have worked their way into everyday Argentine speech, but they may be unintelligible at first to those who have learned Spanish elsewhere.*

## CONDUCT AND CUSTOMS

*Porteños*, like New Yorkers, have a stereotyped reputation for brusqueness and some of them complain that, especially in the current crisis, "nobody respects anybody here any more."

Still, politeness goes a long way with officials, shopkeepers, and others with whom you may have contact. It is always good form to offer the appropriate polite greeting *buenos días* (good morning), *buenas tardes* (good afternoon), or *buenas noches* (good evening or good night), depending on the time of day.

In terms of general conduct, both women and men should dress conservatively and inconspicuously when visiting churches, chapels, and sacred sites. This, again, is an issue of respect for local customs, even if *porteños* themselves don't always observe it.

## Women Travelers

Like many other parts of Latin America, Argentine society has strong *machista* (male chauvinist) elements. Though nearly everybody visits and leaves Argentina without experiencing any unpleasantness, women are certainly not exempt from harassment and, rarely, violence. The most common manifestation of machismo is the *piropo*, a sexist remark that can range from clever and humorous to crude and insulting.

If you do receive unwanted attention, the best strategy is to ignore it, and the odds are that the problem will go away on his own. If not, the next best option is to go to your hotel, a restaurant, or some other public place where harassment will be more conspicuous and you're likely to find support. Some women have suggested wearing a bogus wedding ring, but truly persistent suitors might see this as a challenge.

## Gay and Lesbian Travelers

Despite its conspicuous Catholicism, Buenos Aires is a fairly tolerant city for both gays and lesbians, and public displays of affection— men kissing on the cheek, women holding hands—are relatively common even among heterosexuals. When in doubt, though, discretion is advisable.

Certain districts, most notably Recoleta, Barrio Norte, and Palermo, have a number of openly gay entertainment venues. Outlying areas like the Paraná delta are also remarkably tolerant.

# Travel Basics

## Getting There

Most overseas visitors arrive by air, though many also arrive overland from Chile, Bolivia, Uruguay, Paraguay, and Brazil. Almost all of the latter arrive by bus or private vehicle; there is no international rail service. There are ferry connections to Uruguay.

### BY AIR

Buenos Aires has regular air links with North America, Europe, and Australia/New Zealand, plus less-frequent routes from southern Africa across the Atlantic (some via Brazil). It is, however, a relatively expensive destination during peak periods such as Christmas/New Year's and Holy Week holidays; an Advance Purchase Excursion (APEX) fare can reduce the bite considerably, but may have minimum- and maximum-stay requirements, allow no stopovers, and impose financial penalties for any changes. Economy-class (Y) tickets, valid for 12 months, are more expensive but allow maximum flexibility. Travelers staying more than a year, though, have to cough up the difference for any price increase in the meantime.

Discount ticket agents known as consolidators in the United States and "bucket shops" in Britain may offer the best deals, but they often

colectivo (city bus)

have drawbacks—they may not, for instance, allow mileage credit for frequent-flyer programs. Courier flights, on which passengers give up some or all of their baggage allowance to a company sending equipment or documents to overseas affiliates or customers may be even cheaper, but are less common to Latin America than to other parts of the world. These are also available for short periods only, and often leave on short notice.

Other options include Round the World (RTW) and Circle Pacific routes that permit numerous stopovers over the course of much longer multicontinental trips, but putting these itineraries together requires some effort. Two useful resources for researching airfares are Edward Hasbrouck's *The Practical Nomad* (Emeryville, CA: Avalon Travel Publishing, 2000) and the same author's *The Practical Nomad Guide to the Online Marketplace* (Emeryville, CA: Avalon Travel Publishing, 2001).

Many airlines have reduced their services to Buenos Aires in the past year or so. This owes less to post–September 11 hysteria than it does to the fact that, with debt default and devaluation, far fewer Argentines can afford to travel overseas. At the same time, the Argentine market is less attractive to foreign business interests, so they have less incentive to travel to the Argentine capital.

## Airports

Buenos Aires has two airports, both operated by the private concessionaire Aeropuertos Argentinos 2000, tel. 11/5480-6111, www.aa2000.com.ar. The main international facility is Aeropuerto Internacional Ministro Pistarini, 35 kilometers southwest of downtown, popularly called "Ezeiza" after its Buenos Aires province suburb. The other is Aeroparque Jorge Newbery, within the capital's boundaries at Avenida Costanera Rafael Obligado s/n (*sin número,* or unnumbered), Palermo; Aeroparque is primarily domestic but has a handful of international flights from neighboring countries.

International passengers leaving from Ezeiza pay a US$30.50 departure tax, payable in local currency or U.S. dollars, but it's usually included

in the ticket price. On flights of less than 300 kilometers to neighboring countries such as Uruguay, the tax is only US$16.50, and on domestic flights it's US$2. Again, these fees are normally included in the price of the ticket.

**Airport Transportation:** There's a variety of options to and from the airports, ranging from *colectivos* (city buses) to shuttles, taxis, and *remises* (meterless taxis which quote a fixed price for the trip).

*Colectivos* provide the cheapest transportation to and from the airports, but they are more practical for close-in Aeroparque than distant Ezeiza, as they take circuitous routes on surface streets. To Aeroparque (about US$.20), the alternatives are No. 33 from Plaza de Mayo, the Microcentro and Retiro; No. 37-C ("Ciudad Universitaria") from Plaza del Congreso, Avenida Callao, Avenida las Heras, and Plaza Italia; No 45 northbound from Plaza Constitución, Plaza San Martín, or Retiro; and No. 160-C or 160-D from Avenida Las Heras or Plaza Italia. Return buses leave from the Avenida Costanera Rafael Obligado, a short walk outside the terminal.

To Ezeiza (about US$.50), the backpackers' choice is the No. 86-A ("Aeropuerto"), from La Boca to Plaza de Mayo, Plaza del Congreso, Plaza Once, and onward, but the roundabout route takes up to two hours. *Servicio Diferencial* buses cost more (about US$2) but have more comfortable reclining seats. At Ezeiza, both leave from a stop at the Aerolíneas Argentinas terminal, a short distance from the main international terminal.

**Shuttle** services are more expensive but more direct, leaving from offices near Plaza San Martín in Retiro, and using the faster *autopista.* Transfer Express, in the Edificio Kavanagh at Florida 1045, tel. 11/4314-1999 or 800/555-0224, operates 20 shuttles a day to Ezeiza (US$3.50) between 6:30 A.M. and 8:45 P.M.; from Ezeiza, the first operates at 7:15 A.M. It also takes nine trips per day to and from Aeroparque (US$1.40), between 8:50 A.M. and 9:10 P.M.

Manuel Tienda León, Avenida Santa Fe 790, tel. 11/4315-5115, fax 11/4315-5001, tel. 800/777-0078, www.tiendaleon.com.ar, runs 30

## INTERNATIONAL AIRLINES IN BUENOS AIRES

**Aerolíneas Argentinas:** Perú 2, Monserrat, tel. 4340-7777

**AeroMéxico:** Esmeralda 1063, 9th floor, Retiro, tel. 4315-1936

**Air Canada:** Avenida Córdoba 656, Microcentro, tel. 4327-3640

**Air France:** San Martín 344, 23rd floor, Microcentro, tel. 4480-0524

**Air New Zealand:** Marcelo T. de Alvear 590, 10th floor, Retiro, tel. 4315-5494

**Alitalia:** Suipacha 1111, 28th floor, Retiro, tel. 4310-9999

**American Airlines:** Avenida Santa Fe 881, Retiro, tel. 4318-1111

**American Falcon:** Avenida Santa Fe 1713, 4th floor, Recoleta, tel. 4811-0215

**Avianca:** Carlos Pellegrini 1163, 4th floor, Retiro, tel. 4394-5990

**British Airways:** Viamonte 570, 1st floor, Microcentro, tel. 4320-6600

**Cubana de Aviación:** Sarmiento 552, 11th floor, Microcentro, tel. 4326-5291

**Dinar Líneas Aéreas:** Avenida Roque Sáenz Peña 933, Microcentro, tel. 4327-8000**Iberia:** Carlos Pellegrini 1163, 1st floor, Retiro, tel. 4131-1000

**LanChile:** Cerrito 866, Retiro, tel. 4378-2200

**LAPA:** Carlos Pellegrini 1075, Retiro, tel. 4114-5272

**Lloyd Aéreo Boliviano (LAB):** Carlos Pellegrini 141, Microcentro, tel. 4323-1900

**Lufthansa:** Marcelo T. de Alvear 636, Retiro, tel. 4319-0600

**Mexicana:** Avenida Córdoba 755, 1st floor, Retiro, tel. 4000-6300

**Pluna:** Florida 1, Microcentro, tel. 4342-4420

**South African Airways:** Avenida Santa Fe 846, 3rd floor, Retiro, tel. 4319-0063

**Southern Winds:** Avenida Santa Fe 784, Retiro, 0810/777-7979

**Swiss International:** Avenida Santa Fe 846, 1st floor, Retiro, tel. 4319-0000

**Transportes Aéreos de Mercosur (TAM):** Cerrito 1026, Retiro, tel. 4819-4800

**United Airlines:** Avenida Eduardo Madero 900, 9th floor, Retiro, tel. 4315-7622

**Varig:** Avenida Córdoba 972, 3rd floor, Retiro, tel. 4329-9211

**Note:** At press time, Dinar Líneas Aéreas, LAPA, and Southern Winds were experiencing financial difficulties; strikes and cuts in service were common. Currently Aerolíneas Argentinas is the only reliable domestic airline.

buses daily to and from Ezeiza between 4 A.M. and 9:30 P.M. There are 25 buses daily to Aeroparque (US$1.50); most buses from Ezeiza make connections to Aeroparque for domestic flights. Rates to or from Ezeiza are US$4.

**Taxis and *remises*** offer similar services, but taxis are metered and *remises* (generally newer and more spacious vehicles) are not. Offering door-to-door service, they are no more expensive than shuttles for three or more persons. Manuel Tienda León and many other companies, such as Naon Remises, tel. 11/4545-6500, remisesnaon@sinectis.com.ar, offer *remises* to Aeroparque (US$3) and Ezeiza (US$10). Both *remises* and taxis usually add the cost of the toll road to Ezeiza, which is less than US$1.

## From North America
Miami, Atlanta, Washington, D.C. (Dulles), New York, Chicago, and Los Angeles are the main gateways to Buenos Aires. Canadian passengers must make their connections in the US.

Aerolíneas Argentinas is the traditional flagship carrier, but other options include American Airlines, Copa, LanChile, Lloyd Aéreo Boliviano, Mexicana, Southern Winds, Transportes Aéreos Mercosur (TAM), United Airlines, and Varig. Aerolíneas Argentinas, American, and United have the only nonstop services; others require changing planes elsewhere in Central or South America.

## From Mexico, Central America, and the Caribbean
Mexicana flies four times weekly from Mexico City via Cancún. Aerolíneas Argentinas flies twice weekly from Cancún. Lloyd Aéreo Boliviano and Varig also fly to Cancún, but less directly.

Cubana flies four times weekly from Havana, while Avianca has connections to the Caribbean, Central America, and Mexico via Bogotá.

Copa flies daily from Panama, with connections throughout Central America.

## From Europe
From Europe, there are direct services to Buenos Aires with Aerolíneas Argentinas (from Rome and Madrid); Air France (from Paris); Alitalia (from Milan and Rome); British Airways (from London): Iberia (from Barcelona and Madrid); Lufthansa (from Frankfurt); Pluna; and Swiss International (from Zurich). TAM has connections from Paris via Rio de Janeiro and São Paulo.

## From Asia, Africa, and the Pacific
The most direct service from the Pacific has been Qantas's three times weekly service from Sydney via Auckland, but since the recent Argentine crisis Qantas links up with LanChile flights via Tahiti, Easter Island and Santiago, or with LanChile via Los Angeles. Air New Zealand does the same. From Japan, it's easiest to make connections via Los Angeles.

South African Airways flies six times weekly from Johannesburg to Rio de Janeiro, where TAM and Varig offer connections to Buenos Aires.

## Within South America
Buenos Aires has connections to the neighboring republics of Uruguay, Brazil, Paraguay, Bolivia, Chile, and elsewhere on the continent. There are no flights to the Guyanas, however.

**From Neighboring Countries:** Some major international airlines fly to and from Ezeiza to Montevideo, Uruguay, but most flights to the Uruguayan capital leave from close-in Aeroparque. There are also flights from Aeroparque to Punta del Este, Uruguay's popular summer resort and weekend getaway. Aerolíneas Argentinas and Pluna are the main carriers, but LAPA (Líneas Aéreas Privadas Argentinas), American Falcon, and Southern Winds also have a few flights.

To Brazil, the main destinations are São Paulo and Rio de Janiero, but there are also flights to Florianópolis, Porto Alegre, Porto Seguro, Salvador, and other cities. The main carriers are Aerolíneas Argentinas, TAM, and Varig.

Flights to Paraguay go to the capital city of Asunción, with TAM and Varig; some TAM flights continue to Ciudad del Este and São Paulo (Brazil).

Lloyd Aéreo Boliviano flies to the lowland Bolivian city of Santa Cruz de la Sierra and on to the highland capital of La Paz. Aerolíneas also flies to Santa Cruz, and TAM has connections to Santa Cruz and Cochabamba via Asunción.

Discount fares are often available from travel agents but are less common in Latin America than elsewhere; the major exception is the highly competitive Buenos Aires–Santiago de Chile route, where European carriers like Air France and Lufthansa try to fill empty seats between Chile and the Argentine capital, where most transatlantic passengers board or disembark. This has kept fares low on competitors like Aerolíneas Argentinas and LanChile.

**From Other South American Countries:** Flights to Peru, Ecuador, Colombia, and Venezuela are all via capital cities, though some carriers stop elsewhere en route. Aerolíneas Argentinas goes to Lima and Caracas; Aeroméxico goes to Lima en route to Mexico City; and Avianca flies to Bogotá.

## From Elsewhere in Argentina

In addition to international air service, there is a wide network of domestic airports and airlines centered in Buenos Aires; indeed, to fly between Argentine cities, more often than not it's unavoidable to change planes in Buenos Aires. Since none of the excursions in this book requires flying, these destinations and airlines are covered

only generally here. Unless otherwise indicated, all of them use Aeroparque, the city airport.

Please note that in early 2003 Argentine domestic airlines began to charge differential rates for flights within the country, with Argentine residents paying in pesos and foreigners in dollars.

Aerolíneas Argentinas has domestic as well as international flights. Their domestic branch Austral, Perú 2, Monserrat, tel. 4320-2345, flies to destinations ranging from Puerto Iguazú on the Brazilian border to Ushuaia in Tierra del Fuego.

American Falcon, Avenida Santa Fe 1713, 4th floor, Recoleta, tel. 4811-0215, www.americanfalcon.com.ar, flies from Ezeiza to the provincial capital of Córdoba and the Patagonian resort of Bariloche, and may add other Patagonian destinations.

LAPA, Avenida Carlos Pellegrini 1075, Retiro, tel. 4114-5272, serves domestic destinations ranging from Jujuy and Salta in the far northwest to Ushuaia in the south. Southern Winds, Avenida Santa Fe 784, Retiro, tel. 4515-8600, covers most of the same destinations. Dinar Líneas Aéreas, having experienced financial problems and twice been sold, flies to Salta and Jujuy only; the office is at Avenida Roque Sáenz Peña 933, tel. 4327-8000.

## TRAVEL AGENCIES

North of Plaza San Martín, Retiro's **American Express** office, Arenales 707, tel. 11/4310-3535, fax 11/4315-1846, amexbueemp@aexp.com, offers the usual services and cashes its own travelers' checks without additional commission.

**Swan Turismo**, Cerrito 822, 9th floor, Retiro, tel./fax 11/4129-7926, swanturismo@teletel.com.ar, is a full-service travel agency that's earned a reputation for willingness and ability to deal with some of the eccentricities of the Argentine travel system.

There are also several student-oriented travel agencies, such as the nonprofit **Asatej**, in the Galería Buenos Aires at Florida 835, 3rd floor, Retiro, tel. 11/4311-6953, fax 11/4311-6840, asatej@asatej.com.ar, www.asatej.com.ar. Affiliated

with STA Travel, Asatej is transforming its focus to incoming tourism as the Argentine economic crisis has reduced overseas travel by young Argentines. Also the affiliate of Hostelling International, it's good at searching out the best airfares for anyone, not just students.

The competing **Asociación Argentina de Albergues de la Juventud** (AAAJ), Talcahuano 214, tel./fax 11/4372-7094, info@aaaj.org.ar, www.hostelling-aaaj.org.ar, also provides student-travel services. Also university-oriented is **Turismo Unión Buenos Amigos** (TUBA), Sarmiento 1967, 1° "12", tel./fax 11/4953-3773, infotuba@infovia.com.ar, www.tuba.com.ar, in Balvanera (Congreso).

Líneas Aéreas del Estado (LADE), Perú 714 in San Telmo, 4361-7071, is the Argentine air force's heavily subsidized commercial aviation branch. Miraculously surviving budget crises and privatizations, it flies to southern Buenos Aires province and Patagonia on a wing and a prayer.

## BY LAND

### Bus

Buenos Aires' main bus station is Retiro's Estación Terminal de Omnibus, at Avenida Ramos Mejía 1860, tel. 4310-0700, www.tebasa.com.ar. The sprawling three-story building is home to nearly 140 bus companies that cover the entire country and international destinations as well. It's walking distance from the northern terminus of Subte Línea C, at the Retiro train station.

The terminal's ground floor is primarily for freight; buses leave from *andenes* (platforms) on the first floor. Ticket offices, however, are on the second floor. On the first floor, the Centro de Informes y Reclamos, tel. 4310-0700, provides general bus information and also oversees taxis that serve the terminal; direct any complaints about taxi drivers to them. There is also a separate tourist office, open 7:30 A.M.–1 P.M. only.

For international buses, reservations are a good idea, especially during the summer (January and February) and winter (late July) holiday periods, but also on long weekends like *Semana Santa* (Holy Week). Prices vary according to the quality of service, ranging from ordinary reclining seats to more spacious *servicio diferencial* and nearly horizontal *coche cama* (bed car).

Domestic bus services to the provinces do not appear in detail here; for transportation to areas beyond the federal capital, see the appropriate geographical entry in the Excursions from Buenos Aires chapter.

**International Bus Services:** Several companies take the roundabout 600-kilometer route to Montevideo, Uruguay, which takes more time (nine hours) than the ferry but costs less (US$25): Bus de la Carrera (four nightly), tel. 4313-1700; Cauvi (once nightly), tel. 4314-6999; and Gen-eral Belgrano (once nightly), tel. 4315-1226. All leave between 9:30 and 11:30 P.M.

To the Paraguayan capital of Asunción (US$15–22, 21 hours), the main carriers are Nuestra Señora de la Asunción, tel. 4313-2349, and Chevalier Paraguaya, tel. 4313-2325. For Brazilian destinations such as Foz do Iguaçu (US$33, 18 hours), Porto Alegre (US$39, 20 hours), São Paulo (US$56, 40 hours) and Rio de Janeiro (US$64, 44 hours), try Pluma, tel. 4313-3893, or Rápido Iguazú, tel. 4315-6981.

For the trans-Andean crossing to Santiago, Chile (US$23, 21 hours), carriers include Fénix Pullman Norte, tel. 4313-0134, and Transporte Automotores Cuyo (TAC), tel. 4313-3627. For the Peruvian capital of Lima (via Chile, US$100, a 68-hour marathon), the choices are El Rápido Internacional, tel. 4315-0804, and Ormeño Internacional, tel. 4313-2259.

### Train

There are no international rail services to or from Buenos Aires and only a few long-distance domestic services, mostly to the Atlantic beach resorts of southern Buenos Aires province.

See the Getting Around entry later in this chapter for information on suburban and long-distance trains.

### Car, Motorcycle, and Bicycle

Overland travel from North America or elsewhere is problematical because Panama's Darien Gap to Colombia is impassable for motor vehicles, time-consuming, very difficult and potentially dangerous even for those on foot, and passes through areas controlled by drug smugglers, guerrillas, and/or brutal Colombian paramilitaries.

For travelers whose primary interest is the city, a vehicle is unnecessary, as public transport is cheap and excellent and parking is next to impossible. Those visiting other parts of the continent, however, may want to consider shipping a vehicle, which is recommended over renting a car for extended trips. While rental cars are easy to find in both Argentina and Uruguay, crossing borders with them can be complicated (though not impossible) and requires extra expense for insurance and notarial documents. To locate a shipper, check the Yellow Pages of your local phone directory under Automobile Transporters. These are normally freight consolidators rather than the companies that own the ships—the latter will charge higher container rates. Since many more people ship vehicles to Europe than to South America, it may take patience to find the right shipper; one recommended North American consolidator is McClary, Swift & Co., 360 Swift Avenue, South San Francisco, CA 94080, 650/872-2121, swift@unitedshipping.com, home.netcom.com/~mcswift/home.html, which has agents at many U.S. ports.

Argentine customs has improved in recent years, so shipping a vehicle into the country is easier than it used to be. Vehicles arrive at the Estación Marítima Buenos Aires at Dársena B, at Avenida Ramon Castillo and Avenida Maipu, Retiro, tel. 4311-0692, 4317-0675, or 4312-8677; here it is necessary to present your passport, vehicle title, and the original *conocimiento de embarque* (bill of lading), and to fill out a customs application. You will then obtain an appointment with a customs inspector to retrieve the vehicle, which will cost about US$300 for port costs and another US$200 for the shipper; if the vehicle has been in port longer than five days, there will be additional charges. The vehicle can remain legally in Argentina for eight months, with an eight-month extension possible; of course, any visit to a neighboring country restarts the clock. In event of any difficulty, consult a private *despachante de aduana* (customs broker), such as José Angel Vidal Labra, tel. 4345-7887, vidla@sinectis.com.ar.

Another possibility is the ports of Chile, which are less bureaucratic and safer for the vehicle than those of Argentina. The recommended and most probable ports of entry are San Antonio (southwest of Santiago), and Valparaíso (northwest of the capital). It pays to be there within a couple days of the vehicle's arrival, or storage charges can mount up. Leave the gas tank as nearly empty as possible (for safety's sake) and leave no valuables—including tools—in the vehicle.

To arrange a shipment from San Antonio or Valparaíso, contact the Santiago consolidator Ultramar, Moneda 970, 18th floor, Santiago Centro, tel. 2/63001817, fax 6986552, italia@ultramar.cl. For a trustworthy customs agent to handle the paperwork, contact the office of Juan Alarcón Rojas, Fidel Oteíza 1921, 12th floor, Providencia, Santiago, tel. 2/2252780, fax 2/2045302, alrcon@entelchile.net; Chile's country code is 56.

Bicycles, of course, can be partially dismantled, packaged and easily be shipped aboard airplanes, sometimes for no additional charge. There is rarely any additional paperwork for bringing a bike into the country, but many of the same concerns apply as to any other overland travel, like bad road conditions and drivers.

**Vehicle Documents, Driver's License, and Equipment:** Most South American countries, including Argentina, Chile, Uruguay, and Brazil, have dispensed with the cumbersome *Carnet de Passage en Douanes* that required depositing a large bond in order to import a motor vehicle. Officials at the port of arrival or border post will issue a 90-day permit on presentation of the vehicle title, registration, bill of lading (if the vehicle is being shipped), and your passport. For shipped vehicles, there are usually some small but relatively insignificant port charges (unless the vehicle has been stored more than a few days).

Before traveling to Argentina, obtain an International or Interamerican Driving Permit. (Travelers intending to visit Uruguay should note that that country officially recognizes only the latter, though in practice they appear more flexible.) These permits are available through the American Automobile Association, (AAA) or its counterpart in your home country, and are normally valid for one calendar year from date of issue. Strictly speaking, they are not valid without a state or national driver's license, but Argentine police usually ignore the latter. Another form of identification, such as a national ID card or passport, is also necessary.

The police pay close attention to vehicle documents—*tarjeta verde* ("green card") registration for Argentine vehicles, customs permission for foreign ones, and liability insurance (though many Argentines drive without it, it is reasonably priced from the Automóvil Club Argentino, the national automobile club, and other insurers). Vehicles without registration may be impounded on the spot. Argentine vehicles should have proof of a *verificación técnica* (safety inspection).

At roadside checkpoints, the police are also rigid about obligatory equipment such as headrests for the driver and each passenger, *valizas* (triangular emergency reflectors), and *matafuegos* (one-kilo fire extinguishers). In any instance of document irregularity or minor equipment violation, provincial police in particular may threaten fines while really soliciting *coimas* (bribes). A firm but calm suggestion that you intend to call your consulate may help overcome any difficulty.

**Road Hazards:** Buenos Aires traffic is so fast and ruthless that it's amazing that Jorge Luis Borges, or any other blind person, could survive it—it's tough enough on sighted people in prime physical condition. According to municipal authorities, 65 percent of the city's traffic fatalities are pedestrians; most of the culprits, unsurprisingly, are male drivers between 19 and 35 years of age.

*Porteño* drivers in the city and stray cattle in the provinces might seem enough to deal with, but the economic crisis of 2001–2002 lead to a major increase of *piquetes* (roadblocks) of demonstrators protesting unemployment and other issues. *Piqueteros* (picketers), while they tend to focus on stopping commercial traffic, manage to slow down everything else as well; never try to run a *piquete;* doing so can raise the wrath of the picketers. Rather, try to show solidarity and, in all likelihood, you'll pass without incident.

# BY RIVER

From Buenos Aires, there are ferry connections across the river to the Uruguayan capital of Montevideo, but also to the resort town of Piriápolis (in summer only) and to the charming 18th-century town of Colonia. From the suburban river port of Tigre, there are launches to the Uruguayan river ports of Carmelo and Nueva Palmira.

## Buenos Aires to and from Montevideo

Buquebus, tel. 4316-6500 or 4316-6550, www.buquebus.com, has its main terminal at Puerto Madero's Dársena Norte, but also has a ticket outlet at Patio Bullrich, Avenida Libertador 750, Retiro. It coordinates services and schedules with Ferryturismo, whose slow ferry *Eladia Isabel* sails to Colonia (2.75 hours, US$13 pp tourist, US$19 pp first class) at 12:30 A.M. daily except Sunday and at 9 A.M. daily; the faster hydrofoil *Atlantic III* (50 minutes, US$24 tourist; US$35 first class) sails at 11:30 A.M. and 7 P.M. daily. For direct service to Montevideo (2.5 hours, US$44 tourist class; US$54 first class), the high-speed ferries *Juan Patricio* and *Patricia Oliva III* sail at 8 A.M. daily and 3:30 P.M. weekdays except Monday, and 6 P.M. weekdays only. There are also summer sailings to the port of Piriápolis, midway between Montevideo and the fashionable Atlantic beach resort of Punta del Este.

## Tigre to and from Carmelo and Nueva Palmira

The northern Buenos Aires province suburb of Tigre has international connections with the Uruguayan towns of Carmelo and Nueva Palmira. See the appropriate geographical entries in the Excursions from Buenos Aires chapter for details.

# Getting Around

Even as automobiles clog the streets of Buenos Aires and other cities, most Argentines still rely on public transportation to get around. Services in the capital and Gran Buenos Aires are frequent and reasonably well-integrated, but not perfectly so.

A local miracle, at least for visitors who can understand Spanish, is the free service (tel. 131 from any public or private telephone) that tells you the best Subte or bus route between any two points in the city; simply tell the operator exactly where you are, and he or she will tell you the closest stop.

## COLECTIVOS (BUSES)

More than 200 separate bus routes serve the *capital federal* and Gran Buenos Aires, but most visitors and even residents need to know relatively few of them to get around easily. It is useful, however, to have one of the annually updated city atlases, such as the *Guía Lumi* or the *Guía T,* which include detailed descriptions of bus routes. There are also abbreviated pocket versions of the bus lines. All are readily available at newsstand kiosks and bookstores.

Route signs at fixed stops often but not always indicate the bus's itinerary. If you don't have a written guide, ask someone for help—*porteños* often know the system by heart and are generous with information. Fares depend on distance traveled, but within the capital most are US$.30 or less; after you tell the driver your destination, he will enter the fare in the automatic ticket machine, which takes only coins but does give small change. Though the driver will often give warning of your stop, his politeness may cease when he hits the accelerator.

> *South America's first underground railway, the Subte, has modernized and expanded in recent years, but its antique cars, with their varnished but worn woodwork and elaborately tiled but chipped murals, recall the prosperity and optimism of early-20th-century Argentina.*

## TRAIN

Buenos Aires has two types of rail systems: the subway or Subte that serves the *capital federal,* and a series of surface commuter trains, run by several private companies, that connects downtown with more distant suburbs.

### Subte

Privatized in 1994 and popularly known as the Subte, the Buenos Aires subway opened in 1913. South America's first underground railway, the 13th in the world, it has modernized and expanded in recent years, but its antique cars, with their varnished but worn woodwork and elaborately tiled but chipped murals, recall the prosperity and optimism of early-20th-century Argentina. The Subte is still the fastest way to get around the capital.

Metrovías, the private concessionaire, www.metrovias.com.ar, operates the five existing underground lines and is building a sixth tranverse line from Retiro through Recoleta, Once, and the southern part of the city, which will shorten many trips by reducing the need to transfer in the Microcentro. At present there are 67 stations for 39.5 kilometers of track within the capital; in 2001, the systems carried more than 241 million passengers.

Since taking over the system, Metrovías has also improved the rolling stock, extended existing lines, modernized many stations, and built new ones. Electronic tickets have replaced the traditional Subte *fichas* (tokens) but, while this is perhaps more efficient than in the past, it means lots of litter. Another negative development is the system of SUBTV monitors that show nonstop advertising. Ventilation remains poor in many stations, though some of the newest cars are air-conditioned.

# RIDING THE SUBTE

Operated by the private concessionaire Metrovías, the state-owned Subterráneos de Buenos Aires comprises five alphabetically designated lines, four of which (A, B, D, and E) begin in Monserrat or the Microcentro and serve outlying northern and western barrios, with numerous stations in between. Línea C is a north-south connector line between major railway stations at Retiro and Constitución.

An additional north-south connector line, Línea H, is under construction between Retiro and outlying southern barrios, beneath Avenida Pueyrredón and Avenida Jujuy. Three other lines have been proposed, but construction has not yet begun.

Subte hours are 5 A.M. to about 11 P.M. Monday through Saturday, but the system opens later (around 8 A.M.) and closes earlier (about 10:30 P.M.) Sundays and holidays, when services are less frequent. Fares are 70 centavos; to save time, purchase magnetic tickets in quantities of two, five, 10,

and 30 rides. Two or more people may use the same ticket (legally) by passing it back and forth across the turnstile; you do not need a ticket to exit the system.

Before going through the turnstiles, be sure of the direction you're headed; at some stations, trains in both directions use the same platform, but at others the platforms are on opposite sides. Some stations have one-way traffic only; in those cases, the next station down the line usually serves one-way traffic in the other direction.

For complaints or problems, contact Metrovías's Centro de Atención al Pasajero toll-free at tel. 0800/555-1616.

## Subte Routes

**Línea A** begins at Plaza de Mayo in Monserrat, and runs beneath Avenida Rivadavia to Primera Junta, in the barrio of Chacarita.

**Línea B** begins at Avenida Leandro Alem in the Microcentro, and runs beneath Avenida Corrientes to Federico Lacroze in the barrio of Chacarita, where it connects with the suburban Ferrocarril Urquiza. Two new stations are under construction, at Tronador and Avenida los Incas, on a northwesterly extension that is due to reach Villa Urquiza.

**Línea C** connects Retiro (which has northern suburban commuter surface rail lines) with Constitución, the transfer point for southern suburban commuter surface lines; Línea C also has transfer stations for all other Subte lines.

**Línea D** begins at Catedral on Plaza de Mayo, and runs beneath Avenida Santa Fe and Avenida Cabildo through Palermo and Belgrano to Congreso de Tucumán, in the barrio of Núñez.

**Línea E** begins at Bolívar on the Avenida de Mayo, and goes to Plaza de los Virreyes, in the barrio of Flores. At Plaza de los Virreyes there is a light-rail extension known as the Premetro.

Presently under construction, **Línea H** should open soon; the economic crisis has slowed but not halted progress. The first stretch will begin at Inclán, in the southern barrio of Parque Patricios, and connect with Plaza Miserere (Once), on Línea A; it will eventually extend north to Recoleta and Retiro, and south to Nueva Pompeya; the extension should be complete by 2005.

entrance to Subte Línea A, at Plaza de Mayo

© WAYNE BERNHARDSON

TRAVEL BASICS

## Suburban Trains

With a few exceptions, suburban trains are less useful to short-term visitors than they are to commuters who live in Buenos Aires province. They are very cheap and, while they may be improving, most are not improving nearly so fast as the Subte is.

The most useful and best is the Ferrocarril Mitre, operated by Trenes de Buenos Aires (TBA), tel. 11/4317-4400, www.tbanet.com.ar, which connects the classic Estación Retiro, Avenida Ramos Mejía 1302, with Belgrano and Zona Norte suburbs including Vicente López, Olivos, Martínez, San Isidro, and Tigre. Another branch of the line goes to Villa Ballester, for connections to Reserva Natural Estricta Otamendi.

TBA also operates the Ferrocarril Sarmiento from Estación Once at Avenida Pueyrredón y Bartolomé Mitre (Subte: Plaza Miserere), which goes to western destinations like Moreno, with connections to Luján. Unlike the immaculate, state-of-the-art Mitre, this is a rundown line on which vendors even sell switchblades.

**Driving in Buenos Aires has its risks.**

Transportes Metropolitano, tel. 800/666-358736, operates the Ferrocarril Roca from Estación Constitución, at Avenida Brasil and Lima, to the Buenos Aires provincial capital of La Plata and intermediate points.

## TAXIS AND REMISES

Buenos Aires has an abundant fleet of taxis, painted black with yellow roofs. Since a spate of robberies that began some years ago, nearly all of them are now so-called **radio taxis** (which means you may call in advance for a cab). Some people prefer the security of phoning for a cab, but many if not most *porteños* still flag them down in the street. If in doubt, lock the back doors so that no one can enter the cab by surprise.

All regular cabs have digital meters. It costs about US$.40 to *bajar la bandera* ("drop the flag," i.e. switch on the meter) and another US$.04 per 100 meters. Verify that the taxi meter is set at zero.

Drivers do not expect tips and sometimes, to avoid having to make change, will even round the fare *down*. It's best to carry small bills rather than have to rely on the driver's making change, especially if he has just come on shift. Since there is a handful of dishonest drivers, before handing over the bill you may want to ask if he has the proper change for a large note, stating the amount of the note you're handing over.

*Remises* are radio taxis that charge an agreed-upon rate based on distance; the dispatcher will let you know the fare when you call, based on the pickup and dropoff points.

Hotels, restaurants, and other businesses will gladly ring taxis and *remises* for customers and clients.

## CAR RENTAL

Aggressive drivers, traffic congestion, and lack of parking make driving in Buenos Aires inadvisable, but some visitors may consider this option for excursions beyond the capital. To rent a car, you must show a valid driver's license and a valid credit card, and be at least 21 years old.

## CAR RENTALS

The following rental agencies have representatives in Buenos Aires:

**Ansa International (AI):** Paraguay 866, Retiro; tel. 4311-0220

**Avis:** Cerrito 1527, Retiro; tel. 4378-9640

**Dollar:** Marcelo T. de Alvear 523, Retiro; tel. 4315-8800

**Hertz:** Paraguay 1122, Retiro; tel. 4816-8001

**Localiza:** Maipú 924, Retiro; tel. 4315-8334

**Tauro:** Posadas 1590, Recoleta; tel. 4807-1002

**Thrifty:** Avenida Leandro N. Alem 699; tel. 4315-0777

Both local and international agencies maintain offices in Buenos Aires, where rental costs are typically lower than elsewhere in the country but higher than in North America. Since the devaluation of 2002, prices are more volatile, but they usually involve a fixed daily amount plus a per-kilometer charge; unlimited mileage deals are normally for rentals of a week or longer. Insurance is additional.

Prior to devaluation, Argentina had some of the most expensive gasoline in the Americas except for Uruguay, but prices have fallen in dollar terms—at least temporarily, even as they rose in peso terms. Regular gasoline now goes for about US$.50 per liter, premium for about US$.55 per liter, and super for about US$.60 per liter. *Gasoil* (diesel) is typically cheaper than gasoline, about US$.35 per liter, but the differential is shrinking. Because gasoline prices are unregulated, they may rise quickly.

Anyone driving in Buenos Aires should know that the Microcentro, bounded by Avenida Leandro Alem, Avenida Córdoba, Avenida de Mayo, and Avenida 9 de Julio is off-limits to private passenger vehicles, 7 A.M.–7 P.M. weekdays.

## BICYCLE

Cycling may not be the safest way of getting around Buenos Aires' chaotic traffic, but the number of cyclists is growing rapidly with the economic crisis. According to city government statistics, the number of cyclists rose by more than 50 percent from 2000 to 2001. For trips of less than five kilometers, according to their calcuations, the bicycle is both cheaper and faster than public transportation.

If riding around Buenos Aires, side streets may be safer than fast-moving avenues, but they are also narrower, with less room for getting out of the way. Traffic is not so wild on weekends as on weekdays, and parts of downtown are virtually deserted on Sunday.

There are few dedicated bike paths, except for the *bicisenda* that runs from Palermo to Retiro parallel to Avenida Figueroa Alcorta and Avenida Libertador. Cyclists should exit west at the *fin bicisenda* sign to avoid the *villa miseria* (shantytown) behind the Retiro train and bus stations. New bike lanes are being established on Avenida San Juan and Avenida Independencia, to be shared with automobiles, which must observe a speed limit of 40 kilometers per hour.

The capital's main bicycle advocacy organization is the Asociación de Ciclistas Urbanos, Avenida Díaz Vélez 5563, Caballito, tel./fax 4981-0578, acubici@yahoo.com, www.geocities.com/acubicicleta/index.html.

## WALKING

Thanks partly to its gentle topography, Buenos Aires is a walker's city or, one might even say, a jaywalker's city. Jaywalking is endemic, perhaps because it's not much more dangerous than crossing at the crosswalk with the light—for an overwhelming majority of *porteño* drivers, crosswalks appear to be merely decorative. While making turns, drivers weave among pedestrians rather than slowing or stopping to let them pass.

That said, in congested areas, pedestrians can often move faster than automobiles. In addition, barrios like San Telmo, La Boca, Recoleta, Palermo, and Belgrano (with their shady sidewalks and expansive parks) are particularly rewarding to urban explorers on foot; the summer heat and humidity, though, make it essential to consume plenty of fluids. Thundershowers make an umbrella advisable.

## ORGANIZED TOURS

Some of the best guided tours of the city are available through the municipal tourist office on Saturday and Sunday, often but not always with English-speaking guides. The *Buenos Aires Herald's* Friday "getOut!" section and *Clarín's* event section both contain listings, but the complete schedule also appears in *Viva Bue,* a monthly giveaway guide to the capital. In case of rain, the tours are canceled.

For conventional tours of the capital and vicinity, including the Microcentro, Recoleta and Palermo, and San Telmo and La Boca, the usual choices are **Buenos Aires Tour,** Lavalle 1444, Oficina 10, tel. 11/4371-2304, buenosairestour@sinectis.com.ar, and **Buenos Aires Visión,** Esmeralda 356, 8th floor, tel. 11/4394-2986, bavision@ssdnet.com.ar.

Several city operators provide thematically oriented tours, with English-speaking and other guides available. Though primarily oriented toward outdoor activities, **Lihué Expediciones,** Paraguay 880, 7th floor, Retiro, tel./fax 11/4315-0906, viajes@lihue-expeditions.com.ar, also offers walking tours focused on literary figures like Borges and Julio Cortázar.

Borges' widow María Kodama leads fortnightly Borgesian tours, free of charge, sponsored by municipal tourism authorities and her own **Fundación Internacional Jorge Luis Borges,** Anchorena 1660, tel. 4822-8340; phone for schedules.

**Historical Tours,** Paraguay 647, 6th floor, Retiro, tel. 11/4311-1019, histours@sinectis.com.ar, is also theme-oriented, placing emphasis on subjects such as immigration in its visits to La Boca and San Telmo.

**Travel Line Argentina,** Esmeralda 770, 10th floor, Oficina B, tel. 11/4393-9000, fax11/ 4394-3929, info@travelline.com.ar, www.travelline .com.ar, conducts specialty excursions such as its "Evita Tour," which takes in the CGT labor headquarters, Luna Park Stadium, the Perón and Duarte residences, and other locales associated with Evita's reign.

# Visas and Officialdom

Citizens of neighboring countries—Bolivians, Brazilians, Uruguayans, and Paraguayans—need only national identity cards, but most other nationalities needs passports. Citizens of other Latin American countries, U.S. and Canadian citizens, along with citizens of the European Union and Scandinavian countries, Switzerland, Israel, Australia, and New Zealand need passports but not advance visas. Citizens of nearly all African and Asian countries, with the exceptions of South Africa and Japan, need advance visas.

Regulations change, however, and it may be helpful to check the visa page of Argentina's Ministerio de Relaciones Exteriores (Foreign Relations Ministry), at the website www.mrecic.gov.ar/ consulares/pagcon.html. See also the Special Topic "Argentine Consulates in Other Countries" in this chapter for addresses and telephone num-

bers of the most important overseas Argentine embassies and consulates.

Argentina routinely grants 90-day entry permits to foreign visitors, in the form of tourist cards that, theoretically, must be surrendered on departure from the country; in practice, it's the passport stamp that counts. For US$100, the entry is renewable for 90 days at the Dirección Nacional de Migraciones, Avenida Argentina 1355, Retiro, tel. 11/4317-0237. Hours are 8 A.M.–1 P.M. weekdays only.

In the provinces, renewal can be done at any office of the Policía Federal (Federal Police), but in smaller towns the police may not be accustomed to conducting renewals. Buenos Aires visitors may find it cheaper and simpler to take a day trip on the ferry to Colonia, Uruguay, which will reset the 90-day period.

## FOREIGN CONSULATES IN ARGENTINA

As a major world capital, Buenos Aires has a full complement of embassies and consulates that provide services to foreign visitors. A country's embassy and consulate often share an address, but when the addresses are separate the list below provides the address of the consulate, as they are primarily responsible for dealing with individuals traveling for either business or pleasure.

**Australia:** Villanueva 1400, Palermo, tel. 4777-6580

**Belgium:** 8th floor, Defensa 113, Monserrat, tel. 4331-0066

**Bolivia:**; Avenida Belgrano 1670, 1st floor, Monserrat, tel. 4381-0539

**Brazil:** 5th floor, Carlos Pellegrini 1363, Retiro, tel. 4515-6500

**Canada:** Tagle 2828, Palermo, tel. 4805-3032

**Chile:** San Martín 439, 9th floor, Microcentro, tel. 4394-6582

**Denmark:** 9th floor, Leandro N. Alem 1074, Retiro, tel. 4312-6901

**France:** 3rd floor, Santa Fe 846, Retiro, tel. 4312-2409

**Germany:** Villanueva 1055, Palermo, tel. 4778-2500

**Ireland:** 6th floor, Avenida del Libertador 1064, Recoleta, tel. 5787-0801

**Israel:** 10th floor, Avenida de Mayo 701, Monserrat, tel. 4338-2500

**Italy:** Marcelo T. de Alvear 1125, Retiro, tel. 4816-6132

**Japan:** Bouchard 547, 17th floor, Microcentro, tel. 4318-8220

**Mexico:** Arcos 1650, Belgrano, tel. 4789-8826

**Netherlands:** Olga Cossentini 831, 3rd floor, Edificio Porteño Plaza 2, Puerto Madero, tel. 4338-0050

**New Zealand:** Carlos Pellegrini 1427, 5th floor, Microcentro, tel. 4328-0747

**Norway:** 3rd floor, Esmeralda 909, Retiro, tel. 4312-2204

**Paraguay:** Viamonte 1851, Balvanera, tel. 4815-9801

**Peru:** 11th floor, Avenida Córdoba 1345, Retiro, tel. 4816-0646

**Spain:** Guido 1760, Recoleta, tel. 4811-0070

**Sweden:** Tacuarí 147, Monserrat, tel. 4342-1422

**Switzerland:** 10th floor, Santa Fe 846, Retiro, tel. 4311-6491

**United Kingdom:** Dr. Luis Agote 2412, Recoleta, tel. 4576-2222

**United States of America:** Colombia 4300, Palermo, tel. 5777-4533

**Uruguay:** Avenida Las Heras 1915, Recoleta, tel. 4807-3040

Formally, arriving visitors must have a return or onward ticket, but enforcement is inconsistent—if you have a Latin American, North American, or Western European passport, for instance, it is unlikely you will be asked to show the return ticket (in the western hemisphere, only Cubans need a visa to enter Argentina). The author has entered Argentina dozens of times over many years, at Buenos Aires' international airport and some of the most remote border posts, without ever having been asked for the return or onward ticket.

Airlines, however, may feel differently and not permit a passenger without a roundtrip ticket to board a flight to Argentina. Likewise, if the arriving passenger comes from an Eastern European, Asian, or African country, he or she may be asked for proof of return transport. Immigration officials have a great deal of discretion in these matters.

Always carry identification, since federal and provincial police can request it at any moment, though they rarely do so without a reason. Passports are also necessary for routine transactions like checking into hotels, cashing travelers' checks, and even payment by credit card.

Dependent children under age 14 traveling without both parents presumably need notarized parental consent, but the author's daughter has visited Argentina many times with only one parent, and has never been asked for such a document.

Argentine-born individuals, even if their parents were not Argentines or if they have been naturalized elsewhere, sometimes experience obstacles from immigration officials. Generally, they may enter the country for no more than 60 days on a non-Argentine document. Argentine passports renewed outside the country expire on reentry, making it necessary to renew them with the Policía Federal, which can be a bothersome and time-consuming process on a short trip.

## LOST OR STOLEN PASSPORTS

Visitors who suffer a lost or stolen passport must obtain a replacement at their own embassy or consulate. After obtaining a replacement passport, it's necessary to visit the Dirección Nacional de Migraciones (see details earlier in this section) to replace the tourist card.

## CUSTOMS

Notorious for truly egregious corruption, Argentine customs has improved from the days of the so-called *aduana paralela* (parallel customs) and normally presents no obstacle to tourists. Short-term visitors to Argentina may import personal effects including clothing, jewelry, medicine, sporting gear, camping equipment and accessories, photographic and video equipment, personal computers, and the like, as well as 400 cigarettes, two liters of wine or alcoholic beverages (adults over 18 only), and up to US$300 of new merchandise.

Customs inspections are routine, but at Buenos Aires' international airports, river ports and at some land borders, incoming checked baggage may have to pass through X-ray machines; do not put photographic film in checked baggage. Fresh food will be confiscated at any port of entry.

At some remote border posts, the Gendarmería Nacional (Border Guard) handles all formalities, from immigration to customs to agricultural inspections. Visitors arriving from drug-producing countries like Colombia, Peru, and Bolivia may get special attention at border posts.

## POLICE AND MILITARY

Argentina is notorious for police corruption. For this reason, *porteños* and other Argentines scornfully call both federal and provincial police *la cana*—an insult that should never be used to their faces.

The Policía Federal (Federal Police) are marginally more professional than provincial forces like that of Buenos Aires province; the latter is almost universally detested for harassing motorists for minor equipment violations and, even worse, for their *gatillo fácil* (hair-trigger) response to minor criminal offenses. This behavior is not completely unwarranted, however—many police officers have died at the hands of well-armed

# ARGENTINE CONSULATES IN OTHER COUNTRIES

Argentina has wide diplomatic representation throughout the world, even though economic difficulties have reduced this presence over the past couple of decades. In capital cities, embassies and consulates often, though not always, share an address; people planning a visit to Argentina should go to consulates rather than embassies for visas and other inquiries.

**Australia:** Embassy—John McEwen House, 2nd floor, 7 National Circuit, Barton ACT, tel. 02/6273-9111
Consulate—44 Market Street, 20th floor, Sydney NSW, tel. 02/9262-2933

**Bolivia:** Sánchez Lima 2103, La Paz, tel. 242-2912

**Brazil:** Praia Botafogo 228, Entreloja, Rio de Janeiro, tel. 21/2533-1646
Avenida Paulista 1106, 9th floor, São Paulo, tel. 3282-1366

**Canada:** Suite 620, 90 Sparks St, Ottawa, Ontario K1P 514, 613/236-2351
1 First Canadian Place, Suite 5840, Toronto, Ontario M5X 1K2, 416/955-9075
2000 Peel St, Montréal, Québec H3A 2W5, 514/842-6582

**Chile:** Vicuña Mackenna 41, Santiago, tel. 2/222-6853
Cauquenes 94, 2nd floor, Puerto Montt, tel. 65/253966
21 de Mayo 1878, Punta Arenas, tel. 56/261532

**France:** 6 Rue Cimarosa, Paris, tel. 1/4434-2209

**Germany:** Dorotheenstrasse 89, 3rd floor, Berlin, tel. 30/226-6890

**New Zealand:** 142 Lambton Quay, 14th floor, Wellington, tel. 472-8330

**Paraguay:** 1st floor, Banco Nación, Palma 319, Asunción, tel. 21/442151
Carlos Antonio López 690, Encarnación, tel. 71/201066

**Switzerland:** Tödistrasse 5, 1st floor, Zurich, tel. 1/284-2050

**United Kingdom:** 27 Three Kings Yard, London W1Y 1FL, tel. 20/7318-1349

**United States of America:** 1811 Q Street NW, Washington, D.C. 20009, 202/238-6460
5550 Wilshire Blvd, Suite 210, Los Angeles, CA 90036, 323/954-9155
800 Brickell Avenue, Penthouse 1, Miami, FL 33131, 305/373-1889
245 Peachtree Center Avenue, Suite 2101, Atlanta, GA 30303, 404/880-0805
205 N. Michigan Avenue, Suite 4209, Chicago, IL 60601, 312/819-2610
12 W. 56th Street, New York, NY 10019, 212/603-0403
3050 Post Oak Boulevard, Suite 1625, Houston, TX 77056, 713/871-8935

**Uruguay:** Wilson Ferreira Aldunate 1281, Montevideo, tel. 2/902-8623
Avenida General Flores 226, Colonia, tel. 52/22093
Calle 25 (Arrecifes) No. 544, Punta del Este, tel. 42/441632

TRAVEL BASICS

criminals (who are sometimes themselves police officers).

Police officers often solicit *coimas* (bribes) at routine traffic stops. To avoid paying a bribe, either state your wish to consult your consulate, or use broken Spanish even if you understand the language well. Either one may frustrate a corrupt official sufficiently to give up the effort.

Since the end of the 1976–83 military dictatorship, the Argentine military has lost prestige and appears to have acknowledged its inability to run the country, despite the occasional clamor of fringe groups in favor of a coup. Still, security is heavy around military bases and photography is taboo—it's common to see signs that say No Photography.

## Money

While traveling in Argentina, it makes sense to have a variety of money alternatives. International credit cards are widely accepted, and foreign ATM cards work almost everywhere. Because ATMs are open 24 hours a day, many visitors prefer this alternative, but economic instability and recent regulations that limit cash withdrawals for Argentines have made Argentine ATMs iffy at times; it makes sense to have a cash reserve in U.S. dollars. Traveler's checks may be the safest way to carry money, since they're refundable in case of loss or theft, but changing them outside Buenos Aires is a nightmarish experience even when stability reigns.

Prices throughout this book are given in U.S. dollars because of the instability of the Argentine peso, but normally travelers will be paying in pesos. Nevertheless, merchants and services will often accept dollars at the prevailing exchange rate or sometimes at an even better rate.

If carrying an emergency cash reserve, use an inconspicuous leg pouch or money belt (not the bulky kind that fits around the waist, which thieves or robbers easily recognize, but a zippered leather belt that looks like any other).

### CURRENCY

Throughout the 1990s, money was a simple matter. The Argentine peso was at par with the U.S. dollar, which circulated almost interchangeably alongside it, but the economic collapse of 2001–2002 has complicated matters. Many merchants still accept cash dol-

lars, but exchange rates vary and any change will come in pesos.

Banknotes exist in denominations of 5, 10, 20, 50, and 100 pesos. Coins exist in denominations of 1, 5, 10, 25 and 50 centavos (cents), but one-centavo coins are rare and most businesses generally round off prices to the nearest five or 10 centavos.

One major complication is the increasing use of *bonos*, bonds issued by provincial governments in lieu of cash for salaries and other obligations. Known as *patacones* (in Buenos Aires province), *lecop* (in many provinces), *lecor* (in Córdoba province), and by other names as well, these bonds circulate alongside the peso but many businesses and services do not accept them. When getting change, insist on pesos.

Counterfeiting of both U.S. and foreign currency appears to be increasing. Merchants will often refuse any U.S. banknote with the smallest tear or writing on it, but they will accept any peso note that is not flagrantly *trucho* (bogus). On any banknote, look for the conspicuous watermark with the initials of the historical figure depicted on it—J.S.M for José de San Martín on the five-peso note, for instance.

## EXCHANGE RATES

Following the debt default of early 2002, the government of caretaker president Eduardo Duhalde devalued the peso from 1 to 1.4 pesos per dollar but, when that proved unsustainable, the president floated the currency in mid-February of 2002. By midyear, the peso had fallen to 3.5 pesos to the dollar before stabilizing, but there are so many uncertainties in the Argentine economy that its ability to maintain that level is doubtful.

For the most up-to-date exchange rates, consult the business section of your daily newspaper or an online currency converter such as www.oanda.com.

In Buenos Aires, the best sources on exchange rate trends are the financial dailies *Ambito Financiero* and *Buenos Aires Económico*.

## CHANGING MONEY

During the 1990s (when the peso was at par with the dollar) changing money was a nonissue, as the two were virtually interchangeable. The floating of the peso in early 2002, however, made banks, *casas de cambio* (exchange houses), and surreptitious exchanges relevant again.

ATMs, abundant and becoming universal except in a few remote areas, match the best bank rates and are accessible 24/7. Unfortunately, in the aftermath of devaluation and a run on deposits, the government has declared bank holidays on which it has been difficult or impossible to withdraw cash from them, and there is no guarantee this will not happen again.

Foreign ATM cardholders are not subject to the banking controls known as the *corralito*, which limit withdrawals from Argentine accounts. Many banks, though, have limited hours and access because of protests known as *escraches,* and some have covered their doors and windows with plywood and even sheet metal. (One *porteño* psychiatrist, interviewed for U.S. National Public Radio, suggested that the people's bank accounts had a Freudian symbolism comparable to the penis, and that when Argentines were unable to withdraw their funds they felt castration anxieties.)

During bank holidays, or when exchange-rate policies create an active black market, street changers known as *arbolitos* (little trees, because they are planted in one spot) are a common sight in the Microcentro's financial district, known as La City, along Calle San Martín.

ATMs, unfortunately, generally dispense large banknotes, often of 100 pesos and rarely smaller than 50 pesos. One way around this problem is to punch in an odd amount, such as 290 pesos, in order to ensure getting some smaller notes.

## TRAVELERS' CHECKS AND REFUNDS

Despite the safeguards they offer, travelers' checks have many drawbacks in Argentina. In addition to the time-consuming bureaucracy of changing them at banks and exchange houses, they often carry a substantial penalty in terms of commission—up to three percent or even more in many cases. Businesses other than exchange houses rarely accept them under any circumstances and, in out-of-the-way places, nobody will. Travelers' checks, unfortunately, should be a last-resort means of carrying and changing money here; cash (despite its shortcomings) and ATM cards are better options.

## BANK TRANSFERS

Many Argentine exchange houses, post offices, and other businesses are affiliated with Western Union, making it relatively straightforward to send money from overseas. For a list of Western Union affiliates in Argentina, see their website at www.westernunion.com.

TRAVEL BASICS

The American Express Money Gram is another alternative. Amex has a large office in Retiro and affiliates throughout the country.

In an emergency, it is possible to forward money to U.S. citizens via the U.S. embassy in Buenos Aires by establishing a Department of State trust account through its Overseas Citizens Services, Washington, D.C. 20520, tel. 202/647-5225; there is a US$20 service charge for setting up the account. It is possible to arrange this as a wire or overnight mail transfer through Western Union, 800/325-6000 in the United States; for details see the State Department's website at www.travel.state.gov.

## CREDIT AND DEBIT CARDS

Credit cards have been common currency for many years and, in the aftermath of the recent peso crisis, when Argentines could not withdraw their savings, their use became even more widespread. Visa and MasterCard are most widely accepted, but there are inconsistencies— a significant number of businesses prefer American Express, sometimes to the exclusion of the others, or even Diner's Club. Debit cards are also widely accepted, at least those with Visa or MasterCard affiliation.

There are possible drawbacks to using credit cards, however. During the boom years of the 1990s, Argentine merchants generally refrained from the *recargo,* a surcharge on credit card purchases because of slow bank payments; many have reinstituted the *recargo,* which can be up to 10 percent, to cut their losses due to the peso's loss of value between the customer's payment and the bank's reimbursement. Note that hotels in particular may offer equivalent discounts for payments in cash.

Fluctuating exchange rates may also affect the charge that eventually appears on your overseas account. If the rate has changed in the interim between your payment in Buenos Aires and its posting to the home account, it may be either greater or smaller in terms of dollars (or other foreign currency), depending on the strength of the peso.

In general, *propinas* (gratuities) are *not* be added to charges for restaurant meals. Keep some cash, either dollars or pesos, for tips.

To deal with lost or stolen cards, the major international credit card companies have local representatives: American Express, Arenales 707, Retiro, tel. 11/4310-3000; Diner's Club, Avenida Santa Fe 1148, Retiro, tel. 11/4814-5627; MasterCard, Perú 143, Monserrat, tel. 11/4331-2088 or 800/555-0507; and Visa, Avenida Corrientes 1437, 3rd floor, tel. 11/4379-3300.

## COSTS

For most of the 1990s, Argentina was South America's most expensive country, so much so that even North Americans and European found it costly. Wealthy Argentines, for their part, partied in Miami, Madrid, Rome, and other inexpensive destinations.

This anomaly was a function of the fixed exchange rate instituted by former economy minister Domingo Cavallo, which reduced previous hyperinflation to near zero. Cavallo's "convertibility" policy, however, also froze prices at a relatively high but unsustainable level that eventually made Argentine exports noncompetitive and brought the default of late 2001.

Since the peso float of February 2002, and banking restrictions that limited the amount of money in circulation, Argentina has been a bargain for visitors who bring dollars or other hard currency. According to the Economist Intelligence Unit, Buenos Aires fell from being the 22nd most expensive city in the world to the 120th (of 131 surveyed). A crippling four-year recession, with unemployment exceeding 20 percent, has kept prices from skyrocketing in spite of devaluation. Businesses such as restaurants have had to keep prices relatively low, attempting to sell more at a lower margin.

By global standards, travel in Argentina and Buenos Aires is inexpensively priced, but much depends on the traveler's expectations. There are suitable services for everyone from barebones budget backpackers to pampered international business travelers. Budget travelers will find hotel rooms for less than US$10 pp and some excellent values for only a little more money. Hotels and resorts of international stature, like the Hyatt and Sheraton chains and their local equivalents, normally charge international prices, but even these have had to lower their rates during the crisis.

Likewise, meals range from a couple dollars or even less at the simplest *comedores,* but restaurants with sophisticated international cuisine can charge a lot more; even the latter, however, often serve moderately priced lunchtime specials.

As of press time, shoestring travelers could get along on US$20 per day or conceivably even less for accommodations and food. For US$50 per day it's possible to live very comfortably and eat well, and a budget of US$100 is extravagant. It's worth adding, though, that the volatility of Argentina's economy—hyperinflation was a recurrent phenomenon in the last half of the 20th century—makes it impossible to guarantee that prices will not rise. Check out a website like www.oanda.com to get the current exchange rate.

## TAXES

Argentina imposes a 21 percent *impuesto de valor agregado* (IVA, value added tax or VAT) on all goods and services, though this is normally included in the advertised price; if in doubt, ask for clarification ( *"¿Incluye los impuestos?"*). Tax evasion is a national sport, however, and hotel owners will often ignore the tax for payments in cash.

Foreign visitors making purchases intended for export can often get a legal IVA rebate on leaving the country.

## TIPPING

In restaurants with table service, a 10 percent gratuity is customary, but in smaller family-run eateries the practice is rare. Taxi drivers are customarily not tipped, but rounding off the fare to the next-highest convenient number is appropriate. Where there is no meter, this is not an issue.

## BARGAINING

Bargaining is not the way of life in Argentina that it is in some other Latin American countries, but in flea markets or crafts markets the vendor may start at a higher price than he or she expects to receive—avoid insultingly low offers, or such a high offer that the vendor will think you a fool. Depending on your language and bargaining skills, you should be able to achieve a compromise that satisfies everybody.

Even in some upscale shops in Buenos Aires, prices for items like leather jackets may be open to negotiation.

## STUDENT DISCOUNTS

Student discounts are relatively few, and prices are so low for most services that it's rarely worth arguing the point. In the case of foreign travel, however, students may be eligible for discount international airfares; consult student-oriented travel agencies and see the sections Getting There and Getting Around for details.

## Health and Safety

Midlatitude Buenos Aires and vicinity offer no major health risks beyond those associated with any large city; public health standards are good and tap water is potable. In some parts of northernmost subtropical Argentina, though, there is a small risk of malaria or similar tropical diseases.

A good general source on foreign health matters is Dr. Richard Dawood's *Travelers' Health* (New York: Random House, 1994), a small encyclopedia on the topic. Dr. Stuart R. Rose's *International Travel Health Guide* (Northampton, MA: Travel Medicine Inc., 2000) is annually updated and regionally focused. Try also Dirk G. Schroeder's *Staying Healthy in Asia, Africa and Latin America* (Emeryville, CA: Avalon Travel Publishing, 2000).

For up-to-date information on health issues in Chile and elsewhere in the Southern Cone, see the U.S. Centers for Disease Control (CDC) Temperate South America regional page, www.cdc.gov/travel/temsam.htm, which covers Chile, Argentina, Uruguay, and the Falkland Islands. Another good source is the United Kingdom's Department of Health website, www.doh.gov.uk/traveladvice/index.htm, which provides a chart of recommended prophylaxis by country.

At present, thanks to devaluation of the peso, quality medical care is so cheap that in some cases it might justify a trip to Buenos Aires. The author, for instance, paid US$100 for a magnetic resonance image (MRI) that would have cost at least six times that in California. A half-hour visit with a top orthopedist cost US$10, and a series of x-rays less than US$20. Such favorable prices may not continue as the economy recovers.

Visitors considering medical care, however, should choose private hospitals and clinics, especially since the economic crisis has strained the resources of public hospitals. One good choice is the Clínica Fleni, Montañeses 2325, Belgrano, tel. 11/5777-3200, www.fleni.org.ar; the clinic's focus is pediatrics and neurology, but it also has outstanding specialists in orthopedics. Another possibility is the Fundación Favaloro, Avenida Belgrano 1746, Monserrat, tel. 4378-1200, www.fundacionfavaloro.org, whose specialty is cardiology. Nearly all the doctors at both are English-speaking.

## BEFORE YOU GO

Theoretically, no vaccinations are obligatory for entry to Argentina, but if you are coming from a tropical country where yellow fever is endemic, authorities could ask for a vaccination certificate.

Traveling to Argentina or elsewhere without adequate medical insurance is risky. Before leaving your home country, obtain medical insurance that includes evacuation in case of serious emergency. Foreign health insurance may not be accepted in Argentina, so you may be required to pay out of your own pocket for later reimbursement. Often, however, private medical providers accept international credit cards in return for services.

Numerous carriers provide medical and evacuation coverage; an extensive list, including Internet links, is available at the U.S. State Department's website, www.travel.state.gov/medical.html.

## GENERAL HEALTH MAINTENANCE

Common-sense precautions can reduce the possibility of illness considerably. Washing the hands frequently with soap and water, and drinking only bottled, boiled, or carbonated water will all help diminish the likelihood of contagion for short-term visitors—though Argentine tap water is potable almost everywhere.

Where purified water is impossible to obtain, such as back-country streams where there may be livestock or problems with human waste, pass drinking water through a one-micron filter and further purify it with iodine drops or tablets (but avoid prolonged consumption of iodine-purified water). Non-pasteurized dairy products, such as goat cheese, can be problematic and are best avoided.

## FOOD OR WATERBORNE DISEASES

While relatively few visitors to Argentina run into problems of this sort, contaminated food and drink are not unheard of. In many cases, it's simply exposure to different sorts of bugs to which your body soon becomes accustomed, but if symptoms persist the problem may be more serious.

### Traveler's Diarrhea

Colloquially known as *turista* in Latin America, the classic traveler's diarrhea (TD) usually lasts only a few days and almost always less than a week. Besides "the runs," symptoms include nausea, vomiting, bloating, and general weakness. The usual cause is the notorious *Escherichia coli* (more commonly called *E. coli*) bacterium from contaminated food or water; in some cases *E. coli* infections can be fatal.

Fluids, including fruit juices, and small amounts of bland foods such as freshly cooked rice or soda crackers, may help relieve symptoms and aid you in regaining your strength. Dehydration is a serious problem, especially for children, who may need to be treated with an oral rehydration solution (ORS) of carbohydrates and salt.

Over-the-counter remedies like Pepto-Bismol, Lomotil, and Imodium may relieve symptoms but can also cause problems. Prescription drugs such as doxycyline and trimethoprim/sulfamethoxazole can also shorten the cycle. These may not, however, be suitable for children, and it's better for everyone to avoid them if at all possible.

Continuing and worsening symptoms, including bloody stools, may mean dysentery, a much more serious ailment that requires a physician's attention.

### Dysentery

Bacterial dysentery, resembling an intense form of TD, responds well to antibiotics, but amoebic dysentery is far more serious, sometimes leading to intestinal perforation, peritonitis, and liver abscesses. Like diarrhea, its symptoms include soft and even bloody stools, but some people may be asymptomatic even as they pass on *Entamoeba hystolica* through unsanitary toilet and food preparation practices. Metronidazole, known by the brand names Flagyl or Protostat, is an effective treatment, but a physician's diagnosis is advisable.

### Cholera

Resulting from poor hygiene, inadequate sewage disposal, and contaminated food, contemporary cholera is less devastating than its historic antecedents, which produced rapid dehydration, watery diarrhea, and imminent death without almost equally rapid rehydration. While today's cholera strains are highly infectious, most carriers do not even come down with symptoms. Existing vaccinations are ineffective, so international health authorities now recommend against them.

Treatment can only relieve symptoms. On average, about five percent of victims die, but those who recover are immune. It is not a common problem in Argentina, but it's not unheard of either, especially in northern subtropical areas.

### Hepatitis A

Usually passed by fecal-oral contact under conditions of poor hygiene and overcrowding, hepatitis A is a virus. The traditional gamma globulin prophylaxis has limited efficacy and wears off in just a few months. New hepatitis A vaccines, though, are more effective and last longer.

### Typhoid

Typhoid is a serious disease common under unsanitary conditions, but the recommended vaccination is an effective prophylaxis.

## INSECT-BORNE DISEASES

Argentina is not quite malaria-free but there is no danger in or around Buenos Aires; a few other insect-borne diseases may be present if not exactly prevalent.

## Dengue Fever

Like malaria, dengue is a mosquito-borne disease of the lowland tropics, but it's less common than malaria and rarely fatal. Often debilitating in the short term, its symptoms include fever, headache, severe joint pain, and skin rashes, but most people recover fairly quickly though there is no treatment. Uncommon but often fatal, the more severe dengue hemorrhagic fever sometimes occurs in children, particularly those who have suffered from the disease previously.

Eradicated in Argentina in 1963, the mosquito vector *Aedes egypti* is once again present as far south as Buenos Aires. There were several hundred confirmed cases of dengue in lowland subtropical areas of Salta province in 1997, and health authorities believe outbreaks are possible in Buenos Aires. The best prophylaxis is to avoid mosquito bites by covering exposed parts of the body with insect repellent or appropriate clothing.

## Chagas' Disease

Also known as South American trypanosomiasis, Chagas' disease is most common in Brazil but affects about 18 million people between Mexico and Argentina; 50,000 people die from it every year. Not a tropical disease per se, it has a discontinuous distribution—Panama and Costa Rica, for instance, are Chagas'-free.

Since it is spread by the bite of the conenose or assassin bug, which lives in adobe structures and feeds at night, avoid such structures (these still exist in the countryside); if it's impossible to do so, sleep away from the walls. Insect repellents carrying deet offer some protection. Chickens, dogs, and opossums may carry the disease.

Chagas' initial form is a swollen bite which may be accompanied by a fever that soon subsides. In the long run, though, it may cause heart damage leading to sudden death, intestinal constipation, and difficulty in swallowing; there is no cure. Charles Darwin may have been a chronic Chagas' sufferer.

# HANTAVIRUS

Hantavirus is an uncommon but very deadly disease contracted by breathing, touching, or ingesting feces or urine of the long-tailed rat. Primarily a rural phenomenon and most prevalent in the southern Patagonian area, the virus thrives in enclosed areas; avoid places frequented by rodents (particularly abandoned buildings). The disease normally loses its potency when exposed to sunlight or fresh air, but note that there have been apparent cases in which hikers and farm workers have contracted the disease in open spaces.

It is not a serious problem in urban Buenos Aires, but in July 2002 a veterinarian contracted the disease in the vicinity of the provincial capital of La Plata and later died.

# RABIES

Rabies, a virus transmitted through bites or scratches by domestic animals (like dogs and cats) and wild mammals (like bats), is a concern; many domestic animals in Argentina go unvaccinated, especially in rural areas. Human prophylactic vaccination is possible, but may be incompatible with malaria medication.

Untreated rabies can cause an agonizingly painful death. In case of an animal bite or scratch, immediately clean the affected area with soap and running water, and then with antiseptic substances like iodine or 40 percent-plus alcohol. If possible, try to capture the animal for diagnosis, but not at the risk of further bites; in areas where rabies is endemic, painful post-exposure vaccination may be unavoidable.

# SNAKEBITE

The federal capital does not have poisonous snakes, but the aggressive and highly venomous *yarará* (*Bothrops neuwiedi* is a pit viper found in parts of Buenos Aires province and elsewhere in the country. The timid but even more venomous coral snake (*Micrurus coralinus*) is found is humid areas such as the Paraná delta.

The *yarar* whose venom paralyzes the nervous sytem, is responsible for most snakebite incidents in the country, but incidents are not common. Death is not instantaneous and antivenins are available, but the wisest tactic is to be alert and avoid confrontation. If bitten, get to medical facilities as quickly as possible, but avoid excessive movement, which helps the venom circulate.

## SEXUALLY TRANSMITTED DISEASES

While AIDS is by far the most hazardous of sexually transmitted diseases (STDs) and certainly gets the most press, other STDs are far more prevalent and also serious if left untreated. All are spread by unprotected sexual conduct; the use of latex condoms can greatly reduce the possibility of contracting sexually transmitted diseases, but not necessarily eliminate it.

Most STDs, including gonorrhea, chlamydia, and syphilis, are treatable with antibiotics, but some strains have developed immunity to penicillin and alternative treatments. If taking antibiotics, be sure to complete the prescribed course, since an interrupted treatment may not kill the infection and could even help it develop immunity.

The most common of STDs is **gonorrhea,** characterized by a burning sensation during urination and penile or vaginal discharge; it may cause infertility. **Chlamydia** has milder symptoms but similar complications. **Syphilis,** the only major disease that apparently spread to Europe from its American origins in the aftermath of the Spanish invasion, begins with ulcer and rash symptoms that soon disappear; long-term complications, however, can include cardiovascular problems and even mental derangement. **Herpes,** a virus that causes small but irritating ulcers in the genital area, has no effective treatment. It is likely to recur, easily spread when active, and can contribute to cervical cancer. **Hepatitis B,** though not exclusively a sexually transmitted disease, can spread through the mixing of bodily fluids such as saliva, semen, and menstrual and vaginal secretions. It can also spread through insufficiently sanitary medical procedures, inadequately sterilized or shared syringes, unsterile body piercing, and similar circumstances. Like Hepatitits A, it can lead to liver damage but is more serious; vaccination is advisable for high-risk individuals, but is expensive.

### HIV/AIDS

As in most countries, HIV/AIDS (AIDS is *SIDA* in Spanish) is an issue of increasing concern. According to Argentina's Health Ministry, there are at least 20,000 full-blown AIDS cases and 130,000 HIV-infected individuals, but concerns are that the figure may be substantially higher—many carriers are probably unaware that they are infected.

HIV/AIDS is not exclusively a sexually transmitted disease (intravenous drug users can get it by sharing needles), but unprotected sexual activity is a common means of transmission; the use of latex condoms can reduce the possibility of infection.

Buenos Aires has two AIDS-support organizations: Cooperación, Información y Ayuda al Enfermo de SIDA (Coinsida), Finocchieto 74, Constitución, tel. 11/4304-6664; and Línea SIDA, Zuviría 64, Parque Chacabuco, tel. 11/4922-1617.

### SUNBURN

Since Buenos Aires and vicinity lie within temperate latitudes comparable to those in the northern hemisphere, sunburn is not quite the serious problem it is in subtropical northern Argentina, where nearly vertical solar rays are far more intense, or in southernmost Patagonia and Tierra del Fuego, where ozone-destroying aerosols have permitted the entry of ultraviolet radiation, causing skin problems for people and even for livestock such as cattle and sheep.

Still, sun worshippers in Argentina put themselves at risk whenever the sun shines through the clouds. If you dress for the beach, use a heavy sun block; on city streets, walk in the shade whenever possible.

## TOBACCO

Approximately 40 percent of Argentines smoke, including nearly half of the male population; tobacco is the direct cause of 45,000 deaths per annum. According to one survey, three out of every 10 Argentine *cardiologists* smoke, and few of those make any recommendation against smoking to their own patients.

Still, there is widespread recognition that the habit is unhealthy, and effective smoking restrictions are in force on public transportation and in a few other environments. If faced with second-hand smoke in one of the few places where it's prohibited, such as buses or taxis, appeal to courtesy with a white lie such as *"Soy asmático"* (I'm asthmatic).

Sin Pucho, Tucumán 3527, tel. 4862-6913, sinpucho@infovia.com.ar, is an ex-smokers' support group.

## LOCAL DOCTORS

Top-quality medical services, with the latest technology, are readily available in Buenos Aires. Foreign embassies sometimes maintain lists of English-speaking doctors, who may have overseas training and are numerous in the capital and other large cities.

It is possible, though, that the economic crisis may make it impossible to keep technology up to date, as devaluation has nearly quadrupled the cost of imported equipment in dollar terms.

Public hospitals include the Hospital Rivadavia, Avenida Las Heras 2670, Recoleta, tel. 11/4809-2002, and the Hospital Municipal Juan Fernández, Cerviño 3356, tel. 11/4808-2600. Public hospitals, however, are under severe personnel and budget constraints in dealing with their Argentine patients; if possible, consider a private hospital or clinic.

The Hospital Británico, Perdriel 74, Barracas, tel. 11/4304-1082, is a highly regarded private hospital. One of the city's best private clinics is Belgrano's Clínica Fleni, Montañeses 2325, tel. 5777-3200, www.fleni.org.ar. It's where Argentine presidents have had arthroscopies and soccer star Diego Maradona went for detox, but it does not serve every specialty.

## PHARMACIES

Pharmacies serve an important public health role, but also carry certain risks. Pharmacists may provide drugs on the basis of symptoms that they may not completely comprehend, especially if there is a language barrier; while the cumulative societal impact may be positive, be aware that individual recommendations may be erroneous.

Note that many medications available by prescription only in North America or Europe may be sold over the counter in Argentine pharmacies. Travelers should be cautious about self-medication even when such drugs are available; check expiration dates, as many expired drugs are never cleared off the shelf.

In large cities and even some smaller towns, pharmacies remain open all night for emergency prescription service on a rotating basis. The *farmacia de turno* and its address will usually be posted in the window of other pharmacies, or advertised in the newspaper.

## CRIME

Even though many Argentines believe assaults, rapes, homicide, and crimes against property are increasing, Buenos Aires is a safe city by almost any standard. Because *porteños* keep late hours, there are plenty of people on the street at most times—rarely will you find yourself walking alone down a dark alleyway.

Still, certain precautions almost go without saying—most crimes are crimes of opportunity. Never leave luggage unattended, store valuables in a hotel safe, keep a close watch on your belongings at sidewalk cafés, and carry a photocopy of your passport that shows your date of entry into the country. Do not carry large amounts of cash (money belts or leg pouches are good alternatives for hiding cash), do leave valuable jewelry at home, and do keep conspicuous items such as still-photo cameras and video cameras out of sight when possible. Do not presume that any area is totally secure.

If you should be accosted by anyone with a firearm or other weapon, do not resist. Although guns are uncommon—knives are the weapon of choice—and truly violent crime against tourists is unusual, the consequences of a misjudgment can be lethal.

Certain barrios are more crime-prone than others. Parts of La Boca are inadvisable even during daylight hours, so keep alert as to your surroundings. San Telmo is reasonably secure during daylight hours, but requires caution at night, even though there are many restaurants and clubs in the area.

One phenomenon that has disturbed Argentines in recent years is the so-called *secuestro exprés* (express kidnapping), in which criminals hold an individual for a small ransom or, alternatively, force someone to withdraw money from an ATM. Far more common in Buenos Aires province than in the capital, these crimes have *not* targeted tourists—rather, they appear to concentrate on individuals whose movements are familiar to the kidnapper.

More common are crimes of distraction, in which an individual bumps into a victim and spills a substance like ice cream or mustard; while the perpetrator apologizes profusely, his or her accomplice surreptitiously lifts valuable items. Pickpocketing is also common on crowded public transportation; carry wallets and other items of value in a front trouser pocket or, even better, an interior jacket pocket.

## Information and Services

### COMMUNICATIONS

Buenos Aires is a modern city, and as such the communications infrastructure is similar to what you'd expect in other large cities around the developed world.

#### Postal Services

Since the privatization of Correo Argentino, the Argentine post office, service is more reliable than in the past. Domestic services are generally cheap, international services more expensive. Major international couriers provide fast, reliable services at premium prices.

Correo Argentino operates the Correo Central, Sarmiento 189, a landmark building that's worth a visit in its own right, and many other branch post offices. Open weekdays 9 A.M. to 7:30 P.M., the main building occupies an entire block bounded by Sarmiento, Avenida L.N. Alem, Avenida Corrientes, and Bouchard.

General delivery at Argentine post offices is *lista de correos*, literally a list arranged in alphabetical order. There is a small charge for each item addressed to you.

Note that in Spanish-language street addresses the number follows rather than precedes the name; the U.S. address "1343 Washington Avenue," for example, would read "Avenida Washington 1343" in Argentina. Argentines and other Spanish speakers normally omit the word *calle* (street) from addresses; whereas an English speaker might write "499 Jones Street," a Argentine would simply use "Jones 499," for example. It is not unusual for street addresses to lack a number, as indicated by *s/n* (*sin número*, without a number), especially in the provinces.

International parcels that weigh in excess of one kg must leave from the Correo Internacional, on Antártida Argentina near the Retiro train station, tel. 4316-7777. Hours are 11 A.M.–5 p,m. weekdays only.

Private couriers include DHL International, Moreno 927, Monserrat, tel. 11/4630-1110, and Federal Express at Maipú 753, tel. 11/4393-6054, in the Microcentro.

#### Telephone and Fax

Argentina has two major telephone companies, Telecom (north of Avenida Córdoba) and Telefónica (south of Avenida Córdoba). The country code is 54; the *característica* (area code) for the Capital Federal and Gran Buenos Aires is 11, but there is a bewildering number of area codes for individual cities, smaller cities and towns, and rural areas. All telephone numbers in the

Capital Federal and Gran Buenos Aires have eight digits, while those in other provincial cities and rural areas vary. When calling out of the area code, it's necessary to dial zero first.

Cellular phone numbers in Buenos Aires all have eight digits and the prefix 15. Certain toll-free and other specialty numbers have six or seven digits with a three-digit prefix.

Public telephones are abundant; some of them operate with coins only, but most also accept magnetic phone cards or rechargeable-account cards. The basic local phone rate is 25 centavos (about US$.09) for five minutes or so; domestic long distance is considerably more expensive. Magnetic cards are convenient for in-country calls but less useful for more expensive overseas calls.

For long distance and overseas calls and fax services, it's simplest to use *locutorios* (call centers), which are abundant in both Buenos Aires and the provinces. Prices are increasingly competitive, and now tend to be much cheaper than placing *cobro revertido* (collect) or *tarjeta de crédito* (credit card) calls to the United States or any other country. Calls are more expensive during peak hours, 8 A.M.–8 P.M. weekdays and 8 A.M.–1 P.M. Saturdays.

It's also possible to make credit card calls to your home country, however, through overseas operators. There are contact numbers for Australia, tel. 800/555-6100; Canada, 800/222-1004 or 800/888-3868; France, tel. 800/555-3300; Germany, tel. 800/555-4900; Italy, tel. 800/555-3900; United Kingdom (British Telecom), tel. 800/555-4402. The United States has several different carriers: AT&T, 800/222-1288 or 800/555-4288; MCI, 800/555-1002 (from Telecom) or 800/222-6249 (from Telefónica); and Sprint, 800/222-1003.

**Cellular Phone Rental:** Opening a cell phone account without a permanent Argentine address is something of a nuisance, but phones are available to rent from Nolitel, tel. 11/4311-3500, reservas@nolitelgroup.com.

### Internet Access

In the last few years, public Internet access has become both abundant and so cheap that, if price trends continue, providers will be paying customers to use their services. Rarely does access cost more than US$1 per hour, and it is often even cheaper. Many *locutorios* offer access, but there are also numerous Internet cafés. Some Internet service providers, most notably AOL, Compuserve, and Earthlink, have local dial-up numbers in Argentina, but these often collect a surcharge.

One of Buenos Aires's best Internet outlets is Cosmos Internet Service Center, Avenida Las Heras 2305, Recoleta, which is open 24 hours, has comfortable seating and fast connections, and is extraordinarily cheap at US$.35 per hour. There are countless others, however, especially in the Microcentro and in areas frequented by tourists.

## MEDIA

### Newspapers and Magazines

Historically, freedom of the press has been tenuous, as Argentine governments have controlled the supply of newsprint and withheld official advertising from newspapers and magazines that have published items not to their liking. Nevertheless, since the end of the 1976–83 dictatorship, the trend has been largely positive for liberty of expression. Many of the newspapers and periodicals below have websites listed in the Internet Resources section in the back of this book.

The middle-of-the-road tabloid *Clarín*, the Spanish-speaking world's largest-circulation daily, sells nearly 600,000 copies weekdays and more than a million on Sundays, but its circulation is more sensitive to hard economic times than papers with a steadier niche clientele. Part of a consortium that includes TV and radio outlets, it also publishes the sports daily *¡Ole!*

According to Anglo-Argentine journalist Andrew Graham-Yooll, until your obituary appears in *La Nación,* you are not really dead—a comment that reflects the social standing of the capital's most venerable and center-right daily, dating from 1870. With a circulation of about 200,000—twice that on Sundays when it has an exceptional cultural section—the paper was the creation of Bartolomé Mitre, who later became president.

stresses commerce and finance, but also produces intelligent analyses of political and economic developments; its Sunday edition includes material from the *The New York Times* and Britain's *Guardian Weekly*.

The German-language *Argentinisches Tageblatt* began as a daily in 1889 but is now a Saturday weekly with a circulation of about 10,000.

## Magazines and Newsletters

*Noticias* is the *porteño* counterpart to English-language weeklies like *Time* and *Newsweek*. *Trespuntos*, however, is more critical and innovative. *La Maga* is an arts-oriented monthly, and *El Porteño* has similar content but is more politically oriented.

## Radio and Television

What was once a state broadcast monopoly is now far more diverse, thanks to privatization and the advent of cable, but conglomerates like the Clarín and El Cronista groups now control much of the content. Both radio and TV tend to stress entertainment at the expense of journalism.

Radio Rivadavia, Argentina's most popular station (AM 630), plays popular music and also hosts talk programs. Radio Mitre (AM 790) is the voice of the Clarín group. FM Tango 92.7 plays all tango all the time, and Radio Folclorísimo (AM 1410) plays folk music 24/7.

The Clarín and El Cronista groups also control TV stations and some cable service (where overseas media like CNN, ESPN, BBC, Deutsche Welle, and others are available). TV news coverage, however, can be surprisingly good, and there is even a 24-hour tango channel on cable.

# MAPS

The Automóvil Club Argentino (ACA, Argentine Automobile Club), has its home office at Avenida del Libertador 1850, Palermo, tel. 11/4808-4000, www.aca.org.ar; it publishes the country's most comprehensive series of maps, including the city road map *Carta Vial de Buenos Aires y Alrededores*. It also publishes excellent highway maps, including major city plans, of all Argentine provinces. Members of overseas automobile clubs

© WAYNE BERNHARDSON

Many *porteños* get their daily newspapers and magazines at corner kiosks.

*Página 12* is the tabloid voice of Argentina's intellectual left and, while its outspokenness is admirable, it would benefit from more rigorous editing—many articles are far too long and err on the side of hyperanalysis. Political columnist Horacio Verbitsky is one of the country's most famous and capable journalists, however.

*Crónica*, with a weekday circulation of 400,000 but far fewer on weekends, is a sensationalist tabloid that focuses on celebrities and crime. *Diario Popular* is somewhat less sensationalist, but in the same vein.

The capital has three financial newspapers, which publish weekdays only: the morning *Ambito Financiero*, which also publishes an outstanding arts and entertainment section; the afternoon *El Cronista*, and *Buenos Aires Económico*.

With a circulation of only about 8,000, Graham-Yooll's own *Buenos Aires Herald* is an English-language daily that has suffered from the drop in tourist and business travel, as its niche market correlates highly with hotel occupancy. It

like the AAA in the United States and the AA in Britain can buy these maps at discount prices.

ACA has branches at Avenida Belgrano 1749, Monserrat, tel. 11/4384-8910; at Godoy Cruz and Demaría, Palermo, tel. 11/4771-3408; and at Avenida Cabildo and Virrey Arredondo, Belgrano, tel. 11/4783-5424. The entry on Getting Around earlier in this chapter has more information on ACA.

For topographic maps, the Instituto Geográfico Militar is at Avenida Cabildo 301, Palermo, tel. 11/4576-5576, www.igm.gov.ar.

## TOURIST INFORMATION

The Secretaría Nacional de Turismo maintains an information office at Avenida Santa Fe 883 in Retiro, tel. 11/4312-2232 or 800/555-0016, www.turismo.gov.ar; it's open 9 A.M.–5 P.M. weekdays only; there's a branch at Aeropuerto Internacional Ministro Pistarini (aka Ezeiza), tel. 11/4480-0224, and another at Aeroparque Jorge Newbery, tel. 11/4773-9891. Both airport branches are open 8 A.M.–8 P.M. daily.

The municipal Subsecretaría de Turismo maintains information kiosks at Florida and Diagonal Roque Sáenz Peña in the Microcentro, open 9 A.M.–5 P.M. daily except May to September, when it's open weekdays only; at Puerto Madero's Dique 4, tel. 4313-0187, open 10 A.M.–6 P.M. daily; and at the Retiro bus terminal, tel.

11/4311-0528, open daily except Sunday 7 A.M.–1 P.M. All distribute maps and brochures, and usually have English-speaking staff.

El Viajero, Carlos Pellegrini 1233 in Retiro, tel. 4394-7941, www.elviajero.com, is a combination bookstore, coffee shop, and private tourist information center, with its own free library. The staff is happy to answer queries on Buenos Aires and other Argentine destinations; it's open 10 A.M.–7:30 P.M. weekdays, 10 A.M.–1 P.M. Saturday.

## FILM AND PHOTOGRAPHY

Color print film is widely available, color slide film less so. In any event, it tends to be cheaper in North America and Europe than in Argentina, so it's best to bring as much as possible. If purchasing film in Argentina, check the expiration date to make sure it's current, especially in out-of-the-way places. In the capital and larger tourist centers, competent print-film processing is readily available and moderately priced, but it's better to hold slide film until your return to your home country if possible (but store it under cool, dark, and dry conditions), or to visit a specialist such as Kinefot, Talcahuano 250, tel. 4374-7445. For prints, try Le Lab, Viamonte 624, tel. 4322-2785.

Environmental conditions can affect the quality of your photographs and the type of film you should use. Bright sun can wash out photographs;

## PHOTOGRAPHIC ETIQUETTE—AND A WARNING

Most Argentines, especially *porteños,* are not exactly camera-shy, but do be cautious about photographing political protests—the police are notorious for cataloging dissidents, so protestors may be suspicious of people with cameras. Likewise, avoid taking photographs in the vicinity of military installations, although "the sentry will shoot" signs are mostly a thing of past.

Generally, if a person's presence in a photograph is incidental, as in a townscape, it's unnecessary to ask permission, but avoid the in-your-face approach. If in doubt, ask; if rejected, don't insist. If you're purchasing something from a market vendor, he or she will almost certainly agree to a photographic request.

There is one absolute no-no, however—without express permission, do not even think about photographing Israeli or Jewish community sites anywhere in Argentina. Since car-bomb attacks on Retiro's Israeli Embassy in 1992 and Once's Jewish cultural center in 1994, federal police are stationed outside all of these sites. They will politely or, if necessary, not-so-politely discourage would-be photographers.

clouds, but can result in a dark foreground if you're not careful.

Gerardo Föhse, in the basement of Retiro's Galería Buenos Aires, Florida 835, Local 37, tel. 4311-1139), can do basic camera repairs. Dependable José Norres, Lavalle 1569, 4th floor, Oficina 403, tel. 4373-0963, can perform more complex repairs except on some of the latest electronic equipment, and service is quick.

## LIBRARIES

The Biblioteca Nacional (National Library) is at Agüero 2502, Recoleta, tel. 11/4808-6000, www.bibnal.edu.ar. Open 9 A.M.–8 P.M. weekdays, noon–6 P.M. weekends, it holds frequent special exhibitions, lectures, literary events, and free concerts. Guided tours take place at 4 P.M. weekdays only.

The United States Information Agency's Biblioteca Lincoln is at the Instituto Cultural Argentino-Norteamericano, Maipú 672, in the Microcentro, tel. 4322-3855 or 4322-4557.

## BOOKSTORES

Buenos Aires has countless general-interest bookstores, as well as specialist shops that deal with academic and rare books, and others with English-language materials.

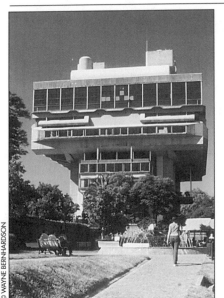

© WAYNE BERNHARDSON

**Recoleta's harsh Biblioteca Nacional (National Library) occupies the site of the demolished presidential residence.**

in these circumstances, it's best to use a relatively slow film, around ASA 64 or 100, and a polarizing filter to reduce glare. A polarizing filter also improves contrast, dramatizing the sky and the

# Weights and Measures

## TIME

Argentina is three hours behind GMT for most of the year, and does not observe daylight savings time (summer time). When the U.S. Eastern Time Zone is on daylight savings during the northern-hemisphere summer and Argentina is on standard time, the hour is identical in New York and Buenos Aires.

## ELECTRICITY

Throughout the country, nearly all outlets are 220 volts and 50 cycles, so converters are necessary for North American appliances such as computers and electric razors. Plugs are two rounded prongs. Adequately powered converters are hard to find, so it's better to bring one from overseas.

## MEASUREMENTS

The metric system is official, but Argentines use a variety of vernacular measures in everyday life. Rural folk often use the Spanish *legua* (league) of about five kilometers as a measure of distance, and the *quintal* of 46 kilos is also widely used, especially in wholesale markets and agricultural statistics.

# What to Bring

## LUGGAGE

What sort of luggage you bring depends on what sort of trip you're planning, how long you'll be traveling, and where you're planning to go. For shoestring travelers planning months in Argentina and neighboring countries, for instance, a spacious but lightweight backpack is the best choice; a small daypack for local excursions is also a good idea.

Even though traveling on airplanes, shuttles, and taxis can be logistically simpler than buses alone—door-to-door service is the rule—light luggage is also advisable for nonbackpackers. A small daypack for excursions is also convenient.

Small but sturdy lightweight locks are advisable for all sorts of luggage, if only to discourage temptation.

## CLOTHING

A good rule of thumb is to bring appropriately seasonal clothing for comparable latitudes in the northern hemisphere. Buenos Aires's climate is mild in spring and autumn, hot, wet, and sticky in summer, and cool but not cold in winter—though the humidity and winter wind can make it feel colder than it is. For summer, light cottons are the rule, while a sweater and perhaps a light jacket suffice for spring and autumn. A warm but not polar-strength jacket and rain gear are advisable for winter. Frost is almost unheard of.

Much depends, of course, on what sort of activities you will be undertaking—for events at the Teatro Colón, for instance, formal clothing is obligatory. Likewise, individuals conducting business in the capital will dress as they would in New York or London, with suit and tie for men and comparably appropriate clothing for women. A compact umbrella is a good idea at any time of year.

## ODDS AND ENDS

Since public toilets sometimes lack toilet paper, travelers should always carry some, even though it's readily available within the country. Many budget hotels have thin walls and squeaky floors, so ear plugs are a good idea.

Leg pouches and money belts are good options for securing cash, travelers' checks, and important documents. A compact pair of binoculars will come in handy for bird-watchers and others who enjoy wildlife and the landscape.

# Special Interests

## WORK

In an imploding economy with 25 percent unemployment, remunerative work is hard to come by even for legal residents, let alone visitors on tourist or student visas. Nevertheless, foreigners have found work teaching English or another foreign language, working in the tourist industry, or doing casual labor in bars or restaurants. The problem with such jobs is that they either require time to build up a clientele (in the case of teaching), and may be seasonal (in the case of tourism) or poorly paid (in the case of restaurants, except in a handful of places where tips are high). Language teachers may find that few *porteños* can afford the luxury of one-on-one lessons.

Ideally, obtaining a work permit from an Argentine consulate is better than attempting to obtain one in-country, as employment may not begin until the permit is actually granted. Either way, the process requires submitting documents and takes some time.

## BUSINESS

There are few if any legal limitations on foreign businesses operating in Argentina, but the recent business climate, thanks largely to the government's debt default and *corralito* banking restrictions, has not been conducive to investment. In by-country investment risk assessments, featured like sports scores on the front page of many *porteño* newspapers, Argentina ranks among the world's highest investment risks—by mid-2002, this key statistic had soared to over 6,000 compared to 1,200 for its beleaguered neighbor Uruguay, and only 150 for Chile.

Corruption remains an issue, as a Transparency International survey for 2002 ranked Argentina 70th of 102 countries evaluated. Political officeholders have an unfortunate reputation for shaking down foreign companies for bribes, and customs procedures can be trying despite increasing professionalization of the service. Intellectual property rights for computer software, CD and cassette recordings, and DVDs and video tapes are problematic.

The businesses dailies mentioned in the Media section of this chapter are good background sources on business, at least for those who read Spanish, as are and the magazines *Apertura* (www.apertura.com), *Mercado* (www.mercado.com.ar), and *Negocios* (www.negocios.com.ar). The most accessible English-language source is the U.S. State Department's Country Commercial Guide service (www.usatrade.gov/website/CCG.nsf), though it often lags behind events. Its best bets for investment include travel and tourism services, computer equipment and software, management consulting, medical equipment, energy technology, building materials and supplies, and biotechnology. It is open to question, though, whether the economy will be able to support imports in its present state.

Nevertheless, some investors are convinced that Argentine businesses may offer high yields on investments because devaluation has depressed prices in dollar terms. Residential real estate, for instance, has been a bargain, but sellers have shown increasing reluctance to sell except in a true emergency. In any event, before signing any business deal, consult a local lawyer recommended by your embassy, your consulate, or a trusted friend.

## Business Etiquette

Conducting business is as much a personal and social activity as an economic one; even though initial contacts may be formal, with appointments arranged well in advance, topics such as family and sports are often part of the conversation. Formality in dress and appearance is not so rigid as it once was, but in sectors like banking it's still the rule.

An ability to speak Spanish well is a plus, even though many Argentine business figures speak English (more than a few have been educated in English-speaking countries). The best months for business travel are April through November; in January and February, when school lets out and *porteños* take their summer vacations, the city can seem deserted.

## Useful Organizations

One critically important and unavoidable contact is the Administración Nacional de Aduanas, the national customs headquarters at Azopardo 350, Monserrat, tel. 11/4338-6400, fax 11/4338-6555. If importing equipment for permanent use, it's essential to deal with them through a *despachante de aduanas* (private customs broker).

The Cámara de Comercio de los Estados Unidos en Argentina (U.S. Chamber of Commerce in Argentina) is at Viamonte 1133, 8th floor, Microcentro, tel. 11/4371-4500, fax 11/4371-8400, amcham@amchamar.com.ar, www.amchamar.com.ar.

The Cámara Argentina de Comercio (Argentine Chamber of Commerce) is at Avenida Leandro N. Alem 36, Planta Baja (ground floor), Microcentro, tel. 11/5300-9000, fax 11/5300-9058, centroservicios@cac.com.ar, www.cac.com.ar.

The Cámara de Importadores de la República Argentina (Argentine Chamber of Importers) is at Avenida Belgrano 427, 7th floor, Monserrat, tel./fax 4342-1101/0523, cira@cira.org.ar, www.cira.org.ar.

The Bolsa de Comercio de Buenos Aires (Buenos Aires Stock Exchange) is at Sarmiento 299, 1st floor, Microcentro, tel. 11/4316-7000, saber@bolsar.com, www.bcba.sba.com.ar.

The Sociedad Rural Argentina (Argentine Agricultural Association) is at Florida 460,

Microcentro, tel. 11/4324-4700, sra@rural.org.ar, www.ruralarg.org.ar.

## LANGUAGE STUDY

The Universidad de Buenos Aires (UBA) offers limited instruction at its Laboratorio de Idiomas, 25 de Mayo 221, tel. 4343-1196, fax 4343-2733, idlab@filo.com.ar, www.idiomas.filo.uba.ar. It also offers more intensive programs (15 hours weekly, US$400) at the Centro Universitario de Idiomas, Junín 508, 3rd floor, Balvanera, tel. 11/4372-9674, internacional@cui.com.ar, www.cui.com.ar.

Tradfax, Avenida Callao 194, 2nd floor, Balvanera, tel. 11/4371-0697, fax 11/4373-5581, tradfaxcultural@hotmail .com, www.tradfax.com, offers 2.5-hour daily classes in general Spanish for US$180 per week; commercial Spanish classes cost about US$30 more per week, while individual classes cost US$18 per hour. The organization also arranges lodging in nearby hotels from US$210/245 per week s/d.

The Centro de Estudio del Español, Reconquista 715, 11th floor, tel./fax 11/4315-1156 or 11/4312-1016, spanish@cedic.com.ar, www.cedic .com.ar. Two hours daily instruction for four weeks costs US$320 plus US$20 in course materials, while shorter courses cost around US$8 per hour plus materials. Individual tutoring costs US$9 hourly.

The Instituto de Lengua Española para Extranjeros (ILEE), Avenida Callao 339, 3rd floor, tel./fax 11/4782-7173, info@argentinailee.com, www.ilee.com.ar, offers conversation-based courses at various levels for for US$200 per week, plus private classes for US$16 per hour. It will also help arrange accommodations.

For individual private tutoring, contact English-speaking Dori Lieberman, tel./fax 4361-4843, dori@sinectis.com.ar.

> *Foreign parents may find it unusual that even toddlers may be out on the swings and slides with their families at 11 P.M. or even later. Porteño kids are also playing in the neighborhood and traveling independently on the Subte at a young age.*

## TRAVEL WITH CHILDREN

In most ways, Argentina is a child-friendly country and Buenos Aires is a child-friendly city. In fact, since many Argentines have large extended families, they may feel little in common with people in their late 20s and older who do *not* have children—traveling with kids can open doors.

Many of the capital's parks and plazas have playground equipment, and it's easy to mix with Argentine families there. What foreign parents may find unusual is that even toddlers may be out on the swings and slides with their families at 11 P.M. or even later. Additionally, *porteño* kids are playing across the street, around the neighborhood, and even traveling on the buses and Subte at ages when nervous North American parents are driving their kids three blocks to school.

On public transportation, strangers may spontaneously but gently touch small children and even set them on their laps. While this may be disconcerting to non-Argentines, it's not necessarily inappropriate in cultural context.

Many cultural activities are child-oriented, particularly during the winter school holidays in late July. Oddly enough, the Friday edition of the financial daily *Ambito Financiero* has the most complete listing of family events.

The northern barrios of Recoleta, Palermo, and Belgrano, with their spacious parks and playgrounds, are particularly good for children. Palermo's zoo is a favorite.

## FEMALE TRAVELERS

Like other Latin American societies, Argentina has a strong *machista* (chauvinist) element. Argentine women are traditionally mothers, homemakers, and children's caregivers, while men are providers and decision-makers, but there are increasing numbers of professional and other working women.

Many Argentine men view foreign women as sexually available, but they view Argentine women the same way. Harassment often takes the form of *piropos,* sexist comments which are often innocuous and can even be poetic, but are just as likely to be vulgar. It is best to ignore the comments, which are obvious by tone of voice even if you don't understand them; if they're persistent, seek refuge in a café or *confitería.*

Despite problems, women have acquired political prominence. The most prominent and notorious, of course, was Evita Perón, but her rise was an unconventional one. The highest-profile female in current politics is populist legislator and presidential candidate Elisa Carrió, a vociferous anti-corruption campaigner who, unfortunately, seems better at identifying problems than at offering solutions.

## GAY AND LESBIAN TRAVELERS

Like other Latin American countries, Argentina is culturally Catholic, but Buenos Aires has an active, visible gay scene focused around Barrio Norte, Recoleta, and Palermo Viejo. There are, however, gay-friendly venues throughout the city and even in the Paraná delta.

Demonstrative contact such as kissing between males (on the cheek, at least) and holding hands for females does not have the same connotation as it might in North America or some European countries. This does not mean that homosexuals can always behave as they wish in public—the police, never the most enlightened sector of society, have beaten and jailed individuals who have offended their sense of propriety. If in doubt, be circumspect.

The capital's leading homosexual organization is the Comunidad Homosexual Argentina (CHA), Tomás Liberti 1080, tel. 11/4361-6352, La Boca. There is a Marcha de Orgullo Gay (Gay Pride Parade) from the Plaza de Mayo to Congreso in early November.

## TRAVELERS WITH DISABILITIES

For people with disabilities, Buenos Aires can a problematical country. The narrow, uneven sidewalks in the capital, not to mention the fast-moving traffic, are unkind to people with disabilities, especially those who need wheelchairs.

Public transportation can rarely accommodate passengers with disabilities, though the capital's newer Subte stations have elevators and others are being refitted. Avis has recently introduced rental vehicles that feature hand controls.

Few older buildings are specifically equipped for handicapped people, but many of the buildings are low and can often accommodate people that have disabilities. Newer hotels are often highrises, and disabled access is obligatory.

# Sights

For sightseers, Buenos Aires is a paradise of diversity. Like New York City, it is a city of barrios—48 of them, officially—but that designation is a little misleading. Many barrios consist of smaller neighborhoods with distinct identities and some, such as Barrio Norte (more a real estate term or a state of mind for its mostly upper-class residents), overlap official barrios.

For much of the 20th century, the Plaza de Mayo and surrounding Monserrat were the nerve center of Argentine politics, the site of spectacle for the Peróns and their successors. The colonial quarter of San Telmo is the home of the tango, while the working-class La Boca neighborhood combines its passion for soccer with a conspicuous commitment to the arts.

Downtown Buenos Aires, the "Microcentro," is the city's traditional business, shopping, and theater district, with many museums and landmark buildings. To the north, the mansions of Retiro and chic Recoleta are home to the *porteño* elite and some of the city's best and newest museums. For wide open spaces, *porteños* visit the parks of Palermo, an area with its own share of museums and monuments.

On weekends, Buenos Aires's municipal tourist office offers free theme-oriented walking tours of many neighborhoods; some but not all have English-speaking guides. For each week's offerings, check the Friday getOut! section of the *Buenos Aires Herald* or the entertainment section of *Clarín*. In case of rain, the tours are canceled.

Puente Calatrava, Puerto Madero

# ORIENTATION IN BUENOS AIRES

Gran Buenos Aires (Greater Buenos Aires) is a sprawling metropolitan area that takes in large parts of surrounding Buenos Aires province. The Ciudad Autónoma de Buenos Aires (Autonomous City of Buenos Aires), also known as the Capital Federal (Federal Capital), lies within the boundaries formed by the Río de la Plata, its tributary the Riachuelo, and the ring roads of Avenida General Paz and Avenida 27 de Febrero.

Buenos Aires may be a major megalopolis, but its barrios give it a neighborhood ambiance, even in areas like the downtown financial district. Its historic center is the Plaza de Mayo, in the barrio of **Monserrat,** the locus of Spanish colonial power and site of major public buildings like the Catedral Metropolitana (which is the reason the barrio also goes by the name Catedral al Sur, or South of the Cathedral). Except for the remains of the Cabildo, those colonial buildings are long gone from the Plaza de Mayo, but several others survive in the vicinity. The original grid stretches in all directions except where modern thoroughfares such as the east-west Avenida de Mayo and the broad north-south Avenida 9 de Julio have obliterated narrow colonial streets.

To the immediate north, the **Microcentro** is the hub of commercial Buenos Aires, and includes neighborhoods like the financial district of La City; also known as Catedral al Norte (North of the Cathedral), Microcentro and vicinity are part of the barrio of San Nicolás, which extends north to Avenida Córdoba and west to Avenida Callao. To the east, stretching north-south along the river, redeveloped **Puerto Madero** is the city's newest barrio.

South of Monserrat, colonial **San Telmo** was a prestigious address until the elite abandoned it during the yellow fever outbreaks of the 19th century; today it's one of the city's most popular tourist attractions, a Bohemian blend of the colonial barrio, peopled with artists and musicians, plus a scattering of old-money families and more than a scattering of *conventillos* (tenements) abandoned

by old money. To the southeast, along the Riachuelo, the immigrant working-class barrio of **La Boca** has never been prosperous, but it has a colorful history, an extravagantly colorful vernacular architecture, and a sense of community that few city neighborhoods can match.

West of Monserrat and San Nicolás, the barrio of **Balvanera** subdivides into several smaller but significant neighborhoods including Congreso (home to the Argentine legislature), Once (the largely Jewish garment district), and the Abasto (which gave the city tango legend Carlos Gardel). Farther west, middle-class **Caballito** is the city's geographical center, but was once its periphery.

Across Avenida Córdoba, **Retiro** marks a transition to the upper-middle-class residential barrios to the north and northwest; still tony, it was once far more elegant than it is today. Immediately to the northwest, **Recoleta** retains that elegance in the area around its legendary necropolis, the Cementerio de la Recoleta. Barrio Norte, a mostly residential area that overlaps Retiro and Recoleta, is not a juridical barrio but rather an imprecise real estate concept.

Beyond Recoleta, the northbound arteries of Avenida Santa Fe, Avenida Las Heras and Avenida del Libertador lead to **Palermo**, the city's largest barrio; its wooded parks were once the country estate of dictator Juan Manuel de Rosas. One of the most rapidly changing parts of the city, it subdivides into several smaller but distinct units: the embassy row of Palermo Chico between Avenida del Libertador and the river; the residential and nightlife zone of Palermo Viejo across Avenida Santa Fe, which further subdivides into Palermo Soho and Palermo Hollywood; and Las Cañitas, on the border with Belgrano.

Once a separate city, **Belgrano** prizes its distinct residential identity, but its leafy streets also host an assortment of museums and other cultural resources. Further outlying barrios have scattered points of tourist interest, including museums, parks, and *ferias* (street fairs).

# Monserrat/Catedral al Sur and Vicinity

In 1580, Juan de Garay reestablished Pedro de Mendoza's failed settlement on what is now the **Plaza de Mayo.** Garay platted the rectangular Plaza del Fuerte (Fortress Plaza), which became the Plaza del Mercado (Market Plaza) and then the Plaza de la Victoria (Victory Plaza), following victory over the British invaders in 1806 and 1807. Its present name derives from the date of the May Revolution of 1810, but its fame comes from the massive and spectacular demonstrations that have taken place there in support and protest of the Peróns, the Falklands/Malvinas War, and other political causes.

Buenos Aires's oldest barrio takes its name from the Catalonian Nuestra Señora de Monserrat, a sacred image hidden in the mountains near Barcelona to protect it from Muslim invaders. Found after a century of weathering, the darkened madonna resonated with Buenos Aires's black slave population, who feted her every September 8. Monserrat was also known as Barrio del Tambor for the drums Afro-Argentines played during Carnaval.

Monserrat encompasses substantial parts of the **Congreso** neighborhood, which overlaps the barrios of San Nicolás and Balvanera. Its southern border with San Telmo, while juridically precise, is a more subtle transition on the ground itself—some businesses technically within Monserrat's limits vocally proclaim their affinity with tourist-friendly San Telmo.

Most major Argentine institutions surround the Plaza de Mayo, which has undergone major transformations since its colonial origins to reach its present status as the city's civic heart. The barrio's axis is the **Avenida de Mayo,** the city's first major boulevard, which links the **Casa Rosada** presidential palace (1873–1898) with the **Congreso Nacional** (National Congress, 1906); the Avenida 9 de Julio runs perpendicular to the Avenida de Mayo and splits Monserrat in half.

At the northwest corner of the plaza, the imposing **Catedral Metropolitana** (1827) gives the barrio its alternative nomenclature. At the southwest corner, construction of the Avenida

de Mayo required demolition of part of the colonial **Cabildo de Buenos Aires** (1725–1765), but a representative segment of the building remains.

At the northeast corner, the **Banco de la Nación** (1939), designed by renowned architect Alejandro Bustillo, occupies the original site of the Teatro Colón, the opera house that moved to Plaza Lavalle early in the 20th century; if the Argentine economy were as solid as the neoclassical construction of this state-run bank, the country would still be a global economic power.

Across the **Plaza de Mayo, immediately south of the Casa Rosada, the marble facade of the Ministerio de Economía** (Economy Ministry) still bears marks from the navy planes that strafed these and other public buildings in the 1955 Revolución Libertadora that sent Juan Domingo Perón into exile. On the east side of Avenida Paseo Colón, generations of military-coup planners plotted against constitutional governments in the **Edificio Libertador** before belatedly realizing they were no more capable of governing than the civilians they overthrew.

As the Avenida de Mayo obliterated several city blocks in 1894 to become Buenos Aires's first boulevard at 30 meters wide, it experienced a major building boom, and several landmarks survive. First among them, perhaps, is the **Café Tortoni,** a *porteño* institution since 1858, at Avenida de Mayo 825 (the original entrance was on Rivadavia, on the opposite side of the building). One of the most fiercely if quietly traditional places in town, it's made no concessions to the 21st century and only a few to the 20th: upholstered chairs and marble tables stand among sturdy columns beneath a ceiling punctuated by stained-glass light fixtures, the wallpaper looks original between the stained wooden trim, and walls are decorated with pictures, portraits, and *filete,* the traditional calligraphy of *porteño* sign-painters. Among the patrons acknowledged on the walls are tango singer Carlos Gardel, La Boca painter Benito Quinquela Martín, dramatists Luigi Pirandello and Federico García Lorca, and pianist Arthur Rubinstein; more recently, the Tortoni has hosted King Juan Carlos I of Spain and Hillary Rodham Clinton.

Reopened in 1994 after nearly being destroyed by fire in 1979, the **Teatro Avenida,** Avenida de Mayo 1212, is second only to the Teatro Colón as a classical music and dance venue. When the famed Spanish dramatist Federico García Lorca came to Buenos Aires in 1933, his classic *Bodas de Sangre* (Blood Weddings) played here. The **Hotel Chile** (1907), Avenida de Mayo 1295, is a prime example of the Art Nouveau architecture that was fashionable in the early 20th century.

Occupying part of the former Hotel Majestic, the **Museo y Archivo Histórico de la Dirección General Impositiva,** Avenida de Mayo 1317, 5th floor, tel. 4384-0282, focuses on the theme of taxation in a country renowned for money laundering and similar subterfuges. Alternatively known as the Museo de la Administración Federal de Ingresos Públicos, it's open 11 A.M.–5 P.M. weekdays only. Admission is free.

The avenue's most literal landmark is Mario Palanti's marvelously detailed **Pasaje Barolo** (1923), a recently restored office building topped by a high-powered rotating semaphore visible from Montevideo's Palacio Salvo (the work of the same architect). In 1923, when Argentine heavyweight Luis Angel Firpo fought Jack Dempsey in New York, the Barolo erroneously announced a Firpo victory with a green light from the tower; director Russell Mulcahy shot parts of the ill-fated 1986 sequel to *Highlander* in the building.

At the west end of the avenue, the **Plaza del Congreso** (officially Plaza de los dos Congresos, 1904), another frequent site for political demonstrations, faces the **Congreso Nacional** (1908), home to Argentina's notoriously dysfunctional national legislature. The plaza itself houses the **Monumento a los Dos Congresos,** commemorating the meetings in Buenos Aires (1813) and Tucumán (1816), which achieved the country's independence. Two Belgians, sculptor Jules Lagae and architect Eugene D'Huique, created the monument, which reflects Argentina's geography: the eastern fountain symbolizes the Atlantic Ocean, and the granite stairways signify the

Andes mountains that form Argentina's western border with Chile.

On the south side of the plaza, the **Biblioteca del Congreso de la Nación** is a resource for elected politicians. Two blocks south, at Moreno 1749, the **Mercado del Congreso** is one of few functioning old-style neighborhood markets, architecturally distinguished by details such as its *guardapolvos* (dust guards), stone carvings of crops and livestock.

South of the Plaza de Mayo, nearly all of Monserrat's major landmarks are colonial, though most have undergone major modifications. The most significant attraction is the **Manzana de las Luces:** several ecclesiastical and educational institutions that occupy an entire block bounded by Alsina, Bolívar, Moreno and Perú; see the Manzana de las Luces entry later in this chapter for detail. Two blocks west, at Alsina and Piedras, the **Iglesia San Juan Bautista** was one of elite churches of the 18th-century and drew upper-class parishioners.

At opposite corners of Alsina and Defensa are the **Capilla San Roque** (1759), a colonial chapel, and the **Farmacia La Estrella** (1900), a classic apothecary with magnificent woodwork and health-themed ceiling murals. The Farmacia's exterior windows display materials from the **Museo de la Ciudad,** upstairs in the same building; see the museum's entry later in this chapter for more detail.

A block to the south, the **Museo Etnográfico Juan B. Ambrosetti,** Moreno 350, has become one of the country's best anthropological museums. The **Museo Nacional del Grabado,** Defensa 372, occupies the **Casa de la Defensa,** which played a key role in repelling the British occupations of 1806 and 1807. See the entry later in this section for more detail on both.

Half a block south, at the corner of Avenida Belgrano, the 18th-century **Iglesia y Convento de Santo Domingo** (see separate entry) shares grounds with the Instituto Nacional Belgraniano, a patriotic research institute that contains the grave of General Manuel Belgrano, a soldier of questionable competence who distinguished himself by designing the Argentine flag.

Two blocks south, at the corner of Defensa

SARMIENTO

PERÓN

SAN NICOLAS

TALCAHUANO

LIBERTAD

MONTEVIDEO

PARANA

BARTOLOME MITRE

URUGUAY

CERRITO

CARLOS PELLEGRINI

AV — 9 — DE — JULIO

SUIPACHA

PLAZA R. ARLT

CAFÉ TORTONI ★

To Congreso ← Nacional

HOTEL NAPOLEÓN

AV RIVADAVIA

MUSEO Y ARCHIVO HISTORICO ★

HOTEL CHILE

Lima

GRAN HOTEL HISPANO

Piedras

PLAZA

25 DE MAYO

EL HISPANO ▼

CASTELAR HOTEL AND SPA

Avenida de Mayo

REQUIEM

@LTERNATIVA

PLAZA DEL CONGRESO

LOREA

Sáenz Peña

AVILA BAR

PASAJE BAROLO

MILHOUSE YOUTH HOSTEL

HIPOLITO YRIGOYEN

LIMA

← To Biblioteca del Congreso de la Nación

TEATRO AVENIDA ★

HOTEL INTERCONTINENTAL ●

VIRREY

STATUS ▼

PRESIDENTE

ADOLFO ALSINA

SANTIAGO DEL

SALTA

BERNARDO - DE - YRIGOYEN

IGLESIA SAN JUAN ★ BAUTISTA

CAVALLOS

LUIS SAENZ

SAN JOSE

To Mercado ← del Congreso

HOTEL PALACE CEVALLOS

MORENO

ESTERO

MONSERRAT

TACUARI

PEÑA

CLUB VASCO FRANCÉS ▼

Moreno

AV BELGRANO

LAURAK BAT ▼

CAMPO DEI FIORI ▼

PLAZA MAYOR ▼

VENEZUELA

DIABLADA ▼

FRIDDA ▼

MÉXICO

# MONSERRAT/CATEDRAL AL SUR AND VICINITY

CHILE

MUSEO DEL TRAJE ★

← To Penélope (restaurant)

AV INDEPENDENCIA

Independencia (Línea E)

Independencia (Línea C)

ESTADOS UNIDOS

MICROCENTRO

AV ROQUE SAENZ PEÑA

FLORIDA

MAIPU

SAN MARTIN

RECONQUISTA

25 DE MAYO

AV LEANDRO N ALEM

AV ROSALES

EDUARDO MADERO

AV

ALICIA MOREAU DE JUSTO

JUANA MANUELA GORRITI

Dique 3

CATEDRAL METROPOLITANA ★

BANCO DE LA NACIÓN ■

○ *Catedral*

RIVADAVIA

ESMERALDA

EL TÚNEL ■

LONDON CITY ■

○ *Perú*

CABILDO DE BUENOS AIRES ★

○ *Bolívar*

CHACABUCO

AV JULIO A ROCA

HOTEL NOGARÓ ●

ADOLFO ALSINA

MANZANA DE LAS LUCES ★

BOLÍVAR

PERÚ

EL QUERANDÍ ■

PLAZA DE MAYO

CASA ROSADA/ CASA DE GOBIERNO ★

Parque Colón

○ *Plaza de Mayo*

HIPÓLITO YRIGOYEN

NH CITY HOTEL ●

BALCARCE

★ MINISTERIO DE ECONOMÍA

AV PASEO COLÓN

EDIFICIO LIBERTADOR

ESPORA

AV INGENIERO

FARMACIA DE LA ESTRELLA/MUSEO DE LA CIUDAD ■

LIBRERÍA DE ÁVILA ■

DEFENSA

★ CAPILLA SAN ROQUE

MORENO

VIEJOS TIEMPOS ■

★ MUSEO ETNOGRÁFICO JUAN B AMBROSETTI

★ ARTE INDÍGENA

PLAZA A.P. JUSTO

CUSTOMS ■

DOMINGUÍN ■

CÁMARA DE IMPORTADORES DE LA REPÚBLICA ARGENTINA ■

★ MUSEO NACIONAL DEL GRABADO

BLVD VILLAFLOR

AZOPARDO

HUERGO

AV BELGRANO

○ *Belgrano*

PERÚ

IGLESIA Y CONVENTO DE SANTO DOMINGO ■

S DE JULIO

LA TRASTIENDA ▽

VENEZUELA

CENTRO CULTURAL PLAZA DEFENSA ■

BALCARCE

LA SAL ▽

MÉXICO

PIEDRAS

★ EX-BIBLIOTECA NACIONAL

EX-CASA DE LA MONEDA ■

TROTAMUNDOS SAN TELMO ▽

BAR SEDDON ■

CAFÉ MOLIÈRE ▽

AV PASEO COLÓN

CHILE

BOLÍVAR

DEFENSA

SAN LORENZO

AV INDEPENDENCIA

DR J M GIUFFRA

PLAZA CORONEL OLAZÁBAL

FACULTAD DE INGENIERÍA

BLVD ROSARIO PEÑALOZA

ESTADOS UNIDOS

| 0 | 200 yds |
| 0 | 200 m |

SIGHTS

ɔ, the erstwhile **Casa de la Moneda** (National Mint, 1877) now houses the army's **Instituto de Estudios Históricos del Ejército** (Army Institute of Historical Studies). Within a couple of years, though, this handsome 10,000-square meter building is due to become a contemporary science museum with emphasis on astronomy, robotics, information technology, electronics, environment, and biotechnology, as well as Argentine history and geography.

Two blocks west, the former **Biblioteca Nacional** (National Library, 1901), México 564, originally housed the national lottery; after the library moved to Recoleta in 1992, this neoclassical building became the Centro Nacional de la Música (National Music Center).

## PLAZA DE MAYO

Colloquially known as the Plaza de Protestas for its frequent, large and often contentious political demonstrations, the Plaza de Mayo has often been center-stage in Argentine history. Juan and Eva Perón used it for spectacle, convoking hundreds of thousands of the fervent *descamisados* (shirtless ones) who comprised their underclass disciples.

Internationally, though, the plaza became notorious for some of the smallest gatherings ever to take place there. During the late 1970s, a handful of Argentine mothers marched silently every Thursday afternoon to demand the return of their adult children kidnapped by the armed forces and paramilitary gangs. Most of the *desaparecidos* (disappeared) died at the hands of their captors, but, in the absence of a complete accounting, the Madres de la Plaza de Mayo still parade every Thursday at 3:30 P.M. around the **Pirámide de Mayo,** the plaza's small central obelisk. Nobel Prize winner V.S. Naipaul chronicled the mothers' bravery while making caustic comments on Argentine society in his long essay *The Return of Eva Perón.*

Ironically, emotional throngs cheered the 1976–83 dictatorship in the Plaza de Mayo following the April 1982 occupation of the British-ruled Falkland Islands, which Argentina still claims as the Malvinas. Soon, however, the crowds turned on the de facto government of General Leopoldo Galtieri as it became obvious that the war was going badly. The military collapse brought a quick return to constitutional government.

Following Argentina's economic meltdown in December 2001, the Plaza de Mayo witnessed major protests and a police riot that killed several demonstrators and brought about the resignation of President Fernando De la Rúa, an honest but indecisive leader who was undercut by the opposition Peronists. Since then, occasionally heated demonstrations have taken place, both by leftist groups who deplore the so-called free-market capitalism ostensibly imposed by the International Monetary Fund (IMF) and other lending agencies, and bank depositors outraged at the *corralito* that limits access to their savings.

## CATEDRAL METROPOLITANA

At the northeast corner of the plaza, at Avenida Rivadavia and San Martín, the capital's cathedral occupies the site of the original colonial church designated by Juan de Garay in 1580. It opened in 1836 in its present form; the 1862 bas-reliefs by Joseph Dubourdieu on the pediment above its Hellenic columns symbolically compare the biblical reconciliation of Joseph and his brothers with the results of the battle of Pavón, in which Buenos Aires forces under Bartolomé Mitre defeated caudillo Justo José Urquiza in the province of Santa Fe.

Even more significant for Argentines, a separate chapel contains the **Mausoleo del General José de San Martín,** the burial site of the country's independence hero. Disillusioned with the country's post-independence turmoil, San Martín spent the rest of his life in exile in Boulogne-sur-Mer, France, where he died in 1850; his remains were returned to Argentina in 1880, after President Nicolás Avellaneda ordered construction of this elaborate tomb, marked by an eternal flame outside the cathedral's eastern-most entrance.

## MUSEO DEL CABILDO

The plaza's only remaining colonial structure, the Cabildo, was a combination town council and prison, and the site where *criollo* patriots deposed Spanish viceroy Baltasar Hidalgo de Cisneros in 1810. The present structure preserves part of the *recova* (arcade) that once ran the width of the plaza.

Unfortunately, the museum itself is thin on content—a few maps, paintings, and photographs of the Plaza de Mayo and its surroundings, along with a portrait gallery of figures in the British invasions 1806–7 and the Revolution of May 1810. The real star is the building; it's good that part of it, at least, survived 19th-century mayor Torcuato de Alvear's wrecking ball, which opened the route of the Avenida de Mayo to connect the Casa Rosada with the Congreso Nacional.

The Museo del Cabildo, Bolívar 65, tel. 4343-4387, is open 11:30 A.M.–6 P.M. Wednesday through Friday, 2–6 P.M. Saturday and 3–7 P.M. Sunday. Admission costs US$.35. The interior has a small confitería, and occasionally hosts live music events.

## CASA ROSADA (CASA DE GOBIERNO NACIONAL)

For better or worse, the presidential palace, which faces the Plaza de Mayo, has been the site of political spectacle—it's the place where Juan and Evita Perón summoned the cheering masses who later jeered the ruthless military dictatorship after the Falklands War in 1982; most recently, it witnessed the shooting of demonstrators by federal police under the De la Rúa administration in December 2001. The building owes its distinctive pink hue to President Domingo F. Sarmiento, who proposed the blend of Federalist red and Unitarist white as a symbol of reconciliation between the two violently opposed factions of 19th-century Argentine politics.

The Casa Rosada was not originally a single building; in 1884, Italian architect Francesco Tamburini (who later worked on the Teatro Colón) merged the original Casa de Gobierno with the Correo Central (Central Post Office) to create the present, somewhat asymmetrical structure. On the building's east side, facing Parque Colón, pedestrians can view the excavated ruins of the colonial **Fuerte Viejo** (old fortress) and early

© WAYNE BERNHARDSON

**Plaza de Mayo and Casa Rosada**

customs headquarters (buried beneath landfill during port improvements in the 1890s).

The Casa Rosada has experienced many low points, but one of the lowest must have been the appearance of pop singer Madonna on its balcony in director Alan Parker's film version of the stage musical *Evita*. In the basement, entered from the south side on Hipólito Yrigoyen, the **Museo de la Casa de Gobierno** contains memorabilia from Argentine presidents but, unfortunately, its charter prohibits inclusion of material any more recent than 30 years ago. Visitors can stroll among the colonial catacombs which are also visible from the pedestrian mall outside.

The **Museo de la Casa de Gobierno,** Hipólito Yrigoyen 219, tel. 4344-3804, info@museo.gov.ar, www.museo.gov.ar, is open 10 A.M.–6 P.M. weekdays, 2–6 P.M. Sunday; admission is free. Guided tours, also free of charge, take place at 11 A.M. and 4 P.M. weekdays, at 3 and 4:30 P.M. Sunday. The museum also contains a 17,000-volume library, an archive, and newspaper and magazine collections.

Guided tours of the Casa Rosada itself take place weekdays at 5 P.M. These are free, but make reservations at the museum at least two hours ahead of time, and show identification.

## MANZANA DE LAS LUCES

Ever since the mid-17th century, when the Jesuit order established itself on the block bounded by the present-day streets of Bolívar, Moreno, Perú, and Alsina, Monserrat has been a hub of intellectual life in the capital. Although the Jesuits were perhaps the most intellectual of all monastic orders, they were also the most commercial, and architect Juan Bautista Ronoli designed the five buildings of **Procuraduría** (two of which survive fronting on Alsina) to store products from their widespread missions.

The Jesuit structures, which also housed missionized indigenous people who came to Buenos Aires from the provinces, contained a number of defensive tunnels; the tunnels were rediscovered in 1912, and are now open to the public. After the Jesuits' expulsion from the Americas in 1767, the buildings served as the Protomed-

icato, which regulated medical practice in the city. Following independence, they housed at various times the Biblioteca Pública (Public Library, 1812); the Cámara Legislativa (Provincial Legislature, 1821); the Universidad de Buenos Aires (1821); the Academia de Medicina (Medical Academy, 1822); the Sociedad Literaria (Literary Society, 1822); the Banco de la Provincia de Buenos Aires (Buenos Aires Provincial Bank, 1822); the Museo Público de Buenos Aires (Public Museum, 1823); the Congreso Nacional (1824); the Museo de Historia Natural (1854); the Departamento de Ciencias Exactas (Department of Exact Sciences, 1865); the Facultad de Ciencias Exactas, Físicas, y Naturales (Faculty of Exact, Physical, and Natural Sciences, 1881), and others. After 1974, the Comisión Nacional de la Manzana de Las Luces attempted to salvage the historical buildings for cultural purposes, opening the tunnels to the public and restoring part of the "Universidad" lettering along the facade on the Perú side.

The deteriorating **Iglesia San Ignacio,** which was begun in 1661 and finished in 1675, was replaced in 1722 by a new structure of the same name. The new building briefly served as the cathedral after the Jesuits' expulsion, while the permanent cathedral underwent repairs. The Jesuits returned in 1836, at an invitation from dictator Juan Manuel de Rosas; in 1955, at the instigation of Juan Perón, mobs trashed the building, but it has since been restored.

The church has one common wall with the **Colegio Nacional de Buenos Aires** (1908), the country's most prestigious and competitive secondary school, taught by top university faculty. Another notable feature of the complex is the re-created **Sala de Representantes,** the province's first legislature.

For US$.50 pp, the **Instituto de Investigaciones Históricas de la Manzana de las Luces Doctor Jorge E. Garrido,** (Perú 272, tel. 4331-5934, http://manzana.fwd.com.ar) conducts a series of guided tours Monday at 3 P.M., Tuesday through Friday at 1 and 3 P.M., and weekends at 3, 4:30, and 6 P.M. There is also a light-and-sound dramatization of the complex's history at 6:30 P.M. Saturday and Sunday, for US$1 pp.

## MUSEO ETNOGRÁFICO JUAN B. AMBROSETTI

Affiliated with the Universidad de Buenos Aires, the city's ethnographic museum has first-rate archaeological, ethnographic, and ethnohistorical material on Argentina's Andean Northwest (on the periphery of the great civilizations of highland Peru), the Mapuche of northern Patagonia, and the archipelago of Tierra del Fuego. Well organized, with good narration in Spanish only, it does a lot with what it has—and what it has is pretty good.

The Museo Etnográfico, Moreno 350, tel. 4331-7788, is open 2:30–6:30 P.M. Wednesday through Sunday. Admission costs US$.35, but retirees get in free. There are guided tours Saturday and Sunday at 3 P.M. (19th-century Tierra del Fuego), 4 P.M. (Northwestern Argentine archaeology), and 5 P.M. (the pampas and Patagonia, 19th century).

## MUSEO DE LA CIUDAD

Upstairs in the same building as the remarkable Farmacia La Estrella, the city museum specializes in themes dealing with the city proper and elements of everyday life, including architecture, postcards, furniture, and floor tiles; the pharmacy's exterior windows have been turned into display cases. Actress Niní Marshall once resided here; for more information on her, see the separate entry for San Telmo's Museo del Cine later in this section.

The Museo de la Ciudad, entered from Defensa 219, tel. 4343-2123 or 4331-9855, is open 11 A.M.–7 P.M. weekdays, 3–7 P.M. Sunday; it is closed in February. Admission costs US$.35 except Wednesday, when it's free.

## MUSEO NACIONAL DEL GRABADO (CASA DE LA DEFENSA)

Occupying one of the historic buildings from which *porteños* routed British invaders in 1806–7 by pouring boiling oil and water from the roof, Buenos Aires's museum of engraving offers rotating exhibits, often of very high quality, from Argentine artists in the field.

The Museo Nacional del Grabado, Defensa 372, tel. 4345-5300, museodelgrabado@yahoo.com, is open 2–6 P.M. daily except Saturday. Admission is free on Sunday.

## MUSEO DEL TRAJE

Buenos Aires's Museo del Traje (Museum of Dress) might more accurately be called the Museo de Moda (Museum of Fashion), as it concentrates largely but not exclusively on women's clothing from colonial times to the present. In a middle-class *casa chorizo* ("sausage house," so called because of its deep narrow lot), the museum features three large patios typical of the mid-19th century; part of the building still awaits restoration.

The Museo del Traje, Chile 832, tel. 4343-8427, is open 4–8 P.M. Tuesday through Saturday. Admission is free, but donations are welcome.

## IGLESIA Y CONVENTO DE SANTO DOMINGO

Shortly after the Dominican order arrived in Buenos Aires in 1601, it acquired a large block of land stretching from present day Avenida Belgrano and Defensa to the riverfront, which it used for vegetable gardens, livestock corrals, and a primitive chapel and convent. The Dominicans finally laid the cornerstone for the present church and convent in 1751, but the second of its twin towers went uncompleted until 1858; its altars and artwork date from 17th and 19th centuries.

Santo Domingo (also known as the Iglesia de Nuestra Señora del Rosario) witnessed some of Argentine history's most dramatic events. It still contains banners captured by Viceroy Santiago de Liniers from the Highlanders Regiment No. 71 during the initial British invasion of 1806, and the facade and left-side tower still show combat damage from the British occupation of the church the following year. General Manuel Belgrano donated flags of the defeated Royalists to the collection after the independence wars. On

SIGHTS

the east side, near the entrance to the church, an eternal flame burns near sculptor Héctor Ximenes's **Mausoleo de Belgrano** (1903), the burial site of Argentina's second-greatest hero, Belgrano; by most accounts, Belgrano was an indifferent soldier, but he did design the Argentine flag.

Following independence, President Bernardino Rivadavia secularized the church, turning the main building into a natural history museum and one of its towers into an astronomical observatory. In 1955, during the overthrow of Juan Perón, anti-clerical Peronists set it afire.

SIGHTS

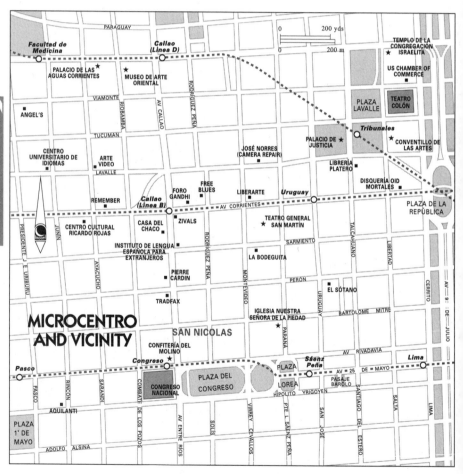

# Microcentro and Vicinity

Formally known as San Nicolás, the area bounded by Avenida Córdoba on the north, Avenida Eduardo Madero on the east, Avenida Rivadavia on the south, and Avenida Callao to the west encompasses much of the city's traditional financial, commercial, and entertainment center. The area between Avenida 9 de Julio and the riverfront, immediately north of the Plaza de Mayo, is commonly called the Microcentro or the Catedral al Norte. Calle San Martín, with its concentration of banks and exchange houses between Avenida Rivadavia and Avenida Corrientes, is the main axis of the financial district, colloquially known as La City.

Named for Argentina's independence day, the broad **Avenida 9 de Julio** separates the

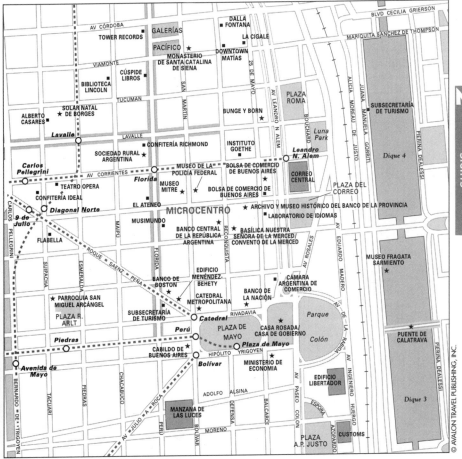

SIGHTS

Microcentro from the rest of the barrio—literally so, as only a world-class sprinter could safely cross its 16 lanes of seemingly suicidal drivers anticipating the green lights. Fortunately for pedestrians, there are several traffic islands, as well as subterranean passageways for those wishing to minimize their exposure to high-speed traffic.

West of Avenida 9 de Julio are important areas like **Tribunales** (the area surrounding the courts of law), home to several major landmarks including the Teatro Colón and the **Congreso,** which overlaps the barrios of Balvanera and Monserrat.

One of the Microcentro's foci is the pedestrian **Calle Florida,** which runs north from Rivadavia and crosses Avenida Córdoba into the barrio of Retiro. Florida first became a *peatonal* in the early 20th century, but for only a few hours each day; when it was completely closed to automobile traffic, it became the city's smartest shopping area, sporting stores like the now-closed

**Harrod's,** which opened in 1913 as a subsidiary of the famous London retailer but became a legally separate entity in the 1960s. The store once boasted 47,000 square meters of floor space in a seven-story building, but just before its closure in the late 1990s it was operating on the ground floor only.

As a shopping district, Florida is less fashionable than it once was, with one major exception: the restored **Galerías Pacífico,** an architectural and historical landmark that occupies most of a city block bounded by Avenida Córdoba, San Martín, and Viamonte. See the Galerías Pacífico entry later in this chapter for more detail.

On Florida and in its vicinity are several other notable sites. Originally a private residence, the headquarters of the **Sociedad Rural Argentina** (1910), Florida 460, houses an organization that has voiced the interests of large-scale landowners—many Argentines would say "the oligarchy"—since 1866. Other oligarchs included the financial and commercial house of **Bunge y Born,** with headquarters at 25 de Mayo 501.

During the invasions of 1806 and 1807, British forces occupied the **Monasterio de Santa Catalina de Siena** (1745), the first women's convent in the city, at San Martín and Viamonte. The Asociación Cristiana Femenina de Buenos Aires (the Buenos Aires equivalent of the YWCA), Tucumán 846, occupies the **Solar Natal de Borges,** the birthplace of Jorge Luis Borges, Argentina's most internationally famous literary figure.

East-west **Avenida Corrientes,** the traditional center of *porteño* nightlife, has recently taken a back seat to trendier areas like Puerto Madero and Palermo; several cinemas have closed and, while some traditional cafés and restaurants have survived beneath gaudily atraditional illuminated signs, others seem to be hanging on by a thread. Likewise, the cinema district along the Lavalle pedestrian mall, which crosses Florida one block north of Corrientes, has experienced an unfortunate diversification—while movie multiplexes have taken up the slack of some traditional cinemas, others have become bingo parlors, evangelical churches blaring amplified hymns, and raucous video arcades.

© WAYNE BERNHARDSON

**The Obelisco is a major landmark along the broad Avenida 9 de Julio.**

At the foot of Corrientes, occupying an entire block also bounded by Avenida Leandro N. Alem, Bouchard, and Sarmiento, the **Correo Central** (central post office, 1928) is a beaux arts landmark whose original architect, Norberto Maillart, based his design on New York City's General Post Office. After Maillart's departure, the Ministerio de Obras Públicas (Public Works Ministry) got hold of the plans, they changed to include a Francophile mansard; the Correo Central remains, though, an elegant addition to the *porteño* cityscape.

Directly west of the post office, architect Alejandro Christopherson's **Bolsa de Comercio de Buenos Aires** (Stock Exchange, 1916), 25 de Mayo 375, is one of La City's key institutions. Half a block east is the **Archivo y Museo Histórico del Banco de la Provincia de Buenos Aires Dr. Arturo Jáuretche,** Sarmiento 364, occupies part of the contemporary headquarters of the provincial bank (1980; see separate entry later in this section).

Argentina's central bank, the Italianate **Banco Central de la República Argentina,** has identical facades at both San Martín 265 and Reconquista 266. The Reconquista entrance offers access to the bank's **Museo Numismático Dr. José E. Uriburu,** a notable museum dedicated to the country's volatile economic history; see the separate entry later in this chapter for more detail.

At the south end of Florida, in La City, angry bank depositors left graffiti on the corrugated aluminum that covered the windows of financial institutions to express their *bronca* after the events of late 2001 and early 2002. Even sturdy, secure buildings such as the elegant Spanish Renaissance **Banco de Boston** (1924), at the intersection with Diagonal Roque Sáenz Peña, suffered defacement at the hands of *corralito* protestors. In 1936, Jorge Fioravanti (1896–1977) sculpted the statue of Sáenz Peña, the Argentine president who initiated universal male suffrage during his term (1910–1913), on a small triangular plaza opposite the entrance.

Immediately southeast of the bank, the **Edificio Menéndez-Behety** (1926), Diagonal Roque Sáenz Peña 543, was the Buenos Aires command center for multinational wool merchants who, in Patagonia and Tierra del Fuego, were more powerful than the Argentine and Chilean governments under which they operated.

Not all the La City's landmarks reflect lucre. Jesuit architect Andrés Blanqui's **Basílica Nuestra Señora de la Merced** (1779, remodeled 1889–1900 by the Italian Antonio Buschiazzo), Reconquista 207, is undergoing a major restoration. Half a block north, at Reconquista 269, the adjacent **Convento de la Merced** offers shelter from the financial district's bustle. The building, possibly the site of Eva Perón's first office, was expropriated by the state in 1822 and returned to the Mercedarians in 1963. Parts of the convent are open to the public as an art space, a small theater, and offices. Three blocks west of Banco de Boston, the **Parroquia San Miguel Arcángel** (1788), Mitre 866, is a national historical monument.

There is also a handful of monuments and museums that have nothing to do with finance. The **Museo Mitre,** San Martín 366, was the home of soldier, president, and journalist Bartolomé Mitre; the **Museo de la Policía Federal** is across the street at San Martín 353. See the section on the Museo de la Policía Federal for more detail.

At the intersection of Avenida 9 de Julio and Corrientes, rising above the oval Plaza de la República, the 67.5-meter **Obelisco** (Obelisk, 1936) is a city symbol erected for the 400th anniversary of Pedro de Mendoza's initial encampment on the banks of the Río de la Plata. There are 206 steps to the top, but the structure is rarely open.

From the Obelisco, the Diagonal Roque Sáenz Peña ends at **Plaza Lavalle,** which stretches north for three woodsy blocks along Talcahuano and Libertad between Lavalle and Avenida Córdoba. Occupying an entire block fronting on Talcahuano, the **Palacio de Justicia** (commonly known as *Tribunales* or Law Courts, 1904) has lent its colloquial name to the neighborhood. At 9:53 A.M. every Monday since 1994, the capital's Jewish community gathers to observe a moment of silence to protest judicial inaction on the bombing of the Asociación Mutualista Israelita Argentina (AMIA), which took place on July 18 1994; more recently, it has been the site of protests

# UNDERGROUND CULTURE

In his short story *Text in a Notebook,* Julio Cortázar imagines a life of pallid people who never leave the Subte system—"their existence and their circulation like leukocytes." Filmmaker Gustavo Mosquera went even farther in his 1996 movie *Moebius,* which depicts a Subte train and its passengers in an endless loop beneath the city.

In reality, there is an underground culture in the city's subways, but nothing quite so enigmatic as Cortázar and Mosquera concocted. Beginning in the 1930s, builders embellished Subte stations with tiled ceramic murals; more recently, the private operator Metrovías has begun to restore some of these faded glories and, at the same, commission new ones and even construct mini-museums with rotating or permanent art and history exhibits at newer stations.

Every Sunday at 2 P.M., a group of three guides that goes by the name "Flor de Buenos Aires," tel. 15/4049-3337, offers a two-hour tour of various Subte stations on the A, C, and D lines, which takes in a broad sample of murals. The starting point is Pasaje Roverano, on the 500 block of Avenida de Mayo, a short distance from Línea A's Estación Perú. Advance reservations are advisable for these tours, which cost US$1.50 pp and include an annotated map of the main murals in the network.

The Subte provides a means to see both classic and contemporary Argentine art on the move. Visitors who prefer their own means can use the following details to orient themselves to this artistic legacy.

## Línea A

Buenos Aires's oldest subway line, originally the Compañía de Tranvías Anglo Argentina (Anglo-Argentine Tramway Company) or Línea Anglo (Anglo Line) is its least decorated, though its classic wooden cars are works of art in their own rights. Nevertheless, the *vidrieras* (display cases) at Estación Perú and Estación Congreso often hold items of historical interest. The walls of the passageway linking Línea A and Línea C contain Hermenegildo Sábat's three-part *Músicos de Buenos Aires* (June 2000).

## Línea B

Línea B, though it has some of the newest and most comfortable cars in the system, is also short on decoration. The Abasto district's remodeled Estación Carlos Gardel, however, features a ceramic mural of an *orquesta típica* (typical orchestra), on its northern platform. More-contemporary works include Carlos Páez Vilaró's *Homenaje a Buenos Aires* (Homage to Buenos Aires) and *Mi Querida Buenos Aires* (My Dear Buenos Aires, after a popular tango) and Andrés Compagnucci's *Gardel por Tres* (Gardel Times Three) and *Abasto,* depicting the old but recently rehabilitated market building.

## Línea C

Imported Spanish tiles adorn the so-called Línea de los Españoles (Spanish Line) opened in 1934 with Iberian scenes, but more recent additions provide some balance. The most venerable pieces are a series of ceramic *Paisajes de España,* depicting landscapes from Lérida, Segovia, Sevilla, and other locales at Estación Avenida de Mayo, Estación Independencia, Estación Lavalle, and Estación Moreno. Martín Noel and Manuel Escasany were among the Argentine artists involved in the project.

The line is also notable for its Moorish masonry and elegant friezes, such as the ceramic coats of arms at Estación San Juan, the decorative dragon at Estación Moreno, and the Arabic script, also at Estación Moreno, of the aphorism "there is no greater victor than God."

More recent works are more self-consciously Argentine, such as Rodolfo Medina's *La Gesta Sanmartiniana* (1969), a series of eight narrative murals in polychrome cement, on the accomplishments of national icon General José de San Martín. Appropriately enough, it covers the walls of the general's namesake station, which also includes a recent mural by Luis Benedit.

Since 1998, reproductions of three of *gauchesco* caricaturist Florencio Molina Campos's paintings have lined the western platform of Estación Constitución: *El de Laj Once y Sais,* which depicts gauchos awaiting a train in the Pampas; *Pa'*

*Nuevos Horizontes,* which shows a gaucho family on a horsecart loaded with personal belongings, bound for a new *estancia* (ranch); and *Beyaquiando Juerte,* an illustration of a gaucho breaking a new mount. Molina Campos titled his pieces in the gaucho dialect.

Renovated Estación Retiro includes three murals by painter Fernando Allievi, also dating from 1998: *Historia de Sábado* (Saturday Story), a family on a city outing); *Las Primeras Luces* (First Light), a bedraggled shoeshine boy and his dog at daybreak; and the surrealistic *Las Máscaras* (The Mask).

## Línea D

In contrast to the Iberian-themed murals of Línea C, most murals on Línea D are more strictly nationalist, dealing with Argentine landscapes, legends, traditions, and native customs interpreted by artists like Léonie Matthis de Villar, Rodolfo Franco, and Alfredo Guido. The line opened in 1937, so this change of focus may reflect events of the Spanish Civil War and the military regime then ruling Argentina. The thematic exception is Estación Palermo, whose ceramic vestibule mural resembles those of Línea C's *Paisajes de España.*

On the north platform of Estación Catedral, *Buenos Aires 1936* reflects the construction of the modern city, with its subways and skyscrapers. In the same station, the ceramic *Buenos Aires en 1830* displays the city of early republican times.

Ceramic murals at the Estación Facultad de Medicina offer insight into provincial cities with *Rosario 1836, Santa Fe 1836,* and *Rosario 1938.* Estación Agüero's *Camino a Córdoba del Tucumán* shows the rigors of travel between provincial capitals in the 19th century.

Estación Bulnes's *Las Leyendas del País de la Selva* (Legends of the Forests) has a folkloric focus, and *Arqueología Diaguita* portrays northwestern Argentina's archaeological heritage. Estación Scalabrini Ortiz's *Evocaciones de Salta* depicts the far northwestern province.

Among the best works on this line is the Estación Plaza Italia's *La Descarga de los Con-*

*voyes,* a series of port scenes based on sketches by Benito Quinquela Martín, which cover the platforms themselves.

The spacious, well-lighted new stations on the Línea D extension—José Hernández, Juramento, and Congreso de Tucumán—all feature custom-made display cases with rotating exhibits of historical and cultural artifacts and artwork such as sculptures. Estación José Hernández features several 1997 reproductions of Raúl Soldi murals originally created elsewhere in the city: *La Música* (Music), *El Ensayo* (The Rehearsal), *Los Amantes* (The Lovers), and *En el Jardín* (In the Garden. Estación Juramento displays a reproduction of Cándido López's 19th-century *Batalla de Curupaytí.*

## Línea E

Opened in 1944, Línea E reflects even more nationalistic times, coinciding with the rise of Juan and Evita Perón. Estación San José is the only station to celebrate the country's scenic treasures, *Las Cataratas del Iguazú* (Iguazú Falls) and *Los Lagos del Sur* (The Southern Lake District).

Estación Entre Ríos, though, glorifies *La Conquista del Desierto,* General Julio Argentino Roca's 19th-century campaign of genocide against the Patagonian Indians, and the *Fundación de Pueblos en la Pampa,* the founding of the towns that displaced the indigenes.

Estación Jujuy represents its namesake province and people in *Jujuy, Sus Riquezas Naturales* (Jujuy's Natural Riches) and *Los Gauchos Norteños* (the Northern Gauchos). Estación General Urquiza acknowledges the achievements of the provincial warlord who overthrew the dictator Rosas in a reproduction of Cándido López's *La Batalla de Caseros* and *La Entrada Triunfal del General Urquiza en Buenos Aires* (General Urquiza's Triumphant Entry into Buenos Aires).

Estación Boedo, by contrast, contains more everyday scenes like *Boedo a Mediados del Siglo XIX,* showing economic activities in the barrio in the mid-19th century. It also contains the ceramic lunette *Niños Jugando* (Children at Play).

against judicial decisions favoring the unpopular *corralito* banking restrictions.

Across the plaza from the Tribunales, originally built as law offices, the kaleidoscopic confines of the **Conventillo de las Artes** (1907), Libertad 543, are now home to a motley assortment of artists and writers. In its present state, the Conventillo is a dramatic contrast to Italian-born architect Carlo Morra's sober neoclassical **Escuela Presidente Roca** (1902), three doors north at Libertad 581, which is distinguished by massive granite columns quarried at Tandil. (Morra designed some 25 Argentine schools in similar styles.) It's an even more dramatic contrast to the stately **Teatro Colón** (1908), Libertad 621; for more information on the Colón, see the separate entry later in this chapter.

At the north end of Plaza Lavalle, fronting on Libertad and protected by bulky concrete planter boxes, architect Alejandro Enquín's **Templo de la Congregación Israelita** (1932) is home to a conservative congregation that's the capital's largest synagogue; it also holds the **Museo Judío de Buenos Aires Dr. Salvador Kibrick,** which deals with Jewish history both within and beyond Argentina. Do not photograph this or any other Jewish community site in Buenos Aires without express permission from that site. For more detail on the museum, see the separate entry later in this chapter.

Five blocks west of the Obelisco, at Avenida Corrientes 1560, the **Teatro General San Martín,** is the capital's only notable cultural facility of the second half of the 20th century. Its facade is unimpressively modern, but its facilities—three theaters, a repertory cinema, and exhibition halls including a branch of San Telmo's Museo de Arte Moderno—are first-rate.

Three blocks south of the theater, in the Congreso neighborhood, the colonial **Iglesia Nuestra Señora de la Piedad,** Mitre 1502, dates from 1769.

## GALERÍAS PACÍFICO

As Calle Florida developed into an elegant shopping district in the late 19th century, Francisco Seeber and Emilio Bunge were the main shareholders in the proposed Bon Marché Argentino, inspired by Milan's Galleria Vittorio Emmanuelle II. Unfortunately for Seeber and Bunge, their French investors backed out because of the global recession of the early 1890s, but Seeber resurrected the project by 1894 as the Galería Florida, which housed a variety of shops and other businesses.

At one time or another, the distinctive building, divided into four discrete sectors by perpendicular galleries with a central cupola and a glass ceiling, held the Museo de Bellas Artes (Fine Arts Museum) and the Academia Nacional de Bellas Artes (National Fine Arts Academy), artists' studios, and even government offices. One of the tallest and broadest buildings of its era, with a double basement and four upper stories, it covered an entire city block bounded by Florida, Avenida Córdoba, San Martín, and Viamonte.

In 1908, however, the British-run Ferrocarril de Buenos Aires al Pacífico, which operated the railroad that ran from the capital to the western city of Mendoza, acquired the sector fronting on Córdoba for its business offices; within two years, it controlled the rest of the building. It later passed into the hands of Ferrocarriles Argentinos, the state railroad enterprise created when Juan Perón nationalized the sector in 1948.

During a remodel in 1945, Argentine artists gave the cupola its most dramatic feature: some 450 square meters of murals including Lino Spilimbergo's *El Dominio de las Fuerzas Naturales* (the Dominion of Natural Forces), Demetrio Urruchúa's *La Fraternidad* (Brotherhood), Juan Carlos Castagnino's *La Vida Doméstica* (Domestic Life), Manuel Colmeiro's *La Pareja Humana* (The Human Couple), and Antonio Berni's *El Amor* (Love). Linked to famous Mexican painter Davíd Alfaro Siqueiros through Spilimbergo, all belonged to the socially conscious Nuevo Realismo (New Realism) movement; the murals have twice been restored, in 1968 under Berni's direction and then again by an Argentine-Mexican group in 1991.

For most of the 1980s, though, the Galerías languished in times of economic disorder until, in 1992, the murals became a highlight of the building's transformation into one of the capital's most fashionable shopping centers—appropriately enough, the purpose for which it was originally conceived. Well worth a visit even for nonshoppers, the tastefully modernized Galerías offers guided tours Wednesdays at 6:30 P.M. from the central information desk at street level. On the basement level, it has a high-quality food court and, in addition, the best public toilets in the city.

## ARCHIVO Y MUSEO HISTÓRICO DEL BANCO DE LA PROVINCIA DE BUENOS AIRES DR. ARTURO JÁURETCHE

Before Argentina existed as a true country (until the federalization of Buenos Aires in the 1880s it was really a loose confederation of provinces, some of them governed by ruthless warlords), the provincial bank was its main financial institution. It held that status from 1822 until 1891, and issued the first Argentine and Uruguayan banknotes.

The museum provides an even longer-term perspective than its nearly 70 years of operation. It covers Argentine economic and monetary history since viceregal times, with displays of banknotes, coins and medallions that offer insights on topics such as early economic geography, the financial mechanisms and consequences of independence (including controversial loans from the British Baring Brothers house), counterfeiting, and the hyperinflation of the 1980s.

The first of its kind in the country, the Museo Jáuretche (Sarmiento 362, tel. 4331–1775 or 4331-7943, bpmuseo@bapro.com.ar) has operated since 1904, but its current facilities are the best it's ever had. Hours are 10 A.M.–6 P.M. weekdays, 2–6 P.M. Sundays and holidays. Admission is free; guided tours are available by appointment.

## MUSEO NUMISMÁTICO DR. JOSÉ E. URIBURU

If the Banco Central de la República Argentina could manage the country's monetary policy as well as it has organized this museum, which tells the story of Argentine currency from colonial times to the chaotic present, Argentina might not be in such dire economic straits. Its most unusual exhibit consists of coins minted in Buenos Aires and postage stamps printed for Romanian engineer and adventurer Julio Popper, who attempted to establish an empire of his own on the island of Tierra del Fuego in the 1880s. A historical display of provincial bonds is a reminder that "funny money" has a long history in Argentina.

Resembling in some ways the museum of the Banco de la Provincia, the Museo Numismático, reached through the Reconquista 266 entrance of the Banco Central, tel. 4393-0021, is open 10 A.M.–3 P.M. weekdays only. Admission is free, but the federal police guarding the gate demand identification from those climbing to the first-floor museum.

## MUSEO MITRE

Bartolomé Mitre (1821–1906), Argentina's first president under the Constitution of 1853, spent a good part of his 1862–1868 term fighting Paraguayan dictator Francisco Solano López in the War of the Triple Alliance, which pitted a seemingly overmatched Paraguay against Argentina, Brazil, and Uruguay. Also a significant historian and pioneer journalist, Mitre founded the daily La Nación, a porteño institution for well over a century.

Mitre rented the building that now houses the museum, a late 18th-century structure with several patios, before receiving it as a gift from the city upon completing his term. Mitre lived there the rest of his life with his family; to what was originally a single story building, he added an upper floor with a bedroom, bathroom, and private office. A side door led to the La Nación offices.

Museum exhibits cover Mitre's military and civilian careers, and there is an 80,000-volume research library that includes many original documents from figures such as independence heroes José de San Martín and Manuel Belgrano. The Museo Mitre, San Martín 366, tel. 4394-8240, museomitre@ciudad.com.ar, is open 1–6 P.M. weekdays, 2–6 P.M. Sundays. Admission costs US$.50.

# MUSEO DE LA POLICIA FEDERAL

It's faint but fair praise to say that Argentina's federal police are the most scrupulous police in the country, if only because provincial forces are so notoriously corrupt as to seem beyond salvation. This museum tells only part of the story. It focuses on material items like uniforms, badges, and weapons over the centuries, as well as the force's role in monitoring and controlling gambling, robbery, drugs, counterfeiting, con artists, and faith healers. There is also a truly gruesome room dedicated to forensic medicine, which includes dismembered bodies and other unpleasant sights.

Still, the museum is as notable for what it excludes as for what it includes. There is only the briefest of mention of its repressive role in events like the anarchist uprisings of the 1920s and the Dirty War of the 1970s. The museum gives no attention to the issue of police corruption—even if the feds are virtually angels compared to the Buenos Aires provincial police, they still have plenty to answer for.

*Teatro Colón is one of the most ornate buildings in the country. Its Gran Hall is outfitted with Verona and Carrara marble; the Salón de los Bustos features the busts of famous musicians and composers; and the Salón Dorado (Golden Salon) is modeled on palaces like Paris's Versailles and Vienna's Schoenbrunn.*

The Museo de la Policía Federal, San Martín 353, 7th floor, tel. 4394-6857, is open Tuesday through Friday, 2–6 P.M. Children under age 16 and the very squeamish of any age are not permitted in the goriest exhibits. Admission is free.

# TEATRO COLÓN

Arguably the most important performing-arts venue on the entire continent, the ornate Teatro Colón (1908), is approaching its centenary down but not out in the face of Argentina's acute economic crisis. Unable to pay for top-tier international opera, ballet, and symphonic performers because of devaluation, it still manages to present top-flight local talent in those and other performance media.

Lyric theater in Argentina dates from the early 19th century, immediately after the May Revolution of 1810, and its first European artists arrived in the 1820s. In 1825, Rossini's *Barber of Seville* was the first opera ever staged in the country, but artistic development in the country stagnated under the Rosas dictatorship.

The original Teatro Colón, on the northeast corner of the Plaza de Mayo, seated almost 2,500 people and opened with Verdi's *La Traviata* in 1857. As the original theater became the Banco Nacional (later to become the still-existent Banco de la Nación), the city chose one of the country's first railway station sites, on the west side of Plaza Lavalle, for the new facility. Architect Francesco Tamburini was responsible for the original Italian Renaissance design, but on his death Víctor Meano, another Italian, took charge of the project.

Occupying a lot that's larger than 8,000 square meters and boasting nearly 38,000 meters of floor space on seven levels, the new Colón opened in 1908 with a performance of Verdi's *Aída*. Seating 2,478 patrons with standing room for another 700, it is one of the most ornate buildings in the country. It has a **Gran Hall** outfitted with Verona and Carrara marble; a **Salón de los Bustos** studded with busts of famous figures like Beethoven, Bizet, Gounod, Mozart, Rossini, Verdi, and Wagner; and a **Salón Dorado** (Golden Salon) modeled on palaces like Paris's Versailles and Vienna's Schoenbrunn. In 1961, Raúl Soldi replaced the Marcel Jambon's earlier cupola murals with canvas paintings of singers, dancers, and actors; the paintings cover 318 square meters of wall space.

The main theater follows lines of French and Italian classics with world-class acoustics; its stage is 35.25 meters wide, 34.5 meters deep, and 48 meters high. A rotating disc makes it possible to change scenes rapidly. The orchestra accommodates up to 120 musicians. The seating ranges from comfortably upholstered rows to luxury boxes, including a presidential box with its own phone line to the Casa Rosada, and a separate exit to Tucumán. Presidential command performances take place on the winter patriotic holidays of May 25 and July 9.

Since the Colón's opening, notable performers have included the composers Richard Strauss, Igor Stravinsky, Camille Saint-Saëns, Manuel de Falla, and Aaron Copland; conductors Otto Klemperer, Wilhelm Furtwaengler, Herbert von Karajan, Arturo Toscanini, and Zubin Mehta; singers Enrico Caruso, Lily Pons, Ezio Pinza, María Callas, José Carreras, Frederika von Stade, Kiri Te Kanawa, Plácido Domingo, and Luciano Pavarotti; dancers Anna Pavlova, Vaslav Nijinsky, Rudolf Nureyev, Margot Fonteyn, and Mikhail Barishnikov; and choreographer George Balanchine.

Foreign dance companies that have appeared at the Colón include the Ballet de Montecarlo, London's Festival Ballet, the Opera Privée de París, the Ballet de la Opera de París, and the Ballet de la Opera de Berlín; orchestras include the New York Philharmonic, the London Philharmonic, and the Washington Philharmonic. Soloists include Arthur Rubinstein, Pablo Casals, Yehudi Menuhim, Mstislav Rostropovich, Isaac Stern, Itzhak Perlman, Yo-Yo Ma, Andrés Segovia, and Anne Sofie Mutter. At times, though, the administration has let its hair down to accommodate performers like politically conscious folksinger Mercedes Sosa, the *porteño* rhythm-and-blues unit Memphis La Blusera, and rock guitarist-songwriter Luis Alberto Spinetta.

The Teatro Colón, Libertad 621, tel. 4378-7344, boleteria@teatrocolon.org.ar, www.teatro-colon.org.ar, presents some 200 events each year in a season that runs from May to November. About 100 shows are opera; the remaining shows comprise about 65 orchestra concerts and 35 ballet performances. The theater fills an entire block bounded by Tucumán, Viamonte, and

Cerrito (Avenida 9 de Julio); the ticket office is open 10 A.M.–8 P.M. Thursday through Saturday, 10 A.M.–5 P.M. Sunday, and 5 P.M. until the beginning of the performance (if there is one) Monday. Although the main entrance is on Libertad, tours enter from the Viamonte side.

Guided tours, always available in Spanish and English and sometimes available in French, German and Portuguese, take place at 11 A.M. and 3 P.M. weekdays, and 9, 10, and 11 A.M. and noon Saturdays. For reservations, contact the Colón at Viamonte 1168, tel. 4378-7132, visitas@teatrocolon.org.ar. Admission costs US$3 for non-resident adults, US$1.50 for Argentine residents, and US$.75 for children up to age 10; tours last 50 minutes and take you behind the scenes for glimpses of sculptors, seamsters and seamstresses, set-builders, wigmakers, and the like.

## MUSEO JUDÍO DE BUENOS AIRES DR. SALVADOR KIBRICK

Alongside Plaza Lavalle's imposing synagogue, and named for its founder, the Jewish museum contains a small but impressive collection of medieval Judaica, along with documents, photographs and recordings dealing with the Jewish presence in Argentina. There is also a gallery of Jewish and Jewish-themed art by Argentine artists.

The Jewish community in Buenos Aires began to acquire prominence in 1862, with the founding of its first synagogue. The major impetus toward immigration came with the German-born Baron Maurice Hirsch's project to resettle persecuted Russian Jews in the Argentine countryside in the 1890s, and his achievements attract considerable attention here.

The Museo Judío, Libertad 769, tel. 4374-7955, is open Tuesday and Thursday from 3:30–5:30 P.M., with guided tours in Spanish, English, and Hebrew. Tours include a visit to the adjacent synagogue, reached by an interior door. Admission costs US$5 pp, and identification is obligatory; knock loudly. Male visitors to the temple, even non-Jews, must wear a yarmulke (which is provided).

# Puerto Madero

Born in controversy and corruption in the 19th century and designated a separate barrio in 1991, modern Puerto Madero is an attempt to reclaim the riverfront, which languished off-limits during the military dictatorship of 1976–83. Comparable in some ways to Baltimore's Inner Harbor and London's Docklands, it has recycled several of the handsome brick warehouses around its four large *diques* (basins, one of which has become a yacht harbor) into stylish lofts, offices, restaurants, bars, and cinemas. One measure of its success is that director Fabián Bielinsky used the promenade for a uniquely entertaining chase scene in his con-man film *Nine Queens*.

Built on landfill east of the river's *barrancas,* what is now Puerto Madero expanded during the dictatorship as the military dumped the debris from its massive public works projects east and southeast of the *diques*. Ironically enough, as plants and animals colonized this expanse of rubble and rubbish, it became the **Reserva Ecológica Costanera Sur,** now a popular destination for Sunday outings.

Sequentially numbered from south to north, the rectangular basins stretch from Retiro in the north to La Boca in the south. Dique No. 3 holds the 450-berth yacht harbor; its **Buque Museo *Fragata A.R.A. Presidente Sarmiento*** is a national historical monument. The newest feature along the basins is the modernistic **Puente Calatrava,** a modernistic pedestrian suspension bridge whose center section rotates to allow vessels to pass between Dique No. 3 and Dique No. 2. Permanently anchored at the southernmost Dique No. 1, the **Buque Museo A.R.A. Corbeta *Uruguay*** (1874) rescued Norwegian explorers Carl Skottsberg and Otto Nordenskjöld from Antarctica in 1903.

Several original cranes remain in place along the west side of the basins, where British engineers designed the handsome but practical red brick *depósitos* (warehouses), now recycled into some of the barrio's bars, restaurants, and entertainment venues, as well as apartments

The old warehouses along the Puerto Madero waterfront have been redeveloped into upscale lofts and restaurants.

and offices. Work on the east-side buildings has been slower to progress, especially during the economic crisis, but the riverfront is finally making a contribution to Buenos Aires's liveability.

## MUSEO DE LA INMIGRACIÓN

Toward the north end of the barrio, the **Hotel de Inmigrantes,** Avenida Antártida 1355, was Argentina's Ellis Island for European immigrants. From 1911 until 1953, arrivals from the Old World could spend three nights in the building before heading into the great Argentine unknown. By all accounts, it was an exemplary facility.

© WAYNE BERNHARDSON

Recently reopened to the public as the **Museo de la Inmigración,** it's still a work in progress, but is off to a good start with displays of sample family histories and panels showing the evolution of Argentine immigration and the treatment of new arrivals. The only parts open to the public as of this writing are the reception area and the dining room, where there is a computer database that visitors can search for information on the 3.7 million immigrants from 60 countries who have arrived by boat since 1882. The upstairs accommodations—actually large dormitories—are currently undergoing restoration.

Admission to the museum is free of charge; it's open 10 A.M.–5 P.M. weekdays, 11 A.M.–5 p.m. weekends.

## RESERVA ECOLÓGICA COSTANERA SUR

Plans to create a satellite city on landfill east of Puerto Madero were part of the Proceso, but the Falklands fiasco of 1982 short-circuited military projects to transform the city and the country. A few years after the return to representative government, lobbying from the Fundación Vida Silvestre, the Fundación Amigos de la Tierra, and the Asociación Ornitológica del Plata persuaded the city government to declare the area a nature reserve.

Now covered with volunteer trees, shrubs, and grasses, the Costanera Sur offers hiking and bicycle trails, ample habitat for migratory wildfowl such as black-necked swans, and for reptiles like river turtles. It has also become a cruising area for the capital's homosexuals.

At the foot of Avenida Belgrano, the Reserva Ecológica Costanera Sur, Avenida Tristán Achával Rodríguez 1550 tel. 4893-1597/1588, reserva_cs@buenosaires.gov.ar, is open 8 A.M.–7 P.M. daily except Monday; there are guided tours weekends and holidays at 10 A.M. and 3 P.M. There are also moonlight tours, at 8:30 P.M. on designated Fridays—by reservation only on the previous Monday.

## BUQUE MUSEO FRAGATA A.R.A. PRESIDENTE SARMIENTO

Built in Birkenhead (one of the biggest English shipbuilding ports) in 1887, the frigate *Sarmiento* takes its name from Domingo F. Sarmiento, the Argentine president who founded the country's Escuela Naval (Naval School) in 1872. Its bowsprit, an effigy of the patriotic symbol La Libertad Argentina (comparable to the U.S. Statue of Liberty), crowns an iron-framed 85-meter vessel with wooden siding and copper veneer that undertook 37 international training voyages from 1899 to 1938 and served in Argentine waters in 1960. It also served a diplomatic function. It was present at the coronations of Edward VII in England and of Alfonso XIII in Spain, the centenary of Mexican independence, and the opening of the Panama Canal, among other occasions.

So famous as to be the subject of an Argentine feature film, the *Sarmiento* is now a museum that honors the ship's commanders and crew—including the stuffed cadaver of its pet, Lampazo. (Embalming of human bodies is rare in Argentina; the most notorious instance of embalming is the body of Eva Perón.) The Buque Museo *Fragata A.R.A. Presidente Sarmiento,* Dique No. 3, tel. 4334-9386, is open 9 A.M.–10 P.M. Tuesday to Friday, 9 A.M.–midnight Friday, Saturday, and Sunday; admission costs US$.35, but children under age 5 enter free.

## BUQUE MUSEO A.R.A. CORBETA URUGUAY

Built in Birkenhead in 1874, this motorized corvette served mostly as a coastal patrol vessel and a training ship until 1902, when it was up for decommissioning. The apparent loss the next year of Otto Nordenskjöld's Swedish Antarctic expedition, on which the Argentine ensign José María Sobral was an officer, intervened, however. Under the command of Lt. (later Admiral) Julián

Irízar—whose namesake icebreaker helped rescue the crew of the stranded German supply vessel *Magdalena Oldendorff* in the austral winter of 2002—the reinforced and refitted *Uruguay's* successful rescue mission marked the beginning of Argentina's Antarctic presence.

After years of abandonment, restoration of the *Uruguay* began in 1953 on the 50th anniversary of its Antarctic mission, and ended in 1955. Declared a national monument in 1967, it was anchored in La Boca until the mid-1990s, when it moved here. It is the oldest Argentine vessel still afloat.

The Buque Museo A.R.A. Corbeta Uruguay, Dique No. 1, tel. 4314-1090, is open 9 A.M.–9 P.M. weekdays, 10 A.M.–9 P.M. weekends. Admission costs US$.35.

## San Telmo and Vicinity

Tourist-friendly San Telmo, with its narrow colonial streets, antique shops, and street fairs, is a favorite barrio among Argentines and foreigners alike. Six blocks south of the Plaza de Mayo, bounded by Chile on the north, Piedras to the west, Puerto Madero to the east, and Avenida Brasil, Parque Lezama, and Avenida Caseros to the south, it's one of the best walkers' neighborhoods in the city—especially on Sunday, when most of Calle Defensa is closed to motor vehicles.

Once a prime residential area, San Telmo declined in the 1870s after a devastating yellow fever epidemic drove elite families to higher ground in northern barrios like Palermo and Belgrano. Like La Boca, to the south, it became an area where impoverished immigrant families could establish a foothold in its *conventillos,* abandoned mansions where large groups crowded into small spaces—often single rooms. Today San Telmo is a mixed neighborhood where conventillos still exist, but young professionals have also recycled crumbling apartment buildings and even industrial sites into stylish lofts.

San Telmo is the barrio most closely identified with tango—at least the tango of high-priced spectacle and professional dancers. Otherwise its nightlife is less impressive than that of other areas such as Palermo, in part because some *porteños* perceive San Telmo as crime-ridden. Nevertheless, improvements are taking place, with increasing numbers of sidewalk cafés, wine bars, and restaurants popping up in the barrio's picturesque setting.

Although the Spanish Laws of the Indies dictated city plans with rectangular blocks of equal size, in practice things were not quite so regular. North-south **Calle Balcarce,** for instance, doglegs several times between Chile and Estados Unidos, crossing the cobblestone alleyways of **Pasaje San Lorenzo** and **Pasaje Giuffra.** At Pasaje San Lorenzo 380, the **Casa Mínima** takes the *casa chorizo* (sausage house) style to an extreme: the width of this now-unoccupied and unfortunately deteriorating two-story colonial house (given to a freed slave by his former owner) is barely greater than the armspread of an average adult male.

Befitting its reputation as an artists' colony, San Telmo is home to a large and growing number of murals, usually collective efforts. One notable piece, at Avenida Independencia and Bolívar, depicts the Afro-Argentine **Carnaval.** Two blocks east, at Avenida Independencia and Balcarce, the restored mural *Tango* covers the walls behind the **Plazoleta Leonel Rivera.** Six blocks south, at the corner of Avenida Juan de Garay and Avenida Paseo Colón, the stylized *Educación y Esclavitud* (Education and Slavery) tackles the sensitive topic of Argentina's authoritarian political heritage.

To the east, where Avenida Paseo Colón narrows toward La Boca, Rogelio Yrurtia's massive sculpture *Canto al Trabajo* (Ode to Labor), on the elliptical **Plaza Coronel Olazábal,** is a welcome antidote to many of the pompously heroic monuments elsewhere in the city. Unfortunately, a metal fence intended to dissuade vandalism blunts the impact of this tribute to hard-working pioneers, originally erected on Plaza Dorrego. On the east side of the plaza, the Universidad

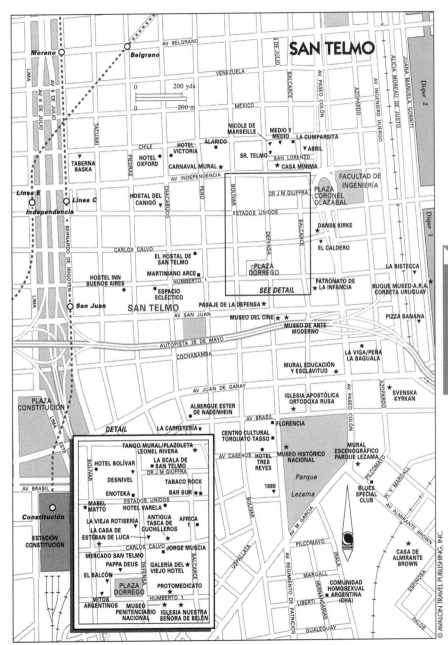

SIGHTS

© AVALON TRAVEL PUBLISHING, INC.

de Buenos Aires's neoclassic **Facultad de Ingeniería** originally housed the Fundación Eva Perón, established by Evita herself to aid the poor—and her own political ambitions.

Buenos Aires has many immigrant communities, but one of the least expected must be the Scandinavians, who nonetheless have left a mark in San Telmo. The Danish architects Rönnow and Bisgaard designed the distinctive red-brick, neo-Gothic **Dansk Kirke** (Danish Lutheran Church, 1931), Carlos Calvo 257; its interior is known for its chandeliers. Five blocks southeast rises the comparable **Svenska Kyrkan** (Swedish Lutheran Church, 1944), Azopardo 1428, looking as if it were airlifted intact from Stockholm.

One block west of the Danish church, the **Antigua Tasca de Cuchilleros,** Carlos Calvo 319, is an intriguing colonial house that houses a

San Telmo's Casa Mínima, barely two meters wide, was reportedly a gift from a slaveholder to his freed slave.

bad restaurant—look but don't eat. To the west, the unassuming *ochava* (corner entrance) at the **Mercado San Telmo** (1897), at Carlos Calvo and Bolívar, opens into a roomy market where barrio residents shop for produce.

San Telmo's heart, though, is the **Plaza Dorrego,** site of the hectic weekend flea market at the corner of Defensa and Humberto Primo; it's a more leisurely place during the week, when shaded tables replace the crowded stalls and it's easier to enjoy lunch. Antique shops line both sides of Defensa, north and south from the plaza.

Half a block east of Plaza Dorrego, at Humberto Primo 378, the **Museo Penitenciario Nacional** was originally a convent of the colonial **Iglesia Nuestra Señora de Belén** (1750); it became a women's prison after independence. Across the street, at Humberto Primo 343, the **Protomedicato** (1858) was the capital's first medical school.

San Telmo is a neighborhood where the upwardly and downwardly mobile mix. The **Pasaje de la Defensa** (1880), Defensa 1179, originally belonged to a single wealthy family but housed upwards of 30 families before being turned into a shopping gallery. The **Galería del Viejo Hotel,** Balcarce 1053, is a similar cluster of workshops, studios, shops, and a bar/restaurant around a courtyard; until its present incarnation around 1980, though, it served at various times as a hotel, hospital (during the yellow fever epidemic), conventillo, and even an *albergue transitorio* (a by-the-hour hotel). Nearby, the former **Patronato de la Infancia,** Balcarce 1170, was a conventillo until early 2003, when city authorities cleared out the squatters.

Across Avenida San Juan are two more significant museums: the **Museo de Arte Moderno,** in a cavernous recycled warehouse at Avenida San Juan 350, and the **Museo del Cine,** the cinema museum at Defensa 1220. One of the barrio's more unsettling sights, on Paseo Colón beneath the Autopista 25 de Mayo (the freeway to Ezeiza) the so-called **Club Atlético** is a grisly archaeological dig, whose basement cells belonged to a building used as a torture center during the military dictatorship of 1976–83 before being demolished to build the autopista.

At the corner of Defensa and Avenida Brasil, a graffiti-covered statue of Pedro de Mendoza guards the entrance to **Parque Lezama**, where Mendoza ostensibly founded the city in 1536. It is also the site of the **Museo Histórico Nacional,** the national history museum; for more details on the park and museum, see the entry later in this section. Across from the park, architect Alejandro Christopherson designed the turquoise-colored onion domes and stained-glass windows of the **Iglesia Apostólica Ortodoxa Rusa** (Russian Orthodox Apostolic Church, 1904), Avenida Brasil 315, built with materials imported from St. Petersburg.

Adjacent southern barrios such as Constitución and Barracas have fewer conspicuous points of interest. Just to the west of San Telmo, across Avenida 9 de Julio, the **Plaza Constitución** is a mess as a transit hub for city buses. The bus stops are due to move beneath the nearby freeway, allowing authorities to redevelop the plaza as open space. **Estación Constitución,** the station for the former Ferrocarril Roca rail line that now serves mostly southern suburban destinations, is also undergoing a major and badly needed facelift.

To the southwest, at the corner of Salta and Echagüe, the **Edificio Crítica** (1915), now the home of the Fundación Cinemática Argentina (Argentine Cinema Foundation), housed one of the capital's early important newspapers. The **Centro Cultural del Sur,** Avenida Caseros 1750, occupies a colonial-style house that once served as a plant nursery and today hosts major tango and other cultural events. The adjacent **Jardín Botánico del Sur** is more a park than a true botanical garden, but it has merged with Plaza España to form a large green and shady area.

## PLAZA DORREGO

Six days a week, Plaza Dorrego is a nearly silent shady square where *porteños* sip *cortados* (small espressos with milk) and nibble lunches from nearby cafés. On weekends, though, when municipal authorities close Calle Defensa between Avenida San Juan and Avenida Independencia, it swarms with Argentine and foreign visitors who stroll among dozens of antiques stalls at the **Feria de San Telmo** (formally Feria de San Pedro Telmo), the most famous and colorful of the capital's numerous street fairs. Items range from antique soda siphons to brightly painted *filete* plaques displaying *piropos* (aphorisms), oversized early radios, and many other items.

The plaza and surrounding side streets fill with street performers like the ponytailed Pedro Benavente, known as El Indio, a smooth *tanguero* (dancer) who with various female partners entrances locals and tourists alike—even though his music source is a boom box. Up and down Defensa there are also live tango musicians and other dancers, not to mention puppet theaters, hurdy-gurdy men with parrots, and a glut of *estatuas vivas* (living statues or costumed mimes), some of whom are remarkably original and others of whom are trite. The author's favorite, though, is the trio who (for a small donation) will jabber in *cocoliche,* the Italian-Spanish pidgin that has had a large influence on the Argentine language since the late 19th century.

The Feria de San Telmo takes place every Sunday, starting around 9–10 A.M. and continuing into late afternoon. Even with all the antiques and crafts stands, there's room to enjoy lunch and the show from the sidewalk cafés and balconies overlooking the plaza.

## MUSEO PENITENCIARIO ARGENTINO ANTONIO BALLVÉ

Once poorly organized, Buenos Aires's penal museum has undergone recent improvements, and now includes thematic exhibits including cell doors from various prisons throughout time and typically outfitted cells, including one from the women's prison this once was. Historically, the most intriguing items are photographs, such as Anarchist Simón Radowitzky's release from the world's most southerly prison at Ushuaia, in Tierra del Fuego, and an elaborate wooden desk that Ushuaia inmates carved for Roberto M. Ortiz (no doubt to show their affection) during his 1938–42 presidency. Note the large wooden apothecary cabinet in the same room as Ortiz's desk.

Half a block east of Plaza Dorrego, the museum occupies the former convent wing of the **Iglesia Nuestra Señora de Belén** (1750), a colonial structure that has experienced several remodelings; taken over by Bethlemites after the Jesuit expulsion of 1767, it became a men's prison under secular President Bernardino Rivadavia and then a women's house of detention until 1978.

Still lacking interpretive materials, the Museo Penitenciario, Humberto Primo 378, tel. 4362-0099, is not worth a special trip, but can justify a stop if you're in the area and it's open. Hours are Tuesday and Friday 2–6 P.M., Sunday 2–7 P.M. Admission costs US$.35.

## MUSEO DE ARTE MODERNO

San Telmo's modern art museum showcases contemporary Argentine artists in a spacious converted warehouse with high ceilings; exhibits tend toward the abstract, with works from figures like Antonio Berni, León Ferrari, and Kenneth Kemble.

The Museo de Arte Moderno, Avenida San Juan 350, tel. 4361-1121, fax 4300-1448, mamba@xlnet.com.ar, is open 10 A.M.–8 P.M. Tuesday to Saturday, 11 A.M.–8 P.M. Sunday. Admission costs about US$.35 but is free on Wednesdays; guided tours take place Tuesday, Wednesday, Friday, and Sunday at 5 P.M. It's closed in January.

## MUSEO DEL CINE PABLO A. DUCRÓS HICKEN

Dramatically improved in its new quarters, the Argentine movie museum has special exhibits devoted to director María Luisa Bemberg, actress Niní Marshall, and sexpot Isabel Sarli, along with a collection of antique cameras and a small cinema that shows Argentine classics for free (no subtitles, though, and on the oldest films the soundtrack can be difficult even for those with a command of *porteño* Spanish). The upper floor is devoted to Argentine films from the 1970s on, from the years of early turmoil through the Proceso, the return to constitutional government, and increasing liberty of expression.

The Museo del Cine, at Defensa 1220 around the corner from the modern art museum, tel. 4361-2462, fax 4307-3839, museodelcine @abaconet.com.ar, is open 10 A.M.–6 P.M. weekdays, 3–6:30 P.M. Sunday. It also contains a library on Argentine cinema.

## PARQUE LEZAMA

The rumored (but improbable) site of Pedro de Mendoza's founding of the city, famed landscape architect Carlos Thays's Parque Lezama is an irregular quadrilateral on the banks above the old rivercourse, which has long been covered by landfill. Shaded by mature palms and other exotic trees and studded with monuments, it's the place where aging *porteños* play chess, working-class families have their weekend picnics, and a Sunday crafts fair stretches north from the park along Calle Defensa to Avenida San Juan. The park appears better-maintained than in recent years, despite its severe feral cat problem—a dilemma it shares with many other city parks.

On the capital's southern edge in colonial times, the property came into the hands of Carlos Ridgley Horne and then Gregorio Lezama, whose widow sold it to the city in 1884. Horne built the Italianate mansion (1846) which is now the **Museo Histórico Nacional,** the national history museum; at the northwest entrance to the park, Juan Carlos Oliva Navarro sculpted the *Monumento a Don Pedro Mendoza* (1937) to mark the 400th anniversary of Buenos Aires's original founding—a year too late.

### Museo Histórico Nacional

From the permanent exhibits at Parque Lezama's national history museum, it's hard to tell that Argentina lived through the 20th century, let alone made it to the 21st. Mostly chronological, it offers a token account of pre-Columbian Argentina and a brief description of the founding of Spanish cities; its most vivid exhibits are the meticulous 19th-century illustrations of Buenos Aires and the surrounding Pampas by Royal Navy purser Emeric Essex Vidal.

The museum offers a perfunctory account of independence and the 19th century caudillos (provincial warlords), plus a substantial if stereotypical nod to the gaucho. Its low point is a chauvinistic version of the so-called Conquista del Desierto (Conquest of the Desert), which expanded the country's territory on the Patagonian frontier at the expense of the indigenous population in the late 19th century.

One entire salon is devoted to the maturation of the iconic independence hero José de San Martín, but a superficial narrative of the conservative republic of the 19th century—consisting mostly of presidential portraits—ends abruptly with the deposed Hipólito Yrigoyen, victim of the country's first modern military coup in 1930. There is no information whatsoever on Juan Domingo Perón, his equally charismatic wife Evita, the Dirty War of the 1970s, the democratic restoration of the 1980s, or the failed boom of the 1990s.

Despite its shortcomings as a museum, the building itself is a well-kept landmark whose subterranean gallery hosts special exhibits, and on occasion there are weekend concerts. The Museo Histórico, Defensa 1600, tel. 4307-1182, museohistoriconacional@hotmail.com, is open 11 A.M.–6 P.M. Tuesday through Friday, 2–7 P.M. Saturday, and 1–7 P.M. Sunday; admission costs US$.35. There are guided tours at 3:30 P.M. Saturday and Sunday.

# La Boca

On the west bank of the twisting Riachuelo, which separates the capital from Buenos Aires province, the working-class barrio of La Boca owes its origins to mid-19th century French Basque and Genovese immigrants who settled here to work in packing plants and warehouses during the beef-export boom. Perhaps more than any other neighborhood in the city, it remains a community symbolized by fervent—most would say fanatical—identification with the Boca Juniors soccer team (the team's nickname Xeneizes, by the way, comes from the Genovese dialect).

La Boca is, in a literal sense, the city's most colorful neighborhood, thanks to the brightly painted houses with corrugated zinc siding that line the pedestrian **Caminito** and other streets. Initially, these bright colors came from marine paints salvaged from ships in the harbor. The colors are inviting, but the poorly insulated buildings themselves can be unbearably hot in summer and frigid in winter.

Still one of the country's—and perhaps the world's—most polluted waterways, the **Riachuelo** is finally undergoing a cleanup; authorities are gradually removing the corroded hulks that ooze much of the contamination along the landmark meander known as the **Vuelta de Rocha.** A new high **malecón** (levee), with improved lighting, a bicycle path, and incipient landscaping, has made the riverside more appealing, but it's still not for sensitive noses. Historically, La Boca has been vulnerable to floods—so much so that many residents keep rowboats—and there remain many other elevated sidewalks.

Socially and politically, La Boca also has a reputation. British diplomat James Bryce, writing in the early 20th century, described the barrio as

*a waste of scattered shanties . . . dirty and squalid, with corrugated iron roofs, their wooden boards gaping like rents in tattered clothes. These are inhabited by the newest and poorest of immigrants from southern Italy and southern Spain, a large and not very desirable element among whom anarchism is rife.*

It is also, however, an artists' colony, thanks to the late Benito Quinquela Martín, who lived in La Boca and sympathetically portrayed its hardworking inhabitants in his oil paintings. *Porteños* may still claim that the barrio is dangerous, but anyone with basic street smarts should be able to visit without incident. There is, however, far more graffiti on the walls than in past years and more dog droppings on the sidewalks—perhaps signs of a declining sense of community. Some

SIGHTS

locals blame the police, who they say view the job not as a vocation but rather as a last-chance option. For this reason, some visitors prefer guided tours, which often start at the Caminito.

La Boca's real gateway, though, is Avenida Almirante Brown, at the southeast corner of Parque Lezama. There, the *Mural Escenográfico Parque Lezama*, a three-dimensional mural erected by the barrio's Catalinas del Sur theater group, depicts community life through colorful caricatures. Three blocks southeast, the **Casa de Almirante Brown,** also known as the **Casa Amarilla** (Yellow House) replicates the country house of the Argentine navy's Irish founder.

Only a block east of the avenue, the parallel **Calle Necochea** houses a traditional cluster of gaudy and raucous cantinas that were once brothels, but this area's tourist appeal is slowly declining. From the foot of the avenue, where it intersects Avenida Pedro de Mendoza at the Riachuelo, the remaining massive girders of the former **Puente Nicolás Avellaneda** (1940), towering above the river, are a civil-engineering landmark; the current namesake bridge parallel to the girders is a concrete construction that leads into the capital's major industrial suburb. To avoid climbing the massive structure, especially in the summer heat, many

pedestrians hire rowboats for the short crossing to Avellaneda.

The starting point for most visits to the barrio remains the cobbled, curving **Caminito**, once the terminus of a rail line and now a pedestrian mall where artists display their watercolors (there are more artists there on weekends than on weekdays). Taking its name from a popular tango, the Caminito may once again sing with the sound of the rails—a new tourist train to the **Plaza de Bomberos** (Firemen's Plaza) is due to connect to Puerto Madero.

On either side of the Caminito, along Avenida Pedro de Mendoza, are several landmarks that lend character to the neighborhood. Immediately to the east, high relief sculptures stand out above the display window of the ship chandler A.R. Constantino. Across the avenue, at permanent anchor, the former ferry *Nicolás Mihanovich*, which linked Buenos Aires to Uruguay, now houses a cultural center and crafts market.

A short distance east stands the **Museo de Bellas Artes de La Boca**, in Quinquela Martín's former studio; one block farther east, the former restaurant **La Barca** retains a batch of Vicente Walter's well preserved bas reliefs on nautical themes.

Immediately south of the Caminito, also fronting on Avenida Pedro de Mendoza, the **Fundación Proa** is one of the capital's best galleries for abstract and figurative art. Beyond several sidewalk cafés, colorfully decorated with *filete* signboards, the **Barracas Descours y Cabaud** (1902) is a former warehouse that now houses the Teatro Espejo, a performing arts venue.

For residents, though, the barrio's key landmark is the **Estadio Doctor Camilo Cichero,** better known by its nickname **La Bombonera,** at the corner of Brandsen and Del Valle Iberlucea; murals of barrio life cover the walls along the Brandsen side of the stadium. It is now home

> *Perhaps more than any other neighborhood in the city, La Boca remains a community symbolized by fervent—most would say fanatical—identification with the Boca Juniors soccer team. It's also the city's most colorful neighborhood, with brightly painted houses lining the streets.*

to the appropriately named **Museo de la Pasión Boquense** (Museum of Boca's Passion), which integrates the history of the soccer team with its role in the community.

Numerous *colectivos* (city buses) from throughout the city either pass through or end their routes at La Boca, most notably the No. 86 from Congreso, but also No. 29 (from Belgrano and Palermo), No. 33 (from Retiro), No. 64 (from Belgrano, Palermo, and Congreso) and No. 152 (from Belgrano, Palermo, and Retiro).

## MUSEO DE BELLAS ARTES DE LA BOCA BENITO QUINQUELA MARTÍN

Boca's very own artist-in-residence, Benito Quinquela Martín (1890–1977), was an orphan who became a son of his barrio, living and painting in the building that is now a homage to his life and work promoting the community. His well-lighted studio displays a collection of his oils of working-class life (Quinquela himself labored as a stevedore before devoting himself to painting). There is also a collection of brightly painted bowsprits that reflects the barrio's maritime orientation, and a selection of works by other notable Argentine painters, including Antonio Berni, Raquel Forner, Eduardo Sívori, and Lino Spilimbergo.

The Museo de Bellas Artes, Pedro de Mendoza 1835, tel. 4301-1080, is open daily except Monday, 10 A.M.–5:45 P.M.. Admission costs US$.40. It shares a street-level entrance with the Escuela Pedro de Mendoza, an elementary school.

## MUSEO HISTÓRICO DE CERA

The only one of its kind in the country, La Boca's historical wax museum re-creates events, scenes, and significant figures in Argentine history. Among its themes are the founding of the city, the gaucho, the tango, and even *candombe* (an Afro-Argentine dance style); the latter serves as an open acknowledgement of the capital's once-substantial black community. In addition to historical and political figures like Pedro de Mendoza, Juan Manuel de Rosas, and Guillermo Brown, there are representations of indigenous leaders such as Calfucurá and San Ceferino Namuncurá, and of cultural icons like Carlos Gardel, Juan de Dios Filiberto (composer of the tango *Caminito*), and the artist Quinquela Martín.

The Museo de Cera occupies a century-old Italian Renaissance residence at Del Valle Iberlucea 1261, tel. 4301-1497, fax 4303-0563, info@museo-cera.com, www.museo-cera.com. It's open 10 A.M.–6 P.M. weekdays, 11 A.M.–8 P.M. weekends. Admission costs US$1.

## FUNDACIÓN PROA

For the most part, La Boca trades on nostalgia, but the Vuelta de Rocha's cavernous Fundación Proa has become an ultra-modern display space, in a recycled three-story Italianate house that hosts rotating exhibitions by both Argentine and international artists. In addition to painting and sculpture, there are also displays of artisans' crafts and of photography. Occasional concerts and films also take place here.

On weekends there are guided tours for individuals, in Spanish only; tours in English cost an additional US$25 for groups up to 25 persons and must be arranged in advance. The Fundación Proa, Avenida Pedro de Mendoza 1929, tel. 4303-0909, info@proa.org, www.proa.org, is

open 11 A.M.–7 P.M. daily except Monday. Admission costs US$1 for adults, US$.35 for children and seniors; children under age 12 accompanied by an adult do not pay.

## MUSEO DE LA PASIÓN BOQUENSE

In the catacombs of La Bombonera, Boca's newest museum is a thunderous interactive homage to the barrio's passion for soccer and its role in the community. Professionally organized, this state-of-the-art facility's 1,800 square meters include photographs of almost every individual who every played for the team, ranging from single-match nobodies to Robert Morizo, who played in 426 matches; the museum also includes roster cards, trophies, and even a photograph of Eva Perón in a blue-and-gold Boca jersey. The ultimate icon and idol of Boca, though, remains retired striker Diego Maradona who, despite his drug problems and other erratic behavior, can seemingly do no wrong in the eyes of his fans.

Interactive video timelines attempt to integrate local, national, and international events—even the Dirty War that the military dictatorship waged as Argentina hosted the World Cup in 1978—with those in the sporting world. In the end, though, it's uninteresting to non-soccerfans except for its depiction of the barrio.

The Museo de La Pasión Boquense is at Brandsen 805, tel. 4362-1100, www.telefonica.com.ar/corp/externos/terra-boca.htm. Admission costs US$2, or US$3.50 with a full guided tour of the stadium itself. Hours are 10 A.M.–7 P.M. daily except Monday.

# Once and the Abasto (Balvanera)

West of Avenida Callao between Avenida Córdoba and Avenida Independencia, the most obvious attractions of Balvanera are major public buildings like the **Congreso Nacional,** which faces the Plaza del Congreso from Avenida Entre Ríos, and architectural landmarks like the sadly neglected **Confitería del Molino,** a national monument at the corner of Avenida Callao and Avenida Rivadavia. In contrast to this neglect is the magnificently preserved **Palacio de las Aguas Corrientes,** the former city waterworks, which fills an entire block at the northern end of the barrio. Immediately east of the waterworks, the **Museo de Arte Oriental,** Riobamba 785, is a new presence in the barrio.

Rarely mentioned by its official name, Balvanera subsumes several smaller neighborhoods with scattered points of interest: the bustling area commonly known as Congreso overlaps the barrios of Monserrat and San Nicolás, while the Once and Abasto neighborhoods have their own distinctive identities.

Once, roughly bounded by Avenida Córdoba, Junín, Avenida Rivadavia, and Avenida Pueyrredón, is the city's garment district; it takes its colloquial name from the **Estación 11 de Septiembre,** the station for the westbound Ferrocarril Sarmiento, which has both commuter rail service and a few remaining long-distance trains. It is one of the most densely populated parts of town, with little green space, but its **Plaza Miserere,** along the station, and **Plaza 1° de Mayo** are undergoing renovation.

Ethnically, Once is the capital's most conspicuously Jewish neighborhood, where men and boys in yarmulkes and Orthodox Jews wearing suits and beards are common sights, especially in the area east of Pueyrredón between Córdoba and Corrientes. There are several Jewish schools, noteworthy for the heavy concrete security posts outside them, as Once was the site of the notorious 1994 bombing of the **Asociación Mutualista Israelita Argentina (AMIA),** at Pasteur 633 between Viamonte and Tucumán. This terrorist act, which killed 87 people, is still under investigation, but there are apparent links to Iran and the Buenos Aires provincial police.

West of Once, the Abasto district was the home of tango legend Carlos Gardel. Gardel's former residence at **Jean Jaurés 735** opened as a museum in early 2003. During his time, the magnificent **Mercado del Abasto** (1893), bounded by Avenida Corrientes, Anchorena, Agüero and Lavalle, was a wholesale produce market that fell into disrepair before its rescue as a modern shopping center by international financier George Soros in the late 1990s. For more detail, see the separate entry later in this chapter.

Immediately east of the Mercado, the **Pasaje Carlos Gardel,** a block-long pedestrian mall, attempts to capitalize on Gardel's legacy, but most of its storefronts remain vacant among various conventillos, except for the restored **Chanta Cuatro,** where Gardel often lunched. San Juan sculptor Mariano Pagés created the larger-than-lifesize bronze statue of Gardel, *El Morocho del Abasto*; despite being 2.4 meters high and weighing 300 kg, it's less impressive than Gardel's tomb at Chacarita.

## PALACIO DEL CONGRESO NACIONAL

Balvanera's largest landmark, the neoclassical Congreso Nacional, is the centerpiece of the Congreso area, which overlaps parts of Monserrat and San Nicolás. One of the last major public works projects undertaken before Francophile architecture became the norm, the Italianate building faces the Plaza del Congreso and, in the distance, the Casa Rosada.

Argentines typically view their legislators with skeptical and even cynical eyes, and the *Congreso* has given them good reason from the start. The progressive if authoritarian mayor Torcuato de Alvear chose the site in 1888, after the city's designation as federal capital, but in 1895 there was a controversial international design competition

© WAYNE BERNHARDSON

Plaza del Congreso and Congreso Nacional

won by the Italian Vittorio Meano who, his rival Alejandro Christopherson wrote decades later, did not prepare the sketches submitted for the competition. The project went far over budget, leading to a major congressional investigation, and Meano died mysteriously, shot by his maid in 1904. The building was functional by 1906, but not until 1946 were the final touches applied.

The Congreso's 80-meter-high bronze cupola still bears marks from the military coup of 1930 against Hipólito Yrigoyen. Presidents who have died in office, such as Perón, have lain in state here, as did Perón's wife Evita.

Phone at least an hour ahead for guided tours of the Senado (upper house), entered at Hipólito Yrigoyen 1849, tel. 4959-3000, Ext. 3855. Tours take place Monday, Tuesday, Thursday, and Friday at 11 A.M., 5 P.M., and 7 P.M. in Spanish; for English and French speakers, there are tours at 11 A.M. and 4 P.M. on the same days.

Guided visits to the Cámara de Diputados (lower house), entered at Avenida Rivadavia 1864, tel. 4370-7532, ceremonial@hcdn.gov.ar, take place Monday, Tuesday, Wednesday, and Friday at 11 A.M. and 5 P.M., in Spanish only. The congressional website, www.congreso.gov.ar,

has separate entries for the Senado and the Cámara de Diputados.

## PALACIO DE LAS AGUAS CORRIENTES (OBRAS SANITARIAS)

Arguably the capital's most photogenic building, the former city waterworks (1894) glistens with 170,000 rust-colored tiles and 130,000 enameled bricks imported from Britain, crowned by a Parisian mansard. Filling an entire city block bounded by Avenida Córdoba, Riobamba, Viamonte, and Ayacucho, the extravagant exterior of the building popularly known as Obras Sanitarias (Sanitary Works) conceals a far more utilitarian interior of 12 metallic tanks that held more than 60 million liters of the growing city's potable water supply. There were similar, though not quite so conspicuously lavish, structures in the barrios of Caballito and Villa Devoto.

Swedish architect Karl Nystromer conceived the building, whose tanks became superfluous as engineers developed a series of subterranean tunnels for moving water through the city.

© WAYNE BERNHARDSON

**The Palacio de las Aguas Corrientes, the onetime city waterworks also known as Obras Sanitarias, is one of the capital's most striking buildings.**

Since its privatization as part of Aguas Argentinas in the 1990s, the building has housed offices and the small but interesting **Museo del Patrimonio Aguas Argentinas,** tel. 6319-1104, a waterworks museum open 9 A.M.–noon weekdays only.

The museum, which offers excellent guided tours in Spanish only, displays an astonishing assortment of antique plumbing fixtures ranging from taps, tubs, pipes, and sinks to bidets and urinals, many of them imported and all of which had to be approved by what was then a state-run bureaucracy. The old storage tanks now hold the archives of maps and plans of the city that were created in conjunction with the waterworks.

The Palacio's street address is Riobamba 750, but the entrance to the museum is on the Riva-davia side; follow the arrows to the elevator, which takes you to the first floor.

## MUSEO DE ARTE ORIENTAL

Now opposite the waterworks, the capital's Asian art museum had occupied a "provisional" site in the Palacio Errázuriz, on Avenida Libertador, for nearly 40 years. It closed in 2001 after a major scandal when an inventory failed to account for up to 400 pieces, some on loan from China and Japan, that were either missing or damaged. Some had apparently been replaced with credible fakes, but former director Osvaldo Svanascini has vociferously denied any responsibility.

As of the writing of this handbook, the museum was in the process of moving to its new quarters, at Riobamba 785, but the scandal added further uncertainty to an already uncertain economic atmosphere.

## MERCADO DEL ABASTO

Until 1893, the area bounded by Avenida Corrientes, Anchorena, Agüero, and Lavalle was a sprawling open-air market for wholesale fruits, vegetables, and meats. In that year, however, the Italian Devoto family's construction of the Mercado de Abasto made room for merchants displaced by mayor Torcuato de Alvear's ambitious transformation of the city's civic axis along the newly created Avenida de Mayo.

Rebuilt in 1934 under the auspices of the influential Bunge & Born conglomerate by Italian architect José Luis Delpini, the cavernous Abasto served its purpose until the 1970s, when the military dictatorship moved its functions to the new and more spacious—if clearly misnamed—Mercado Central in La Matanza, over the border in Buenos Aires province.

In 1998, after nearly two decades of neglect, the Mercado del Abasto reopened in 1998 as a four-story shopping center with 120,000 square meters of display space, 186 shops, 12 cinemas, parking, and a food court (with a kosher McDonalds!). Part of a project for rejuvenating the Abasto area, sponsored by U.S.-Hungarian financier George Soros (who has since bowed out of Argentina), this adaptive reuse saved a noteworthy building from demolition. Unfortunately, it is notoriously noisy and less appealing than competing centers like the Galerías Pacífico and Patio Bullrich; for most visitors the restored exterior is all that's worth seeing.

One unique feature is its children's museum, the Museo de Niños Abasto, Corrientes 3247, 2º nivel, 4861-2325, www.museoabasto.org.ar, which amuses and educates the children when they tire of toy shopping. Hours are 1–8 P.M. daily except Monday; admission costs US$2 pp, but there are packages available for families with children (comprising most of the museum's patrons).

## MUSEO FORENSE DE LA MORGUE JUDICIAL DR. JUAN BAUTISTA BAFIGO

Definitely not for the squeamish, the Forensic Museum of the Morgue is primarily a resource for students from the nearby medical school. It consists of a single large hall filled with glass cases displaying mutilated body parts from famous criminal cases or suicides (some of the remains are from tattooed prisoners).

Though not quite so grisly as it sounds, the Museo de la Morgue, Junín 760, tel. 4344-2035, has a serious purpose and is thus not open to casual drop-ins. It's open 9 A.M.–2 P.M. weekdays only, for groups of 10 or more, but by phoning at least a day ahead between 10 A.M. and 3 P.M., it's possible to join an existing group. Admission is free; photography is prohibited.

## CASA MUSEO BERNARDO A. HOUSSAY

Bernardo Houssay, Argentina's 1947 Nobel Prize winner in physiology, resided at what is now the Casa Museo Bernardo A. Houssay, Viamonte 2790 in the Once, tel. 4961-8748 (Subte: Facultad de Medicina). It's open 2–6 P.M. weekdays only.

# Caballito and Vicinity

Now precisely in the center of the federal capital, the middle-class barrio of Caballito once lay on its western fringes. It takes its name ("little horse") from the design of a weathervane placed by Italian immigrant Nicolás Vila on the roof of his *pulpería* (general store) at Avenida Rivadavia and Cucha Cucha; Vila's establishment was a landmark in an area of country-style houses with large gardens.

Today, sculptor Luis Perlotti's replica of Vila's weathervane sits atop a flagpole at **Plazoleta Primera Junta,** now the terminus of Línea B of the Subte. Immigration and the Subte have transformed Caballito into a residential barrio for downtown workers, with notable open spaces. One of those open spaces, **Parque Rivadavia,** was formerly the *quinta,* or country estate, of Ambrosio Lezica, cofounder of the influential *porteño* daily *La Nación.*

In the vicinity of Parque Rivadavia are several significant buildings, such as the **Liceo de Señoritas,** immediately to the north at Avenida Rivadavia 4950. Across the street, the **Parroquia Nuestra Señora de Caacupé,** a restored Romanesque building at Rivadavia 4879 that was once part of a convent, is particularly dear to Paraguayans, to whom the Virgin of Caacupé is patron saint. Particularly attractive in the late afternoon light, it holds an image of the saint that, legend says, was carved by an Indian who pledged to do so if he escaped his enemies. Down the block, the rococo **Club Italiano** (1910), Rivadavia 4731, sports a mansard dome and an ornate ballroom with parquet floors.

Caballito is also the site of Buenos Aires's last operating tramway, the **Tranvía Histórico,** which operates on weekends only from the corner of Avenida Rivadavia and Emilio Mitre (the car itself had to be imported from Portugal since all other city tramlines have been torn up and the cars scrapped). The suburban Ferrocarril Sarmiento still runs through the barrio from Once, and north of the tracks is the **Museo de Esculturas Luis Perlotti,** a small but outstanding art museum. See the museum's specific section later in this chapter for details.

On Caballito's northern edge, the nearly circular **Parque Centenario** is well known for its **Museo de Ciencias Naturales** (Natural Sciences Museum), its **Observatorio Astronómico,** and its open spaces. See the section on the park later in this chapter for more information.

## PARQUE RIVADAVIA

Extending several blocks along Avenida Rivadavia, between Doblas and Beauchef, today's Parque Rivadavia formed part of the Ambrosio Lezica estate but became municipal property in 1920; one reminder of its country origins is the remains of a *noria* or well, from which a water wheel irrigated the grounds (according to legend, one of Lezica's washerwomen was murdered here, and her ghost can still be seen carrying her own head).

Parque Rivadavia has a handful of monuments, such as José César Avanti's **Monumento a Bolívar,** which won the competition for the 1934 centenary of Venezuelan independence; finished in 1942, it is unfortunately covered with graffiti. Sculptor Luis Perlotti, whose museum is a few blocks northwest of here, carved the **Escultura a la Madre** (The Mother). There is a small shrine to the Virgin of Luján, the symbol of Argentine Catholicism.

Parque Rivadavia also has a large Sunday book fair, which began spontaneously but has since been formalized. In the economic crisis of 2002, unfortunately, it also became the site of the so-called *Feria de los Desocupados,* (Jobless Fair) in which unemployed middle-class families from the barrio sold their personal belongings to pay their rents and mortgages.

## MUSEO DE ESCULTURAS LUIS PERLOTTI

Luis Perlotti, an Italo-Argentine who traveled widely in the Andean highland countries of Peru and Bolivia, adapted the themes of these early American civilizations into exceptional *indigenista* (Indianist) sculptures, with strong social

content but realist and naturalistic style. Perlotti (1890–1969), a friend and contemporary of La Boca painter Benito Quinquela Martín, and his wife donated their Caballito house, along with about 1,000 pieces of his and others' work, to the city.

Despite its out-of-the-way location, this municipally run museum is a worthwhile detour. It's located at Pujol 644, tel. 4433-3396, museo_perlotti@buenosaires.gov.ar; hours are 11 A.M.–7 P.M. Tuesday through Friday, 10 A.M.–1 P.M. and 4–8 P.M. weekends and holidays. Admission costs US$.35, but is free on Wednesday.

## PARQUE CENTENARIO

Caballito's largest open space, Parque Centenario, is a heavily used park in a mostly residential neighborhood. Also well-maintained, with a small artificial lake, the park attracts joggers, cyclists, sunbathers and dogs. It includes the city's most important natural history museum (see the entry later in this chapter for details) and a separate **Observatorio Astronómico,** Avenida Patricias Argentinas 550, tel. 11/4863-3366; the observatory's telescopes are open to the public from 9–10 P.M. Friday and Saturday nights when the weather is clear. Admission costs US$1 for adults, slightly less for children.

### Museo Argentino de Ciencias Naturales Bernardino Rivadavia

Housing one of the largest and best-maintained natural history collections in the country, this museum veers between the traditional stuff-in-glass-cases approach and more sophisticated exhibits that provide ecological, historical, and cultural context. Its equally impressive quarters, dating from 1937, are only one-third the size of the original grandiose project, but they have some beautiful decorative details such as bas relief spiderwebs around the main entrance, and sculpted owls flanking the upper windows.

The main floor contains exhibits on geology and paleontology (including a reconstruction of the massive Patagonian specimens *Giganotosaurus carolini,* the world largest carnivorous dinosaur,

M

SIGHTS

and the herbivore *Argentinosaurus huinculensis,* whose neck alone measures about 12 meters. Other prized exhibits are meteorites from the Campo de Cielo field in Santiago del Estero province. There is also an aquarium, plus material on marine flora, mollusks, and deep-sea creatures, a diorama of seagoing megafauna such as sharks, rays, giant squid, and sailfish, and Antarctic fauna, plus the cranium of a sperm whale.

The second floor stresses mostly South American mammals (including marine mammals), comparative anatomy, amphibians and reptiles, birds, arthropods, botany, and an ecology exhibit in preparation.

The Museo Argentino de Ciencias Naturales Bernardino Rivadavia, Angel Gallardo 490, Caballito, tel./fax 4982-1154, postmast@musbr .org.secyt.gov.ar, www.macn.secyt.gov.ar, is open 2–7 P.M. daily. Admission costs US$.60 for patrons seven years and older.

There is also a library, open 11 A.M.–4 P.M. weekdays.

## Retiro

Retiro commonly refers to the area surrounding the **Plaza San Martín,** but the barrio includes all the terrain north of Avenida Córdoba, also bounded by Uruguay, Montevideo, Avenida Presidente Ramón S. Castillo, San Martín, and Avenida Eduardo Madero. It also overlaps the sector known as Barrio Norte—not a true barrio but a vague designation that's more a real estate contrivance, though Barrio Norte is closely identified with Recoleta and even extends into Palermo by some accounts.

Well north of Juan de Garay's refounded Buenos Aires of 1580, Retiro (literally, a retreat) was home to an isolated monastery in the 17th century. The name Retiro, though, does not appear formally until 1691, when Spanish Governor Agustín de Robles built a house on the *barranca* (terrace), where Plaza San Martín now sits, above the river. Later, the Compañía Real de la Guinea Francesa (Royal Company of French Guinea) established a domestic slave market on the site, but it was soon superseded by the Compañía Inglesa del Mar del Sud (English South Seas Company) which, in addition to slaves, dealt in contraband.

Confiscated and probably sold by the Spanish government, the site became a bull ring and, during the wars of independence, a cavalry barracks. Following independence and the rejection of all things Spanish, bullfights were halted and the ring demolished. For a time, Retiro became a zone of *quintas* or country houses, but by 1862 the erection of General San Martín's equestrian statue marked its definitive urbanization. In 1878, the centenary of the Liberator's birth, Robles's original property was declared **Plaza San Martín;** progressive mayor Torcuato de Alvear was responsible for turning it into a large public park.

Beginning in the late 19th century, the streets surrounding Plaza San Martín became the city's most elite residential area. The most extravagant residence, without question, was the **Palacio Paz** (1909), Avenida Santa Fe 750, a 12,000-square-meter Francophile mansion built for *La Prensa* newspaper founder Jose C. Paz. Like many of the sumptuous residences on Plaza San Martín, it became state property during the Great Depression of the 1930s, and passed into the hands of the army as its **Círculo Militar;** part of the building serves as the **Museo de Armas** (Weapons Museum), entered at Maipú 1030; see separate entry later in this chapter. It dwarfs the nearby **Palacio Haedo,** a neo-Gothic residence that in any other context would seem truly lavish. The Palacio Haedo fills a triangular lot bounded by Maipú, Avenida Santa Fe, and Marcelo T. de Alvear; the present occupant is Argentina's national park service.

On the north side of the plaza, the Art Nouveau **Palacio San Martín** (1905), Arenales 761, was originally a complex of three houses built for the Anchorena family. Purchased by the state in 1936 for the Ministerio de Relaciones Exteriores y Culto (Foreign Ministry), it serves primarily protocol and ceremonial purposes since the ministry moved to sparkling new headquarters across the street. The Palacio San Martín is open for public visits; see separate entry.

At the southeast edge of the plaza, the **Edificio Kavanagh** (1935), Florida 1035, is a 33-story building that was Buenos Aires's first skyscraper. Built in 14 months, it was inspired by the Chicago skyscrapers of the 1920s and a symbol of the capital's modernization. Unfortunately, it obscures the nearby **Basílica Santísimo Sacramento** (1916), San Martín 1035, which is based on its Parisian namesake and sponsored by Mercedes Castellano de Anchorena (who built and lived in the Palacio San Martín with her children and their families).

Plaza San Martín's most recent major addition is the **Monumento a los Caídos de Malvinas,** a marble monument that lists the names of those who died in the 1982 war with Britain over the Falkland (Malvinas) Islands. Across Avenida del Libertador to the northeast, the **Plaza Fuerza Aérea Argentina, Plaza del Carril,** and **Plaza Canadá** are extensions of Plaza San Martín. Plaza Fuerza Aérea Argentina, once known as Plaza Britania, was renamed after the war, in which the air force was the only branch of the Argentine military that performed credibly; its centerpiece, though, is still architect Ambrose Poynter's **Torre de los Ingleses** (1916), a clocktower resembling London's Big Ben that was a donation of the once-substantial but now diminishing Anglo-Argentine community.

Immediately across Avenida Ramos Mejía is the **Estación Retiro** (1915), a recently restored relic of the British-run railroad era, where trains once ran to Argentina's northern and northwestern provinces. Today, however, it receives mostly suburban commuter trains on the Mitre and San Martín lines. To the northeast, long-distance buses from the **Estación Terminal de Omnibus** (1982) have replaced the long-distance trains; much of area immediately north of the bus terminal is a dubious *villa miseria* (shantytown).

To the northwest, several impressive mansions that did not become state property were acquired by foreign diplomatic missions. These mansions include the **Palacio Pereda,** Arroyo 1130, now occupied by the Brazilian Embassy. In March of 2002, Israeli ambassadors from all over Latin America came to the dedication of the **Plaza Embajada de Israel,** at Arroyo and Suipacha, where a car-bomb blast in 1992 destroyed the embassy that had occupied the site since 1950 (Israeli foreign minister Shimon Peres had to withdraw from the dedication because of the situation between Israel and Palestine). The outlines of the destroyed embassy are still visible on the wall of the building next door, while 22 freshly planted trees commemorate the diplomatic personnel and passersby who lost their lives here.

South of Plaza San Martín are a handful of other landmarks, most notably the beaux arts **Centro Naval** (Naval Center, 1914) at the corner of Avenida Córdoba and Florida. Literary great Jorge Luis Borges resided in the apartment building at **Maipú 994,** immediately south of the Museo de Armas. Across Avenida 9 de Julio, opposite Plaza Lavalle at the corner of Libertad, the sumptuous plateresque **Teatro Nacional Cervantes** (1921) is one of the capital's most important theater venues; state-run, it also houses the **Museo Nacional del Teatro** (National Theater Museum), tel. 11/4815-8883, Ext. 195, open 10 A.M.–6 P.M. weekdays.

Prosperous Retiro is a barrio where people purchase rather than make art, and its numerous contemporary galleries around Plaza San Martín are almost all worth a look; for details, see the Shopping chapter. Retiro is the site of one major museum, the **Museo Municipal de Arte Hispanoamericano Isaac Fernández Blanco,** Suipacha 1422 between Arroyo and Avenida del Libertador; see the entry later in this chapter for details. At the southwestern edge of the barrio, a block north of the Teatro Nacional Cervantes, the **Museo de la Shoá,** Montevideo 919, is Argentina's Holocaust museum; see the separate entry later in this chapter for details.

## MUSEO DE ARMAS DE LA NACIÓN

A field day for gun fetishists and other weapons zealots, the army's museum displays weapons and armor from medieval and colonial Europe, firearms from the 15th century on, antique

SIGHTS

M

0    200 yds
0    200 m

HAEDO

AYACUCHO

AV CALLAO

RODRIGUEZ PEÑA

AV ALVEAR

MONTEVIDEO

GUIDO

VICENTE LÓPEZ

PRESIDENTE QUINTANA

PARERA

POSADAS

AV DEL LIBERTADOR

LIBERTAD

AUTOPISTA PRESIDENTE A U ILLA

PATIO BULLRICH

CAESAR PARK HOTEL

GALERÍA ZURBARÁN

HOTEL PARK PLAZA KEMPINSKI

CERRITO

SUKHOTHAI ▼

GUADALAJARA DE NOCHE ▼

MUSEO MUNICIPAL DE ARTE HISPANOAMERICANO ISAAC FERNÁNDEZ BLANCO ★

ARROYO

★ PALACIO PEREDA

PLAZA EMBAJADA DE ISRAEL

LA QUERENCIA ▼

■ CHRISTIE'S

ASOCIACIÓN ARGENTINA DE CULTURA INGLESA ■

JUNCAL

ANTIQUE BOOK SHOP ■

PLAZA VICENTE LÓPEZ

PARANÁ

PIAZZA DANTE ▼

RECOLETA ● YOUTH HOSTEL

IMPALA ● HOTEL

RETIRO

■ EL VIAJERO

PALACIO SAN MARTÍN ★

GALERÍA AGUILAR ■

AMERICAN EXPRESS ■

TALCAHUANO

ARENALES

GRAN BAR ■ DANZÓN

CARLTON ● HOTEL

GALERÍA VERMEER ■

GALERÍA ■ RUBBERS

SARGENTO CABRAL

AV SANTA FE

CASA DE JUJUY ■

CASA DE MISIONES ■

San Martín

SECRETARÍA NACIONAL DE TURISMO ★

CRILLÓN HOTEL ■

MILIÓN ●

URUGUAY

AMÉRICAS TOWERS HOTEL ●

LIBERTAD

LOS CHILENOS ▼

SUIPACHA

PAYANCA ▼

LA QUERENCIA ▼

PALACIO PAZ ■

SUPERMERCADO DISCO ▼

LO DE ALVARADO ▼

MARCELO T DE ALVEAR

■ THE TEMPLE BAR

MANUEL TIENDA LEÓN ■

HOTEL DE LAS AMÉRICAS ●

LOS INMORTALES ▼

PLAZA LIBERTAD

CERRITO

AV 9 DE JULIO

AV 9 DE JULIO

CARLOS PELLEGRINI

HOTEL ● CONQUISTADOR

ESMERALDA

MONTEVIDEO

MUSEO DE LA SHOÁ ★

PARAGUAY

TEATRO NACIONAL CERVANTES ★

HOTEL ● PRESIDENTE

LA CHACRA ▼

LIBRERÍA L'AMATEUR ■

LA ESQUINA DE LAS FLORES ▼

▼ LOTOS

AV CÓRDOBA

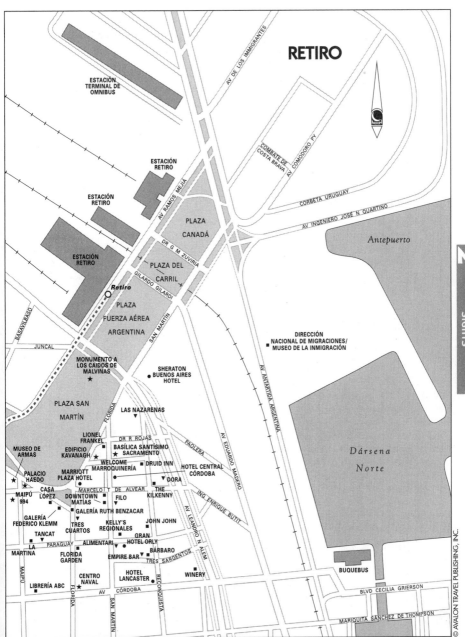

SIGHTS

artillery, and a few more events-oriented items: a diorama of the British landing at Ensenada de Barragán in 1807 prior to the occupation of Buenos Aires, photographs of General Julio Argentino Roca's genocidal *Campaña del Desierto* (Desert Campaign) against the Mapuche of northern Patagonia in the late 19th century, and a nod to the Falklands war, in which the Argentines seem to have produced an inordinate number of heroes for a country that lost so badly. There is also a roomful of antique Asian—mostly Japanese—weapons and armor.

For a while, though, the exhibits were less impressive than they had been. In July of 2002, federal police arrested former director José María González, a retired army colonel, for sneaking at least 28 antique pieces out of the museum and into his private collection. González, in a textbook example of what Argentines call *viveza criolla,* (roughly translatable as "cunning" or perhaps "artful deception") had himself reported the missing items after an inventory just prior to his retirement from the museum. (An even more colorful example of the *viveza criolla* phenomenon was the convicted counterfeiter who, in the early independence years, falsified his own release papers from jail but had the misfortune to be executed for it.) The federal police also found a substantial illegal arsenal of modern firearms on the properties of González's presumed civilian accomplice.

The controversial General Roca himself founded the museum in 1904. All the exhibits are well presented and labeled, though like many Argentine museums this one is short on interpretation. The Museo de Armas de la Nación, Avenida Santa Fe 702, tel. 4311-1070, Int. (*interno,* or extension) 179, is open 2:30–7 P.M. weekdays only. Admission costs US$.70.

## PALACIO SAN MARTÍN

Mercedes Castellano de Anchorena, matriarch of one of Argentina's most powerful families, ordered the construction of the three interconnected beaux arts residences that constitute the Palacio San Martín. Designed by renowned architect Alejandro Christopherson and finished in 1912, the three houses share imposing gates and a common circular courtyard, but each has its own separate entrance, marble staircases and balustrades, elaborate stained-glass windows, immense dining rooms (still used for state functions), and other elements of Parisian-style opulence. The satellite plaza immediately south of the palace was, de facto at least, the Anchorena family's private garden.

Sold to the foreign ministry for 1.5 million pesos in 1936, the building has served diplomatic purposes ever since; however, due to construction of the new highrise *cancillería* (chancellery) across Esmeralda immediately to the west, it no longer houses permanent offices. Now open to the public, it provides an unmatched opportunity to experience the style in which the Argentine oligarchy lived. It also holds a small museum of pre-Columbian antiquities from northwestern Argentina and works by famous Latin American artists including the Argentine Antonio Berni, Uruguayan Pedro Figari, and Chilean Roberto Matta. One of the gardens holds a chunk of the Berlin Wall.

When not needed for official functions, the Palacio San Martín, Arenales 761, tel. 4819-8092, is open for guided tours Thursday at 11 A.M. in Spanish only, and Friday at 3, 4, and 5 P.M. in Spanish and English. Admission is free of charge.

## MUSEO MUNICIPAL DE ARTE HISPANOAMERICANO ISAAC FERNÁNDEZ BLANCO

Housing the extensive colonial and independence-era art collections of its namesake founder, the municipal art museum contains an impressive array of Spanish- and Portuguese-American religious painting and statuary, as well as exquisite silverwork and furniture. It occupies the Palacio Noel, an impressive neocolonial residence built for city mayor Carlos Noel by his brother Martín in 1921—with its nods to Andalucía, Arequipa (Perú), and especially Lima for its balconies, the building was an overdue antidote to the fashionable Francophile architecture of the time, especially in this neighborhood.

The Museo Municipal de Arte Hispanoamericano Isaac Fernández Blanco, Suipacha 1422, tel. 4327-0272/0228, www.buenosaires.gov.ar/areas/cultura/museos/museoblanco.asp#museo, is open 2–7 P.M. Tuesday–Sunday; it's closed Monday. Holiday hours are 3–7 P.M.. Admission costs US$.35 except Thursday, when it's free. There are guided tours at 4 P.M. Saturday and Sunday, and occasional concerts and other cultural events. It may close during the summer months of January and February.

## MUSEO DE LA SHOÁ

Opened in October 2001, Buenos Aires's Holocaust museum is a highly professional endeavor with both permanent collections and rotating exhibits on topics such as the Warsaw ghetto and the Danish resistance to deportation of the Jews. Its bright explanatory panels, illustrated with photographs and documents, intertwine events in Europe with those in Argentina (there were in fact Argentine victims of the Holocaust). In addition, there is a Sala de la Memoria (Memorial Hall) that honors Argentine Jews who died in the European carnage.

The Museo de la Shoá, Montevideo 919, tel. 4811-3537, info_fmh@fibertel.com.ar, www.fmh.org.ar, is open 10 A.M.–7 P.M. Monday through Thursday, 10 A.M.–5 P.M. Friday. Admission costs US$.35. Note that even when the museum is open, the heavy metal door is closed for security purposes, and the friendly but muscular young men at the entrance are a further deterrent to potential malefactors.

# Recoleta and Barrio Norte

Recoleta, where the line between vigorous excess and serene but opulent eternity is thin, is one of Buenos Aires's most touristed barrios. In everyday usage, Recoleta refers to the area in and around the celebrated **Cementerio de la Recoleta** (Recoleta Cemetery); the Recoleta area is also one of the capital's prime dining and nightlife areas. Formally it's a sprawling barrio that includes all the territory bounded by Montevideo, Avenida Córdoba, Mario Bravo, Avenida Coronel Díaz, Avenida General Las Heras, Tagle, the Belgrano railway line, and the new northbound Autopista Illía to the eastward prolongation of Montevideo.

Recoleta also encompasses large sections of Barrio Norte, a mostly residential area of vague boundaries that extends westward from Retiro and north into Palermo. Neither a formal barrio nor even a state of mind, Barrio Norte is more a real estate concept, but one which is widely accepted by both its residents and those of other parts of the capital.

Once a bucolic outlier of the capital and known primarily for its Franciscan convent, Recoleta urbanized rapidly after the yellow fever outbreaks of the 1870s, when upper-class *porteños* concluded that low-lying San Telmo was too unhealthy for their families. Originally the site of a Franciscan convent (1716), it is internationally known for the **Cementerio de la Recoleta** (Recoleta Cemetery, 1822), whose elaborate crypts and mausoleums cost more than many, if not most, *porteño* houses. Historically, the cemetery has sheltered the remains of the elite (the exception being Eva Perón, who was of humble origins). Flanking the cemetery is the colonial **Iglesia de Nuestra Señora de Pilar** (1732), a Jesuit-built baroque church that's a national historical monument.

Surrounding much of the church and cemetery are several sizable green spaces including the **Plaza Intendente Alvear** and the **Plaza Francia,** the latter home to a growing Sunday crafts fair that is gradually working its way toward the cemetery; there are also many street performers and a legion of *paseaperros* (professional dog walkers), some with a dozen or more canines under their control. On the southeastern corner, along Robert M. Ortiz, are some of Buenos Aires's most exclusive cafés, most notably **La Biela** and **Café de la Paix.**

Despite the existence of these mainstays, parts of the area have plunged into commercial kitsch.

You can now visit Hooter's, a place called Dakar that is guarded by an Indiana Jones figure on an antique motorcycle, and even the inevitable sore thumb McDonald's. Immediately across from the southwestern wall of the cemetery, the weekend decibel level along the new Vicente López pedestrian mall could raise Evita from the dead.

Recoleta has other attractions, however. Alongside the church is the **Centro Cultural Ciudad de Buenos Aires,** one of the capital's most important cultural centers with an interactive museum, exhibition halls, and a full events calendar; see the entry on the Centro Cultural Ciudad de Buenos Aires later in this chapter for details. Facing Plaza Francia, the **Museo Nacional de Bellas Artes** (1933) is the national fine arts museum, described in greater detail later in this chapter. Several other plazas stretch northwest of the museum, along Avenida del Libertador toward Palermo.

The apartment building at **Posadas 1567,** between Ayacucho and Callao, was the residence of Eva Perón. The **Palais de Glace,** a former skating rink, now houses the **Salas Nacionales de Cultura,** Posadas 1725, tel. 4804-1163, a museum with a steady calendar of artistic and historical exhibitions, plus cultural and commercial events (see the current schedule on the website at www.artesur.com/links/palais.htm). It's open 1–8 P.M. weekdays, 3–8 P.M. weekends. The price of admission depends on the program.

Recoleta's other landmarks and attractions are scattered around the barrio. A block west of the cemetery, the neo-Gothic **Facultad de Ingeniería** occupies an entire block fronting on Avenida Las Heras between Azcuénaga and Cantilo. Four blocks farther north, architect Clorindo Testa's **Biblioteca Nacional** occupies the grounds of the former presidential palace; the last head of state to actually live there was Juan Domingo Perón, along with his wife Evita. See the entry later in this chapter for more detail.

Facing the Plaza Rodríguez Peña, one of Barrio Norte's most striking buildings is the **Palacio Pizzurno,** now occupied by the Ministerio de Cultura y Educación (Culture and Education Ministry). Originally built as a girls' school, the

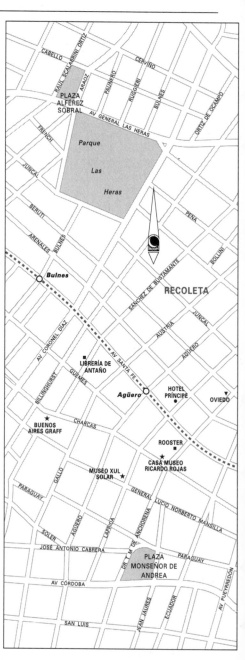

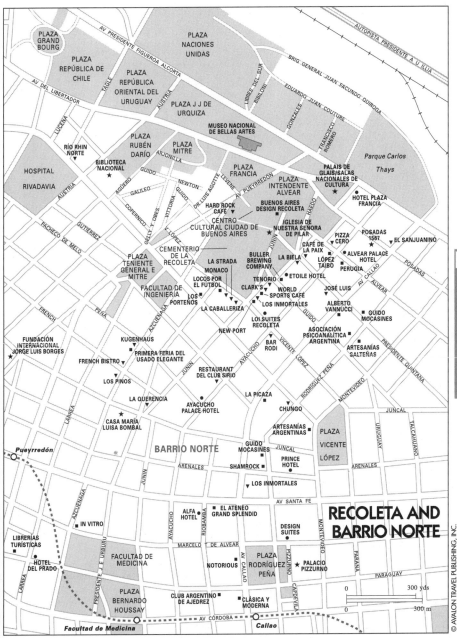

PLAZA GRAND BOURG

PLAZA NACIONES UNIDAS

PLAZA REPÚBLICA DE CHILE

PLAZA REPÚBLICA ORIENTAL DEL URUGUAY

PLAZA J J DE URQUIZA

AV PRESIDENTE FIGUEROA ALCORTA

AUTOPISTA PRESIDENTE A U ILLIA

BRIG GENERAL JUAN FACUNDO QUIROGA

EDUARDO JUAN COUTURE

TAGLE

AV DEL LIBERTADOR

LUCENA

AUSTRIA

LIBRES DEL SUR

BIBILONI

GONZALES

FRANCISCO ROMERO

MUSEO NACIONAL DE BELLAS ARTES

Parque Carlos Thays

RÍO RHIN NORTE ▼

PLAZA RUBÉN DARÍO

PLAZA MITRE

ARJONILLA

PLAZA FRANCIA

PALAIS DE GLAIS/SALAS NACIONALES DE CULTURA ★

HOTEL PLAZA FRANCIA

HOSPITAL RIVADAVIA

BIBLIOTECA NACIONAL ★

AGUERO

GUIDO

GALILEO

NEWTON

DE LUIS AGOTE LEVENE

AV PUEYRREDON

PLAZA INTENDENTE ALVEAR

COPERNICO

GELLY Y OBES

VITTORIA

V LÓPEZ

GUIDO

HARD ROCK CAFE ▼

BUENOS AIRES DESIGN RECOLETA

TOLEDO

AUSTRIA

PACHECO DE MELO

GUTIERREZ

CENTRO CULTURAL CIUDAD DE BUENOS AIRES

IGLESIA DE NUESTRA SEÑORA DE PILAR

CAFÉ DE LA PAIX ▼

PIZZA CERO ●

POSADAS 1587 ★

● EL SANJUANINO

CEMENTERIO DE LA RECOLETA

LA STRADA

JUNÍN

LA BIELA ●

LÓPEZ TAIBO

ALVEAR PALACE HOTEL ★

POSADAS

PLAZA TENIENTE GENERAL E MITRE

MONACO

BULLER BREWING COMPANY

PERUGIA

AV CALLAO

FRENCH

PEÑA

FACULTAD DE INGENIERÍA

LOCOS POR EL FÚTBOL

LOS PORTEÑOS

CLARK'S ●

TENORIO ●

WORLD SPORTS CAFÉ

ETOILE HOTEL ●

JOSÉ LUIS ●

ALBERTO VANNUCCI ■

● GUIDO MOCASINES

AV ALVEAR

AZCUENAGA

LA CABALLERIZA

LOS INMORTALES

GUIDO

LOI SUITES RECOLETA

NEW PORT

ASOCIACIÓN PSICOANALÍTICA ARGENTINA ■

ARTESANÍAS SALTEÑAS ■

PRESIDENTE QUINTANA

FUNDACIÓN INTERNACIONAL JORGE LUIS BORGES ★

KUGENHAUS ▼

PRIMERA FERIA DEL USADO ELEGANTE

JUNÍN

AYACUCHO

BAR RODI ▼

VICENTE LÓPEZ

RODRÍGUEZ PEÑA

MONTEVIDEO

FRENCH BISTRO ▼

RESTAURANT DEL CLUB SIRIO ■

LOS PINOS ▼

LA QUERENCIA ▼

AYACUCHO PALACE HOTEL ●

LA PICAZA ■

CHUNGO

JUNCAL

LARREA

CASA MARÍA LUISA BOMBAL ●

BARRIO NORTE

GUIDO MOCASINES ●

JUNCAL

ARTESANÍAS ARGENTINAS ■

PLAZA VICENTE LÓPEZ

URUGUAY

TALCAHUANO

Pueyrredón ○

JUNÍN

ARENALES

SHAMROCK ■

PRINCE HOTEL

ARENALES

LOS INMORTALES ▼

AV SANTA FE

AZCUENAGA

IN VITRO ■

ALFA HOTEL ●

EL ATENEO GRAND SPLENDID ■

DESIGN SUITES ●

RECOLETA AND BARRIO NORTE

LIBRERÍAS TURÍSTICAS ■

AYACUCHO

RIOBAMBA

MARCELO T DE ALVEAR

AV CALLAO

MONTEVIDEO

PARANÁ

HOTEL DEL PRADO ●

FACULTAD DE MEDICINA

NOTORIOUS ■

PLAZA RODRÍGUEZ PEÑA

PALACIO PIZZURNO ★

CAPEVILA

PARAGUAY

LARREA

PRESIDENTE J URIBURU

PLAZA BERNARDO HOUSSAY

CLUB ARGENTINO DE AJEDREZ ■

CLÁSICA Y MODERNA ■

0    300 yds

0    300 m

Facultad de Medicina

AV CÓRDOBA

Callao

N

SIGHTS

© AVALON TRAVEL PUBLISHING, INC.

© WAYNE BERNHARDSON

**Iglesia de Nuestra Señora de Pilar**

building owes its blend of Spanish and German styles to architects Hans and Carlos Altgelt. Officially known as the Palacio Sarmiento after Argentina's education-oriented 19th-century president, it takes its popular name from three career teachers, all brothers, for whom the blocklong street immediately behind it was named.

Four blocks west, fronting on Paraguay, the Universidad de Buenos Aires's **Facultad de Medicina** lends its name to this part of Barrio Norte. The multistory building contains two museums, the **Museo Houssay de Ciencia y Tecnología,** named for Argentina's 1947 Nobel Prize winner, and the morbidly intriguing **Museo de Anatomía José Luis Martínez,** which displays every possible human organ pickled in formaldehyde. The latter is open noon–4 P.M. weekdays whenever classes are in session, and admission is free (UBA med students, by the way, are notorious for pranks and practical jokes with stray body parts). For more details on the Museo Houssay, see the separate entry later in this section.

Barrio Norte's western sector boasts a substantial literary and artistic tradition. A plaque marks the **Casa María Luisa Bombal,** on Juncal between Azcuénaga and Uriburu, where the Buenos Aires-based Chilean novelist (1910–1980) lived for many years. Jorge Luis Borges's widow María Kodama established the **Fundación Internacional Jorge Luis Borges,** Anchorena 1660, tel. 4822-8340, which has begun a series of Borges-focused tours of the city. Writer Ricardo Rojas lived at the **Casa Museo Ricardo Rojas,** Charcas 2837.

The innovative paintings of Borges's close friend Alejandro Schulz Solari are on display at the **Museo Xul Solar,** Laprida 1212, tel. 4824-3302; for more detail, see the separate entry later in this chapter. For equally spontaneous but more contemporary work, see the elaborate spray-can street art by **Buenos Aires Graff,** covering the walls from the corner of Charcas and Sánchez de Bustamante; the organization has its own website: www.bagraff.com.

## EVITA ON TOUR

**E**va Perón became famous for her visit to Europe in 1947 when, as representative of an Argentina that emerged from WWII as an economic power-house, she helped legitimize a shaky Franco regime in Spain and, despite missteps, impressed other war-ravaged European countries with Argentina's potential. But even her death five years later did not stop her from touring.

Millions of *porteños* said "adiós" to Evita in a funeral cortege that took hours to make its way up Avenida de Mayo from the Casa Rosada to the Congreso Nacional, where her corpse lay in state before finding a temporary resting place in the headquarters of the Confederación General del Trabajo (CGT), the Peronist trade union. There, the mysterious Spanish physician Pedro Ara gave the body a mummification treatment worthy of Lenin, in preparation for a monument to honor her legacy.

Evita remained at the CGT until 1955, when the vociferously anti-Peronist General Pedro Aramburu took power, ordered her removed, and eventually (after a series of whistle stops that included a visit to an officer who apparently became infatuated with the mummy) exiled her to an anonymous grave near Milan, Italy. For Aramburu, even Evita's presence as a cadaver was a symbolic reminder of Peronism's durability.

Despite banning the Peronist party, Aramburu had reason to worry. For many years, Argentines dared not even speak Perón's name, while the former strongman lived in luxury near Madrid. In 1970, though, as Argentine politics were coming undone in an era of revolutionary ferment, the left-wing Peronist Montoneros guerrillas kidnapped Aramburu and demanded to know Evita's whereabouts.

When Aramburu refused to answer, they executed him and issued a public statement that they would hold the retired general's body hostage until Evita was returned to "the people." A common slogan of the time was "Si Evita viviera, sería Montonera" (If Evita were alive, she would be a Montonera), but Perón himself detested the leftists even as he cynically encouraged their activism to pave the way for his return to power.

The police found Aramburu's body before the proposed postmortem prisoner-swap could take place, but a notary in whom Aramburu had confided came forward with information as to Evita's whereabouts. In September 1971, Perón was stunned when a truck bearing Evita's casket and corpse arrived at his Madrid residence; remarried to dancer María Estela (Isabelita) Martínez, he neither expected nor wanted any such thing. His bizarre spiritualist adviser José López Rega, though, used the opportunity to try to transfer Evita's essence into Isabelita's body, as the mummy remained in the attic.

Perón returned to popular acclaim in 1973—leaving Evita in Madrid—and was soon elected president with Isabelita as his vice president. Meanwhile, the Montoneros once again kidnapped Aramburu—this time from his crypt in Recoleta cemetery—until the return of Evita.

Angry but increasingly ill and senile, Perón died the following year, but now-president Isabelita brought Evita's corpse on a charter flight from Madrid to the presidential residence at Olivos, in Buenos Aires province. It stayed there until March of 1976, when the brutal military junta of General Jorge Rafael Videla overthrew Perón's living legacy.

Evita, for her part, finally achieved the "respectability" that she so resented during her rise to power. Though she was an illegitimate child who went by her mother's Basque surname Ibarguren, she landed in the family crypt of her father Juan Duarte (a provincial landowner)—only a short walk from the tomb of Aramburu.

Even that may not be the end of Evita's wanderings. In mid-2002, there were rumors of yet another move—to the Franciscan convent at Defensa and Alsina in San Telmo. (Ironically, the convent was set afire by Peronist mobs in 1955, and is also the place where her confessor Pedro Errecart is buried). Another possibility is Juan Perón's *quinta* (country house) in the northern suburb of San Vicente, where a new mausoleum would reunite the two (Perón presently rests at Chacarita cemetery). The major obstacle to the move, it seems, is that Peronist politicians like the idea better than the Duarte heirs do.

## CEMENTERIO DE LA RECOLETA

For the living and the dead alike, Recoleta is Buenos Aires's most prestigious address. The roster of residents within its cemetery walls represents wealth and power as surely as the inhabitants of surrounding Francophile mansions and luxury apartment towers hoard their assets in overseas bank accounts. Arguably, the cemetery is even more exclusive than the neighborhood—enough cash can buy an impressive residence, but not a surname like Alvear, Anchorena, Mitre, Pueyrredón, or Sarmiento.

Seen from the roof of the Centro Cultural Recoleta immediately to the east, the cemetery seems exactly what it is—an orderly necropolis of narrow alleyways lined by ornate mausoleums and crypts that mimic the architectural styles of the city's early 20th-century belle epoque. Crisscrossed by a few wide diagonals but with little greenery, it's a densely *de*populated area that receives hordes of Argentine and foreign tourists.

Many, if not most, go to visit the crypt of Eva Perón, who overcame her humble origins with a relentless ambition that brought her to the pinnacle of political power with her husband, general and president Juan Perón, before her sudden and painful death from cancer in 1952. Even Juan Perón, who lived until 1974 but spent most of his post-Evita years in exile, failed to qualify for Recoleta and lies across town in the more democratic Cementerio de la Chacarita.

There were other ways into Recoleta, however. One unlikely tomb is that of boxer Luis Angel Firpo (1894–1960), the "wild bull of the Pampas," who nearly defeated Jack Dempsey for the world heavyweight championship in New York in 1923. Firpo, though, had pull—one of his sponsors was Félix Bunge, a powerful landowner whose family owns some of the most ornate constructions in the cemetery.

The economic crisis of the past several years has had an impact on one of the world's grandest graveyards. Even casual visitors will notice that more than a few mausoleums have fallen into

Cementerio de la Recoleta, Buenos Aires's world-famous cemetery

disrepair, as once-moneyed families can no longer afford their maintenance. Municipal authorities, recognizing the cemetery's importance to tourism, have intensified overdue repairs to sidewalks and the most significant sculptures, but budget problems limit their impact.

The Cementerio de la Recoleta, Junín 1790, tel. 4803-1594, is open 7 A.M.–6 P.M. daily. Many private travel agencies offer guided tours on demand; there are occasional free weekend tours sponsored by the municipal tourist office.

## CENTRO CULTURAL CIUDAD DE BUENOS AIRES

In the 1980s, architects Clorindo Testa, Jacques Bedel, and Luis Benedit turned the 18th-century Franciscan convent alongside the Iglesia Nuestra Señora del Pilar into one of Buenos Aires's major cultural centers; it now boasts exhibition halls, a cinema, and an auditorium that is one of the most important sites for March's Festival de Tango. In addition, outside the center proper, the architects added the **Plaza del Pilar**, a stylish arcade housing the upscale Buenos Aires Design shopping mall and a gaggle of sidewalk restaurants and cafés.

Immediately after Argentine independence, General Manuel Belgrano established an art school on the site. Thereafter, though, it served as a beggars' prison until reformist mayor Torcuato de Alvear cleaned up the site in the 1880s; Italian architect Juan Buschiazzo turned the chapel into an auditorium and gave adjacent walls and terraces an Italianate style. Until its 1980s remodel, it served as the Hogar de Ancianos General Viamonte, a retirement home.

The Centro's other facilities include the **Museo Participativo de Ciencias,** tel. 4807-3260, a participatory science museum for children, open 9 A.M.–4 P.M. weekdays, 3–8 P.M. weekends and holidays; and a **Microcine** (small cinema) with repertory film cycles.

The Centro Cultural Ciudad de Buenos Aires, Junín 1930, tel. 4803-1040, www.centroculturalrecoleta.org, is open 2–9 P.M. weekdays except Monday, and 10 A.M.–9 P.M. weekends and holidays. Admission is free except for the Museo Participativo, which costs US$2 pp for those age five and older. There are also charges for some film programs.

## MUSEO NACIONAL DE BELLAS ARTES

Argentina's traditional fine arts museum mixes works by well-known European artists such as Degas, El Greco, Goya, Kandinsky, Klee, Monet, Picasso, Renoir, Rodin, Tintoretto, Toulouse-Lautrec, and Van Gogh with their Argentine counterparts including Antonio Berni, Cándido López, Ernesto de la Cárcova, Raquel Forner, Benito Quinquela Martín, Prilidiano Pueyrredón, and Lino Spilimbergo.

In total, it houses about 11,000 oils, watercolors, sketches, engravings, tapestries, and sculptures. Among the most interesting are the works of López, who re-created the history of the war with Paraguay (1864–70) in a series of remarkably detailed oils despite losing his right arm to a grenade.

Oddly enough, architect Julio Dormald designed the building, in a prime location on the north side of Avenida del Libertador, as a pumphouse and filter plant for the city waterworks in the 1870s, but the renowned architect Alejandro Bustillo adapted it to its current purpose in the early 1930s. The collections are generally stronger on classic than contemporary art.

The Museo Nacional de Bellas Artes, Avenida del Libertador 1473, tel. 4803-0802, info @mnba.org.ar, www.mnba.org.ar, is open weekdays except Monday from 12:30–7:30 P.M.; weekend hours start at 9:30 A.M. Admission is free; there are guided tours Tuesday–Friday at 4 and 6 P.M., and weekends at 5 and 6 P.M.

Immediately behind the museum, the Asociación Amigos del Museo Nacional de Bellas Artes, Avenida Figueroa Alcorta 2280, tel. 4803-4062 or 4804-9290, asamuba@lvd.com.ar, www.aamnba.com.ar, regularly sponsors well-attended interviews with well-known Argentine artists such as Guillermo Kuitca, Juan Carlos Distéfano, Aldo Sessa and others. Check their website for the most current events, which are normally free of charge.

# BIBLIOTECA NACIONAL

On the site of the former presidential residence (which moved to the northern suburb of Olivos in 1958), Italian architect Clorindo Testa's national library is a concrete monolith whose construction took more than three decades before its formal inauguration in 1992. Barely a decade later, it's already showing plenty of wear and tear, in part because its pathways and pyramids have proved a serendipitous godsend to *porteño* skateboarders and stunt bikers.

Still, the library makes a major contribution to the capital's cultural life, hosting lectures by literary figures, exhibits by local artists, and major expositions like 2002's "Evita, una vida, una historia, un mito"—a remarkably thorough and thoroughly remarkable retrospective on Evita's life and influence, on the 50th anniversary of her death.

At the Las Heras entrance, designed with readers in mind, the library's **Plaza del Lector** features comfortable benches, cobbled pathways, and a fountain, but not much shade from the afternoon sun. Its latest acquisition is a bronze monument to Evita herself. The **Café del Lector,** on the Agüero side, serves moderately priced lunches.

The Biblioteca Nacional, Agüero 2502, tel. 4806-4729, www.bibnal.edu.ar, is open 10 A.M.– 9 P.M. weekdays and noon–9 P.M. weekends. The website has a regularly updated calendar of events.

# MUSEO HOUSSAY DE CIENCIA Y TECNOLOGÍA

This small but engaging museum at the UBA's Facultad de Medicina contains primarily educational and experimental equipment, instruments, and documents relating to Argentine medicine. Presently undergoing a long-overdue reorganization, it takes its name from physiologist Bernardo Houssay, the son of French immigrants and winner of the Nobel Prize (1947) in medicine. The museum also features some remarkable scientific curiosities, including an extraordinary German-built mechanical model of the eye dating from the late 19th century.

The Museo Houssay, Paraguay 2155, 1st floor, tel. 5950-9500, Int. 2102, www.fmed.uba.ar/depto/histomed/houssay.htm, is open noon– 4 P.M. weekdays only when the university is in session. Houssay's residence, also a museum, is nearby in Once.

# CASA MUSEO RICARDO ROJAS

Ricardo Rojas (1882–1957) was a poet, essayist, and playwright who, unlike many Argentine intellectuals who saw their society as a struggle between civilization and barbarism, tried to reconcile indigenous and immigrant aspects of South American development. Perhaps because of his provincial origins in the Andean northwestern city of Tucumán, he considered the pre-Columbian civilizations of highland South America equal to those of Europe.

Rojas's 1929 house, designed by architect Angel Guido to the author's specifications, incorporates architectural elements from both places. Its facade is a colonial-style replica of the Tucumán house in which the country now known as Argentina declared its independence in 1815. Yet Rojas consciously incorporated Incaic ornamentation into the building design, according to his *doctrina euríndica* (Euro-Indian doctrine), which posited a harmonious fusion of indigenous, Hispanic, creole, and cosmopolitan influences.

Donated to the state by Rojas's wife Julieta Quinteros a year after the author's death, the house features an impressively decorated vestibule, a patio embellished with bas-reliefs of Incan and Spanish colonial origins, and a Cuzco-style balcony. The furniture, in colonial style, is of dark polished wood.

The Casa Museo Ricardo Rojas, Charcas 2837, tel. 4824-4039, is open 10 A.M.–5 P.M. weekdays, 1–5 P.M. Saturday, and 10 A.M.–2 P.M. Sunday. Admission costs US$.35 pp for guided tours conducted by motivated, congenial personnel.

# MUSEO XUL SOLAR

Despite his blindness, Jorge Luis Borges left vivid descriptions of the paintings of his friend Alejandro Schulz Solari, better known as Xul

Solar. Obsessed with architecture and the occult, Xul Solar (1897–1963) was an abstract artist who produced vivid oils and watercolors. During his lifetime, he showed his work in Buenos Aires, Brasil, France, and Italy; after his death, it also appeared in Miami, New York, London, Madrid, Stockholm, and other European cities.

The Xul Solar museum displays a large assortment of his work, mostly smallish watercolors, in utilitarian surroundings with sheetrocked walls and relatively dim light that contrast dramatically with the painter's intense colors. It also shows personal effects such as postcards directed to famous writers like Nietzsche.

The Museo Xul Solar, Laprida 1212, tel. 4824-3302, fax 4821-5378, xulsolar@ciudad.com.ar, www.xulsolar.org.ar, is open noon–8 P.M. weekdays only, and is closed in the summer months of January and February. Admission is US$1 except for children under age 12 and retired persons, who pay only US$.35.

# Palermo

Buenos Aires's largest barrio, Palermo enjoys the widest open spaces in the city, thanks to 19th-century dictator Juan Manuel de Rosas, whose private estate stretched almost from Recoleta all the way to Belgrano, between present-day Avenida del Libertador and the Río de la Plata. Beaten at the battle of Caseros by rival caudillo Justo José de Urquiza, a onetime confederate from Entre Ríos province, Rosas spent the rest of his life in British exile. The property passed into the public domain and, ironically enough, the sprawling **Parque Tres de Febrero** takes its name from the date of Rosas's defeat in 1852.

Even apart from its parkland, Palermo is a large and diverse barrio. Formally, its boundaries zigzag along La Pampa, Avenida Figueroa Alcorta, Avenida Valentín Alsina, Zabala, Avenida Cabildo, Jorge Newbery, Cramer, Avenida Dorrego, Avenida Córdoba, Mario Bravo, Avenida Coronel Díaz, Avenida Las Heras, Tagle, the tracks of the Ferrocarril Belgrano, Salguero, and the Avenida Costanera Rafael Obligado.

Once part of the capital's unsavory *arrabales* (margins), its street corners populated by stylish but capricious *malevos* (bullies) immortalized in the short stories of Jorge Luis Borges, Palermo hasn't entirely superseded that reputation—in some areas, poorly lighted streets can still make visitors uneasy. Yet it also has exclusive neighborhoods such as **Barrio Parque,** also known as **Palermo Chico,** across Avenida del Libertador immediately north of Recoleta.

Home to many embassies and enormous mansions still occupied by single families, Barrio Parque boasts some of Buenos Aires's highest property values. One of its landmarks is the **Instituto Nacional Sanmartiniano,** housing the research institute on national hero José de San Martín's life, on **Plaza Grand Bourg.** Built to mimic San Martín's home-in-exile in Boulogne sur Mer, France—but a third larger—it no longer serves as a museum, since its collections have moved to San Telmo's Museo Histórico Nacional.

Barrio Parque has several other museums, however, including the gaucho-oriented **Museo de Motivos Argentinos José Hernández,** Avenida del Libertador 2373. The beaux arts **Palacio Errázuriz** (1918), Avenida del Libertador 1902, is a former private residence and national historical monument that contains the **Museo Nacional de Arte Decorativo.** The new kid on the block, though, is the state-of-the-art **Museo de Arte Latinoamericano de Buenos Aires** (Malba), Avenida Figueroa Alcorta 3415, which concentrates on contemporary Latin American artists and their works.

Across Avenida del Libertador from Barrio Parque, the **Botánico** is an upper-middle-class neighborhood that takes its name from the **Jardín Botánico Carlos Thays,** though it also abuts the **Jardín Zoológico** (zoo) and **Parque Las Heras** (the former site of a federal prison). Once a neighborhood of imposing *palacetes,* (mansions, or "small palaces") the Botánico is still affluent but no longer so exclusive as when, in

1948, Eva Perón enraged the neighbors by appropriating one of those mansions to create the **Hogar de Tránsito No. 2,** a home for single mothers that now houses the **Museo Eva Perón,** at Lafinur 2988. For a glimpse of what the neighborhood used to look like, visit the **Edificio La Colorada** (1911), Cabello 3791, a 24-unit apartment building of imported British brick; created for workers on the British-run railways, it features a skylighted central patio that was unusual in its time.

South of Parque Las Heras and across Avenida Santa Fe (one of Palermo's main traffic arteries) **Alto Palermo** is a densely built area that has given its name to one of the city's major shopping centers. The real center of action, though, is slightly northwest at **Palermo Viejo,** where the **Plaza Serrano** (also known as **Plaza Cortázar**) is a major axis of *porteño* nightlife; its stylishly inventive restaurants and bars, plus its clothing and furniture outlets, have made it one of the city's most fashionable neighborhoods. Jorge Luis Borges set his poem "La Fundación Mítica de Buenos Aires" (The Mythical Foundation of Buenos Aires) on the Palermo Viejo block bounded by Guatemala, Serrano, Paraguay, and Gurruchaga.

Palermo Viejo further subdivides into **Palermo Soho,** a trendy term to describe the area south of Avenida Juan B. Justo, and the more northerly **Palermo Hollywood,** where many *porteño* television and radio producers have located their facilities. Shaded by sycamores, many of Palermo Viejo's streets still contain lowrise *casas chorizos* (sausage houses) on deep narrow lots. Borges himself lived at **José Luis Borges (formerly Serrano) 2135,** a street recently renamed for the literary great (though still marked by a plaque, the house here is a recent replacement for Borges's residence). The nondescript modern apartment building at **Aráoz 2180** shares the onetime address of legendary revolutionary Ernesto Guevara, but is not the house in which "Che" lived. One of the most interesting private residences is the **Casa Jorge García,** Gorriti 5142, whose garage facade features Martiniano Arce's *filete* caricatures of the García family.

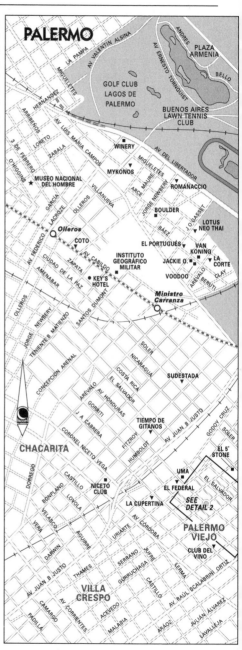

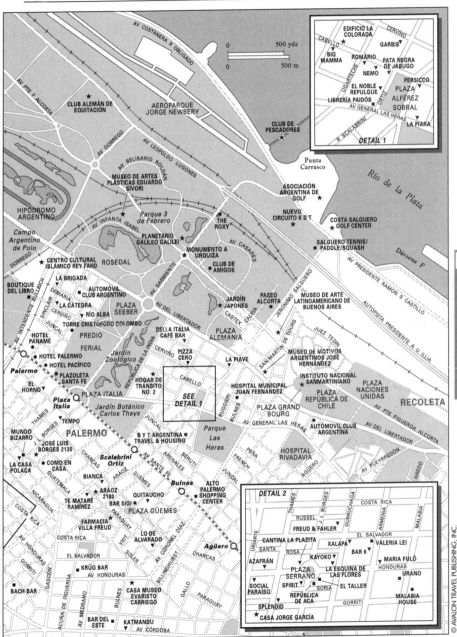

**DETAIL 1**

EDIFICIO LA COLORADA
CERVINO
CABELLO
GARBIS
BIG MAMMA
ROMARIO
PATA NEGRA DE JABUGO
NEMO
PERSICCO
EL NOBLE REPULGUE
PLAZA ALFÉREZ SOBRAL
LIBRERÍA PAIDÓS
AV GENERAL LAS HERAS
R SCALABRINI
LA PIARA

AV COSTANERA R OBLIGADO

AV PTE F ALCORTA

CLUB ALEMÁN DE EQUITACIÓN

AEROPARQUE JORGE NEWBERY

CLUB DE PESCADORES

Punta Carrasco

Río de la Plata

AV DORREGO
AV LEOPOLDO LUGONES
AV BELISARIO ROLDÁN

ASOCIACIÓN ARGENTINA DE GOLF

NUEVO CIRCUITO K D T

COSTA SALGUERO GOLF CENTER

MUSEO DE ARTES PLÁSTICAS EDUARDO SÍVORI

HIPÓDROMO ARGENTINO

Campo Argentino de Polo

Parque 3 de Febrero

AV INFANTA ISABEL

PLANETARIO GALILEO GALILEI

THE ROXY

MONUMENTO A URQUIZA

AV CASARES

SALGUERO TENNIS/ PADDLE/SQUASH

Dársena F

SIGHTS

CENTRO CULTURAL ISLÁMICO REY FAHD
ROSEDAL

CLUB DE AMIGOS

AV PRESIDENTE RAMON S CASTILLO

BOUTIQUE DEL LIBRO

LA BRIGADA
AUTOMÓVIL CLUB ARGENTINO
DEMARIA
LA CÁTEDRA
CERVINO
RÍO ALBA
PLAZA SEEBER

AV SARMIENTO

JARDÍN JAPONÉS

PASEO ALCORTA

MUSEO DE ARTE LATINOAMERICANO DE BUENOS AIRES

AUTOPISTA PRESIDENTE A U ILLIA

JERÓNIMO SALGUERO

TORRE CRISTÓFORO COLOMBO
AV DEL LIBERTADOR

CASTEX CALVA

PREDIO

HOTEL PANAMÉ
FERIAL
Jardín Zoológico
BELLA ITALIA CAFÉ BAR

REPÚBLICA DE LA INDIA

CERVINO

PLAZA ALEMANIA

JUEZ TEDIN

DE TOURS

MUSEO DE MOTIVOS ARGENTINOS JOSÉ HERNÁNDEZ

HOTEL PALERMO
HOTEL PACÍFICO
PLAZOLETA SANTA FE
PIZZA CERO
LA PIAVE
SAN MARTÍN
INSTITUTO NACIONAL SANMARTINIANO
PLAZA NACIONES UNIDAS

Palermo
EL HORNO
Plaza Italia
PLAZA ITALIA

CABELLO

SEE DETAIL 1

HOGAR DE TRANSITO NO. 2

RUGGIERI
BULNES

HOSPITAL MUNICIPAL JUAN FERNANDEZ

PLAZA REPÚBLICA DE CHILE

RECOLETA

Jardín Botánico Carlos Thays

JUNCAL

Parque Las Heras

PLAZA GRAND BOURG

AV GENERAL LAS HERAS

AUTOMÓVIL CLUB ARGENTINA

AV PTE FIGUEROA ALCORTA
AV DEL LIBERTADOR

THAMES
J L BORGES
TEMPO
PALERMO

B Y T ARGENTINA TRAVEL & HOUSING

PEÑA
FRENCH

HOSPITAL RIVADAVIA

AV PUEYRREDON

MUNDO BIZARRO
JOSÉ LUIS BORGES 2135
Scalabrini Ortiz
AV SANTA FE
BERUTI
JUNCAL
HAEDO

LA CASA POLACA
COMO EN CASA
CHARCAS
ARENALES

Buines

ALTO PALERMO SHOPPING CENTER

GUATEMALA
NICARAGUA
COSTA RICA

BIANCA
ARÁOZ
TE MATARÉ RAMÍREZ
ARÁOZ 2180
BAR SIGI
QUITAUCHO
PLAZA GÜEMES

GUEMES
PARAGUAY

AV HONDURAS

FARMACIA VILLA FREUD
LO DE ALVARADO
VIDT
SOLER
AV CORONEL DIAZ
CHARCAS
Agüero

COSTA RICA
EL SALVADOR
GORRITI
GASCON
AV MEDRANO

KRÜG BAR
AV HONDURAS

CASA MUSEO EVARISTO CARRIEGO

ACUÑA DE FIGUEROA
BULNES
GALLO
PARAGUAY
BILLINGHURST

BACH BAR
BAR DEL ESTE
KATMANDU
AV CÓRDOBA

**DETAIL 2**

THAMES
J L BORGES
GURRUCHAGA
COSTA RICA
ARMENIA
MALABIA

RUSSEL
FREUD & FAHLER
EL SALVADOR
URIARTE
SANTA ROSA

CANTINA LA PLAZITA
XALAPA
VALERIA LEI

AZAFRÁN
KAYOKO
BAR 6
MARIA FULÓ
HONDURAS
URANO

SOCIAL PARAISO
SPIRIT
PLAZA SERRANO
LA ESQUINA DE LAS FLORES
SORIA
EL TALLER
MALABIA HOUSE

SPLENDID
REPÚBLICA DE ACÁ
GORRITI

CASA JORGE GARCÍA

© AVALON TRAVEL PUBLISHING, INC.

In addition to Borges, Palermo has a wide literary tradition. Guevara was a prolific if politically polemical writer. Additionally, the **Casa Museo Evaristo Carriego,** Honduras 3784, tel. 4963-2194, open 10 A.M.–6 P.M. weekdays, was the residence of a *porteño* poet and Borges contemporary who died young (1883–1912).

North of the Zoológico, the Sociedad Rural Argentina has rented out the historic **Predio Ferial** as the site of events ranging from traditional livestock shows to book fairs. The area's most conspicuous new landmark is the controversial **Centro Cultural Islámico Rey Fahd,** built with Saudi money on land acquired from the Menem administration, on Avenida Intendente Bullrich.

At the northern end of the barrio, overlapping Belgrano, **Las Cañitas** is a new gastronomic and nightlife area challenging Palermo Viejo among *porteño* partygoers; the nearby **Museo Nacional del Hombre** complements Monserrat's Museo Etnográfico.

## PARQUE TRES DE FEBRERO

Argentine elites got their revenge on José Manuel de Rosas with the creation of Parque Tres de Febrero. Not only does the equestrian **Monumento a Urquiza,** at Avenida Sarmiento and Avenida Figueroa Alcorta commemorate Rosas's conqueror at the battle of Caseros, but Unitarist President Domingo F. Sarmiento's name graces one of the park's main avenues. Sarmiento, an implacable enemy of Rosas, oversaw the estate's transformation during his presidency (1868–1874).

In the early 20th century, British diplomat James Bryce described what the area had become:

> On fine afternoons, there is a wonderful turnout of carriages drawn by handsome horses, and still more of costly motor cars, in the principal avenues of the Park; they press so thick that vehicles are often jammed together for fifteen or twenty minutes, unable to move on. Nowhere in the world does one get a stronger impression of exuberant wealth and extravagance. The Park itself, called Palermo, lies on the edge of the city towards the river, and is approached by a well-designed and well-planted avenue.

Today, by contrast, the park is a more democratic destination. There are no more carriages and the few automobiles go slower than elsewhere in the city. On weekends, in particular, it gets plenty of picnickers, walkers, joggers, in-line skaters, and bicyclists who enjoy its verdant serenity and other recreational and cultural attractions.

Among those attractions are the **Jardín Japonés** (Japanese Gardens), at Avenida Casares and Avenida Adolfo Berro, opposite Plaza Alemania; the **Planetario Galileo Galilei,** at the intersection of Avenida Sarmiento and Belisario Roldán; the **Rosedal** (Rose Garden) at Avenida Iraola and Avenida Presidente Pedro Montt; the nearby **Museo de Artes Plásticas Eduardo Sívori,** a painting and sculpture museum; the **Hipódromo Argentino** (racetrack) at Avenida del Libertador and Avenida Dorrego; and the **Campo Argentino de Polo** (polo grounds) directly across Avenida del Libertador.

At the northeast corner of the park, the **Nuevo Circuito KDT** is a velodrome where cyclists can work out without worry about the pace of motor-vehicle traffic. To its north, beyond the park boundaries, the landmark **Club de Pescadores** sits at the end of a long pier that extends into the river. The park's greatest drawback is the proximity of **Aeroparque Jorge Newbery,** the city's domestic airport; its relocation, proposed but apparently stalled, would open up an even larger area to public use.

### Jardín Japonés

An oasis of calm in the rush of the city, Buenos Aires's Japanese garden opened in 1967, when Crown Prince Akihito and Princess Michiko visited Argentina. Administratively part of the Jardín Botánico (see separate entry later in this chapter), it enjoys far better maintenance and, because there's chicken wire between the exterior hedges and the interior fence, it's full of chirping birds rather than feral cats.

Like Japanese gardens elsewhere, it mimics nature in its large koi pond (a bag of fish food goes for US$.20), *taki* (waterfall), and *shinzen jima* (isle of the gods), but also culture in its *sambashi* (pier), *tourou* (lighthouse), *yatsuhashi* (bridge of fortune), *taiko bashi* (curved bridge), *tobi ishi* (path of stones), and *yusanju no to* (tower of thirteen eaves). There is also a *vivero kadan* (plant nursery) with bonsai trees at reasonable prices.

In addition, the garden contains a **Monumento al Sudor del Inmigrante Japonés** (Monument to the Effort of the Japanese Immigrant), erected during the military dictatorship of 1976–83 and still bearing the name of dictator Jorge Rafael Videla as "president." Argentina has a small but well-established Japanese community in the capital and in the suburban community of Escobar.

The Jardín Japonés, at Avenida Casares and Avenida Adolfo Berro, tel. 4801-4922, www.jardinjapones.com.ar, is open 10 A.M.–6 P.M. daily. Admission costs US$.70 for adults, US$.35 for children; there are guided tours at 3 and 4 P.M. Saturdays. In addition to the garden features, it includes a confitería/restaurant and an exhibition hall.

### Museo de Artes Plásticas Eduardo Sívori

Shifted from downtown Centro Cultural San Martín in 1995, the Museo Sívori occupies a Bavarian-style house (1912) with a newer cement-block annex designed specifically for painting and sculpture, along with a separate sculpture garden. Argentine artists whose work is on display include Ernesto de la Cárcova, Lino Spilimbergo, and Luis Seoanes; there are also special exhibitions in fields such as photography.

The Museo de Artes Plásticas Eduardo Sívori, Avenida Infanta Isabel 555, tel. 4772-5628, is open noon–6 P.M. daily except Mondays. Admission costs US$.35, but is free Wednesdays.

### Rosedal

Reached by a gracefully arching bridge over a narrow neck of the **Lago del Rosedal,** an artificial lake, Parque Tres de Febrero's rose garden contains a diversity of both bush roses and climbers on pergolas. Its southeast corner contains the **Jardín de los Poetas,** a sculpture garden of famous literary figures, mostly Spanish speakers such as Argentina's Jorge Luis Borges and Alfonsina Storni and Guatemala's Miguel Angel Asturias, but also global greats such as Shakespeare.

### Planetario Galileo Galilei

Since it opened in 1967, Buenos Aires's planetarium has introduced more than 10 million visitors, mostly school children, to the night skies projected on its interior dome in a 360-seat auditorium, though it also has a telescope for viewing the stars directly. There is a small artificial lake outside, the **Lago del Planetario.**

The Planetario Galileo Galilei, at Avenida Sarmiento and Belisario Roldán, tel. 4771-6629, www.earg.gov.ar/planetario, is open 9 A.M.–5 P.M. weekdays, 1–7:30 P.M. weekends. Admission is free except for guided tours at 3, 4:30, and 6 P.M. weekends and holidays, which cost about US$1 pp.

## MUSEO DE MOTIVOS ARGENTINOS JOSÉ HERNÁNDEZ

It's tempting to call this the "museum of irony," as Argentina's most self-consciously gaucho-oriented institution sits smack in the middle of what may be the country's single most urbane, affluent, and cosmopolitan neighborhood, also home to many international diplomatic missions. Named for the author of the epic *gauchesco* poem *Martín Fierro,* it specializes in rural Argentiniana, regional history, and occasional special exhibitions on similar themes.

Even more ironically, the land-owning oligarch Félix Bunge built the house, a derivative French-Italianate building with marble staircases and other extravagant features. Originally known as the Museo Familiar Gauchesco de Carlos Guillermo Daws after the family who donated its contents, it became the Museo de Motivos Populares Argentinos (Museum of Argentine Popular Motifs) José Hernández until the military dictatorship of 1976–83 deleted the ostensibly inflammatory word "popular" (which in this context also means "people's") from the official name. Thus, perhaps, it could justify depictions of Argentine gentry like the Martínez de Hoz family—one of whose scions was economy minister during the dictatorship—as representatives of a bucolic open-range lifestyle.

That said, the museum has many exhibits worth seeing, ranging from magnificent silverwork and vicuña textiles created by contemporary Argentine artisans to pre-Columbian pottery, indigenous crafts, and even a typical *pulpería* or rural store. Translations of Hernández's famous poem, some in Asian and Eastern European languages, occupy a prominent site.

The Museo José Hernández, Avenida del Libertador 2373, tel. 4803-2384, museohernandez @ciudad.com.ar, www.naya.org .ar/mujose, is open 1–7 P.M. Wednesday through Sunday. Admission costs US$.35 except Sunday, when it's free of charge. The museum is normally closed in February.

## MUSEO NACIONAL DE ARTE DECORATIVO

Matías Errázuriz Ortúzar and his wife and widow Josefina de Alvear de Errázuriz lived less than 20 years in the ornate four-story beaux arts building (1918) that now houses the national museum of decorative art. Nonetheless, its inventory consists of 4,000 items from the family's own collections, ranging from Roman sculptures to contemporary silverwork, but mostly Asian and European pieces from the 17th to 19th centuries. Many items are anonymous; the best-known artists are Europeans like Manet and Rodin.

The Museo de Arte Decorativo, Avenida del Libertador 1902, tel. 4802-6606, museo@mnad .org, www.mnad.org.ar, is open 2–7 P.M. daily; admission costs US$.70 except Tuesdays, when

it's free. There are guided tours Wednesday, Thursday, and Friday at 4:30 P.M., by appointment only.

## MUSEO DE ARTE LATINOAMERICANO DE BUENOS AIRES (MALBA)

Buenos Aires's newest and most deluxe art museum is a striking steel-and-glass structure dedicated exclusively to Latin American art rather than the European-oriented collections of many—if not most—Argentine art collections. Designed by Córdoba architects Gastón Atelman, Martín Fourcade, and Alfredo Tapia, the building contains one entire floor dedicated to the private collection of Argentine businessman Eduardo F. Constantini, the motivating force behind the museum's creation; the second floor offers special exhibitions— one of which was unfortunately withdrawn when New York City officials decided that sending valuable artwork to Buenos Aires in the current economic crisis was too risky.

> *The Museo de Arte Latinoamericano de Buenos Aires, the city's newest and most deluxe art museum, is a striking steel-and-glass structure dedicated exclusively to Latin American art rather than the European-oriented collections of many—if not most—Argentine art collections.*

The most famous works on display are by the Mexican artists Frida Kahlo and Diego Rivera, but there are also works by Antonio Berni, the Chilean Robert Matta, the Uruguayan Pedro Figari, and others. Given the current crisis, Malba curator Marcelo Pacheco plans to focus on contemporary Argentine art, both for the museum's own exhibitions and those it sends abroad, rather than importing megabucks exhibits from overseas.

The Museo de Arte Latinoamericano de Buenos Aires, Avenida Figueroa Alcorta 3415 in Palermo Chico, tel. 4808 6500, info@malba .org.ar, www.malba.org.ar, is open Monday, Thursday, and Friday noon–8 P.M., Wednesday noon–9 P.M., and weekends 10–8 P.M. Admission costs US$1.10 except Wednesdays, when it's free.

## JARDÍN BOTÁNICO CARLOS THAYS

Originally part of Parque Tres de Febrero, Buenos Aires's botanical garden dates from 1892, when famed French landscape architect Carlos Thays requested its separation from the park to create a roughly eight-hectare space bounded by Avenida Santa Fe, República Arabe Siria (formerly Malabia), and Avenida Las Heras.

One of Buenos Aires's shadiest spots, the Jardín Botánico boasts a wide variety of trees from around Argentina and the world. More than 30 sculptures dot the garden, including those of Thays and Patagonia explorer Francisco P. Moreno; near the Arabe Siria side stands one of the last of the hideous grottos placed around city parks by mayor Torcuato de Alvear in the 1880s. Unfortunately, hundreds of feral cats, especially notable after closing hours, have contributed to a distinctive odor. The park is a (fairly discreet) pickup spot for gay males.

The city's Dirección General de Espacios Verdes also operates a gardening school and a specialized library at the Jardín Botánico, Avenida Santa Fe 3951, which is open 8 A.M.–6 P.M. daily. The main entrance to the fenced and gated triangular garden is at the Plaza Italia end of the property.

## JARDÍN ZOOLÓGICO EDUARDO LADISLAO HOLMBERG

When Palermo was his private preserve, dictator Juan Manuel de Rosas kept his own collection of exotic animals and when, according to one legend, his pet jaguar ran in fright from a group of female visitors, he sarcastically suggested that it was because the animal "had never seen so much ugliness in one place." In the not-too-distant past, because of political cronyism, one could have made a similar comment about the zoo; in the 1990s, though, the once-decrepit Buenos Aires zoo passed into private hands and, rejuvenated, became the facility that is once again a favorite with *porteño* families.

What is now the zoo, an 18-hectare area bounded by Avenida Sarmiento, Avenida Las Heras, República de India, and Avenida del Libertador, was separated from the Parque Tres de Febrero in 1888. Its first director was Eduardo Ladislao Holmberg, who saw it primarily as a research facility, but in the early 20th century it became one of the city's favorite excursions, with more than 150,000 visitors per annum. Beginning in the early 1920s, authorities built decorative fountains and lakes, a monkey island, tanks for hippopotami and crocodiles, an aviary, and other large enclosures in lieu of cages and pits. The concessionaire has also repaired historic structures within the park.

After the 1940s, there were various projects to shift the deteriorating facility to another park on the outskirts of town, given the potential real estate value of such a large property in a prime neighborhood, but local objection in the 1980s kept the zoo in the present location. Today it holds some 2,500 animals of some 350 different reptile, mammal, and bird species; the zoo also includes sculptures of important figures in Argentine natural history, including Domingo F. Sarmiento, Florentino Ameghino, Clemente Onelli, and William Henry Hudson. For children, there is a *granja infanta* (petting zoo), a *calesita* (merry-go-round), a *trencito* (miniature train), and a *laberinto* (maze).

The Jardín Zoológico, with entrances opposite Plaza Italia and at Avenida Sarmiento and Avenida del Libertador, tel. 4806-7412, charges US$1.50 per adult but is free for children under age 13. Hours are 10 A.M.–6 P.M. weekdays, 10 A.M.–6:30 P.M. weekends. Retired and disabled people enter free Tuesday through Friday.

## MUSEO EVA PERÓN

At her most combative, to the shock and disgust of neighbors, Eva Perón chose the upscale Botánico for the **Hogar de Tránsito No. 2,** a shelter for single mothers from the provinces. Even more galling, her Fundación de Ayuda Social María Eva Duarte de Perón acquired architect Estanislao Pirovano's imposing three-story mansion, built for José María Carabassa in 1923, to house the transients in their transition to life in the capital.

Since Evita's death in 1952, the neighborhood has undergone steady if undramatic change, as middle-class multistory apartment blocks have mostly replaced the elegant single-family houses and distinctive apartment buildings that once housed the *porteño* elite (many of whom have since moved to exclusive northern suburbs like Olivos and San Isidro). Fifty years later, on the July 26th anniversary of her death—supporting Tomás Eloy Martínez's contention that Argentines are "cadaver cultists"—Evita's great niece María Carolina Rodríguez officially opened the Museo Eva Perón to "to spread the life, work and ideology of María Eva Duarte de Perón."

Five years in the making, this is the first Argentine museum to focus specifically on a woman. It is also a work in progress, as the country's economic crisis and *corralito* banking restrictions have put much of the work on the shoulders of volunteers.

What it largely lacks, as yet, is a critical perspective that would make it possible, again in Rodríguez's words, "to understand who this woman was in the 1940s and 1950s, who made such a difference in the lives of Argentines"—a goal not necessarily consistent with her other stated aims. Rather than a balanced account of her life, the museum's initial stage is more a homage that divides Evita's life into stages: Eva Duarte (her childhood and adolescence, acting career, and first encounters with Juan Perón), Eva Perón (marriage to Perón, becoming Argentina's first lady, and the Spanish journey that brought her international attention), Evita (as her political influence grew through the Fundación Eva Perón), and her death and legacy.

All this material is professionally presented but, with a couple of minor exceptions, it sidesteps the issue of personality cults that typified both Evita and her husband. One minor exception is the display of the Anglo-Argentine author Mary Main's *The Woman with the Whip*, published in Argentina as *La Mujer del Látigo* under the pseudonym María Flores. Although an obvious hatchet job, this biography at least suggests how Evita polarized Argentine society.

The Museo Eva Perón, Lafinur 2988, tel. 4807-9433, fax 4809-3168, ievaperon@uol.com.ar, is open 10 A.M.–8 P.M. daily except Monday. It also contains a library, a graphic archive, and a film and video library, open 2–8 P.M. weekdays. The museum store has a fine selection of Evita souvenirs, and there is a café-restaurant as well.

## CENTRO CULTURAL ISLÁMICO REY FAHD

Built with Saudi funds on three hectares of land donated by the scandal-ridden administration of President Carlos Menem, Buenos Aires's new Islamic cultural center is a pharaonic project seemingly out of proportion with it surroundings and even its needs. In a high-rent part of town, holding up to 2,300 worshippers, it rarely attracts more than about 300 for Friday prayers.

According to its Saudi director, though, the mosque, its ancillary constructions, and its grounds are intended to become South America's major Muslim cultural center. Guided tours, unfortunately, are pedestrian, offering generalities about Islam but little about Argentina's Muslim community and even less about this particular mosque's origins.

South America's largest Islamic center, Avenida Bullrich 55, tel. 4899-1144, info@centroculturalislamico.org, www.centroculturalislamico.org, is open for guided tours only, Friday noon–1 P.M. and Sun. 11 A.M.–1 P.M. Female visitors must put on tunics—some women have shown up in shorts and other clothing that would be considered truly offensive in the Muslim world—but need not cover their heads.

## MUSEO NACIONAL DEL HOMBRE

Small but well-maintained and -organized, the Museo Nacional del Hombre (National Museum of Man) is a modest but worthy complement to Monserrat's larger and more elaborate Museo Etnográfico. Providing information on the prehistory and contemporary status of Argentina's indigenous peoples, it could use more detailed maps of individual group territories, but its 5,000 pieces are a fine representative sample of indigenous material culture.

Part of the Instituto Nacional de Antropología y Pensamiento Latinoamericano, a research and training institute, the Museo Nacional del Hombre, 3 de Febrero 1370, tel. 4784-9971, is open 10 A.M.–8 P.M. weekdays only. Admission costs US$.35. The museum shop has a small but excellent selection of crafts.

## Belgrano

Readily linked to central Buenos Aires by Subte, bus, and train, Belgrano remains a barrio apart. In fact, before becoming a barrio of the capital, it was a separate city and then, briefly in the 1880s, served as the country's capital. After the Buenos Aires provincial capital moved to the new city of La Plata, Buenos Aires became the federal capital and, in 1887, it absorbed Belgrano into the city.

Belgrano is bordered on the south by Palermo, on the west by Colegiales and Villa Ortúzar, on the north by Coghland and Núñez, and on the east by the Río de la Plata. The actual line zigzags among many streets, but the approximate border with Palermo runs along La Pampa, Avenida Valentín Alsina, and Zabala. The major thoroughfares are Avenida Cabildo, the northward extension of Avenida Santa Fe; Avenida Luis María Campos; and Avenida del Libertador. With the recent extension of the Subte beneath Avenida Cabildo, to Congreso de Tucumán on the border with Núñez, the barrio is more accessible than ever.

Belgrano subdivides into three distinct areas: the wooded residential area of **Belgrano R,** west of Avenida Cabildo (the *R* stands not for "residential," but for the city of Rosario, the ultimate destination of the area's rail line); **Barrancas de Belgrano,** between Avenida Cabildo and the tracks of the Ferrocarril Mitre commuter line to Tigre; and **Bajo Belgrano,** alternatively known as **Belgrano Chico,** between the tracks and the Río de la Plata.

Avenida Cabildo is a disorientingly noisy commercial boulevard, with a cluster of cinemas and theaters as well, but the tree-lined streets immediately to the east contain most points of interest. Only a block off Cabildo, the **Plaza General Manuel Belgrano** hosts a very fine Sunday crafts market; immediately to its east, at Vuelta de Obligado 2042, the landmark **Iglesia de la Inmaculada Concepción** (1865), colloquially known as **La Redonda** for its circular floor plan, figures prominently in Ernesto Sabato's psychological novel *On Heroes and Tombs*.

North of the plaza, the **Museo de Arte Español Enrique Larreta,** Juramento 2291, belonged to the Hispanophile novelist and still contains his private art collection; the museum offers outstanding special programs. When Belgrano was briefly Argentina's capital, both the executive and legislative branches met at what is now the **Museo Histórico Sarmiento,** to the east at Cuba 2079, honoring President Domingo F. Sarmiento. A few blocks northwest of the plaza, **Museo Casa de Yrurtia,** O'Higgins 2390, was the residence of sculptor Rogelio Yrurtia, creator of San Telmo's *Canto al Trabajo.*

The famous landscape architect Carlos Thays turned **Barrancas de Belgrano** proper, on the river terrace three blocks east of Plaza Belgrano, into a shady public park; it now includes a fenced dog park, where *paseaperros* can take their charges for off-leash romps. Just across from the park, the **Museo Libero Badii,** 11 de Septiembre 1990, exhibits the work of one of the country's most innovative sculptors.

Across the tracks from the Barrancas, along Arribeños north of Juramento, Belgrano's **Chinatown** grew rapidly in the 1990s but has languished in the current hard times. The number of Chinese restaurants and other businesses, however, remains higher than it was a decade ago— Belgrano residents who need *feng shui* consultants can find them here.

## MUSEO DE ARTE ESPAÑOL ENRIQUE LARRETA

When many Argentine writers were forging a national literature, Enrique Larreta's novels evoked nostalgia for the Spanish motherland, and his Belgrano house and art collection reflect that orientation. Most of the items either come from Spain or reflect Spanish traditions: polychrome religious carvings and *retablos* (altarpieces), *bargueños* (gilt boxes), tapestries, carpets, braziers, ceramics, paintings, and furniture from the 13th to the 20th centuries. The 19th-century fans, with elaborately painted landscapes, are exceptional.

The museum's rooms are large enough to present an enormous number of artifacts without seeming cluttered. Look for special exhibitions, such as the 2002 display of regional costumes given to Evita Perón during her 1947 tour of Spain—which took place at a time when the Franco dictatorship was desperately seeking legitimacy after the defeat of Nazi Germany and Fascist Italy in World War II.

The grounds are no less impressive, with formal Andalusian gardens and an open-air theater that offers dramatic and musical performances, including tango, in the summer months. The theater entrance is on the Vuelta de Obligado side of the building.

The Museo Larreta, Avenida Juramento 2291, tel. 4783-2640, museolarreta@infovia.com.ar, is open 2–7:45 P.M. daily except Tuesday. Admission costs US$.35, but is free on Thursdays. There are guided tours Sunday at 4 and 6 P.M. Like many other museums, it usually closes for the entire month of January.

## MUSEO HISTÓRICO SARMIENTO

When President Nicolás Avellaneda felt insecure in Buenos Aires in mid-1880, he briefly shifted both the government's executive and the legislative branches to Juan A. Buschiazzo's Italian Renaissance building (1874), originally designed for the Municipalidad de Belgrano. After the congress declared Buenos Aires the federal capital and conflict subsided, the building returned to municipal authorities until 1938, when it became a museum honoring Argentine educator and president (1868–1874) Domingo Faustino Sarmiento—on the 50th anniversary of his death.

Though Sarmiento never lived in this house, the exhibits contains many of his personal possessions and a model of his birthplace, in the province of San Juan. He detested provincial warlords like Rosas and Facundo Quiroga, after whom he titled his polemic *Facundo: Or, Civilization and Barbarism,* still used as a text in many Latin American studies courses in the United States.

In addition to the life of Sarmiento, the museum includes displays on Avellaneda and the near–civil war of the 1880s that resulted in the federalization of Buenos Aires. There is also an 11,000-volume library.

The Museo Histórico Sarmiento, Cuba 2079, tel. 4783-7555, museosarmiento @fibertel.com.ar, is open 2–7 P.M. Tuesday through Friday and 3–7 P.M. Sunday. Admission costs US$.35, but is free Thursdays; guided tours take place Sunday at 4 P.M.

## MUSEO CASA DE YRURTIA

Influenced by Auguste Rodin, sculptor Rogelio Yrurtia (1879–1950) spent much of his career in Italy and France before returning to Buenos Aires in 1921. His signature work, *Canto al Trabajo* (Ode to Labor, 1923) on Plazoleta Olazábal in San Telmo, is a worthy antidote to the pompous equestrian statues that for decades dominated *porteño* public art.

Yrurtia designed, lived, and worked in this mudéjar residence, which he intended as a museum for his sculptures and the paintings of his wife, Lía Correa Morales; there are some works from other artists, most notably Picasso's painting *Rue Cortot, Paris.* The garden features Yrurtia's oversized *Boxers,* which appeared at the 1904 St. Louis World's Fair.

The Museo Casa de Yrurtia, O'Higgins 2390, tel. 4781-0385, museo@casadeyrurtia.gov.ar, www.casleo.secyt.gov.ar/index.htm, is open Tuesday through Friday and Sunday from 3–7 P.M.

Admission costs US$.35. Guided tours, at no additional expense, take place Tuesday through Friday at 3 P.M. and Sunday at 4 P.M.

## MUSEO LIBERO BADII

After the fall of Rosas, jurist Valentín Alsina acquired the property overlooking Barrancas de Belgrano for his *quinta* or country house, but it soon passed into the hands of the Atucha family that build the 1870s Italian Renaissance house that survives, amid highrises, to house this unique museum. The wildly imaginative Italian-born Badii, a naturalized Argentine, specialized in sculpture, engraving, design, collage, and illustration.

Operated under the auspices of the Fundación Banco Francés, the Museo Badii, 11 de Septiembre 1990, tel. 4783-3819, ajusto@bancofrancés.com.ar, also offers special exhibits. It's open 10 A.M.–6 P.M. weekdays only. Admission is free; ring the bell for entry.

# Outer Barrios

Beyond its most touristed barrios, Buenos Aires has a variety of worthwhile sights that range from the relatively mundane to the morbid. Most of them are less easily accessible by Subte, but have regular *colectivo* (city bus) service.

## CEMENTERIO DE LA CHACARITA AND VICINITY

Buenos Aires's second cemetery may be is a more affordable final destination than Recoleta, but eternity at the **Cementerio de la Chacarita** can still mean notoriety. Many high-profile Argentines in fields ranging from entertainment to religion and politics (sometimes the lines between the categories are blurred) reside at Chacarita.

The most universally beloved is tango singer Carlos Gardel, who died in a plane crash in Medellín, Colombia in 1935. Hundreds of admirers from around the globe have left plaques on his tomb, many thanking him for miracles, and every June 26 they jam the streets of Chacarita—laid out like a small city—to pay homage. As often as not, the right hand of his bronze statue holds a lighted cigarette and a red carnation adorns his lapel.

In terms of devotion, probably only Spanish-born faith-healer-to-the-aristocracy Madre María Salomé can match Gardel; on the 2nd of every month—she died October 2, 1928—her tomb is covered in white carnations. She gained fame as the disciple of Pancho Sierra, the *curandero gaucho* (gaucho healer) of Salto, in Buenos Aires province.

Other famous figures entombed at Chacarita include pioneer aviator Jorge Newbery, for whom the city airport is named (he was killed in a plane crash in 1914); tango musicians Aníbal "Pichuco" Troilo (seated playing his *bandoneón*) and Osvaldo Pugliese; poet Alfonsina Storni; La Boca painter Benito Quinquela Martín; and theater and film comedian Luis Sandrini, whose bronze statue often holds a red carnation in its hand.

Certainly the most famous, though, is Juan Domingo Perón, whose remains lie in a vault across town from his equally famous wife Evita. His remains are incomplete, though—in June of 1987, stealthy vandals entered the crypt, amputating and stealing the caudillo's hands in a crime that has never been resolved. People speculated, though there is no evidence, that the thieves sought Perón's fingerprints for access to supposed Swiss bank accounts.

Chacarita's role as the capital's most democratic cemetery dates from its origins in the 1870s, when it buried yellow-fever victims of the 1870s epidemic in then-mosquito-ridden San Telmo and La Boca. The barrio, also known as Chacarita, takes its name from a Quechua term meaning "a small farm;" during the 17th century, it was a Jesuit agricultural property known as La Chacarita de los Colegiales, on the city's outskirts.

The Cementerio de la Chacarita, Guzmán 680, tel. 4553-9338/5086, covers 95 blocks with a total of 12,000 burial vaults, 100,000 gravesites, and 350,000 niches. Hours are 7 A.M.–6 P.M. daily. It's only a short walk from Estación Federico

Lacroze, presently the terminus of the Subte's Línea B (the line, however, is being extended to the northwest).

In addition to Chacarita, there are two contiguous but formally separate cemeteries in the vicinity: the **Cementerio Alemán** (German Cemetery), Avenida Elcano 4530, tel. 4553-3206, and the **Cementerio Británico** (British Cemetery), Avenida Elcano 4568, tel. 4554-0092. Both keep identical hours to Chacarita's.

The Británico is more diverse, with tombs belonging to Armenian, Greek, Irish, Jewish, and many other immigrant nationalities. The Anglo-Argentine Lucas Bridges, son of pioneer Anglican missionaries in Tierra del Fuego and author of the classic Fuegian memoir *The Uttermost Part of the Earth,* was buried here after dying at sea en route from Ushuaia to Buenos Aires. The Alemán features a large but politically neutral monument to Germany's World War II dead—no German or German-Argentine wants to be associated with the Third Reich.

## ESCUELA DE MECÁNICA DE LA ARMADA (ESMA)

Buildings often cause controversy, but none quite so much as the Escuela de Mecánica de la Armada (ESMA, Naval Mechanics' School) in Núñez, beyond Belgrano near the border with Buenos Aires province. It was not the architecture of this handsome neoclassical building that raised havoc, though—rather, it was the fact that during the military dictatorship of 1976–83, more than 5,000 *desaparecidos* passed through the country's most notorious clandestine torture center.

Before his term expired in 1999, President Carlos Menem—himself a victim of the repression though he later pardoned his jailers—relocated the institution to Puerto Belgrano, near the naval town of Bahía Blanca in southern Buenos Aires province. At the same time, he ordered the demolition of the building and construction of a dubious "monument to national unity" in its place.

Menem's decrees infuriated human rights groups and city officials, who saw the former ESMA as the most gruesomely suitable location for a Museo de la Memoria (Museum of Memory) to preserve and present documentary records, oral histories, sound, film, and photographs of the military's brutal *Guerra Sucia* (Dirty War) against its own citizens. Authorized in 1996, the museum still lacks a physical facility; city authorities argued that the ESMA property, originally granted to the navy in 1924, should revert to its original municipal control.

In June of 2000, at the urging of Amnesty International, other human rights organizations, and prominent Argentine intellectuals including Nobel Peace Prize winner Adolfo Pérez Esquivel, artist León Ferrari, and novelist Ernesto Sábato (author of the famous human rights report *Nunca Más*), the city legislature voted unanimously to reacquire the property on which the ESMA sits.

The navy claimed that the Escuela Naval de Guerra (Naval War College) and the Escuela Fluvial (River Navigation School) still operate on the site, and the matter may go to the courts. In November of 2001, joint chiefs of staff press secretary Vicente Engelman confirmed that the military would not surrender the ESMA without a struggle and, in the country's present political and economic dilemma, it's not a high priority.

Meanwhile the ESMA still stands at the 8200 block of Avenida del Libertador. The Museo de la Memoria, as yet, remains only virtual: www .imaginario.org.ar/museo.

## MUSEO HISTÓRICO BRIGADIER GENERAL CORNELIO DE SAAVEDRA

Focusing on 19th-century Argentina, this historical museum occupies the grounds of the one-time rural estate of Luis María Saavedra, nephew of independence hero Cornelio de Saavedra. Expropriated after 1929, the property came under municipal control as the Parque General Paz; the building, "modified for authenticity," became a museum in 1941.

Permanent museum exhibits include silverwork from the private collection of Ricardo Zembo-

## LA FERIA DE MATADEROS

**G**auchesco traditions live in the weekend Feria de Mataderos, where city-bound *paisanos* (countrymen) and would-be *paisanos* immerse themselves in the nostalgia of the *campo,* or countryside. In addition to a diverse crafts selection, this lively street fair features open-air *parrilladas* (mixed grills) and regional delicacies like tamales, plus live music and dancing in rural styles such as *chamamé,* gaucho horseback races, and even—during Carnaval—a neighborhood *murga* (troupe) to kick off the season in the style of northwestern Jujuy province.

Despite occasional exaggeratedly nationalistic overtones, the Feria generates genuine enthusiasm.

It was founded in the mid-1980s under the sponsorship of a Jewish *porteña,* Sara Vinocur, who still directs it as the link between city authorities and residents of the barrio.

In the southwesterly barrio of Mataderos, in the streets surrounding the arcades of the former Mercado de Hacienda at Lisandro de la Torre and Avenida de los Corrales, the Feria (www.feriademataderos.com.ar, info@feriademataderos.com.ar) is about an hour from the Microcentro by *colectivo* No. 180, *ramal* (branch) 155 from Tucumán, Talcahuano, or Lavalle. In summer, it takes place 6 P.M.–midnight on Saturdays; the rest of the year it starts at 11 A.M. Sundays.

---

rain (1872–1912), who willed his possessions to the city; gems, coins, clothing, and furniture from the 18th and 19th centuries; and fashion accessories such as *peinetones* (ornamental combs). Thematically, it covers events of the independence era and the early Argentine confederation.

The Museo Saavedra, Crisólogo Larralde 6309, Saavedra, tel. 4572-0746, www.buenosaires.gov .ar/areas/cultura/museos/museosaavedra.asp, also functions as a cultural center that hosts concerts, films, and dance and theater events. Museum hours are Tuesday through Friday 9 A.M.–6 P.M., weekends and holidays 2–6 P.M. Guided tours take place weekends and holidays at 4 P.M. Admission costs US$.35, but is free on Wednesday.

# Accommodations

Buenos Aires has an abundance of accommodations in all categories, from youth hostel dormitories to extravagant luxury suites and everything in between. There is no camping in the city proper, but many of the excursion destinations in Buenos Aires province and Uruguay do offer that option.

National and municipal tourist officials offer accommodations lists and brochures, but these frequently exclude budget options and may even omit some mid-range and high-end places. Prices, especially since the devaluation of 2001–2002, are often negotiable; do not assume the *tarifa mostrador* (rack rate) is etched in stone. Visitors also should not take hotel ratings too seriously as they often represent an ideal rather than a reality, and some one- or two-star places are better than others that rank higher on paper.

Prices in Buenos Aires proper often fall during the peak summer season of January and February, as business travel slows to a crawl; for excursion destinations, though, prices usually rise as *porteños* flee the capital for sand, sun, and sex on the beach.

The same is true for popular provincial destinations like San Antonio de Areco. Other peak seasons, when prices may rise, are Semana Santa (Holy Week) and July's winter school vacations, which coincide with patriotic holidays.

Alvear Palace Hotel, Recoleta

© WAYNE BERNHARDSON

Note also that Argentine hotels levy 21 percent in Impuesto de Valor Agregado or IVA (Value Added Tax or VAT); there is also IVA in Uruguay—remember this if you take excursions there. Unless otherwise indicated, rates in this book include IVA, but if there's any question at the front desk, ask for clarification to avoid unpleasant surprises when paying the bill.

## CAMPING

Organized camping is a common alternative throughout Argentina and Uruguay, though not in Buenos Aires proper. Still, several of the excursion destinations in this book offer options for those with or without their own vehicles. Devaluation has made modest hotels more than competitive with campgrounds, however.

Argentine and Uruguayan campgrounds are generally spacious affairs, with shade, clean toilets, and bathrooms with hot showers, and even groceries and restaurants. They are often surprisingly central, and they are almost always cheap—rarely more than a couple of dollars per person. In the peak summer season and on weekends, however, the best sites can be crowded and noisy, as families on budgets take advantage of bargain prices. It's usually possible to find a quiet—but less desirable—site on the periphery. But remember that Argentines stay up late—very late—for their barbecues.

## HOSTELS

Buenos Aires proper has a few official Hostelling International (HI) affiliates; there are several more in the province and in Uruguay. The capital also has a growing number of independent hostels. Since the recent devaluation, these are no longer the only budget options, but they do offer an opportunity to get together with like-minded travelers.

For up-to-the-minute information on official Argentine hostels, contact Hostelling International Argentina, Florida 835, 3rd floor,

Oficina 319-B, tel. 11/4511-8712, fax 4312-0089, raaj@hostels.org.ar, www.hostels.org.ar. The competing but rather torpid Asociación Argentina de Albergues de la Juventud (AAAJ), Talcahuano 214, tel./fax 11/4372-7094, info @aaaj.org.ar, www.hostelling-aaaj.org.ar, has a smaller network of affiliates, though there is some overlap.

In Uruguay, the official HI representative is the Asociación de Albergistas del Uruguay, Pablo de María 1583, Montevideo, tel. 598/2-4004245, fax 4001326, aau@adinet.com.uy, www.internet .com.uy/aau/esp/aau00m1.htm.

## OTHER BUDGET ACCOMMODATIONS

Budget accommodations in Buenos Aires, the surrounding provinces, and Uruguay can cost as little as US$5 pp; they go by a variety of names that may be misleading as to their quality—they can range from dingy fleabags with mattresses

### HIGHER PRICES FOR FOREIGNERS

In the aftermath of the peso devaluation of early 2002, price levels fell for nearly everything in Argentina, including accommodations. As the year progressed, however, and the 2003 summer tourist season began, some hotels began to institute differential pricing for Argentine residents and foreign visitors. Consequently, foreign visitors should not be surprised to encounter hotel rates significantly higher than those indicated in this chapter, which are based on research completed before these increases took place. This increase has been particularly noticeable at the top of the accommodations scale, where foreigners may pay 40 percent or so more than Argentines, but much may depend on the individual traveler's language and negotiating skills. The trend in hotel prices is likely a steady move upward, but prices are nevertheless cheaper than they were in the years when the peso and the dollar were at par.

that sag like hammocks to simple but cheerful and tidy places with firm new beds.

*Hospedajes* are generally family-run lodgings with a few spare rooms; *pensiones* and *casas de huéspedes* are comparable, nearly interchangeable terms. All often have long-term residents as well as overnight guests. *Residenciales* (singular *residencial*) are generally buildings constructed with short-stay accommodations in mind, but may also have semi-permanent inhabitants. All of these places may even go by the term *hotel,* though usually that belongs to a more formal category.

There are some exceptionally good values in all these categories. Many will have shared bath and toilet (*baño general* or *baño compartido*), or offer a choice between shared and private bath (*baño privado*); bathtubs are unusual. In some cases, they will have ceiling fans and even cable TV, but there is often an extra charge for cable and almost always a surcharge for air-conditioning (referred to as a/c throughout this book).

Travelers intending to stay at budget accommodations should bring their own towels. Many but by no means all establishments include breakfast in their rates; ask to be certain.

## MID-RANGE ACCOMMODATIONS

Mid-range hotels generally offer larger, more comfortable, and better-furnished rooms (almost always with private bath) than even the best budget places. Ceiling fans, cable TV, and even air-conditioning are common, but they may not have on-site parking. Some have restaurants. Rates can range anywhere from US$30 to US$100 double (d); some are better values than their high-end counterparts.

## HIGH-END ACCOMMODATIONS

Luxury hotels with top-flight service, which can range well upwards of US$100 per night, are few outside the capital and major resort areas. In the capital, these usually offer amenities like restaurants, swimming pools, gym facilities, business centers, Internet connections, and conference rooms; outside the capital, these are mostly resort hotels and lack the business facilities. Invariably they offer secure parking.

Some of the best options in this category are country inn resorts on *estancias,* offering traditional hospitality and ambiance with style unmatchable at other high-end places. Again, prices may be upwards of US$100—often substantially upwards.

## Under US$25

The majority of the capital's budget accommodations are in the vicinity of Plaza de Mayo and Avenida de Mayo, the Microcentro, and in parts of Once and San Telmo.

### MONSERRAT/CATEDRAL AL SUR AND VICINITY

Most budget accommodations in the vicinity of the Plaza de Mayo are only so-so and fairly interchangeable, but there are some exceptions. One of those is the Hostelling International affiliate **Milhouse Youth Hostel,** a refurbished period house at Hipólito Yrigoyen 959, tel. 4345-9604, info@milhousehostel .com, www.milhousehostel.com. It's an immaculate, well-managed, well-located, and secure facility with spacious common areas for US$9 pp with breakfast in dormitory rooms; rooms with private bath go for US$28 d.

**Hotel Palace Cevallos,** Virrey Cevallos 261 in Congreso, tel. 4372-7636, is another budget choice for US$7/9 single/double (s/d) with private bath but without breakfast. **Hotel La Argentina,** Avenida de Mayo 860, tel. 4342-0078, is a budget favorite for US$7/ 11 s/d without TV; rooms with TV cost US$2 more.

Though gradually improving after some ill-advised and improvised remodeling, the interior at **Hotel Reina,** Avenida de Mayo 1120, tel. 4383-2264, belies its ornate Parisian exterior. Rates are US$9/12 s/d with shared bath, US$14/17 with private bath; students recieve a 10 percent discount.

**Hotel Roma,** Avenida de Mayo 1413, tel. 4381-4921, is a no-frills cheapie at US$10/13 s/d. **Gran Hotel España,** at Tacuarí 80 just south of Avenida de Mayo, tel. 4343-5541, fax 4343-5544, is passable for US$12/16 s/d with private bath but without breakfast. The **Novel Hotel,** Avenida de Mayo 915, tel./fax 4345-0504, costs US$14/19 s/d, but offers significant discounts for cash payments.

**Hotel Madrid,** Avenida de Mayo 1135, tel./fax 4381-9021, reserva@hotelmadrid.com.ar, www.hotelmadrid.com.ar, charges US$14/19 s/d with cable TV, a/c, and breakfast. Rates are identical at the **Turista Hotel,** Avenida de Mayo 686, tel. 4331-2281, for rooms with private bath and a/c but without breakfast. The rehabbed **Hotel Central,** south of the Plaza del Congreso at Solís 192, tel. 4373-8785, also charges US$14/19 s/d with private bath.

**Hotel Chile,** Avenida de Mayo 1297, tel./fax 4383-7877, is an art nouveau monument where modernized rooms with private bath and breakfast go for US$14/19 s/d. Corner balcony rooms on the upper floors enjoy panoramic views of the Plaza del Congreso and, by craning the neck a bit eastward, the Plaza de Mayo and Casa Rosada; the decibel level is high because of the location, though.

Rates at **Nuevo Hotel Mundial,** Avenida de Mayo 1298, tel. 4383-0011, fax 4383-6318, mundial@house.com.ar, www.hotel-mundial.com.ar, start at US$15/20 s/d with breakfast, private bath, and a/c, but the rooms are fairly basic; the hotel has a good range of services, though, for a place in its price category.

**Hotel Marbella,** Avenida de Mayo 1261, tel./fax 4383-8566, fax 4383-2388, reservas

*The majority of the capital's budget accommodations are in the vicinity of Plaza de Mayo and Avenida de Mayo, the Microcentro, and parts of Once and San Telmo.*

@hotelmarbella.com.ar, www.hotelmarbella.com.ar, is a well-kept if plain hotel that, for prices of US$15/20 s/d with private bath and cable TV, is perfectly acceptable. **Gran Hotel Hispano,** Avenida de Mayo 861, tel. 4345-2020, fax 4331-5266, hhispano@hhispano.com.ar, www.hhispano.com.ar, is a full-service hotel in a handsome building. Rates are US$17/20 s/d.

Rates at **Hotel Avenida,** Avenida de Mayo 623, tel. 4331-4341, fax 4343-7951, are US$17/23 s/d for rooms with private bath and breakfast. **Hotel Palace Solís,** south of the Congreso at Solís 352, tel./fax 4371-6266, hotelsolis@seconp.com.ar, falls into the US$18/23 s/d range with private bath.

The congenial **Astoria Hotel,** Avenida de Mayo 916, tel./fax 4334-9061, offers improved rooms with private bath, a/c, telephone, and Internet access for US$18/23 s/d.

## MICROCENTRO AND VICINITY

Recent economic conditions have made some pretty good Microcentro hotels more affordable, but this could change if the economy stabilizes.

The independently operated **V&S Hostel Club,** well located at Viamonte 887, tel./fax 4322-0994 or 4327-5131, hostelclub@hostelclub.com, www.hostelclub.com, has dormitory accommodations in a recycled early-20th-century house for as little as US$6 pp; rooms with private bath cost US$10 pp. The building has central heating, a/c, and spacious and attractive common areas including kitchen, dining room, and a *parrilla* for barbecues.

In the Congreso area, the **St. Nicholas Youth Hostel,** Bartolomé Mitre 1691, tel. 4373-5920, became an HI affiliate in early 2003. It has only dormitory accommodations for US$7 pp with breakfast and shared bath. Like the other hostels, it's a rehabbed period house with ample shared spaces.

ACCOMMODATIONS

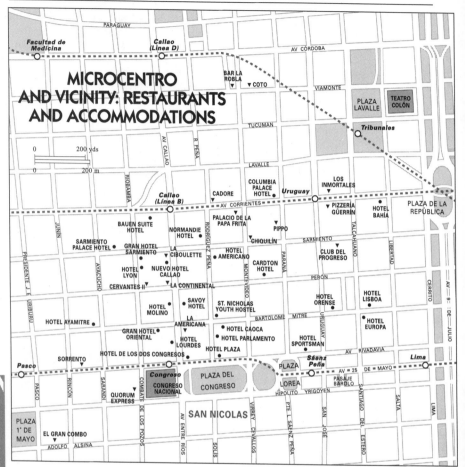

**MICROCENTRO AND VICINITY: RESTAURANTS AND ACCOMMODATIONS**

**Hotel Sportsman,** Rivadavia 1425, tel. 4381-8021, fax 4383-6263, sportsman @mixmail.com, www.hotelsportsman.com.ar, is a moldy backpackers' special whose main attraction is low rates: US$6/9 s/d with shared bath, US$8/11 s/d with private bath (of which there are few); breakfast is extra. There are discounts for longer stays. **Hotel Bahía,** Corrientes 1212, tel. 4382-1280, is also a long-time backpackers' choice for US$9 d, but in Argentina's present predicament there are many better options. Among the cheapest in town, Congreso's no-frills **Hotel Plaza,** Riva-davia 1689, tel. 4371-9747, charges US$6 s or d with shared bath, US$7.50 s or d with private bath.

Long-popular with backpackers for its central location and low prices—despite notoriously cranky management—**Hotel O'Rei,** Lavalle 733, tel. 4394-7112, fax 4393-7186, hotelorei@ yahoo.com.ar, costs US$7 s or d for smallish rooms with shared bath, US$11 s or d with private bath. The kitchen is open to guests.

Catering to overseas visitors, **Hotel Maipú,** Maipú 735, tel. 4322-5142, occupies an attractive but aging building whose utilitarian rooms cost

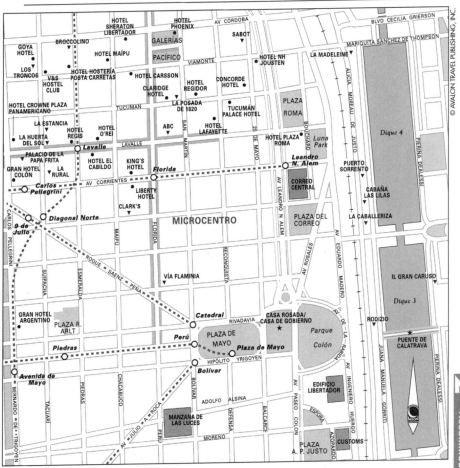

US$9/11 s/d with shared bath, US$11/14 s/d with private bath. Breakfast is not included.

The Deco-style **Hotel Europa,** Bartolomé Mitre 1294, tel./fax 4381-9629, hoteleuropa @elsitio.com.ar, www.europahotel.com.ar, charges US$11/14 s/d for rooms with private bath and central heating. The hotel offers a 10 percent discount with student ID.

Rates at **Hotel Orense,** Mitre 1359, tel. 4372-4441, informes@hotelorense.com.ar, www .hotelorense.com.ar, start at US$12/18 s/d with private bath, telephone, and a/c. **Hotel Lisboa,** one block east at Mitre 1281, tel. 4381-2152,

charges US$12/18 s/d with cable TV and breakfast; prices for larger rooms with a/c are about 20 percent higher.

Japanese-run **Hotel Caoca,** Mitre 1688, tel. 4385-5084, has smallish rooms for US$9/13 s/d with shared bath, US$13/20 s/d with private bath. Across from Hotel O'Rei is **Hotel El Cabildo,** Lavalle 748, tel./fax 4322-6745, which charges US$14/18 s/d with private bath; there are discounts for longer stays.

Opposite the Luna Park stadium, convenient to Puerto Madero's restaurants and cinemas, **Hotel Plaza Roma**, Lavalle 110, tel. 4314-666, fax 4312-0839, info@hotelplazaroma.com.ar, www.hotelplazaroma.com.ar, is an outstanding value for US$17/25 s/d with private bath, breakfast, a/c, cable TV, and telephone. Some rooms enjoy views of the Puerto Madero complex.

Rates at centrally located **King's Hotel,** a 50-room unit at Avenida Corrientes 623, tel. 4322-8461, fax 4322-8334, kingshotel@fullcom .com.ar, are US$17/23 for utilitarian rooms with a/c. The well-located **Tucumán Palace Hotel,** Tucumán 384, tel. 4311-2298, fax 4311-2298, is passable for US$18/23 s/d.

There are several worthy choices in Congreso, including the **Cardton Hotel,** Perón 1555, tel./fax 4382-1697, hotelcardto baires @hotmail.com, for US$15/18 s/d with private bath, breakfast, cable TV, and telephone. Rooms 364 and 368 have good views toward the Plaza del Congreso. Barely a block away, under the same management, **Hotel Americano,** Rodríguez Peña 265, tel. 4382-4223, fax 4382-4229), is a solid choice starting at US$18/23 s/d with breakfast, though the better rooms and suites are more expensive. Nearby, the identically priced **Hotel Parlamento,** Rodríguez Peña 61, tel. 4374-1410, fax 4814-3690, is comparable.

Congreso's finest value, though, is the rejuvenated **Hotel de los dos Congresos,** Rivadavia 1777, tel. 4372-0466, fax 4372-0317, reservas @hoteldoscongresos.com, www.hoteldoscongresos .com; its stately exterior is a misleading approach to the refurbished interior, where spacious and comfortable rooms with cable TV, a/c, telephone, and other standard amenities cost only US$20/22 s/d with buffet breakfast included. Reservations are advisable for one of the stylish loft rooms, which have spiral staircases and jacuzzi-equipped bathtubs.

For US$21/25 s/d with breakfast, **Hotel Regidor,** Tucumán 451, tel. 4314-9516, hotelregidor @arnet.com.ar, is traditionally underpriced for the area; it has cable TV, telephone, and a/c. At times it offers three-nights-for-the-price-of-two specials.

The **Goya Hotel,** Suipacha 748, tel./fax 4322-9311, goyahotel@infovia.com.ar, is one of the Microcentro's best small hotels. Rates start at US$21/25 s/d for rooms with private bath, continental breakfast (if the room payment is in cash), cable TV, and a/c; there are some larger, slightly more expensive rooms.

## SAN TELMO AND VICINITY

San Telmo has several hostels, including the oldest continuously operating one in the city, the **Albergue Ester de Nadenhein,** Brasil 675, tel. 4300-9321, www.hostelling-aaaj.org.ar, near the Constitución train and Subte stations. Its major drawback is that during school holidays it's overrun with groups from the provinces and the kids can get rowdy. Rates are US$4 pp with breakfast but without kitchen privileges.

The casual **Che Lagarto Youth Hostel,** Avenida San Juan 1836 in San Cristóbal, tel. 4304-7618, chelagarto@hotmail.com, www .chelagarto.com.ar, charges US$8 pp for dorm accommodations with breakfast, but also has doubles for US$11 pp. Another possibility in the same range is **Hostel Inn Buenos Aires,** Humberto Primo 820, tel. 4300-7992, fax 4300-7993, www.hostel-inn.com.ar.

**El Hostal de San Telmo,** Carlos Calvo 614, tel. 4300-6899, fax 4300-9028, elhostal@satlink.com, http://webs.satlink.com/usuarios/e/elhostal, is an appealingly cozy—perhaps cramped would be closer to the truth—hostel in a prime location. Dorm rates are US$10 pp; shared amenities include kitchen facilities, cable TV, and Internet access.

Among non-hostel accommodations, **Hotel Varela,** Estados Unidos 342, tel. 4362-1231, hotelvarela@yahoo.com.ar, is a very plain but spotless and reputable backpackers' choice. Rates are US$6 s or d with shared bath, US$7 s or d with private bath. **Hotel Bolívar,** Bolívar 886, tel. 4361-5105, is not quite so plain for US$5/7 s/d with private bath; it also has slightly cheaper rooms with shared bath.

On the southern edge of the barrio, **Hotel Tres Reyes,** Brasil 425 near Parque Lezama, tel. 4300-9456, hotel_tresreyes@yahoo.com, is a two-star hotel that's a respectable alternative. Rates are US$9 d with cable TV, private bath, and breakfast.

Friendly **Hotel Victoria,** Chacabuco 726, tel. 4361-2135, charges US$6/9 s/d with private bath, as well as kitchen and laundry facilities. **Hotel Oxford,** across the street at Chacabuco 719, tel. 4361-8581, costs US$7/10 s/d with breakfast.

The area's most unique accommodations is the German-run **Pop Hotel Boquitas Pintadas,** Estados Unidos 1393 in Constitución, tel. 4381-6064, a flamboyant place that takes its name and inspiration from the even more flamboyant novelist, the late Manuel Puig. Decorated in a pop art mode and offering a popular bar that pumps thumping techno at night and especially on weekends, it charges from US$25 d. The neighborhood is marginal, but the German owners have given the place a remarkable makeover.

## ONCE AND THE ABASTO (BALVANERA)

Most Balvanera budget hotels are within a few blocks of the Congreso Nacional. Amiable **Gran Hotel Sarmiento,** Sarmiento 1892, tel. 4374-8069, fax 4372-8069, hotelgransarmiento@infovia.com.ar, is a modest 30-room place that remains a decent value at US$11/16 s/d with private bath; breakfast costs extra.

**Gran Hotel Oriental,** Bartolomé Mitre 1840, tel./fax 4952-3371, costs US$13/16 s/d for smallish but otherwise good rooms with private bath and breakfast; the streetside rooms have balconies but are noisier than the interior rooms.

**Hotel Lourdes,** barely half a block from the Congreso at Avenida Callao 44, tel. 4952-7467, lourdeshotel@yahoo.com, www.hotelguia.com /hoteles/lourdes, deserves consideration for tidy comfortable rooms at bargain rates—US$13/17 s/d.

In an undistinguished but well-kept multi-story building, **Hotel Ayamitre,** Ayacucho 106, tel./fax 4953-1655, reservas@hotelayamitre .com.ar, www.hotelayamitre.com.ar, charges US$18/23 s/d for soundproofed rooms with cable TV, phone, a/c, and breakfast.

Rates at tidy **Hotel Molino,** Avenida Callao 164, tel. 4374-9112, fax 4374-9152, molinohotel@movi.com.ar, start at US$18/25 for rooms with private bath, telephone and a/c. In a stylish building crowned by a cupola, the recently up-graded **Nuevo Hotel Callao,** Avenida Callao 292, tel./fax 4372-4222, info@hotelcallao.com.ar, www.hotelcallao.com.ar, is an exceptional value at US$22/25 s/d with breakfast.

## RETIRO

True budget accommodations are few in the northern barrios, but the **Recoleta Youth Hostel,** Libertad 1216, tel. 4812-4419, fax 4815-6622, reservas@trhostel.com.ar, www.trhostel.com.ar, boasts the best location in its category (despite the name, it lies geographically within the barrio of Retiro but it is close to Recoleta). Bunks in multi-bedded rooms with shared bath and separate lockers cost US$7 pp.

The salient characteristic at **Hotel Central Córdoba,** San Martín 1021, tel. 4311-1175, fax 4315-6860, is its self-stated centrality—it's a well-located no-frills option with private bath, telephone, cable TV, and breakfast for US$10/13 s/d.

Centrally located **Gran Hotel Orly,** Paraguay 474, tel./fax 4312-5344, info@orly.com.ar, www.orly.com.ar, has become an exceptional value since devaluation, with rates of US$18/20 s/d (there's a 10 percent discount for Internet reservations), breakfast and taxes included.

## RECOLETA AND BARRIO NORTE

Budget accommodations are equally scarce in Recoleta and Barrio Norte, but **Hotel del Prado,** near the Facultad de Medicina at Paraguay 2385, tel. 4961-1192, reservas@hoteldelprado-ba.com.ar, www.hoteldelprado-ba.com.ar, is a simply but tastefully remodeled older building with a quiet interior, good beds, and friendly owner-operators. Rates are US$12/15 s/d for rooms with private bath, cable TV, telephone, and ceiling fans but no a/c. There are discounts of five percent for three to six days, 10 percent for seven to 14 days, and 25 percent for 15 days or more.

The **Alfa Hotel,** Riobamba 1064, tel. 4812-3719, reservas@alfahotel.com.ar, www.alfahotel .com.ar, is a small but well-kept and well-priced Barrio Norte choice for US$18/22 s/d. All rooms have private bath, cable TV, telephone, and a/c, and breakfast is included; there's a 10 percent discount for cash payments.

At the **Prince Hotel,** Arenales 1627, tel./fax 4811-8004, princehotel@arnet.com.ar, www.hotelprince.go.to, rates are US$18/22 s/d for reasonably ample rooms with all the basic comforts in a good location.

## PALERMO

Rates at modern but nondescript **Key's Hotel,** a 25-room hotel at Zapata 315, tel./fax 4772-8371, hotelkeys@ciudad.com.ar, are US$10/14 s/d with breakfast; its best asset is its location, close to public transportation but on a quiet, shady block.

Otherwise, budget accommodations are scarce except in the immediate vicinity of Plaza Italia; though they're generally not bad, with a couple of notable exceptions they're below the standards of other neighborhoods.

**Hotel Panamé**, Godoy Cruz 2774, tel. 4771-4041, info@panamehotel.com.ar, is a respectable choice for US$15/19 s/d with private bath, breakfast, and cable TV; upstairs rooms at this 56-room facility are airier. **Hotel Pacífico,** Santa María de Oro 2554, tel./fax 4771-4071, charges US$16/18 s/d for rooms with a/c and cable TV, breakfast included.

Rates at the modernized **Hotel Palermo** Godoy Cruz 2725, tel./fax 4774-7342, info @hotelpalermo.com.ar, www.hotelpalermo.com .ar, are US$18/24 s/d for smallish but impeccable rooms that lack character. The barrio's oldest hotel, it began as accommodations for *estancieros* who came to the capital for livestock shows at the nearby Predio Ferial.

HI's newest affiliate is the **Tango Backpacker's Hostel**, in the sleep-all-day, party-all-night zone of Palermo Soho at Thames 2212, tel./fax 4776-6871, info@tangobp.com,www .tangobp.com. Rates range from US$8 pp in shared rooms to US$20 s in a small private room. The building itself is a grand old Palermo house, with a rooftop terrace with a *parrilla* for barbecues, a large kitchen, and free Internet access, plus dining and partying recommendations from the staff, who also lead inexpensive guided tours around town.

## BELGRANO AND VICINITY

Accommodations are almost nonexistent in the northernmost residential suburbs. **Hotel Mórdomo**, Ciudad de la Paz 2942, tel. 4544-2711, fax 4545-1263, hotelmordomo@hotmail.com, is actually in the barrio of Núñez, but is barely a block off Avenida Cabildo and close to the Congreso de Tucumán Subte station. Room rates are US$15/18 s/d.

# US$25–50

In the aftermath of the economic meltdown of 2001–2002, there are some extraordinary values in the US$25–50 range.

## MONSERRAT/CATEDRAL AL SUR AND VICINITY

Rooms at **Hotel Napoleón,** Rivadavia 1364, tel./fax 4383-2031, info@napoleon.com.ar, www.hotel-napoleon.com.ar, suffer from garish decor, but the rates of US$22/26 s/d with breakfast, a/c, cable TV, and telephone are competitive.

Devaluation has made the four-star **Hotel Nogaró,** Diagonal Presidente Julio A. Roca 562, tel. 4331-0091, fax 4331-6791, reservas @nogarobue.com.ar, www.nogarobue.com.ar, a bargain at US$38/40 s/d with buffet breakfast included. Dating from 1930 but renovated a few years ago, this French-style, 150-room hotel also offers in-room safes and Internet connections.

## MICROCENTRO AND VICINITY

Rates at the 94-room **Liberty Hotel,** Avenida Corrientes 632, tel./fax 4325-0261, www.liberty-hotel.com.ar, are US$20/26 s/d for accommodations with private bath, a/c; and buffet breakfast. **Hotel Carsson,** centrally located at Viamonte 650, tel. 4322-3601, fax 4322-3551, carsson@datamarkets.com.ar, charges US$28 d for decent rooms with breakfast.

Convenient to the Teatro General San Martín and other prestigious theater venues, the **Columbia Palace Hotel,** Avenida Corrientes 1533, tel./fax 4373-2123 or 4325-7687, reservas@columbiapalacehotel.clm.ar, www.columbiapalacehotel.com.ar, charges US$23/28 s/d, with discounts for extended stays.

In the Congreso district, the **Normandie Hotel,** Rodríguez Peña 320, tel./fax 4371-7001, normandie@hotelnormandie.com.ar, is a respectable midrange choice that charges US$27/32 s/d for rooms with private bath and breakfast. There are discounts for cash payments, however, and for stays longer than five consecutive nights.

The renovated **Hotel Lafayette,** Reconquista 546, tel. 4393-9081, lafayette@sion.com.ar, www.lafayettehotel.com.ar, normally charges US$59/63, but specials can be as low as US$32 s or d for spacious rooms with breakfast. Amenities include cable TV, telephone, and Internet connections, a/c, and the like.

The **Concorde Hotel,** 25 de Mayo 630, tel. 4313-2018, fax 4313-2818, hotelconcorde @arnet.com.ar, www.hotelconcorde.com.ar, is a modernized place whose rates start at US$30/35 s/d. Its 56 rooms often fill with business groups.

Only a few years ago, **Hotel Phoenix,** adjacent to the Galerías Pacífico shopping center at San Martín 780, tel. 4516-0507, fax 4516-0499, info@hotelphoenix.com.ar, www.hotelphoenix .com.ar, overcame decades of neglect in a successful restoration to its early 20th-century heyday, when its guests included the Prince of Wales. Its attractive lobby, classic staircases and elevator, and interior patios are invitations to rooms that sport both antique furniture and contemporary conveniences. Rates are US$31/39 s/d with breakfast, but there are also steep discounts for payment in cash.

Housed in a handsome Art Nouveau building a few blocks south of the Obelisco, **Gran Hotel Argentino,** Carlos Pellegrini 37, tel./fax 4334-4001, info@hotel-argentino.com.ar, www.hotel-argentino.com.ar, charges US$20 s or d with breakfast, but larger rooms fall into the US$40 d category. Either one is a bargain, and there are also discounts for cash and for extended stays.

## ONCE AND THE ABASTO (BALVANERA)

For large families or groups of friends, one of the capital's best options is **Hotel Lyon,** Riobamba 251, tel. 4372-0100, fax 4814-4252, info@hotel-lyon.com.ar, www.hotel-lyon.com.ar, which has spacious apartment-style rooms—the smallest are 40 square meters—for only US$27/32 s/d. For stays longer than three days and paid in cash, there's a 15 percent discount.

Congreso's **Bauen Suite Hotel,** Avenida Corrientes 1856, tel. 4370-0400, fax 4370-0404, reservas@bauensuite.com, www.bauensuite.com, is a highrise hotel with spacious, well-equipped rooms that are ideal for business travelers. Rates are US$34 s/d with breakfast and taxes included; there are discounts for stays longer than 15 days.

Deservedly known for personalized attention, the three-star **Sarmiento Palace Hotel,** Sarmiento 1953, tel. 4953-3404, fax 4953-6247), hsarmiento@redesdelsur.com.ar, www.bookings-americas.com/ar/hotels/sarmientohotel, charges US$36/53 with breakfast.

## RETIRO

The **Impala Hotel,** with its superb location at Libertad 1215, tel./fax 4816-0430, info @hotelimpala.com.ar, www.hotelimpala.com.ar, has smallish but modern, comfortable, and immaculate rooms for US$31 d with breakfast.

Graham Greene, appropriately, once stayed at the British-styled **Hotel Lancaster,** Avenida Córdoba 405, tel. 4312-4061, fax 4311-3021, lancast@infovia.com.ar, www.lancasterhotel-page.com, which figures briefly in his novel *The Honorary Consul.* It has an English-style pub on the ground floor; rates are US$35/38 s/d with breakfast.

The **Carlton Hotel,** Libertad 1180, tel./fax 4812-0080, hotelcarlton@solans.com, www.solans.com, charges US$36/48 s or d with buffet breakfast for pleasant rooms—some with patios—in an equally convenient location.

## RECOLETA AND BARRIO NORTE

Rooms at the modest **Hotel Príncipe,** Laprida 1454, tel. 4821-9818, fax 4821-7425, are really mini-apartments with a refrigerator and sink (but no other kitchen facilities) for US$22/28 s/d with breakfast.

The **Ayacucho Palace Hotel,** Ayacucho 1408, tel./fax 4806-1815, reservas@ ayacuchohotel .com.ar, www.ayacuchohotel.com.ar, offers some of the exterior style of more elegant *porteño* hotels without extravagant prices—in fact, rack rates are only US$20/25 s/d with breakfast included. Its 70 rooms are plainly but comfortably furnished.

## PALERMO

Towering above everything else in the neighborhood, the **Torre Cristóforo Colombo,** Santa María de Oro 2747, tel. 4777-9622, fax 4775-9911, reservas@torrecc.com.ar, www.torrecc.com.ar, contains 160 fully equipped suites with kitchenettes and patios, accommodating from two to four persons. Rates start at US$42 s or d with breakfast and IVA, but the larger units are substantially dearer.

# US$50–100

Most of the accommodations in the US$50–100 range are found in the northern barrios, with a scattering elsewhere.

## MONSERRAT/CATEDRAL AL SUR AND VICINITY

One of the capital's most historic lodgings, dating from 1929, the four-star **Castelar Hotel & Spa,** Avenida de Mayo 1152, tel. 4383-5000, fax 4383-8388; reservas@castelarhotel.com.ar, www.castelarhotel.com.ar, has hosted the likes of Spanish dramatist Federico García Lorca (who lived six months in room 704), Chilean Nobel Prize–winning poet Pablo Neruda, Nobel Prize–winning scientist Linus Pauling, and many Argentine politicians. Embellished with Carrara marble, it offers comfortable, well-equipped rooms with breakfast and access to its own spa for US$51/55 s/d, an outstanding value even in a time of devaluation. There are entire non-smoking floors.

## MICROCENTRO AND VICINITY

**Hotel Regis,** in a handsome building on the pedestrian mall at Lavalle 813, tel./fax 4327-2605, regisventas@orho-hoteles.com.ar, is a good choice for US$50/55 without breakfast.

Rates at **Gran Hotel Colón,** only meters from the Obelisco at Carlos Pellegrini 507, tel. 4320-3500, fax 320-3507 info@colon-hotel.com.ar, www.colon-hotel.com.ar, are US$45/54, but there are substantial discounts for stays of three days or longer. Devaluation has made this business-oriented hotel a bargain.

## RETIRO

Rates at **Crillón Hotel,** a classic Parisian-styled edifice near Plaza San Martín at Avenida Santa Fe 796, tel. 4310-2000, fax 4312-9955, info@hotelcrillon.com.ar, www.hotelcrillon.com.ar, are US$50/59 s/d, with buffet breakfast. Rooms offer all contemporary comforts including a/c, cable TV, telephone, Internet access, and voicemail. The room rate even includes a cell phone.

The business-oriented **Hotel de las Américas,** Libertad 1020, tel. 4816-3432, fax 4816-0418, americas@americas-bue.com.ar, www.americas-bue.com.ar, is a 150-room hotel with king-size beds, telephones, dataports, voicemail, double-paned windows, bar and restaurant, and parking. Rates are US$56/68 s/d with breakfast.

Its sister **Américas Towers Hotel,** Libertad 1070, tel. 4815-7900, fax 4815-9466, towers@americas-bue.com.ar, www.americas-bue.com.ar, is a 100-room facility that has virtually identical services (plus a fitness center) and rates to those at Hotel de las Américas.

## RECOLETA AND BARRIO NORTE

**Hotel Plaza Francia,** Eduardo Schiaffino 2189, tel./fax 4804-9631, contact@hotelplazafrancia.com, www.hotelplazafrancia.com, is a boutique-style hotel closed to Recoleta cemetery, restaurants and entertainment, and open spaces, but still close to downtown. Rates of US$60 s or d include buffet breakfast, Internet connections, a/c, and many other conveniences—thanks to devaluation.

## PALERMO

Palermo Viejo has few accommodations in any category, but the B&Bs in this price range are worth consideration—they're within walking distance to restaurants and nightlife but not so close that it's impossible to sleep at a reasonable hour.

Occupying a painstakingly remodeled 19th-century *casa chorizo,* **Malabia House,** Malabia 1555, tel./fax 4832-3345 or 4833-2410, info@malabiahouse.com.ar, www.malabiahouse.com.ar, is a stylish bed-and-breakfast with magnificent natural light, glistening wood floors, handsome furnishings, and small but attractive patio gardens. Standard ground floor rooms, for US$60 d with breakfast, have external private baths; slightly more expensive upstairs rooms (US$70 d) have a/c and interior baths. There is a 10 percent discount for cash payment.

**Como en Casa,** Gurruchaga 2155, tel. 4831-0517, fax 4831-2664, info@bandb.com.ar, www.bandb.com.ar, is a charming house dating from 1926, with 11 cozy rooms that have high ceilings, attractive common areas, and several shady patios on a narrow but deep lot. Rates, ranging from US$15–30 pp with continental breakfast, depend on whether or not the room has private bath. The establishment offers Internet access and English-speaking personnel, but lacks a/c.

# US$100–150

Some of the best new values in town fall into this category.

## MONSERRAT/CATEDRAL AL SUR AND VICINITY

Part of a highly regarded Spanish luxury business chain, the **NH City Hotel,** just south of the Plaza de Mayo at Bolívar 160, tel. 4121-6464, fax 4121-6450, info@nh-city.com.ar, www.nh-hoteles.com, is a spectacularly modernized 300-room facility (dating from 1931) that had the misfortune to reopen at the nadir of Argentina's economic meltdown of 2001–2002. The bad timing, though, has meant good rates: US$97 s or d, for beautifully appointed rooms with all modern conveniences, plus luxuries like a rooftop pool, gym, and sauna, and a first-rate Spanish restaurant.

## MICROCENTRO AND VICINITY

**Hotel Hostería Posta Carretas,** Esmeralda 726, tel. 4322-8567, fax 4322-8606, www.postacarretas.com.ar, has an older sector with smallish and dark but quiet rooms, and a newer addition with larger, comfier rooms but a noisier exposure to the street. Services include cable TV, a/c, sauna and gym, bar, restaurant, and buffet breakfast. The staff is agreeable, but at US$100 d for two-room suite and US$125 for a more spacious junior site, it's not the best value in town.

Near the Obelisco, the **Hotel Crowne Plaza Panamericano,** Carlos Pellegrini 525, tel. 4348-5000, fax 4348-5251, hotel@crowneplaza.com.ar, www.crowneplaza.com.ar, consists of an older south tower where rates are US$70/110 s/d and a newer north tower where rates are US$110/130 s/d. Both are comfortable but the north tower rooms are technologically superior.

Its restaurant *Tomo I* is widely considered one of the capital's best.

## ONCE AND THE ABASTO (BALVANERA)

Opposite the Mercado del Abasto, the **Holiday Inn Select Abasto Buenos Aires,** Avenida Corrientes 3190, tel. 6311-4466, fax 6311-4465, reservas@holidayinnabasto.com.ar, www.holidayinnabasto.com.ar, is a five-star facility whose rack rates are US$120 s or d.

## RETIRO

**Hotel Presidente,** Cerrito 850, tel. 4816-2222, fax 4816-5985, webmaster@hotelpresidente.com.ar, www.hotelpresidente.com.ar, is a modern highrise hotel with 181 rooms, 28 suites, and 35 apartments, oriented toward business travelers. Rates start at US$106 d with breakfast, cable TV, Internet, gym and sauna, parking, room service, and other amenities.

**Hotel Conquistador,** Suipacha 948, tel. 4328-3012, fax 328-3252, mailhotel@elconquistador.com.ar, www.elconquistador.com.ar, is a modern multistory hotel appealing primarily to business travelers. Rates starting at US$115 s or d include taxes, buffet breakfast, and a PC on request. There are also workout facilities.

More a boutique-style hotel on the edge of fashionable Recoleta, the 54-room **Hotel Park Plaza Kempinski,** Parera 183, tel. 6777-0200, reservas@parkplazahotels.com, www.parkplazahotels.com, has rates starting at US$144 s or d plus IVA.

## RECOLETA AND BARRIO NORTE

The bright, modern **Design Suites,** Marcelo T. de Alvear 1683, tel./fax 4814-8700, design@designsuites.com, www.designsuites.com, is a new boutique-style hotel with a heated pool, a gym, a restaurant, and room service. Each of its 40 rooms has cable TV, telephone, Internet and fax connections, kitchenette, minibar, a/c, strongbox, and jacuzzi; rates start US$96 s/d for standard rooms, but rise to USD$144 s/d for two-room suites.

# US$150–200

Top-end hotels are scattered around town from Plaza de Mayo north, but look for new ones to open as Puerto Madero develops east of the yacht basin.

## MONSERRAT/ CATEDRAL AL SUR AND VICINITY

**Hotel Intercontinental,** Moreno 809, tel. 4340-7100, fax 4340-7199, http://buenos-aires.argentina.intercontinental.com/index.shtml, buenosaires@interconti.com, consistently makes the list of the best hotels in town, according to magazines like *Travel & Leisure.* More than half of the 305 rooms are nonsmoking. Rates are US$180 s or d, but corporate and other discount rates are available.

## MICROCENTRO AND VICINITY

Another affiliate of the Spanish chain, **Hotel NH Jousten,** Avenida Corrientes 240, tel. 4321-6750, fax 4321-6775, info@nh-jousten.com.ar, www.nh-hoteles.com, has 85 rooms in an elegant, tastefully recycled French-style castle. Quiet despite the busy avenue thanks to double-paned windows, each room has cable TV, stereo, telephone, a/c, and a modem connection; rates are US$160 s or d plus 21 percent IVA with buffet breakfast; the hotel's highly regarded basement restaurant serves Spanish cuisine.

One of the capital's classics, dating from 1946 but tastefully modernized, the **Claridge Hotel,** Tucumán 535, tel. 4314-7700, fax 4314-8022, reservations@claridge-hotel.com.ar, www

.claridge-hotel.com.ar, charges US$163 s or d for rooms with the standard amenities in its range, including cable TV, telephone, and a workdesk with Internet connections. Several floors are tobacco-free.

Congreso's prime upscale option is the **Savoy Hotel,** now part of the Dutch Golden Tulip chain, at Avenida Callao 181, tel. 4370-8000, fax 4372-7006, info@hotel-savoy.com.ar, www .gtsavoyhotel.com.ar. Rates start at US$129 s/d plus 21 percent IVA, with suites for US$160 plus IVA; for stays longer than two weeks, there's a 10 percent discount. All windows are double-paned for silence, and include phones (with voicemail), computer connections and other business amenities, and a buffet breakfast.

## RETIRO

Near Puerto Madero, across from the Plaza Fuerza Aérea Argentina, the massive 742-room high-rise **Sheraton Buenos Aires Hotel,** San Martín 1225, tel. 4318-9000, fax 4318-9346, sheraton @sheraton.com.ar, www.starwood.com/redir/ sheraton/buenosaires, gets lots of the international business trade. Rates start at US$165 s or d.

Now under international chain control, the landmark (1909) **Marriott Plaza Hotel,** Florida 1005, tel. 4318-3000, fax 4318-3008, marriott.plaza@ba.net, www.marriott.com, has undergone a significant modernization without losing its German baroque charm. Rates start at US$195 s or d, but that's a function of recent economic conditions.

# Over US$200

## MICROCENTRO AND VICINITY

The **Hotel Sheraton Libertador,** Avenida Córdoba 680, tel. 4322-2095, fax 4322-9703, reserva@libertador-hotel.com.ar, www.starwood .com, charges US$285 s or d plus 21 percent IVA, breakfast not included. It has a business center, restaurant, pool, gym, and other luxuries.

## RETIRO

Belonging to a Mexican luxury hotel chain, the contemporary **Caesar Park Hotel** is at Posadas 1232, tel. 4819-1100, fax 4819-1165, hotel @caesar.com.ar, www.caesar-park.com. Rates start at US$252 s or d with buffet breakfast included.

## RECOLETA AND BARRIO NORTE

Facing Recoleta's famous cemetery, the high-rise **Etoile Hotel,** Roberto M. Ortiz 1835, tel. 4805-2626, fax 4805-3613, reservas@etoile.com.ar, www.etoile.com.ar, starts at US$220 d with taxes. This modern hotel lacks the character of many *porteño* hotels, but compensates with its location and services.

The **Loi Suites Recoleta,** Vicente López 1955, tel. 5777-8950, fax 5777-8999, recoleta @loisuites.com.ar, www.loisuites.com.ar, is the toniest link of a stylish new local three-hotel chain. Rack rates start at US$200 d plus IVA, but rise to US$345 d for the executive suite; the hotel presents some of the most innovative new design approaches in town, with magnificent use of natural light.

Since 1928, the **Alvear Palace Hotel,** Avenida Alvear 1891, tel. 4805-2100, fax 4804-9246, info@alvearpalace.com, www.alvearpalace.com, has symbolized *porteño* elegance and luxury—not to mention wealth and privilege. This hotel, despite devaluation, maintains both its standards and its prices—rack rates start around US$410 s or d and range up to US$3,000 for the royal suite; the hotel's accommodations include Egyptian cotton sheets and Hermés toiletries. Francophobes may find the *ancien régime* decor cloying, but *Travel & Leisure* readers have called it the 18th-best hotel in the world and the second-best in Latin America (2002), and it also made the Condé Nast Gold List as one of the world's finest hotels.

**ACCOMMODATIONS**

# Food and Drink

*Note: For restaurant locations see map* **Microcentro and Vicinity: Restaurants and Accommodations** *pp. 124–125*

Food and drink in Buenos Aires range from the economical and ordinary to the truly elegant. For most of the 1990s, eating well at restaurants was financially challenging except for cheap cafetería lunches and *tenedor libre* (literally, "free fork") buffets, but the peso collapse of 2001–2002 has made it possible to eat diverse and imaginative food for a fraction of its former price—at least for visitors with dollar or Euro salaries.

The stereotype that the Argentine diet consists of beef and more beef is not entirely mistaken. However, the local diet has always had a Spanish touch and, for more than a century, a marked Italian influence including pizza and pasta. Over the past decade, though, the restaurant scene has become far more cosmopolitan, adventurous, and nuanced. Brazilian, Japanese, Thai, Vietnamese, and many other once-exotic cuisines—not to mention high-quality variations on Argentine regional dishes—have entered the scene. Certain neighborhoods, such Palermo Viejo and Las Cañitas, seem to have sprouted stylish and sophisticated new eateries on every corner and in between.

sidewalk dining in Las Cañitas

## WHERE TO EAT

Places to eat range from hole-in-the-wall *comedores* (eateries) or fast-food *bares* (unavoidably but misleadingly translated as "bars") with no formal menu in bus and train stations, to cafés, *confiterías*, (teahouses) and elegant *restaurantes* in Buenos Aires and other major tourist centers. A bar, of course, can also be a drinking establishment; this is usually obvious in context. And a café is both more and less than its English-language equivalent would suggest, though it does serve food. See the Special Topic "Restaurant Terminology" in this chapter for a more complete explanation, and see the Arts and Entertainment chapter for more information on specific locales.

## Buying Groceries

Abundant across Buenos Aires, North American-style supermarkets such as Coto and Disco carry a wide selection of processed foods but often a lesser variety (and quality) of fresh produce than is available in produce markets. Many of them also have cheap cafeterías with surprisingly good food.

In areas where supermarkets are fewer, almost all neighborhoods have corner shops where basic groceries and fresh produce are available, usually within just a few minutes' walk from wherever you're staying. Butchers are numerous, fishmongers somewhat less so.

## What to Eat and Drink

Argentina is famous for beef—in abundance—and grains, but fresh fruit, vegetables, and an underrated wealth of seafood add diversity to the country's cuisine. The stereotypical Argentine beef diet has serious shortcomings, and visitors will have no difficulty finding alternatives, especially in Buenos Aires.

According to historian John C. Super, whatever the negative consequences of the Spanish invasion, it improved a diet that was, by some accounts, nutritionally deficient (often protein-poor) in late pre-Columbian times. In Super's opinion,

> *The combination of European and American foods created diversified, nutritionally rich diets. Crop yields were higher than those in Europe, and longer or staggered growing seasons made fresh food available during much of the year. The potential for one of the best diets in the history of the world was evident soon after discovery of the New World. For Europeans, the introduction of livestock and wheat was an essential step in creating that diet.*

When Europeans first set foot in South America, in the densely populated Andean region the staple foods were beans, squash, and a variety of potatoes and other tubers, but the diet was low in animal protein—only the llama, alpaca, guinea pig, and wild game were readily available, and these not in all areas.

The Spanish introductions blended with the indigenous base to create many of the edibles found on Argentine tables today. Spanish introductions like wheat and barley, which yielded only a four-to-one harvest ratio in Europe, reached at least two to three times that in the Americas. Furthermore, the abundance of seafood, combined with the increase of European livestock and the high productivity of European fruits like apples, apricots, grapes, pears and many others, resulted in a diverse food production and consumption system which, however, is changing today.

Consumption of red meat may be decreasing among more affluent Argentines, but it remains the entrée of choice among lower classes. Thanks to the Italian immigrant influence, an assortment of pastas is available almost everywhere.

FOOD AND DRINK

## RESTAURANT TERMINOLOGY

The term *restaurante* (occasionally *restorán*) usually refers to places with sit-down service, but within this definition there can be great diversity. Most often, the term refers to a place with a printed menu, but this can range from any place with a basic beef and pasta menu to truly formal places with complex cuisine, elaborate wine lists, and professional waiters. It's worth emphasizing that the occupation of waiter is traditionally professional and male in Argentina, rather than a short-term expedient for university students or aspiring actors, but this is changing in the capital—in the new, stylish restaurants of Palermo Viejo and Las Cañitas, servers are just as likely to be young and female.

The usual international fast food villains have franchises in Buenos Aires, but the best cheap food in town is available at *rotiserías* (delicatessens), which serve excellent takeaway food and sometimes have basic seating. Likewise, supermarkets like Coto and Disco have budget cafeterías that are excellent options for visitors on a budget.

*Bares* and *comedores* are generally no-frills eateries with indifferent service, offering *minutas* (short orders); the term *comedor* can also mean a hotel breakfast nook or dining room. A café, by contrast, is a place where *porteños* may dawdle over coffee and croissants, but its de facto purpose is to promote social interaction in personal affairs, business deals, and other transactions; in addition to coffee and pastries, cafés serve snacks, *minutas,* and alcoholic drinks (beer, wine, and hard liquor).

*Confiterías* often serve breakfast, light meals like sandwiches, snacks like cakes and other desserts, and a variety of coffee drinks. Generally, they are more formal than cafés, popular destinations for afternoon tea, and some are prestigious; some have full-scale restaurant menus, often in a separate sector of the establishment.

## GRAINS

*Trigo* (wheat), a Spanish introduction, is most commonly used for *pan* (bread), but it's also common in the form of pasta. *Arroz* (rice) is a common *guarnición* (side order).

*Maíz* (maize or corn) is a main ingredient in many dishes, including the traditional Italian polenta. Maize leaves often serve as a wrapping for traditional dishes like *humitas,* the northwestern Argentine equivalent of Mexican tamales.

## LEGUMES, VEGETABLES, AND TUBERS

Salads are almost invariably safe in Argentina, and all but the most sensitive stomachs probably need not be concerned with catching bugs from greens washed in tap water. (Note that green salads are usually too large for a single person and often sufficient for two.)

*Porotos* (beans of all sorts except green beans) are traditional in families of Spanish descent. Other common legumes include *chauchas* (green beans), *arvejas* (peas), *lentejas* (lentils) and *habas* (fava beans).

In many varieties, *zapallo* (squash) remains part of the traditional diet, as does the *tomate* (tomato). Many Old World vegetables are also widely consumed, including *acelga* (chard), *berenjena* (eggplant), *coliflor* (cauliflower), *lechuga* (lettuce), and *repollo* (cabbage). *Chiles* (peppers) are relatively uncommon; Argentine cuisine is rarely *picante* (spicy) except for dishes from the Andean Northwest, and even those rarely challenge palates accustomed to Mexican or Thai cuisine.

Native to the central Andes, *papas* (potatoes) grow in well-drained soils at higher elevations in northwestern Argentina; *papas fritas* (French fries) are virtually universal, but spuds also appear as *purée* (mashed potatoes) and in Italian dishes as *ñoquis* (gnocchi). Other common tubers include *zanahorias* (carrots) and *rábanos* (radishes).

### Vegetarianism

While vegetarian restaurants are relatively few except in Buenos Aires proper, the ingredients for quality vegetarian meals are easy to obtain,

## DINING VOCABULARY AND ETIQUETTE

Restaurant vocabulary is mostly straightforward. The usual term for menu is *la carta; el menú* is almost equally common, but can also mean a fixed-price lunch or dinner. The bill is *la cuenta. Cubiertos* are silverware, a *plato* is a plate, and *vaso* is a glass. A *plato principal* is a main dish or entrée.

Note that one might ask for a *vaso de agua* (glass of water), but never for a *vaso de vino* (literally but incorrectly, a glass of wine); rather, ask for a *copa de vino.* When speaking English, native Spanish speakers frequently make a similar error in requesting "a cup of wine."

Many but not all Argentine restaurants assess a small *cubierto* (cover charge, not silverware in this case) for dishes, silverware, and bread. This is not a *propina* (tip); a 10 percent tip is the norm, but Argentines themselves often ignore this norm, especially in times of economic crisis. Women in a group will often tip little or nothing, but a good rule of thumb is that anyone able to afford a restaurant meal can afford a tip.

A professional waiter, usually in uniform, is a *mozo;* this term, by the way, is totally innocuous in the Río de la Plata region but an insult in neighboring Chile, where it implies rural servitude. A waitress, regardless of age or marital status, is a *señorita.* When trying to attract a server's attention, it's also possible to use terms such as *señor* or even *jóven* (young man or woman, so long as the individual is not obviously elderly).

and many eateries prepare dishes such as pasta and salads which are easily adapted into a vegetarian format. Before ordering any pasta dish, verify whether it comes with a meat sauce—*carne* means "beef" in the Southern Cone countries (Argentina, Chile, Paraguay, and Uruguay), and waiters or waitresses may consider chicken, pork and similar items as part of another category—sometimes called *carne blanca* (literally, white meat). Faced with a reticent cook, you can always claim *alergia* (allergy).

## FRUITS

Temperate Argentina produces many of the same fruits as northern-hemisphere nations do, often available as delicious fresh juices. Items like *manzana* (apple), *pera* (pear), *naranja* (orange), *ciruela* (plum), *sandía* (watermelon), *membrillo* (quince), *durazno* (peach), *frambuesa* (raspberry), and *frutilla* (strawberry) will be familiar to almost everyone. When requesting *jugo de naranja* (orange juice), be sure it comes *exprimido* (fresh-squeezed) rather than out of a can or box.

Also widely available, though mostly through import, are tropical and subtropical fruits like banana and *ananá* (pineapple). Mango, *maracuyá* (passion fruit), and similar tropical fruits are uncommon but not unknown.

The *palta* (avocado), a Central American domesticate known as *aguacate* in its area of origin, often appears in Argentine salads.

## MEATS AND POULTRY

Prior to the invasion of the Spaniards, South America's only domesticated animals were the *cuy* (guinea pig, rare in what is now Argentina), the llama, the alpaca, and the dog, which was sometimes used for food. The Spaniards enriched the American diet with their domestic animals, including cattle, sheep, pigs, and poultry, including chicken and ducks.

*Carne,* often modified as *carne de vacuno,* or *bife* (beef) is the most common menu item in a variety of cuts. Among them are *bife de chorizo* (sirloin or rump steak), *bife de lomo* (tenderloin), *asado de tira* (rib roast), and *matambre* (rolled flank steak). *Milanesa* is a breaded cutlet or chicken-fried steak that, at cheaper restaurants, can be intolerably greasy.

The widest selection is usually available in the *parrillada* or *asado,* a mixed grill that includes prime cuts but also *achuras,* a broad term that encompasses offal such as *chinchulines* (small intestines), *mollejas* (sweetbreads), *criadillas* (testicles), *morcilla* (blood sausage), and *riñones* (kidneys). *Asado* can also mean a simple roast.

FOOD AND DRINK

*Chimichurri* is a garlic-based marinade that often accompanies the parrillada.

Sausages such as the slight spicy *chorizo* may also form part of the *asado;* in a hot-dog bun, it becomes *choripán. Panchos* are basic hot dogs, and *fiambres* are processed meats.

*Cordero* (lamb), often roasted on a spit over an open fire, is a fairly common item from Argentine Patagonia. *Cerdo* (pork) appears in many forms, ranging from simple *jamón* (ham) to *chuletas* (chops) to *lomito* (loin) and *matambre de cerdo.* *Chivo* (goat) or *chivito* (the diminutive) is a western Argentine specialty that sometimes appears on menus in the capital; note that the Uruguayan *chivito* is very different—a steak sandwich or plate slathered with eggs, fries, and other high-calorie extras.

Stews and casseroles include *carbonada,* which consists of beef, rice, potatoes, sweet potatoes, corn, squash, and fruit like apples and peaches, and *puchero,* of beef, chicken, bacon, sausage, morcilla, cabbage, corn, garbanzos (chickpeas), peppers, tomatoes, onions, squash, and sweet potatoes. Broth-cooked rice serves as a garnish.

*Ave* (poultry) most often means *pollo* (chicken), which sometimes appears on menus as *gallina* (literally, hen) in a casserole or stew; eggs are called *huevos. Pavo* (turkey) is becoming more common.

## FISH AND SEAFOOD

Argentina's fish and seafood may not have the international reputation of its beef, but the country's long coastline, extensive territorial seas, and huge freshwater rivers and lakes provide abundant options. Buenos Aires has some very fine seafood restaurants, but these are less common in provincial cities and towns.

## CATTLE CULTURE ON THE PAMPAS

From his hotel room on the Avenida de Mayo, U.S. poet Robert Lowell once wrote that he could hear "the bulky, beefy breathing of the herds." Ever since feral livestock changed the face of the Pampas in the 16th century, displacing the native guanaco and rhea, cattle have been a symbol of wealth and the foundation of the Argentine diet. Riding across the Pampas, Charles Darwin found the reliance on beef remarkable:

*I had now been several days without tasting any thing besides meat: I did not at all dislike this new regimen; but I felt as if it would only have agreed with me with hard exercise. I have heard that patients in England, when desired to confine themselves exclusively to an animal diet, even with the hope of life before their eyes, have scarce been able to endure it. Yet the Gaucho in the Pampas, for months together, touches nothing but beef. . . . It is, perhaps, from their meat regimen that the Gauchos, like other carnivorous animals,*

*can abstain long from food. I was told that at Tandeel, some troops voluntarily pursued a party of Indians for three days, without eating or drinking.*

Recent research has suggested that this diet has not been quite so universal as once imagined—urban archaeologist Daniel Schávelzon has unearthed evidence that, for instance, fish consumption was much greater in colonial Buenos Aires than people thought—but there is no doubt that the Porteño *parrilla* is a culinary institution. Beef may not be healthy in the quantities that some Argentines enjoy, and many of them will even admit it. But few *porteños* can bypass the capital's traditional restaurants—where flamboyantly clad urban gauchos stir the glowing coals beneath grilled meat on a vertical spit—without craving that savory beef.

For most Argentines, *bien cocido* (well done) is the standard for steak, but *jugoso* (rare) and *a punto* (medium) are not uncommon.

Seafood, among the most abundant sources of animal protein in pre-Columbian times, includes both *pescado* (fish) and *mariscos* (shellfish and crustaceans). The most common fish are *congrio* (conger eel, covering a variety of species), sometimes called *abadejo*, *lenguado* (sole or flounder), *merluza* (hake), and *trucha* (trout); *salmón* (salmon) normally comes from fish farms in Patagonia and in Chile.

Note that the cheapest restaurants often ruin perfectly good fish by preparing it *frito* (overpoweringly deep fried), but on request almost all will prepare it *a la plancha* (grilled, usually with a bit of butter) or *al vapor* (steamed). Higher-priced restaurants will add elaborate sauces, often including shellfish.

Among the shellfish, visitors will recognize the relatively commonplace *almejas* (clams), *calamares* (squid), *camarones* (shrimp), *cangrejo* (crab), *centolla* (king crab), *mejillones* (mussels), and *ostiones* or *callos* (scallops, but beware—the latter word can also mean tripe), *ostras* (oysters) and *pulpo* (octopus). Spanish restaurants normally serve the greatest variety of fish and shellfish.

> *Argentina's fish and seafood may not have the international reputation of its beef, but the country's long coastline, extensive territorial seas, and huge freshwater rivers and lakes provide abundant options.*

## MEALS AND MEALTIMES

Despite some regional differences, Argentina's cuisine is relatively uniform throughout the country, except in Buenos Aires, where diverse ethnic and international cuisine is abundant. Some resort areas in both Buenos Aires province and neighboring Uruguay also have a diverse food scene.

By North American and European standards, Argentines are late eaters except for *desayuno* (breakfast). *Almuerzo* (lunch) usually starts around 2 P.M., *cena* (dinner) around 9 P.M. or later—sometimes much later. *Porteños* often bide their time between lunch and dinner with a late afternoon *té* (tea) that consists of a sandwich or some sort of pastry or dessert; it can be very substantial.

Since *porteños* often eat *after* the theater or a movie, around 11 P.M. or even later on weekends, anyone entering a restaurant before 9 P.M. may well dine alone. One advantage of an early lunch or dinner is that fewer customers means fewer smokers; this is not foolproof, but statistically things are on your side.

### Breakfast and Brunch

Most Argentines eat only a light breakfast of coffee or tea with *pan tostado* (toast, occasionally with ham and/or cheese), *medialunas* (croissants), or *facturas* (pastries, also eaten for afternoon tea); medialunas may be either *de manteca* (buttery and sweet) or *salada* (saltier, baked with oil). *Mermelada* (jam) usually accompanies plain *tostados*.

An occasional side dish, eggs may be *fritos* (fried), *revueltos* (scrambled), or sometimes *duros* (hardboiled). In some fashionable restaurant zones, such as Las Cañitas, a more elaborate Sunday brunch has become an option.

### Lunch

Lunch is often the day's main meal, usually including an *entrada* (appetizer), followed by a *plato principal* (entrée) accompanied by a *guarnición* (side dish) and a *bebida* (soft drink) or *agua mineral* (mineral water) and followed by *postre* (dessert).

Upscale Buenos Aires restaurants sometimes offer fixed-priced lunches that make it possible to eat well and stylishly without busting the budget, but elsewhere this is usually not the case. It's also possible to find local fast-food items like *hamburguesas* (hamburgers), sandwiches, pizza, and pasta without resorting to international franchises.

### Té

*Té*, the fourth meal of the typical Argentine day, can range from a late afternoon sandwich to the equivalent of afternoon tea, with elaborate cakes and cookies, and is often a social occasion as

© WAYNE BERNHARDSON

Sunday morning at Café La Biela, Recoleta

well. Presumably intended to tide people over until their relatively late dinnertime, it often becomes larger and more elaborate than that would imply.

## Dinner

Dinner resembles lunch, but in formal restaurants it may be substantially more elaborate (and more expensive), and it can be a major social occasion. Argentines dine late—9 P.M. is early, and anything before that will likely earn incredulous "What are you doing here?" stares from waiters. The exception to this rule is at tourist-oriented areas like the Puerto Madero complex, where restaurateurs have become accustomed to North Americans and northern Europeans lodged at nearby luxury hotels who often won't wait any later than 7 P.M.

## "Fast Food" Snacks

Argentina has some of the continent's best snack food. The best of the best is the empanada, a flaky phyllo dough turnover most frequently filled with ground beef, hard-boiled egg, and olive, but it may also come with ham and cheese, chicken, onion and (rarely) with tuna or fish. The spicier ground beef *salteña* comes from northwestern Argentina but is available in Buenos Aires; the tangy *empanada árabe* (lamb with a touch of lemon juice) is more difficult to find. Empanadas *al horno* (oven-baked) are lighter than empanadas *fritas* (fried, sometimes in heavy oil).

Argentine pizza is also exceptional, though not so diverse in terms of toppings as in North America. For slices, try the cheeseless *fugazza* with Vidalia sweet onions or its cousin *fugazzeta*, enhanced with ham and mozzarella. *Porteños* embellish their slices with *fainá*, a baked garbanzo dough that fits neatly atop.

## DESSERTS

Many Argentines have a sweet tooth. At home, the favorite *postre* is fresh fruit, ranging from grapes (most single-family homes have their own arbors) to apples, pears, and oranges. In restaurants, this becomes *ensalada de frutas* (fruit salad) or, somewhat more elaborately, *macedonia*. *Postre vigilante*, consisting of cheese and *membrillo* (quince) or *batata* (sweet potato) preserves, is another fruit-based dessert; it also goes by the name *queso y dulce*.

*Arroz con leche* (rice pudding) and *flan* (egg custard, often topped with whipped cream) are also good choices, as is the Spanish custard known as *natillas*. An acquired taste is *dulce de leche*, which one international travel magazine referred to as "its own major food group." Argentines devour this sickly sweet caramelized milk, spread on just about anything and often spooned out of the jar in prodigious quantities in private homes.

> *Dinner in formal restaurants may be substantially more elaborate than lunch and can be a major social occasion. Argentines dine late— 9 P.M. is early, and anything before that will likely earn incredulous "What are you doing here?" stares from waiters.*

Thanks to their Italian tradition, Argentine *helados* (ice cream) are popular everywhere, and the quality can be extraordinary where *elaboración artesanal* (small-scale production) is the rule. *Almendrado*, vanilla ice cream rolled with crushed almonds, is a special treat.

## INTERNATIONAL AND ETHNIC FOOD

Buenos Aires has the greatest variety of international food in the country, though some tourist-oriented areas also have good selections. Italian and Spanish are probably the most common foreign cuisines, but French and Chinese venues are also numerous. Brazilian, Mexican, and Middle Eastern cuisine are less common; some popular world food cuisines, such as Japanese, Thai and Vietnamese, have made significant inroads in recent years.

## BEVERAGES

### Coffee, Tea, and Chocolate

Caffeine addicts will feel at home in Argentina, where espresso is the norm even in small provincial towns. *Café chico* is a dark viscous brew in a miniature cup, supplemented with enough sugar

packets to make it overflow onto the saucer. A *cortado* comes diluted with milk—for a larger portion request a *cortado doble*—and follows lunch or dinner. *Café con leche*, equivalent to a latte, is by contrast a breakfast drink; ordering it after lunch or dinner is a serious faux pas.

*Té negro* (black tea) usually comes in bags and is insipid by most standards. Those wanting tea with milk in the British manner should ask for tea first and milk later; otherwise, they may get a tea bag immersed in lukewarm milk. Herbal teas range from the nearly universal *té de manzanilla* (camomile) and *rosa mosqueta* (rose hips) to *mate de coca* (coca leaf), but *yerba mate*, the so-called "Paraguayan tea," is one of the most deeply embedded customs in the entire country.

Chocolate lovers will enjoy the *submarino*, a bar of semi-sweet chocolate that dissolves smoothly in steamed milk from the espresso machine. Powdered chocolate is also available, but not nearly so flavorful.

### Water, Juices, and Soft Drinks

Argentine tap water is potable almost everywhere except in some of the northerly tropical deserts; ask for *agua de la canilla*. For ice, request it *con hielo*. Visitors with truly sensitive stomachs might consider bottled water, which is widely available. Ask for *agua pura* or *agua mineral;* some brands, such as Eco de los Andes and Villavicencio, are spring water, while others are purified. For carbonated water, add *con gas* or ask for the even cheaper *soda*, which comes in large siphon bottles.

*Gaseosas* (in the plural) are sweetened bottled soft drinks (including most of the major transnational brands but also local versions such as the refreshing tonic water Paso de los Toros).

Fresh-squeezed *jugos* (fruit juices) are exceptionally good though limited in their diversity. *Naranja* (orange) is the standard; to be sure it's fresh, ask for *jugo de naranja exprimido*.

## COOLING DOWN WITH HELADOS

Though it stems from the Italian tradition, Argentine ice cream lacks the high international profile of gelato—when a pair of *porteños* opened an ice creamery in the author's hometown of Oakland, California, they chose the compromise name of Tango Gelato, stressing its Italian origins without suppressing its Buenos Aires way station. Buenos Aires has a remarkable number of high-quality ice creameries, and remarkable diversity of flavors, ranging from the standard vanilla and chocolate (with multiple variations, including white chocolate and bittersweet chocolate) to lemon mousse, *sambayón* (resembling eggnog), the Argentine staple *dulce de leche* (caramelized milk, its own major food group), and countless others.

Buenos Aires has two kinds of *heladerías*. The first is the chain that produces large industrial batches; some of the chains' products are nevertheless very fine, others are truly awful, and most fall in between. The other is the small neighborhood ice creamery that creates *helados artesanales* in smaller quantities.

Gradually overshadowing the fading Freddo, **Chungo,** tel. 0800/888-248646, www.chungo .com.ar, is probably the best industrial-quality ice cream, and is good enough by any standard. It has branches at Avenida Las Heras and Rodríguez Peña in Recoleta, Olleros 1660 in Palermo, and Virrey del Pino 2500 in Colegiales, on the border with Belgrano. **Bianca,** Avenida Scalabrini Ortiz 2295, tel. 4832-3357, is the Palermo franchise of a medium-sized chain that offers a wide selection of flavors. Founded by the former owners of Freddo, always crowded **Persicco,** Salguero 2591,

tel. 4801-5549, is putting up a challenge to the other chains.

Over the past couple of decades **Cadore,** Avenida Corrientes 1695 in Congreso, has been consistently one of the best ice creameries in the city, but its small storefront (often obscured by construction) gives it a much lower profile than chain stalwarts like Freddo and Chungo. Both good and inexpensive, **Sorrento** has branches at Avenida Rivadavia 2051 in Congreso (Balvanera) and at Olavarría 658 in La Boca.

The Microcentro is shorter on ice creameries than might be expected, but **Vía Flaminia,** Florida 121, is a more-than-respectable choice. Monserrat's **Fridda,** Santiago del Estero 502, tel. 4381-1069, is a small but outstanding ice creamery with low prices. Across from Parque Lezama, at the corner of Brasil and Defensa, **Florencia,** tel. 4307-6407, is San Telmo's best. Palermo Viejo's **Tempo,** J.L. Borges 2392, tel. 4775-2392, features unusual fruit flavors like mango and maracuyá. **La Piave,** at Salguero and Seguí, tel. 4801-2346, is also worth a stop.

Belgrano's **Bella Italia** (no relation to the restaurant and café of the same name in Palermo), Avenida Cabildo 2628, tel. 4787-2245, has all the usual flavors plus a few—*crema de yerba mate* and *zanahoria* (carrot)—that are hard to find anywhere (they claim to be the only ice creamery in the city making *mate,* though there are several in Argentine Patagonia that do so). The owners also sell homemade jams and preserves. Other possibilities in Belgrano include **Furchi,** Avenida Cabildo 1506, and especially the hole-in-the-wall **Gruta,** Sucre 2356, tel. 4784-8417.

## Alcoholic Drinks

Argentina is less famous for its wines than Chile is, perhaps because most production is for domestic consumption rather than export; Argentina is the world's fifth-largest wine producer. Most wine-making takes place in the western and northwestern provinces of Mendoza, San Juan, and Salta, but it's increasing in the southerly Patagonian province of Río Negro.

*Tinto* is red wine, and *blanco* is white. Good wine is almost always reasonably priced, even during times of an overinflated peso and high inflation. The best restaurants have a wide selection, usually in full bottles though sometimes it's possible to get a *media botella* (half bottle) or, increasingly frequently, wine by the glass. Argentines often mix their table wines—even reds—with soda water or ice.

An increasing number of wine bars also offer Spanish tapas, sushi, and other light meals. Keep an eye out for *torrontés,* a unique Argentine white varietal from the vineyards around Cafayate, in Salta province.

Since the main wine regions are in western and northwestern Argentina, nowhere close to Buenos Aires, wine tourism is not an easy option from the capital. With production booming across the Río de la Plata in Uruguay, however, that country may soon offer possibilities.

Although Argentine wines are more than worthwhile, Argentines themselves are leaning more toward beer, which tastes best as *chopp* (direct from the tap) rather than from bottles or cans. The most widely available beer is Quilmes, produced in its namesake suburb across the Riachuelo from La Boca.

Hard liquor is not quite so popular, but whiskey, gin, and the like are readily available. *Ginebra bols* (different from gin) and *caña* (cane alcohol) are local specialties.

Argentina's legal drinking age is 18.

# Restaurants

Buenos Aires has a fast-evolving restaurant scene that can be hard to keep up with. One good source for the latest developments is *Los Recomendados,* written and updated annually (in both English and Spanish as of the 2003 edition) by Alicia Delgado and María Esther Pérez and published by Editorial El Ateneo. The publication provides information on 100 of the best restaurants in the capital and Buenos Aires province.

The Friday edition of the daily tabloid *Clarín* offers a variety of restaurant reviews. For English speakers, Dereck Foster's Sunday column in the English-language *Buenos Aires Herald* offers some of the latest suggestions; a separate column covers Argentine wines.

There are good restaurants in many parts of town, but the best barrios for dining out are the Microcentro/Catedral al Sur, Retiro, Recoleta, and Palermo (including the Palermo Viejo and Las Cañitas neighborhoods).

For breakfast options, look at the separate entries for cafés and confiterías in the Arts and Entertainment chapter.

## MONSERRAT/CATEDRAL AL SUR AND VICINITY

In general, the area from Avenida de Mayo south toward San Telmo is less inventive than rejuvenated neighborhoods in the northern barrios, but there are some notable exceptions and some good lunchtime options, especially west of Avenida 9 de Julio.

The southerly sector of Monserrat, along Balcarce, is home to many new restaurants of good but not exceptional quality. **La Sal,** Balcarce 598, tel. 4342-9821, serves fine midday lunches for around US$3.50; you'll get a choice of meat or seafood entrées plus dessert and wine, with good service in a casual atmosphere. Relocated from Recoleta, open for lunch and dinner, **Café Molière,** Chile 299, tel. 4343-2623, offers an international menu, and tango shows on some nights.

Housed in a recycled warehouse that also serves as a venue for live theater and music, **La Trastienda,** Balcarce 460, tel. 4342-7650, is

# THE RITE OF YERBA MATE

It's rarely on the menu, but the single most important social drink in Argentina and most of the Río de la Plata region—including Uruguay, Paraguay, and southern Brazil—is *yerba mate,* the dried, shredded leaf of *Ilex paraguayensis.*

Espresso, in its many forms, may dominate café society, but the *mate* infusion transcends commercialism. Its production is a major industry, but its consumption belongs to home and hearth. Native to the forests of the upper Río Paraná, a relative of the everyday holly, *yerba mate* became a commercial crop in plantations on colonial Jesuit missions.

Transplanted Europeans took to it—the Austrian Jesuit Martin Dobrizhoffer asserted that mate "speedily counteracts the languor arising from the burning climate, and assuages both hunger and thirst"—but, unlike coffee and tea, it never really established markets across the Atlantic or even elsewhere in the Americas, except in parts of Chile.

Production diminished with the Jesuits' expulsion from the Americas in 1767, but the "Paraguayan tea" kept its place in humble households and privileged palaces alike. According to the English sailor Emeric Essex Vidal, who visited Buenos Aires in the 1820s,

> Mate *is in every house all day long, and the compliment of the country is to hand the* mate *cup to every visitor, the same cup and tube serving for all, and an attendant being kept in waiting to replenish for each person. Throughout the provinces, the weary traveler, let him stop at what hovel soever he may, is sure to be presented with the hospitable* mate-*cup, which, unless his prejudices are very strong indeed, will be found a great refreshment.*

In fact, the purpose of *mate* is hospitality; preparing and serving it is a ritual. It is also an equalizer, as everyone sips in turn from the same *bombilla* (metallic tube or straw) placed in the same *yerba*-stuffed *mate* (a term which also means "gourd"),

filled from the *cebador* (brewer) with slightly-below-boiling-temperature water. It is customary to drink the gourd dry, and then return it to the *cebador,* who will pass it clockwise around the group. Note that, in this context, to say *gracias* (thank you) means that you want no more.

Not all rituals are equal, though, and *mate*'s material culture can differ dramatically between social classes. Although having a servant whose sole job was to prepare and serve it is a thing of the past, upper-class households own far more elaborate paraphernalia than working-class families do—just as British nobility have more ornate tea sets than the untitled. Simple *mates* might be made from plain calabashes or from plastic, but others might be made of elaborately carved wood set in silver or even gold; the *bombilla,* likewise, can range from utilitarian aluminum to ceremonial silver.

Most Argentines prefer *mate amargo* (bitter, i.e. without sugar), but northerners often take it *dulce,* with sugar and fragrant herbs known as *yuyos* (literally, weeds). While it's a mostly homebound custom in Argentina, Uruguayans (who consume even more yerba mate than Argentines) make it a public affair as they walk the streets with leather-encased gourds and enormous thermoses. In the ferocious Paraguayan summer, street vendors sell ice-cold *yerba* in the form of *tereré.*

Supermarkets sell *yerba* in bulk packages with engaging designs that look half a century old. It is also available in tea bags as *mate cocido,* which is weaker, and may be more palatable to neophytes, than the first bitter swallows from the freshly prepared gourd. Do not confuse it, however, with *mate de coca,* another innocuous infusion made from the leaf of the notorious coca plant.

Fortunately for its Argentine aficionados, *mate* is inexpensive. No one really has to worry, as Dobrizhoffer did, that:

> If many topers in Europe waste their substance by an immoderate use of wine and other intoxicating liquors, there are no fewer in America who drink away their fortunes in potations of the herb of Paraguay.

mostly standard Italo-Argentine but, surprisingly, lacks stuffed pastas such as ravioli. Lunchtime specials cost around US$3, individual entrées US$2.50–3.50.

In the winter of 2002, the owners of **Trotamundos San Telmo,** Defensa 683, tel. 4343-8342, had the temerity to open a new restaurant in the midst of Argentina's worst economic crisis ever. Open for lunch and dinner daily, their promising "Patagonian bistro" features uncommon items like scallops (around US$4) and Patagonian lamb (US$3), a 6–9 P.M. happy hour at the bar, and even a basement art space.

Peruvian food, uncommon in Buenos Aires, is worth seeking out. **Status,** south of the Plaza del Congreso at Virrey Cevallos 178, tel. 4382-8531, offers inexpensive home-style Peruvian dishes such as *aji de gallina* (chicken in a walnut cream sauce over rice, with potatoes), *lomo saltado* (stir-fried beef with vegetables), and *papa a la huancaína* (a spicy potato dish) in the US$2–4 range. Some of the garnishes are far spicier than most *porteños* can handle.

The Spanish seafood restaurant **Plaza Mayor,** Venezuela 1399, tel. 4383-0788, is part of a complex including the parrilla **Diablada,** Venezuela 1402, tel. 4381-4766, and the Italian **Campo dei Fiori,** San José 491, tel. 4381-8402, www.grupoplazamayor.com. The restaurant has San Telmo style, including filete-painted lamps hanging from high ceilings, and serves an excellent salmon gruyere (US$5) and other more expensive items.

**Penélope,** Avenida Independencia 1702 at Solís, tel. 4381-6715, is a fine new Catalán (Catalonian) restaurant; for US$15, the diverse fish and seafood *parrillada* easily suffices for two diners, but try also the lightly breaded *rabas* (large squid). The staff is professional, the service attentive, and the wine selection ample and reasonably priced.

In the barrio of San Cristóbal, near Monserrat's western edge, **Miramar,** Avenida San Juan 1999 at Sarandí, tel. 4304-4261, is a reliable *rotisería* (rotisserie);it's an unfashionable restaurant unsuitable for a formal meal or romantic night out, but great for inexpensive, unpretentious lunches or dinners with quietly profes-

sional service. Unlike many recently gentrified—or plasticized—*porteño* cafés, this classic corner bar sports fading posters from classic Argentine movies thumbtacked to the walls as a backdrop for surprisingly good entrées like oxtail soup and *gambas al ajillo* (garlic prawns). Prices range US$2–5 for most items.

According to *Buenos Aires Herald* restaurant critic Dereck Foster, the best Spanish food in town comes from the so-new-that-it's-still-nameless restaurant at the **NH City Hotel,** Bolívar 160, tel. 4121-6464. Monserrat has several other Spanish/Basque seafood options, though, including the author's personal favorite **Laurak Bat,** a traditional classic at Avenida Belgrano 1144, tel. 4381-0682. Consider also the **Club Vasco Francés,** Moreno 1370, tel. 4382-0244 and **El Hispano,** Salta 20, tel. 4382-7543.

# MICROCENTRO AND VICINITY

Many of the city's traditional favorites are located downtown and in nearby neighborhoods. One of the most economical choices, though, is the cafetería at the supermarket **Coto,** Viamonte 1571.

**Pizzería Güerrín,** Avenida Corrientes 1372, tel. 4371-8141, is a one-of-a-kind that sells pizza by the slice at the standup counter—the fugazza and fugazzeta are simply exquisite (or exquisitely simple), and the baked chicken empanadas (avoid the fried ones) are exceptional. There are many more options if you choose table service. **La Americana,** Avenida Callao 83, tel. 4371-0202, is a venerable chain pizzería with outstanding empanadas.

The misleadingly named **Palacio de la Papa Frita,** on the pedestrian mall at Lavalle 954, tel. 4322-1559, is a *porteño* classic with a diverse Argentine menu; there's another branch at Avenida Corrientes 1612, tel. 4374-8063. For just US$3, their *arroz a la valenciana,* with chicken, saffron, and a mixture of vegetables, can feed at least two hungry mouths.

Another Microcentro classic is **Los Inmortales,** Avenida Corrientes 1369, tel. 4373-5303, a pizzería seemingly unchanged since the days of Carlos Gardel, whose photographs line the walls. There's another branch at Lavalle 748, tel. 4322-5493.

**Bar La Robla,** Viamonte 1615, tel. 4811-4484, belongs to a small chain of Spanish seafood restaurants, but also has an extensive pasta menu. Entrées range from about US$2 for the simplest pasta dishes to US$4 or so for more elaborate items like paella.

**Broccolino,** Esmeralda 776, tel. 4322-9848, is an unfailingly reliable Italian choice, with impeccable service (all the waiters speak at least two languages) and a diverse menu ranging from pizza and pasta to seafood and beef dishes. Entrées range US$3–6, but most are in the US$4–5 range. It's open for lunch and dinner.

For a 19th-century dining experience with contemporary flourishes, try the **Club del Progreso,** in the same site at Sarmiento 1334 since 1852, tel. 4371-5053, www.clubdelprogreso.com. With its high ceilings, classic library and other features, it served as a location for the film *Imagining Argentina,* with Antonio Banderas and Emma Thompson. For about US$5 pp, the fixed-price dinners are a little bland, but the singing waiters, with their tangos and boleros, are worth the price.

In the same location since 1929, **ABC,** near the junction of the two pedestrian malls at Lavalle 545, tel. 4393-3992, seems a relic of the Austro-Hungarian empire, with its continental atmosphere and focus on sausage, schnitzel, and goulash. It's a popular lunch spot for bankers and businessmen from La City.

Nearby, on the edge of the financial district, lunchtime favorite **La Posada de 1820,** Tucumán 501, tel. 4314-4557, serves a standard but above-average Argentine menu of beef and pasta at reasonable prices (US$3–6 per entrée) in bright, cheerful surroundings accented with burnished wood.

The Microcentro and nearby neighborhoods have several tourist-oriented parrillas that make a fetish out of staking their steaks over hot coals in circular barbecue pits tended by bogus gauchos in full regalia behind picture windows; while they play for the cliché and serve far too many people to be able to give patrons individual attention, their food quality is outstanding

and their prices reasonable. Among the best choices are **La Estancia,** Lavalle 941, tel. 4326-0330; **La Rural,** Suipacha 453, tel. 4322-2654; and the more expensive **Los Troncos,** Suipacha 732, tel. 4322-1295.

For a more characteristic *porteño* experience, though, try one of the cheaper bare-bones parrillas like Congreso's **Pippo,** Paraná 356, tel. 4374-0762, or **Chiquilín,** Montevideo 321, tel. 4373-5163. For an antidote, try the vegetarian **La Huerta del Sol,** Lavalle 893, tel. 4327-2862.

Perhaps the best downtown restaurant of any sort, the banker's favorite **Sabot,** 25 de Mayo 756, tel. 4313-6587, serves Italo-Argentine dishes of the highest quality in a very masculine environment (women are few but not unwelcome) with good-humored but extraordinarily professional service. Moderately expensive by current standards, most entrées like *matambre de cerdo, chivito,* and some fish dishes cost in the US$5–7 range. A pleasant surprise is the *mate de coca* made from fresh coca leaves, for digestive purposes only.

It's not so formal as it once was, but most lunchtime customers are still well-dressed businessmen at the classic **Clark's,** Sarmiento 645, tel. 4325-1960/3624, whose Victorian atmosphere still oozes out of the magnificent mahogany woodwork. With outstanding meat and seafood and impeccable service, it's one of the more expensive choices in town—even ñoquis, one of the cheapest items on most Argentine menus, cost US$7, not including IVA.

# PUERTO MADERO

Over the past few years, redeveloped Puerto Madero has made a big impact on the restaurant scene, but more because of the area's overall tourist appeal than because of its quality—with a couple of exceptions, the food is unimpressive. Most restaurants, though, have outdoor as well as indoor seating, and when the weather's fine it's is a great option for people-watching along the yacht harbor. Because the area is popular with foreigners who stay at nearby luxury hotels, restaurants here are more accustomed to dealing with dinnertimes as early as 7 P.M.

Opposite the northerly Dique No. 4 at Alicia Moreau de Justo 516, tel. 4313-1336, the best parrilla is **Cabaña Las Lilas,** the waterfront branch of the Recoleta favorite. Often packed for lunch despite relatively high prices in the midst of a crisis, it offers complimentary champagne and snacks while you wait; its *bife de chorizo* (US$7) may be the finest in town. Next door, **La Caballeriza,** Alicia Moreau de Justo 580, tel. 4314-2648, is also highly regarded for grilled beef.

At the north end of Dique No. 4, **La Madeleine,** Avenida Alicia Moreau de Justo 102, tel. 4315-6200, serves a respectable but unexceptional beef, chicken, and pasta menu, with lunchtime specials in the US$5 range. **Puerto Sorrento,** Alicia Moreau de Justo 410, tel. 4319-8730, is a the best seafood choice in the area.

On the west side of Dique No. 3, **Rodizio,** Alicia Moreau de Justo 840, tel. 4334-3638. is a Brazilian-style parrilla. Across the basin, **Il Gran Caruso,** Olga Cossentini 791, tel. 4515-0707, is a cavernous Italian restaurant with lunch specials for US$5; normally, pasta and seafood entrées range US$7–9.

Alongside the southernmost Dique No. 1, **La Bistecca,** Alicia Moreau de Justo 1888, tel. 4514-4999, is a popular buffet parrilla with several branches around town. **Pizza Banana,** Alicia Moreau de Justo 2030, tel. 4314-9500, serves the obvious.

## SAN TELMO AND VICINITY

Despite the barrio's tourist allure, San Telmo lags behind other barrios in gastronomic appeal. That's not to say there are no places worth visiting, but for the most part they're better lunchtime bargains than dinnertime indulgences.

The northwestern Argentine provinces of Salta and Jujuy produce spicier-than-normal empanadas and stews like *locro,* available cheaply at **La Carretería,** Brasil 656, tel. 4300-5564.

**Medio y Medio,** Chile 316, tel. 4300-1396, bursts with lunchgoers in search of the Uruguayan caloric overload known as the *chivito,* a steak sandwich embellished with lettuce, cheese, tomato, and bacon; a fried egg crowns the *chiv-*

*ito al plato,* which includes a larger cut of beef and potato salad, green salad, and French fries. The place takes its name from the popular Uruguayan blend of sparkling and white wines.

Sunday visitors to the Plaza Dorrego flea market line up outside **DesNivel,** Defensa 855, tel. 4300-9081, for parrillada and pasta at bargain prices; it's open for lunch (except Mondays) and dinner daily. No-frills **La Vieja Rotisería,** Defensa 963, tel. 4362-5660, is an even more economical choice with a similar menu (entrées US$3–5).

Just north of Plaza Dorrego, in a recycled colonial house, **La Casa de Estéban de Luca,** Defensa 1000, tel. 4361-4338, serves a variety of international dishes along with the conventional parrillada. Prices are mid-range—US$5–8 for entrées.

If you're looking for a traditional San Telmo parrilla with plenty of barrio atmosphere, including *filete* ornaments by Martiniano Arce, visit **1880,** opposite Parque Lezama at Defensa 1665, tel. 4307-2746. Most entrées fall into the US$3–4 range, including pasta dishes like ñoquis.

**Abril,** Balcarce 722, tel. 4342-8000, is a small atractive bistro whose US$4 fixed-price dinners are more diverse and lighter than the average Argentine meal. The service is good and friendly, even when the restaurant is understaffed. **Nicole de Marseille,** Defensa 714, tel. 4362-2340, is a Francophile institution with moderate prices, especially at lunchtime.

Plaza Dorrego's **Pappa Deus,** in a late 18th-century house at Bethlem 423, tel. 4361-2110, is more imaginative than most San Telmo eateries, serving items like arugula and sun-dried tomatoes, and a tremendous pumpkin-stuffed ravioli, but pricey desserts. Entrées cost around US$3–4; the restaurant has both sidewalk and indoor seating.

**Hostal del Canigó,** Chacabuco 863, tel. 4304-5250 or 4300-5252, specializes in Catalonian seafood, other Spanish dishes, and the occasional standard Argentine item. Best at lunch, it occupies the classic dining room—dark mahogany woodwork and Spanish tiles—of the Casal de Catalunya cultural center. The **Taberna Baska,** Chile 980, tel. 4383-0903, serves Basque dishes.

sidewalk café, La Boca

**Sr. Telmo**, Defensa 756, tel. 4363-0100, is an attractive new pizzeria that also serves pasta and meat. **El Caldero,** Carlos Calvo 240, tel. 4300-3883, has a good but mostly run-of-the-mill Argentine menu, with attractive prices around US$2–3 for most entrées, and attentive service.

Several places in the vicinity of Plaza Dorrego offer pretty good tango shows along with Sunday lunch, including **El Balcón,** Humberto Primo 461, which has a US$3 parrillada, and **Mitos Argentinos,** Humberto Primo 489, tel. 4362-7810. The latter hosts live music, including rock bands, late at night on weekends.

## LA BOCA

La Boca is not an enclave of haute cuisine, but there's good enough food to be found for lunch—most people visit the barrio during the daytime—and even an occasional dinnertime foray.

With sidewalk seating on the Vuelta de Rocha, adorned with colorful *filete,* **La Barbería,** Pedro de Mendoza 1959, tel. 4301-8770, serves em-panadas, tapas, pasta, pizza, sandwiches, seafood, and beer and cold hard cider straight from the tap. Prices are moderate, in the US$3–7 range. **El Corsario,** next door at Pedro de Mendoza 1981, tel. 4301-6579, is almost indistinguishable from La Barbería.

The **Caminito Tango Club,** Del Valle Iberlucea 1151, tel. 4301-1520, offers a lunchtime tango show alongside its menu of beef, seafood and pasta, with most entrées in the US$3–6 range. **El Samovar de Rasputín,** Del Valle Iberlucea 1251, tel. 4302-3190, is a cheap restaurant at midday and a lively blues-and-rock venue on weekend evenings.

Across the block from La Bombonera stadium, **La Cancha,** Brandsen 697, tel. 3362-2975, draws soccer fans for standard Argentine fare. Only a block off Avenida Almirante Brown, several garishly painted pizza-and-pasta cantinas draw the Argentine tourist crowd for lunch and dinner: **Tres Amigos,** at Necochea and Suárez, tel. 4301-2441; **Il Piccolo Vapore;** tel. 4301-4455, at the opposite corner of Necochea and Suárez; and **Gennarino,** Necochea 1210, tel. 4301-6617.

In an area where taxis are obligatory at night and maybe even advisable in the daytime though some cabbies have trouble finding it, **El Obrero,** Agustín Cafferena 64, tel. 4362-9912, is where Argentine and foreign celebrities go slumming for steaks. El Obrero draws an international clientele on the order of Bono, Robert Duvall, and others, but it hasn't even taken down the photo of disgraced ex-President Fernando De la Rúa. Its walls are plastered with images of soccer icon Diego Maradona and little additional decor to speak of. There is no printed menu—check the chalkboards scattered around the dining room. No entrée exceeds about US$3–5, and most are cheaper.

> *El Obrero is where Argentine and foreign celebrities go slumming for steaks. It draws international clientele like Bono and Robert Duvall, and its walls are plastered with images of soccer icon Diego Maradona. There is no printed menu— check the chalkboards scattered around the dining room.*

4942-5853 or 4943-6442, occupies an improbable Once location with no other restaurants and few other businesses of any kind. Relatively expensive by current standards, with lunch for US$10 and up, it may be a lesser value than some more recent additions to the Asian scene. It's open noon–2:30 P.M. and 7–11:30 P.M. weekdays, Saturday for dinner only.

Since the 1940s, **La Viña del Abasto,** Jean Jaurés 3007, tel. 4963-4890, has served the Once neighborhood with standard Argentine dishes. Opposite the renovated Mercado del Abasto, and offering a similar menu, **La Recova del Abasto,** Anchorena 557, tel. 4866-4244, is a pioneer on a pedestrian mall that hasn't yet quite matched redevelopers' plans.

## ONCE AND THE ABASTO (BALVANERA)

Congreso's **La Continental,** Avenida Callao 202, has fine chicken empanadas and pizza slices, including a particularly choice *fugazzeta;* there are several other branches around town. **Quorum Express,** Combate de los Pozos 61, tel. 4951-0855, is a buffet-style restaurant with lunch for US$2 and dinner for US$3.

Known for its Pantagruelian portions, **Cervantes II,** Perón 1883, tel. 4372-8869, is the place to load up on carbohydrates like ravioli, gnocchi, and the like. Most entrées are large enough for two people at this utilitarian but agreeable place, whose service is professional. **La Ciboulette,** Sarmiento 1802, tel. 4373-2178, is a well-established vegetarian all-you-can-eat.

The entire diverse menu at the Peruvian **El Gran Combo,** Alsina 2163, tel. 4953-3070, is available only on weekends; otherwise, it offers the most basic dishes like *lomo saltado* and *ají de gallina.* Portions are gigantic, and single diners may have trouble finishing their meals.

Authentically Japanese in minimalist decor and cuisine, **Ichisou,** Venezuela 2145, tel.

## CABALLITO AND VICINITY

The menu at Almagro's **Malevo,** Mario Bravo 908, tel. 4861-1008, is an eclectic mix of wok-fried vegetables and meats, fish, tempura, and the like, with most entrées in the US$3–4 range. Painted in bright Mexican hues, its walls adorned with paintings for sale, it's open for lunch and dinner.

**Pierino,** Billinghurst 809, tel. 4864-5715, is a more traditional sort of place, a cantina whose location goes by the name Esquina Astor Piazzola after the late tango master. Olive-lovers should check the open barrels at **La Casa de las Aceitunas,** Guardia Vieja 3602, tel. 4862-0280.

**Los Sabios,** Avenida Corrientes 3733, tel. 4864-4407, provides a vegetarian alternative.

## RETIRO

**Supermercado Disco,** Montevideo 1037, has an upstairs cafetería that offers a surprisingly good, cheap and diverse selection of fast food. **Alimentari,** San Martín 899, tel. 4313-9382, is a popular breakfast and lunch cafetería.

**La Querencia,** Esmeralda 1392, tel. 4393-3202, prepares excellent spicy Tucumán-style empanadas and other northwestern Argentine dishes. **Lo de Alvarado,** Marcelo T. del Alvear 1521, tel. 4812-3462, serves similar fare from the adjacent province of Salta. Downtown lunchgoers flock to **Payanca,** Suipacha 1015, tel. 4312-5209, for similar salteño cuisine.

**Piazza Dante,** Paraná 1209, tel. 4811-2222, is a slightly upscale Italian venue that still manages a fixed-price lunch for less than US$3, with a far more diverse pasta, pizza, beef, and fish menu a la carte. The barrio branch of the traditional pizza chain **Los Inmortales** is at Marcelo T. de Alvear 1234, tel. 4393-6124, but the hippest and most adventurous pizzeria is the garishly decorated **Filo,** San Martín 975, tel. 4311-0312.

Mexican food is unusual and usually none too good in Buenos Aires, but **Guadalajara de Noche,** Montevideo 1669, tel. 4815-4468, is a respectable representative for ceviche (US$3) and mixed fajitas (US$5), but some Mexican staples like guacamole and enchiladas are not always available. **Sukhothai,** next door at Montevideo 1671, tel. 4811-9442, provides a fixed-price menu (US$3) with a selection of Thai entrées.

Tourist-oriented parrillas are numerous but almost invariably good—two of the best are **Las Nazarenas,** Reconquista 1132, tel. 4312-5559, and **La Chacra,** Avenida Córdoba 941, tel. 4322-1409. **Dora,** a traditional Spanish-Argentine favorite at Avenida L.N. Alem 1016, tel. 4311-2891, often gets attention for the size of its portions, but deserves at least as much recognition for the quality of its beef, seafood, pasta, and desserts. Entrées run in the US$3–4 range.

Retiro also has a pair of vegetarian landmarks. **La Esquina de las Flores,** Avenida Córdoba 1587, tel. 4813-3630, is a Retiro institution not just for its health-food market and upstairs restaurant, but also for its efforts at diversifying the Argentine diet through public workshops and radio and TV programs. Takeaway meals are available. Its next-door competitor is **Lotos,** Avenida Córdoba 1577,

tel. 4814-4552, which is more cafetería-style and also has market produce and takeaway dishes. Both are open for weekday lunches, but the markets proper keep longer hours.

Chile, better known for its diverse seafood and produce than its beef, has a longstanding gastronomic representative in **Los Chilenos,** Suipacha 1042, tel. 4328-3123. It doesn't, however, suggest the variety of recent food developments in the Chilean capital of Santiago, one of South America's welcome surprises.

Even in the midst of economic crisis, **Tancat,** Paraguay 645, tel. 4312-5442, is a first-rate and wildly popular tasca, for lunches around US$3–5 pp; don't miss the *jamón serrano* (ham) appetizer. Reservations are almost essential for tables, which are few, but plenty of people can jam into the long wooden bar, behind which are shelves of wines covered with business cards, posters and photos. Its Spanish owner takes a genuine personal interest in everyone who comes through the door.

The **Empire Bar,** the ex-Lotus Bar at Tres Sargentos 427, tel. 4312-5706, recently split from Las Cañitas's culinary landmark Lotus Neo Thai, but still offers a fine Thai menu with some spicy dishes. Midday specials go for around US$3, most other entrées for US$3–4, and there's a 6–9 P.M. happy hour at the bar. The decor is contemporary.

Highly regarded **Tres Cuartos,** Florida 947, tel. 4314-4045, offers variations on standard Argentine dishes like ravioli (stuffed with hake, for instance), with a midday menu for about US$4. Unfortunately, even though they ceremoniously ask whether you prefer smoking or nonsmoking, enforcement is nil and tobacco junkies light up wherever they feel like it.

## RECOLETA AND BARRIO NORTE

For spicy northwestern Argentine dishes like *locro,* one of the best values in town is **El Sanjuanino,** Posadas 1515, tel. 4804-2909; the empanadas are particularly choice. **La Querencia,** Junín 1308, tel. 4821-1888, is part of a small chain that offers similar fare.

It's fallen well behind other restaurants in the barrio, but the US$3.50 *tenedor libre* at **Río Rhin Norte,** Tagle 2521, tel. 4802-0197, is still a good value for the budget-conscious. **Bar Rodi,** Vicente López 1900, tel. 4801-5230, bursts with Recoleta diners in search of beef and pasta, though it's far less stylish than other nearby eateries.

**Pizza Cero,** Schiaffino 2009, tel. 4807-1919, is an above-average pizza chain in both price and quality. Less chic but more enduring, **Los Inmortales** has branches at Junín 1727, tel. 4803-3331, and at Avenida Callao 1165, tel. 4813-7551.

**José Luis,** Avenida Quintana 456, tel. 4807-0606, is an Asturian seafood restaurant that stresses fresher and lighter dishes than most of its counterparts. Entrées are mostly in the US$7 range; it's open daily for lunch and dinner.

There are several mostly interchangeable mid-range to upscale restaurants in the Village Recoleta complex at Vicente López and Junín, including **La Strada,** Vicente López 2008, tel. 4802-0905, which has good pasta and excellent desserts, sidewalk seating, and somewhat erratic service. **Monaco,** Vicente López 2052, tel. 4807-5330, for pizza and sandwiches; and the more elegant parrilla **La Caballeriza,** Vicente López 2006, tel. 4806-3262.

Across from the cemetery, **Tenorio,** Junín 1793, 4802-6214, is a mid-range parrilla with a self-conscious and even aggressive hipness. It has outdoor seating. Nearby **Clark's,** Junín 1777, tel. 4801-9502, is the Recoleta branch of the Microcentro's Victorian institution, but it lacks the venerable style of the latter.

The Barrio Norte favorite **Los Pinos,** Azcuénaga 1500, tel. 4822-8704, occupies an old-style apothecary, its wooden cases still stocked with antique bottles and rising nearly to the ceiling. It offers fixed-price lunch and dinner specials in the US$3–5 range, with substantial choice; the a la carte menu of beef, seafood and pasta is not much more expensive, as the comparably priced entrées include a side order. The service is well-intentioned but inconsistent.

The **French Bistro,** French 2301, tel. 4806-9331, serves a Gallic international menu in European-style surroundings. **Kugenhaus,** Azcuénaga 1570, tel. 4805-8512, sells Middle European–style pastries and takeout dishes. Charging US$5 pp, the Middle Eastern buffet at the **Restaurant del Club Sirio,** Pacheco de Melo 1902, tel. 4806-5764, is open nightly except Sunday.

Internationally recognized **Oviedo,** Beruti 2602, tel. 4822-5415, specializes in seafood but also serves Patagonian lamb and standards like steak, with most entrées in the US$4–7 range. It's open for lunch and dinner, but unfortunately thinks its air purification system justifies its being a cigar bar as well.

## PALERMO

Palermo is, without question, the center of innovation in Argentine dining. The main geographical areas of interest are Palermo Viejo, subdivided into Palermo Soho, centered around Plaza Serrano (which is also known as Plazoleta Cortázar); Palermo Hollywood, north of Avenida Juan B. Justo; the Botánico, between Avenida Las Heras and Avenida del Libertador; and Las Cañitas, in the area between Avenida Luis María Campos and the Campo Argentino de Polo. That said, there are other options scattered around the city's largest barrio.

One of the cheapest choices, by no means bad, is the citywide supermarket **Coto,** which has a cafetería at Avenida Cabildo 545. **Quitaucho,** Salguero 1857, tel. 4822-4936, makes spicy *salteñas,* the northwestern Argentine version of empanadas, plus other regional specialties like *locro* and *carbonada* (both stews), tamales, and *humitas* at low prices. **Lo de Alvarado,** Mansilla 3428, tel. 4825-1133, also sells *salteñas.*

### Palermo Soho

Plaza Serrano is the heartbeat of Palermo Viejo and, though it's not the best spot for dining, there are acceptable choices like **Cantina La Plazita,** Serrano 1636, with standard Argentine choices for US$2–3. The best option in the immediate vicinity, though, is **Spirit,** Serrano 1550, tel. 4833-4360, a tapas and oyster bar that's crowded even in the midst of economic crisis;

an ample plate of seafood tapas, sufficient for two persons, costs only US$10.

Away from the mad bustle of Plazoleta Cortázar, with minimalist modern decor, **Splendid,** Gorriti 5099, tel. 4833-4477, www.splendidrestaurant.com, prepares perfectly cooked penne pasta with fresh mushrooms, and a fine maracuyá (passion fruit) ice cream with raspberry sauce. Open daily for lunch and dinner, it has first-class service and live jazz Thursday and Saturday around 10 P.M.

Distinctly unhip compared to its neighbors—unless you consider Polish coats-of-arms the latest in cool—**La Casa Polaca,** Jorge Luis Borges 2076, tel. 4899-0514, has a huge and diverse menu based on Polish specialties like pierogi. Meals are inexpensive, the service is friendly, and it's also the place to take Polish classes. Hours are 8 P.M.–12:30 A.M. daily except Sunday and Monday.

**El Horno,** Güemes 4689, tel. 4773-8364, offers even spicier Bolivian salteñas, but for quality-to-price ratio, the hands-down best choice for empanadas and regional dishes is **La Cupertina,** Cabrera 5300, tel. 4777-3711. The service may be inconsistent, but the chicken empanadas and the *humitas en chala* (similar to tamales, wrapped in corn stalks) are exquisite and so cheap that price is no object, even with wine; try also the desserts, especially the Spanish custard *natillas* and *arroz con leche.* It's open for lunch and dinner daily except Monday but closes early, around 11 P.M.

**La Esquina de las Flores,** the capital's vegetarian landmark, has a market and takeaway outlet at Gurruchaga 1632, tel. 4832-8528. Nearby **Kayoko,** Gurruchaga 1650, tel. 4832-6158, serves an exceptional sushi/sashimi mix (US$12) for two, plus other light Japanese dishes, but the ginger is a little sour. In fine weather, try the shady streetside deck; the service is fine. For lunch, try also **Freud & Fahler,** Gurruchaga 1750, tel. 4833-2153, which has a US$3.50 menu with choices like fish, risotto, and ravioli, plus starters and wine.

Attractive **Azafrán,** Honduras 5143, tel. 4832-6487, specializes in slightly more elaborate versions of Argentine standards like ravioli, but hasn't yet reached the level of neighbors like **Social Paraíso,** Honduras 5182, tel. 4831-4556, an intimate nouvelle-cuisine place with a US$3 lunch special that features items like bruschetta and risotto; other entrées fall into the US$4–6 range. Open for lunch and dinner daily except Sunday and Monday, it also has innovative desserts.

**El Federal,** down the block at Honduras 5254, tel. 4832-6500, attracts an upper-class clientele to high-priced versions of regional specialties from throughout the country: potatoes and quinoa from Jujuy, *cabrito* (goat) from the western Cuyo provinces, jabalí (wild boar) from Bariloche, and Patagonia lamb. Open for lunch and dinner, its entrées cost in the US$6–7 range.

Popular **Bar 6,** Armenia 1676, tel. 4833-6807, embodies the modishly recycled Palermo Viejo style, with its high ceilings and loft. Entrées like *ojo de bife* (ribeye steak), stir-fried vegetables, and polenta with goat cheese fall into the US$7 range, but the menu is less diverse than some others in the neighborhood. Reservations are advisable for a table even on weeknights; otherwise eat at the bar. Air quality is mediocre despite the open floor plan.

**Xalapa,** El Salvador 4800, tel. 4833-6102, makes a pretty good guacamole and decent margaritas, but the *carnitas* (pork) are not up to snuff. There's sidewalk seating in good weather, attractive interior decor when it's raining, and inexpensive entrées around US$2.50–3.

Known for live music in its intimate theater-club, the **Club del Vino,** Cabrera 4737, tel. 4833-8330, is also a fine and stylish restaurant with, as its name suggests, an exceptional selection of wines—not to mention an effectively segregated tobacco-free area. The diverse selection of entrées includes the usual beef dishes (US$3–4), but also rabbit stew (US$4), conger eel with tomato and basil (US$3), chicken breast in orange sauce (US$3), and stuffed trout with almonds (US$5).

Palermo also has a brilliant Brazilian restaurant, **Maria Fulô,** Honduras 4795, tel. 4833-4051. For US$4, the *ximxim de galinha* of chicken breast, shrimp, and cashews in coconut milk is exquisite, but the *maracuyá* (passion fruit) mousse may be the best dessert on any menu in the city.

Across Avenida Scalabrini Ortiz, the flamboyant **Te Mataré Ramírez,** Paraguay 4062, tel. 4831-9156, www.tematareramirez, is a self-styled "aphrodisiac restaurant" notorious for suggestive food and decor. Diners are often slow to order as they ogle the salacious menu while contemplating entrées (around US$4–5) like *pecado carnal* ("mortal sin," beef in a cabernet sauce); *grité tanto de dolor como de placer* ("I screamed as much from pain as from pleasure," flounder in bleu-cheese sauce); and *paseaba mi rostro por su pecho* ("my mouth brushed your breast," pork loin in sweet-and-sour sauce). Desserts include *anestesiada por el placer* ("anesthetized by pleasure," a cashew semifreddo), and *un beso ilícito y a oscuras* ("an illicit kiss in the dark," a semisweet chocolate dessert). Open for dinner only daily except Monday, its major drawback is poor air quality—go on weeknights or early before the smokers monopolize the relatively small dining room.

On the western border of the barrio, **Katmandu,** Avenida Córdoba 3547, tel. 4963-1122, serves Indian food, an unusual cuisine in the capital, but it gets high marks from the capital's small Indian community of about 150 people. Most entrées cost about US$3–4; it's open nightly except Sunday for dinner.

## Palermo Hollywood

**Sudestada,** Guatemala 5602, tel. 4776-3777, is one of the city's first and finest Vietnamese and Southeast Asian restaurants. Open for lunch and dinner daily, it has a slow kitchen, but does allow single diners to order half portion of starters.

Run by a pair of documentary filmmakers, appropriately set in Palermo Hollywood, **Tiempo de Gitanos,** El Salvador 5575, tel. 4776-6143, is a bar/restaurant that serves an eclectic mix of Spanish and Middle Eastern dishes. Decorated with souvenirs of the owners' extensive travels, it opens at 5 P.M. daily except Monday and Tuesday. There is live music, mostly jazz, on some nights.

## Botánico and Vicinity

**El Noble Repulgue,** Scalabrini Ortiz 3062, tel. 4809-0423, is a takeaway chain that serves 16 varieties of baked empanadas and 23 of *soufflé* (fried) empanadas. **Big Mamma,** Cabello 3760, tel. 4806-6822, is a small deli chain with large, good sandwiches.

**Romario,** Cabello 3700, tel. 4511-4444, is the Botánico branch of a wildly popular pizza chain that also sells good empanadas. **Pizza Cero**, Cerviño 3701, tel. 4803-3449, is similar, but is more spacious and comfortable.

**La Piara,** Avenida Las Heras 3541, tel. 4807-6342, is a parrilla with a difference—while it serves the usual beef cuts in abundance, the house specialty is a succulent roast pork (US$4), with fish and pasta also on the menu.

**Pata Negra de Jabugo,** Scalabrini Ortiz 3096, tel. 4805-9957, is an attractive *tasca*-style locale, but the tapas portions are small and only so-so. The service is attentive and the wine selection is outstanding. **Garbis**, Scalabrini Ortiz 3190, tel. 4511-6600, has outstanding hummus and a variety of kebabs but stick with the lamb rather than chicken, as the latter tends to dry out. Some more elaborate kebabs (around US$10) are large enough for two, so ask before ordering.

Recently separated from Spirit, the popular Plaza Serrano seafood restaurant, **Nemo,** Cabello 3672, tel. 4803-5678 or 4802-5308, is a small neighborhood spot with spare decor and a diverse but evolving seafood menu, with most entrées in the US$5–8 range. For about US$5, the *cuarto tapeo mare* is an outstanding appetizer.

Probably the best in the vicinity, **Bella Italia Café Bar**, República Arabe Siria 3330, tel. 4807-5120, is the moderately priced café version of the nearby restaurant of the same name. For around US$3, it has outstanding squash gnocchi with a subtle cream sauce, along with fine canelloni and salads. An unlikely outpost of its namesake in Fort Worth, Texas, but with distinctively Argentine touches, it has Mediterranean-villa style decor, friendly management, and good service.

Across Avenida Sarmiento, north of the zoo and near the U.S. Embassy, **La Cátedra**, Cerviño 4699, tel. 4777-4601, is rapidly diversifying what was almost exclusively a parrilla-style menu to include creatively prepared fish, seafood and pasta dishes. Entrées range from around US$3.50 for pasta to US$6 or so for items like rabbit in red wine sauce.

**La Brigada,** Demaría 4711, tel 4777-1515, is one of the barrio's top parrillas, with moderate prices around US$4–5 for most entrées, which include uncommon items such as *chinchulines de chivito* (kid goat intestines). **Río Alba,** Cerviño 4499, tel. 4773-5748, is another fine parrilla.

## Las Cañitas

Newly popular Las Cañitas has acquired a reputation for fashionability, but one of its landmark restaurants is the venerable **El Portugués,** Báez 499, tel. 4771-8699, whose half-portion of *bife de chorizo* some might consider a double—consider sharing and then order more if you're still hungry. Though it dominates the intersection of Báez and Ortega y Gasset with the restaurant, a separate pizzería, and a small grocery, El Portugués, unfortunately, does not see fit to serve wine by the glass.

**Mykonos,** Olleros 1752, tel. 4779-9000, is a Greek/Mediterranean venue that's so far survived the economic crisis. **Romanaccio,** Jorge Newbery 1638, tel. 4511-4300, is a chain pizzería.

**La Corte,** Arévalo 2977, tel. 4775-0999, is a combination restaurant, bar, and chic household-goods outlet that serves Sunday buffet brunch for US$6, but also entrées like stir-fry vegetables (US$2.50) and fresh fish (US$3.50); a la carte portions, though, are small for an Argentine restaurant. It is spacious, with high ceilings and some sidewalk tables, but the service can be absent-minded and the drum-machine music is truly irritating.

**Lotus Neo Thai,** upstairs at Ortega y Gasset 1782, tel. 4771-4449, was the pioneer of Thai food in Argentina and one of few places in the country where it's possible to taste truly spicy dishes. Open for dinner only, a quiet locale with soothing music and imaginative lotus-themed decor, it's relatively expensive at US$4–8 for entrées, even after the steep devaluation.

## BELGRANO

**Holística,** Mendoza 2490, tel. 4786-9871, ecointegral@latinmail.com, is a small natural-foods grocery that also produces inexpensive takeaway meals.

Economical **Cocina Regional 1810,** Mendoza 2320, tel. 4784-3063, serves Tucumán-style empanadas (roquefort and onion, chicken, calabresa, provolone, spicy beef, beef, cheese and onion, chard, ham and cheese, basil with mozzarella and tomato); there are also *humita en chala* and tamales (corn-based plates resembling their Mexican namesake), and stews like *locro*. **La Paceña,** Echeverría 2570, tel. 4788-2282, serves similarly spicy empanadas and the like from northwestern Argentina and Bolivia.

**Contigo Perú,** in a cul-de-sac near the railroad tracks at Echeverría 1627, tel. 4780-3960, is a Peruvian locale which, from humble beginnings, has become a neighborhood success whose ambiance now matches the quality of the food. Prices are moderate, even cheap. Hours are 10 A.M.–midnight daily except Monday. The upside is the attentive service, the downside is dueling TVs—though one could argue that this is authentically Peruvian.

Pizza and pasta are as popular in Belgrano as elsewhere in the city, starting economically at **Pepa's Pizza,** Mendoza 1909, tel. 4788-8673. Other options include **La Siembra,** tel. 4784-4274, Vuelta de Obligado 2501; **La Farola de Núñez,** Avenida Cabildo 2899, tel. 4786-1565; and **Genoa,** Avenida Cabildo 2492, tel. 4784-7784. **Da Orazio,** Cuba 2220, tel. 4786-0088, is a more elegant Italian choice, open for dinner only, with most entrées in the US$5–6 range.

**El Jardín,** Juramento 1640, tel. 4706-0756, is a neighborhood *tenedor libre* with a standard Argentine menu. **La Broqueta de Belgrano,** Cuba 2290, tel. 4786-3349, is a step up in price and quality.

Belgrano's compact Chinatown is home to a gaggle of moderately priced, mostly Cantonese, restaurants. **Cantina Chinatown,** Mendoza 1700, tel. 4783-4173, serves abundant portions and some spicy dishes such as kung pao beef that many not seem quite so spicy to an experienced palate, but extra hot sauce is available. Another recommended choice is **Nuevo Chinatown,** Juramento 1656, tel. 4786-3456.

**Confitería Zurich,** with sidewalk seating at Echeverría 2200, tel. 4784-9808, is good for light meals and snacks. **Cloé,** Cuba 2208, tel. 4784-8436, has similar offerings. Directly opposite Plaza Belgrano and next to La Redonda, **Marco Polo,** Sagasta Isla 2080, tel. 4788-4400, is an ideal spot for a lunch break from the Sunday *feria.*

**Garbis,** Monroe 1799, tel. 4788-2360, serves Middle Eastern specialties like couscous, hummus, and kebabs. For Jewish cuisine, the capital's longstanding option is **Mis Raíces,** in the midst of Chinatown at Arribeños 2148, tel. 4786-6633, open to patrons with reservations only—no drop-ins.

# Arts and Entertainment

In the midst of Argentina's financial crisis and loan default of 2001–2002, the one sector of Argentine society that showed resilience was arts and entertainment. After Tomás Eloy Martínez, a Tucumán native and professor of Spanish at Rutgers, the State University of New Jersey, won the Spanish Alfaguara literary prize (US$175,000) in 2002 for *El Vuelo de la Reina* (a novel about crime and corruption), he remarked, "One of Argentina's riches is forgotten but it is the quality, the leadership of our culture. [In that field] we can speak as equals to the U.S. or France."

Entertainment in Buenos Aires does not mean only events. Cinema, live theater, live music, and discos make the capital a 24-hour city. Still, for many *porteños*, just sitting for hours in a café or

*murga* from Parque Patricios protests and performs at Plaza del Congreso

*confitería* conversing and people-watching is just as important. Sometimes, all these categories may overlap—the world-famous Café Tortoni, for instance, is a traditional meeting place, but it's also a bar and hosts live music and dance events including tango programs.

# Fine Arts

Since independence, Argentina's impact on the arts has been remarkable for a country so geographically remote and with a relatively small population. Many Argentines have been eloquent writers and a much greater number are voracious readers. In the visual arts, particularly modern art, they have been innovative, and their architecture has often been grand even if derivative of Europe. Classical music has always held a place in *porteño* society, but Buenos Aires presently has one of the most vigorous rock-music scenes since 1960s London or San Francisco, creatively adapting polysyllabic Spanish to a frequently monosyllabic music. Likewise, Argentine cinema, theater, and dance have all been influential beyond the country's borders.

## LITERATURE

In the 19th century, even as the free-roaming gaucho was becoming a wage laborer on the *estancias* of the Pampas, Argentine literature enshrined his most positive qualities in José Hernández's epic poem *Martín Fierro* (1872 and 1879), available in many editions and in English translation. The *gauchesco* (gauchesque) tradition has never completely disappeared, and is most memorable in Ricardo Güiraldes's novel *Don Segundo Sombra* (1926). Güiraldes's romanticized fiction is also available in many editions, and has been translated into English and many other languages.

Born of U.S.-immigrant parents in Buenos Aires province, William Henry Hudson (1841–1922) left Argentina for London at the age of 33, but his memoir *Long Ago and Far Away* (1922) has been a staple of Argentine public education. An accomplished amateur field naturalist, he also wrote *Idle Days in Patagonia* (1893) about his explorations in search of birds, plus short stories and even a novel, *Green Mansions* (1904), which is set in the Venezuelan rain forest. Argentines, who translate his forenames into Spanish, know him as Guillermo Enrique Hudson.

A more critical assessment of Argentina and its rural heritage came from the educator and politician Domingo F. Sarmiento. His *Life in the Argentine Republic in the Days of the Tyrants* (1845), an eloquent tirade against rural caudillos that betrays his provincial background, has overcome its polemical origins to become a staple of Latin American history courses in English-speaking countries.

No Argentine author has ever won a Nobel Prize for Literature, but three have won the Premio Cervantes, the Spanish-speaking world's most important literary honor: essayist, poet, and short-story writer Jorge Luis Borges (1979), and novelists Ernesto Sábato (1984) and Adolfo Bioy Casares (1990). Other noteworthy Argentine writers include Julio Cortázar, Victoria Ocampo, Manuel Puig, and Osvaldo Soriano, much of whose work is available in English translation. (Publication dates in this book indicate the Spanish-language original unless otherwise noted.)

Globally, the most prominent is Borges (1899–1986), often mentioned but never chosen for the Nobel. Ironically enough for a classically educated and urbane figure who loathed Perón and Peronism, his short stories, poetry, and essays often focus on urban lowlifes and rural themes, including gaucho violence. Borges never wrote a novel; his most frequently read works are collections such as *Labyrinths* (1970, in English), many of whose stories can seem obscure and even surrealistic.

Sábato (born 1911) acquired some renown in the English-speaking world as the coordinator of *Nunca Más*, an official account of the brutalities of the military dictatorship of 1976–83. Born in Buenos Aires province but long resident in the capital, his best work may be the engrossing psychological novel *On Heroes and Tombs* (1961; New York: Ballantine, 1991), which credibly depicts places and examines people in the city; its subsection "Report on the Blind," capable of standing alone, is truly extraordinary. Sábato's novella *The Tunnel* (1950; New York: Ballantine, 1988), about artistic obsession, is equally absorbing but less conspicuously *porteño* in its approach.

Borges's close friend Bioy Casares (1914–1999) collaborated with the older man on detective stories under the pseudonym Honorario Bustos Domecq, but his own fantastical novella *The Invention of Morel* (Austin: University of Texas Press, 1985) is a purposefully disorienting work that director Eliseo Subiela transformed into the award-winning film *Man Facing Southeast.* Bioy's *Diary of the War of the Pig* (New York: McGraw Hill, 1972) takes place in the barrio of Palermo, mostly within the area popularly referred to as "Villa Freud." His *The Dream of Heroes* (New York: Dutton, 1987) paints a surrealistic portrait of the late 1920s, a time when Carnaval flourished in Buenos Aires.

Son of a diplomatic family, the Belgian-born Cortázar (1914–1984) was a short story writer, experimental novelist, and committed leftist who went into Parisian exile after losing his university post in a Peronist purge. Michelangelo Antonioni turned one of Cortázar's short stories into the famous film *Blow-Up,* but the author is also known for his novels *Hopscotch* (1963; New York: Random House, 1966), the story of a failed Francophile poet in Buenos Aires, and *62: A Model Kit* (1968; New York: Random House, 1972).

Manuel Puig (1932–1990) authored a series of novels concerning popular culture, and specifically the cinema, including *Betrayed by Rita Hayworth* (1968), the detective novel *The Buenos Aires Affair* (New York: Dutton, 1968), and *Kiss of the Spider Woman* (New York: Vintage, 1991), which Brazilian director Héctor Babenco made into an award-winning English-language film starring William Hurt and Raúl

Julia. Puig wrote *Eternal Curse on the Reader of These Pages* (New York: Random House, 1982), about an amnesiac victim of the 1976–83 Proceso dictatorship, in English and later translated it into Spanish.

Journalist and novelist Osvaldo Soriano (1943–1997) wrote satirical novels such as *A Funny Dirty Little War* (Columbia, Louisiana, and London, Readers International, 1989), depicting the consequences of national upheaval in a small community, and *Winter Quarters* (same publisher and year). His *Shadows* (New York: Knopf, 1993), which takes its Spanish title *Una Sombra Ya Pronto Serás* from the lyric of a classic tango, became a surrealistically disorienting road movie under the direction of Héctor Olivera.

Essayist Victoria Ocampo (1891–1979), whose poetess sister Silvina (1909–1994) was Bioy Casares's wife, founded the literary magazine *Sur;* some of her essays appear in Doris Meyer's biography *Victoria Ocampo: Against the Wind and the Tide* (Austin: University of Texas Press, 1990). One of her collaborators at *Sur,* which also became a prestigious publishing house and brought figures like Aldous Huxley, D.H. Lawrence, and even Jack Kerouac to the attention of Spanish-speaking readers, was Borges.

Tomás Eloy Martínez, quoted above on Argentina's cultural resilience and vitality, is author of several novels dealing the Argentine condition through fictionalized biography, most notably *The Perón Novel* (New York: Pantheon Books, 1988)—based partly on his own extensive interiews with the late caudillo. *Santa Evita* (New York: Knopf, 1996), by contrast, can only be called post-biographical, as it traces the odyssey of Evita's embalmed body to Italy, Spain, and back to Buenos Aires.

Novelist Federico Andahazi, also a psychiatrist, outraged industrialist heiress Amalia Fortabat when an independent jury awarded him her self-anointed literary prize for *The Anatomist* (New York: Doubleday, 1998), a sexually explicit (but less than erotic) tale set in medieval Italy.

For a detailed guide to Buenos Aires bookshops, see the Shopping chapter.

## VISUAL ARTS

Because of its small, dispersed settlements, Argentina mostly lacked the great tradition of colonial religious art of the populous central Andean highlands, which developed their own styles of painting and sculpture in the churches of Peru and Bolivia. As a political and demographic entity, the Viceroyalty of the Río de la Plata did not even exist until the late 18th century and, according to *porteño* art critic Jorge Glusberg, "Buenos Aires was practically devoid of any cultural life." Glusberg has gone so far as to claim that the colonial period, "characterized by subordination to the European models currently in vogue," lasted until after World War II.

Glusberg may underrate the work of some pre–World War II figures, but there is no question that innovative Argentine painters and sculptors have flourished artistically, if not always financially, since then—in both figurative and abstract modes. His English-language book *Art in Argentina* (Milan: Giancarlo Politi Editore, 1986), is a readable and well-illustrated introduction to currents in contemporary Argentine art, though it needs an update. The same is true of Rafael Squirru's Spanish-only *Arte Argentino Hoy* (Ediciones de Arte Gaglianone, Buenos Aires, 1983), with color displays of 48 20th-century painters and sculptors.

For an overview of Buenos Aires galleries, which range from prosaically traditional to truly daring, see the Shopping chapter. While gallery-hopping, watch for street art in the form of elaborate graffiti (see the website www.bagraff.com) and *filete,* the traditional line painting that once

## THE REBIRTH OF FILETE

The flamboyant folk art called *filete* began with Sicilian immigrants whose horse carts were art on wheels. Their symmetrical ornamental lines, enriched by elaborate calligraphy, simulated the moldings and wrought-iron ornamentation on late-19th and early-20th-century buildings—the word *filete* derives from the Italian *filetto,* meaning a strip that separates moldings.

Gradually the Argentine capital's *fileteadores* made their craft the standard for commercial sign painting, as it drew attention to fixed businesses like restaurants, cafés, and a variety of other services. It suffered, though, during the dark days of the Proceso dictatorship (1976–83), when the generals banned it from public transportation for its alleged unreadability. Since the return to representative government, though, *filete* has made a comeback, and skilled *fileteadores* can make a handsome living.

To see readymade decorative plaques, visit Plaza Dorrego's Sunday Feria de San Telmo, where typical themes and subjects are tango (and tango legend Carlos Gardel), plus skillfully drawn dragons, flowers, and fruits. Many of these plaques display *piropos,* aphorisms or proverbs.

Perhaps typical of contemporary *fileteadores* is Martiniano Arce, whose San Telmo studio is literally a memorial to his craft—he has already chosen and painted his and his wife's coffins, and keeps them on display in his house. He does not shy away from commercial work, saying that his art is incomplete until someone owns it—in addition to the cover for the cover of rock band Fabulosos Cadillacs' *Fabulosos Calavera* CD, he has commemorated the 10th anniversary of McDonald's in Argentina with a custom design, and even painted a symbolic bottle for Coca-Cola.

Arce and several of his colleagues will produce custom work on commission; a typical plaque of about 20 by 30 centimeters (eight by 12 in.) costs around US$100. Most of their houses studios proclaim their craft conspicuously, but it's best to phone for an appointment unless you just want to admire the shops from the outside. Arce is at Perú 1089, 1st floor, tel. 11/4362-2739, martinianoarce@sinectis.com.ar, http://webs.sinectis.com.ar/martinianoarce. Other artists include Adrián Clara, tel. 11/4381-2676; Jorge Muscia, Carlos Calvo 370, tel. 11/4361-5942; and Mabel Matto, Estados Unidos 510, 1st floor. Eduardo Genovese, tel. 11/4581-0798, www.fileteado.com.ar, teaches classes at various cultural centers around Buenos Aires.

ARTS & ENTERTAINMENT

decorated horsecarts, trucks, and buses; experiencing something of a revival, it now graces many cafés and restaurants.

## Painting

One of the first notable Argentine artists, European-trained Prilidiano Pueyrredón (1823–1870) painted landscapes and people of rural Buenos Aires. Other early painters of note included Eduardo Sívori (1847–1918) and Ernesto de la Cárcova (1866–1927), both of whom manifested concern with social causes such as poverty and hunger.

One of Argentine painting's extraordinary stories, though, is that of Cándido López (1840–1902), a junior army officer who lost his right forearm to gangrene after being struck by a grenade in battle against Paraguay. Remarkably, López painted over 50 oils of war scenes with his left hand; even more remarkably, his paintings were not romanticized scenes of heroism in combat, but vivid landscapes depicting routine activities—ordinary encampments and river crossings, for instance—in addition to the occasional battle.

Benito Quinquela Martín (1890–1977) chronicled the struggles of immigrant factory workers and stevedores in his vivid oils of La Boca, many of which reside in his namesake museum in the barrio. One of modern art's pioneers in Argentina was Borges's friend Xul Solar (1887–1963; real name Alejandro Schulz Solari), who dealt with esoteric and mystical themes in his watercolors, displayed in a Barrio Norte museum in his honor.

One of Argentina's best-known modern artists is the versatile Antonio Berni (1905–1981), who worked in painting, drawing, engraving, collage, and sculpture. His socially conscious canvases, such as *Juanito Laguna Bañándose entre Latas* (Juanito Laguna Bathing in the Trash), have fetched astronomical prices in the international art market. His *Monstruos* (Monsters) is a series of three-dimensional works (1964–71) that depict the nightmares of Ramona Montiel, a prostitute who dreams of war, death, and destruction.

In conjunction with other artists, including Lino Spilimbergo (1896–1964), Juan Carlos Castagnino (1908–1972), Galician-born Manuel Colmeiro (1901–1999), and Demetrio Urruchúa (1902–1978), Berni was an adherent of the politically conscious Nuevo Realismo (New Realism) movement, whose greatest public legacy is the ceiling murals in the recycled Galerías Pacífico shopping center, under the influence of the famed Mexican painter David Alfaro Siqueiros.

Spilimbergo, when not collaborating on such projects, specialized in geometric forms, still lifes, and lighted landscapes. Castagnino specialized in rural, even gauchesque, landscapes, and Colmeiro and Urruchúa were both socially oriented painters and muralists.

Self-taught Jorge de la Vega (1930–1971), influenced by pop art, alternated figurative and abstract geometrical work; in his series of *Monstruos* or *Bestiario,* he attached objects such as coins, sticks, and especially mirrors to his canvases, deforming both the subject and the viewer.

One of Argentina's rising modern painters is Guillermo Kuitca, born in 1960 to a Russian-Jewish immigrant family. Kuitca contrasts small figures with large environments, transforms everyday abstractions such as floor plans and road maps (particularly effectively so in his *Kristallnacht II,* an observation on the Nazi genocide against German Jews), and creates abstract visual expressions of popular music themes like the anti-lynching classic "Strange Fruit" and the Rolling Stones's "Gimme Shelter."

Daniel Barreto (born 1966) adapts popular figures, like the folk saint Difunta Correa of San Juan province and the rural bandit Gaucho Antonio Gil of Corrientes province, into colorful paintings that transcend the kitsch often associated with those figures.

## Sculpture

Buenos Aires is a city of monuments; unfortunately, many if not most of them are pretentious busts of ostensible statesmen and colossal equestrian statues of military men like national icon José de San Martín, caudillo Justo José Urquiza, and Patagonian invader Julio Argentino Roca. The Rodin-influenced Rogelio Yrurtia (1879–1950), though he did create the mausoleum of President Bernardino Rivadavia, displayed his talents better in statues like the larger-than-life-size *The Boxers,* displayed at his house and museum in the barrio of Belgrano; even better is his working-class tribute *Canto al Trabajo* (Ode to Labor), on San Telmo's Plazoleta Olazábal.

Those following Yrurtia have been far more daring. León Ferrari (born 1920) created the prescient *La Civilización Occidental y Cristiana* (Western and Christian Civilization, 1965), a sardonic Vietnam-era work that portrays Christ crucified on a diving F-16. Similarly, Juan Carlos Distéfano (born 1933) blends sculpture and painting in works like *El Rey y La Reina* (1977), a disturbingly lifelike representation of a couple shot to death in an automobile. In the context of its time, it was a thinly disguised portrayal of extrajudicial executions carried out by military and paramilitary death squads after the coup of 1976. Remarkably, the work was shown publicly, on the Florida pedestrian mall, shortly thereafter.

Albert Heredia (born 1924) mocks the pomposity of monumental public art in works such as *El Caballero de la Máscara* (The Masked Horseman). The title is misleading, as this headless parody of an equestrian statue is a collage of materials that ridicules 19th-century strongmen and their modern political counterparts. Heredia originally titled it *El Montonero,* a reference to the Federalist cavalry of that time, but could not exhibit the piece under its original name because the leftist guerrilla group Montoneros was a hot-button issue at the time.

Yoël Novoa, in contrast to politically committed sculptors like Ferrari and Heredia, creates cleverly entertaining caricatures of *porteños* and Buenos Aires street scenes in papier mâché.

# ARCHITECTURE

Because Buenos Aires languished as a backwater of the Spanish colonial empire until the creation of the Viceroyalty of the River Plate in the late 18th century, little remains of its precarious early architecture. (There are older, more impressive early colonial constructions in the northwestern provinces of Jujuy, Salta, Tucumán, and Córdoba).

Nevertheless, the barrios of Monserrat, San Telmo, and some others boast a selection of worthwhile colonial buildings, many but not all of them churches. Vernacular architecture styles include the distinctive *casa chorizo,* a long narrow construction—sometimes barely wider than an adult's armspan—on deep lots. The traditional bright primary colors of the wood-frame, metal-clad houses of La Boca derive from the fact that early residents scavenged their paint from ships on the Riachuelo.

For most of the 19th century, *porteño* architecture evolved from its Spanish colonial origins to an Italianate style. Beginning in the early 20th century, the reigning architectural fashion was a Beaux Arts academicism, both for public buildings and the ornate *palacetes* (mansions) of the landowning oligarchy. Some of these Parisian-style residences became public buildings when the Great Depression bankrupted and impoverished—relatively speaking, of course—Argentina's first families. Many French professionals, including landscape architect Carlos Thays, worked on *porteño* projects in what has been called, perhaps with some exaggeration, "the Paris of the South."

From the 1930s onward, the capital developed greater residential and commercial density with buildings such as the Edificio Kavanagh, a handsome 30-story highrise on Plaza San Martín. Barrios like Recoleta and Palermo that were once almost exclusively single family residences or *propiedades horizontales* (horizontal properties, or *PHs*) are now filled with soaring apartment blocks. Some of these are handsome, others much less so.

The late 20th century saw some hideous developments, such as Italian-born Clorindo Testa's brutalist Biblioteca Nacional (National Library) in Palermo (in fairness, the building's interior is more attractive and practical than it appears from outside). One positive development is the recycling of historical structures, such as the Galerías Pacífico and the Mercado del Abasto into contemporary shopping centers, and the former brick warehouses at Puerto Madero into fashionable restaurants and residential lofts.

The best general guide to Buenos Aires's architecture, the Spanish-language *Buenos Aires: Guía de Arquitectura* (1994), edited by Alberto Petrina, includes suggested walking tours, architectural drawings, and sharp B&W photographs. Readers who know even basic Spanish can benefit from it.

## MUSIC AND DANCE

Argentines are musical people, their interests ranging from folk, pop, rock, and blues to classical. The country's signature sound and dance is the tango, both as instrumental and with lyrics; in its plaintiveness and melancholy, it's a cultural counterpart to the blues.

In their musical interests, Argentine performers are versatile and unselfconscious about crossing boundaries—folksinger Mercedes Sosa, for instance, has sometimes performed with erratic rock musician Charly García. Throughout most of the 1990s, major international artists in both classical and popular music toured the country, but the peso's collapse has placed many of them beyond the public's means. Highly qualified local performers, however, have been able to take up much of the slack even at locales like the Teatro Colón, which traditionally attracts big overseas names. (Refer to the Bars and Clubs section later in this chapter for more information on music and dance venues.)

### Classical Music and Dance

Since its completion in 1908, the **Teatro Colón** has been the preeminent high-culture venue on the continent and perhaps in the entire southern hemisphere (the Sydney Opera House cannot boast the Colón's history). Thanks to the presence of the Colón, the **Teatro Avenida,** and other classical venues, early 20th century Argentina produced an abundance of classical composers, particularly in the fields of opera and ballet.

facade of the Teatro Colón, home to the Buenos Aires opera

Among the notable figures of the time were Héctor Panizza (1875–1967); Constantino Gaito (1878–1945), who produced *gauchesco* ballet such as *La Flor del Irupé* (The Flower of Irupé); Felipe Boero (1884–1958), and Italian-born Pascual De Rogatis (1880–1980). Possibly the most distinguished, though, was Juan José Castro (1895–1968), whose career suffered because of his outspoken opposition to the military government of 1943 and the subsequent Perón regime. Castro's ballets include *Mekhano* and *Offenbachiana*.

The Spanish composer Manuel de Falla (1876–1946) spent the last seven years of his life in Alta Gracia—a provincial Córdoba town that was also the boyhood home of Ernesto "Che" Guevara—following the victory of Perón's ally Francisco Franco in the Spanish Civil War. Franco's regime had executed Falla's friend, playwright Federico García Lorca.

One of the outstanding figures in Argentine ballet is Roberto García Morillo (1911–1996), whose works include *Usher* and *Harrild*. Arnaldo D'Espósito (1897–1945), Luis Gianneo (1897–1968), and Alberto Ginastera (1916–1983) were his contemporaries. A later generation of opera composers includes Valdo Sciamarella (born 1924), Mario Perusso (born 1936) and Gerardo Gandini (born 1936).

Contemporary Argentine classical music boasts figures like Daniel Barenboim (born 1942), a pianist and conductor who has held posts at the Orchestre de Paris, the Chicago Symphony Orchestra, and the Deutsche Staatsoper Berlin among others. Barenboim (also an Israeli citizen who has played in the West Bank in defiance of Israeli government objections) is a versatile figure who has, among other achievements, recorded tango and other popular music. He performed at the Colón during the economic crisis of 2002, when the theater could not afford to pay high-profile international acts.

Pianist Martha Argerich (born 1941), though she lives in Brussels, has sponsored competitions in Buenos Aires. She has drawn rave reviews from *The New York Times* for her Carnegie Hall concerts and has won a Grammy for Best Instrumental Soloist.

US-based Osvaldo Golijov (born 1960) is responsible for classical works like *The St. Mark Passion*, but is flexible enough to work on movie soundtracks (for British director Sally Potter's widely panned *The Man Who Cried*) and even with rock bands like Mexico's Café Tacuba.

Rosario-born but Europe-based tenor José Cura (born 1962) has drawn attention as a credible successor to Luciano Pavarotti on the international opera scene. Among ballet performers, by far the most significant is Julio Bocca (born 1967), a prodigy who has performed in New York, Paris and elsewhere. He has formed his own company, the Ballet Argentino, and continues to perform in Argentina even during the economic crisis.

## Popular Music

Argentine popular music takes many forms, from the folk tradition of the Andean northwest to the accordion-based immigrant *chamamé* of the northeastern lowlands and the hard-nosed *rock nacional* of Buenos Aires. Its centerpiece, though, remains the tango, which overlaps categories—many classical composers and performers (see the preceding Classical Music and Dance section) have incorporated tango into their repertoires.

**Tango:** Tango overlaps the categories of music and dance, and even within those categories there are distinctions. As music, the tango can be instrumental but it gained its initial popularity and international reputation through the *tango canción* (tango song) as projected by the legendary Carlos Gardel and others (though to a lesser degree). One *porteño* songwriter has described the

> *One porteño songwriter has described the tango as "a sad feeling that is danced"; there is no doubt that it appeals to nostalgia for things lost—an old flame or the old neighborhood, perhaps. Tango remains a daily presence in the lives of porteños.*

tango as "a sad feeling that is danced," and there is no doubt that it appeals to nostalgia for things lost—an old flame or the old neighborhood, for instance.

The charismatic Gardel, whose birthdate and birthplace are both topics of controversy, attained immortality after dying young in an aviation accident in Medellín, Colombia in 1935. According to his diehard admirers, "Gardel sings better every day." Uruguayan-born Julio Sosa (1926–1964), who also died young in a car accident, was nearly as important; at a time when Peronism was outlawed, his subtle smile and gestures on stage evoked the exiled caudillo.

Orchestral tango music, as opposed to that of the *tango canción*, is the legacy of bandleaders and composers like Osvaldo Pugliese (1905–1995), Aníbal "Pichuco" Troilo (1914–1975), and especially Astor Piazzola (1921–1992), whose jazz influences are palpable. Important lyricists include Enrique Santos Discépolo (1901–1951), also a composer, and Homero Manzi (1907–1951).

Practiced by skilled and sexy dancers in San Telmo and Monserrat night clubs, the tango floor show is popular with tourists, but tells only part of the story. The tango is not exclusive to the young and lithe—in fact, one could easily argue that its nostalgia lends it to older individuals with longer memories—and a recent revival has made it just as popular with mixed-age audiences at *milongas* (informal dance clubs).

Tango remains a daily presence in the lives of *porteños*, with both a 24-hour FM radio station (FM 92.7) and a cable TV channel, Sólo Tango. Contemporary performers of note include several women, such as Eladia Blásquez (born 1931), Susana Rinaldi (born 1935), and Adriana Varela (born 1958). Pop singers such as Sandro (see the Rock and Pop section) and Cacho Castaña (born 1942) have also sung tango, and the much younger Omar Giammarco produces tango-flavored music using accordion instead of *bandoneón* in his *quinteto*. La Chicana is a tango song group that adds a flute to the traditional instrumental mix, and even works with rock musician Omar Mollo of Los Divididos.

**Folk:** Tango is arguably an urban folk music, but Argentina's true folk tradition stems from *payadores*, gauchos who sang verses with guitar accompaniment; in dance, it sometimes takes the form of the *malambo*, a competitive male-only affair that, despite its identification with the rural pampas, contains echos of flamenco. An older current derives from the northwestern Andean provinces and their link to the Bolivian and Peruvian highlands, featuring the *zampoña* (panpipes) and *charango*, a tiny stringed instrument that uses an armadillo shell as its sound box.

Born in Buenos Aires province, the late Atahualpa Yupanqui (1908–1992) belongs to these purist traditions, as does the Salta-based group Los Chalchaleros, an institution for over half a century. Tucumán native Mercedes Sosa (born 1935) also comes from this tradition, but is less of a purist, having even performed with the brilliant but erratic rock musician Charly García (see the Rock and Pop section). Their contemporary León Gieco (born 1951) crosses the line into folk-rock and even rap.

Tomás Lipán, an Aymará Indian from the northwestern village of Purmamarca in Jujuy province, embodies the region's Andean folk roots, but adds urban touches like the *bandoneón* to create an Argentine hybrid. Soledad Pastorutti (born 1980), who goes by her first name only as a performer, is a self-conscious folkie who sings and dresses in an exaggerated *gauchesco* style.

Immigrant communities have left their mark in *chamamé*, an accordion-based music typical of the humid lowland provinces along the Río Paraná and the Río Uruguay, north of Buenos Aires to the Brazilian and Paraguayan borders. Among the notable performers are Antonio Tárragó Ros and Chango Spasiuk (born 1968); the latter is from a Ukrainian immigrant community in the province of Misiones.

**Peña La Baguala,** la_baguala@hotmail.com, is a folk music collective that has no fixed abode but presents acts such as Tomás Lipán. They often perform at La Viga; see Bars and Clubs later in this chapter.

**Rock and Pop:** It may be no exaggeration to say that Buenos Aires, like London or San Francisco in the mid- to late 1960s, has one of the most vigorous rock scenes ever. Despite the handicap of trying to fit a multisyllabic language into a monosyllabic musical idiom, the practitioners of *rock nacional* have had remarkable success.

In terms of live music, there seems to be something happening every night. The down side to this is that some of the top bands have a small but pugnacious hard core of fans who tend to crowd the stage; most visitors unaccustomed to the scene will probably prefer to stand back a bit.

The pioneer of Argentine rock music is Roberto Sánchez (born 1945), better known by his stage name, Sandro. As an early rock star who became a movie idol with a dominating manager, Sandro draws obvious comparisons with Elvis Presley, but "El Maestro" is also a credible tango singer and the first Argentine to appear at Madison Square Garden. A surprisingly modest individual, he is the honoree of *Tributo a Sandro: Un Disco de Rock,* an exceptional tribute album by Argentine, Chilean, Colombian, and Mexican rock bands.

Charly García (born 1951), a founder of the legendary Sui Generis, transcends generations—many of his fans are in their 20s and often younger. García, who sings and plays mostly keyboards, incorporates women into his backing bands even as lead guitarists and saxophonists; he displays a sense of history in performing classics like Eddie Cochran's "Summertime Blues," the Byrds's "I'll Feel a Whole Lot Better," Neil Young's "Don't Let It Bring You Down," and even the obscure Small Faces gem "Tin Soldier." Rather than strict cover versions, these are adaptations, often with García's own Spanish-language lyrics.

Nearly as revered as Charly is León Gieco, a Dylanesque figure also mentioned in the Folk section of this chapter; his album *Bandidos Rurales* (2002) bears thematic resemblance to Dylan's *John Wesley Harding*. He does an utterly brilliant cover of Sandro's "Si Yo Fuera Carpintero," itself a brilliant Spanish-language adaptation of Tim Hardin's "If I Were a Carpenter."

Fito Páez (born 1963) and García protegé Andrés Calamaro (born 1961) also have major solo careers, but many acts in the *rock nacional* idiom have a stronger group identity than individual identity. Among them are Attaque 77, Babasónicos, Los Divididos (a branch of the earlier Sumo and famous for their versions of the Mexican folk song "Cielito Lindo" and the Doors's "Light My Fire"), Las Pelotas (the other branch of Sumo), Los Piojos, Los Ratones Paranoicos (strongly influenced by the Rolling Stones), and Patricio Rey y Sus Redonditos de Ricota. Almafuerte and the power trio A.N.I.M.A.L are the leading heavy metal bands.

Grammy winners Los Fabulosos Cadillacs (best alternative Latin rock group in 1998) have toured North America, playing salsa- and reggae-influenced rock at venues like San Francisco's legendary Fillmore Auditorium. Others in this idiom include Los Auténticos Decadentes and Los Cafres.

Buenos Aires has a robust blues scene, thanks to individuals like guitarist Pappo and groups like La Mississippi and Memphis La Blusera, who have even taken their act to the stage of the Teatro Colón (to the disgust of classical music critics). The female vocal trio Las Blacanblus treats blues standards in a distinctive style with minimal accompaniment—only guitar and piano. International blues figures such as B.B. King, and many less-famous but still credible foreign artists, have also played in B.A.

In a category of their own are Les Luthiers, an eclectic bunch who make their own unique instruments (which defy description) and caricature the most bourgeois and authoritarian sectors of Argentine society. While musically sophisticated, their shows are as much theater as concert.

**Jazz:** Both traditional and free-form jazz play a part in Argentina's musical history. A fixture in the traditional jazz scene is the Fénix Jazz Band, whose vocalist Ernesto "Cachi" Carrizo says he can't sing blues in Spanish because "the blues in Spanish seems to me as absurd to me as tango in English."

Better known outside strictly Argentine circles is saxophonist Gato Barbieri (born 1932), who also wrote the soundtrack for *The Last Tango in Paris*. Hollywood regular Lalo Schifrin (also born 1932), famous for TV and movie soundtracks like

*Bullitt Cool Hand Luke,* and *Mission Impossible,* originally moved to the United States to play piano with Dizzy Gillespie. Schifrin, who also writes classical music, makes a brief onscreen appearance as an orchestra conductor in the opening sequence of the Hannibal Lecter gorefeast *Red Dragon* (2002); his father, Luis, was concertmaster of the Teatro Colón's orchestra.

## CINEMA

Given the country's political and economic instability, it's surprising that Argentine cinema has been as productive and successful as it has. In the year 2000, for instance, Argentine directors managed to make 30 full-length features and four documentaries. In October 2002, the American Cinemateque showed a dozen new films in the three-day New Argentine Cinema 2002 in Hollywood's Egyptian Theater, with attendance by Argentine directors and actors.

Special effects are generally limited, and it's worth noting that Argentine films, like European ones, tend to be more character- than plot-driven, but there are plenty of outstanding directors and actors. Quite a few films from the last 20 years, in particular, are available on video.

Not only have Argentines made good films, but foreign directors have found Buenos Aires an interesting locale for filming—all the more so now that the peso's collapse has made it inexpensive to shoot in the capital. Readers who know Spanish should look for film critic Diego Curubeto's *Babilonia Gaucha* (Buenos Aires: Editorial Planeta, 1993), on the relationship between Argentina and Hollywood; Curubeto also wrote *Cine Bizarro* (Buenos Aires: Editorial Sudamericana, 1996), on idiosyncratic films from Argentina and elsewhere.

Alquileres Lavalle, Lavalle 1199, tel. 4476-1118, rents and sells Argentine videos in the original Spanish. Argentine videos, however, use European PAL technology, which is incompatible with the North American VHS system.

**Argentine Directors, Movies, and Actors:** In its earliest years, Argentine cinema dealt almost exclusively with *porteño* topics such as Carnaval.

## FOREIGN FILMS ON AND IN BUENOS AIRES

Foreign filmmakers have found Buenos Aires both visually and thematically appealing. Argentine-born but British-based, Martin Donovan made the cult thriller *Apartment Zero* (1989), which brilliantly and even humorously portrays porteño life—its depiction of busybody neighbors in a Buenos Aires apartment building is priceless—even as it deals with the savagery of the Dirty War. British actor Colin Firth plays the protagonist, an Anglo-Argentine cinema manager.

The worst of the worst is Alan Parker's kitschy version of the already kitschy musical *Evita* (1996). Filmed partly in B.A. but also in Budapest, it is most noteworthy for the controversy it caused with Peronist politicians obsessed with Evita's legacy, and for the highly publicized meeting between Madonna and a flagrantly lecherous President Carlos Menem.

Nearly as bad, though, is British director Sally Potter's narcissistic *The Tango Lesson* (1997). For a better cinematic presentation of the tango, despite a weak story line, see Puerto Rican director Marcos Zurinaga's *Tango Bar* (1988); Zurinaga worked with his compatriot, the late Raúl Julia, and a cast and crew of Argentines including *bandoneon* player Rubén Juárez and singer Valeria Lynch.

It's only incidental, but the hero of Dutch director Paul Verhoeven's *Starship Troopers* (1997), a hilarious adaptation of Robert Heinlein's sci-fi novel, is a *porteño*. Buenos Aires, in the process, gets vaporized by alien bugs.

U.S. actor/director Robert Duvall, a frequent visitor to Buenos Aires and a fervent tango aficionado, filmed the thriller *Assassination Tango* (2003) on location in Buenos Aires. British director Christopher Hampton filmed the adaptation of Lawrence Thornton's novel *Imagining Argentina*, starring Emma Thompson and Antonio Banderas, in the capital and the provinces.

Even given the capital's Afro-American traditions, it's startling to see Argentine actors dressed in blackface. Later, tango legend Carlos Gardel worked extensively in Hollywood as well as in Buenos Aires, starring in films such as *El Día Que Me Quieras* (The Day You Love Me, 1935).

Over the years, several Argentine films have made respectable showings at the Oscars. Director Sergio Renán's *La Tregua* (The Truce, 1975), based on a story by the Uruguayan Mario Benedetti, was the first nominated for best foreign-language film; it lost to the tough competition of Federico Fellini's *Amarcord*.

María Luisa Bemberg (1922–1995), astonishingly enough, made her first feature at the age of 58, but made up for lost time with films like *Camila,* nominated in 1984; it was based on the true story of 19th-century heiress Camila O'Gorman, her Jesuit lover, and their persecution by the Rosas dictatorship. In 1985, director Luis Puenzo's *The Official Story* won the Oscar for his treatment of the controversial issue of military adoptions of infant children of "disappeared" parents during the 1976–83 Dirty War; it stars Norma Aleandro, a highly respected theater actress and director. Puenzo drew scorn, though, for the implication that some Argentines were unaware of extrajudicial tortures and murders.

Based partly on Adolfo Bioy Casares's novella *The Invention of Morel,* Eliseo Subiela's *Man Facing Southeast* won a nomination in 1986; the plot of the 2001 Hollywood production *K-Pax,* starring Kevin Spacey and Jeff Bridges, bears a remarkable resemblance to Subiela's work. Most recently, in 2002, Juan José Campanella's maudlin *Hijo de la Novia* (The Bride's Son) received a nomination; Ricardo Darín plays the title role, a type-A *porteño* restaurateur whose father wants to give Darín's Alzheimer's-stricken mother a church wedding.

The Oscars, though, showcase only a small percentage of Argentine films and are not necessarily representative. Often subtly and sometimes overtly political, they are frequently eloquent and passionate but also introspective—partly due, perhaps, to the popularity of psychoanalysis in the capital.

Subiela's *The Dark Side of the Heart* (1992), an erotic love story with both humor and pathos, takes place in Buenos Aires and Montevideo; based loosely on the life on *porteño* poet Oliverio Girondo, it features a cameo by Uruguayan poet Mario Benedetti.

Bemberg also made the English-language *Miss Mary* (1986), the tale of an English governess on an Argentine *estancia,* starring Julie Christie; and *I Don't Want to Talk About It* (1992), a truly peculiar romance starring the late Marcelo Mastroianni and set in a conservative provincial town (the filming took place in the Uruguayan city of Colonia, across the river from Buenos Aires).

Adolfo Aristarain (born 1943) directed the versatile Federico Luppi in the Spanish-language thriller *Time of Revenge* (1981), a labor drama available on video, and in *A Place in the World* (1992). The latter is a socially conscious film that was disqualified for an Oscar nomination because it was unclear whether it was an Uruguayan, Argentine, or Spanish production (most of the filming took place in Argentina's scenic San Luis province). Aristarain also directed the English-language film *The Stranger* (1986), a psychological thriller with Peter Riegert, Bonnie Bedelia, and cameos from a cast of Argentine stars, but its ingenious structure can't compensate for a plot full of holes.

Other films have gotten less international recognition but are worth seeing, such as Bruno Stagnaro's and Adrián Caetano's low-budget *Pizza, Birra, Faso* (1997), an unsentimental story of *porteño* lowlifes trying to get by. Ricardo Darín shares the lead with Gastón Pauls in Fabián Bielinsky's *Nine Queens* (2001), the twist-filled noirish tale of *porteño* con-men who strike up a partnership in crisis-racked Buenos Aires; according to reports, Mel Gibson has bought the rights to an English-language remake.

Politically committed director Fernando "Pino" Solanas (born 1936), a left-wing Peronist, dealt with the theme of expatriation in *The Exile of Gardel* (1985). Tango legend Astor Piazzola wrote the soundtrack and also appears in the film which, appropriately enough for a film whose title figure may have been born in France, takes place in Paris.

## CINEMAS

Buenos Aires' traditional commercial cinema district is in the Microcentro along the Lavalle pedestrian mall west of Florida and along Avenida Corrientes and Avenida Santa Fe. In addition, there are multiplexes in the shopping malls of Puerto Madero, Retiro, and Palermo, and clusters of cinemas in the outer barrios such as Belgrano.

Imported films generally appear in the original language with Spanish subtitles, except for animated and children's movies, which are dubbed into the local language (Cine Los Angeles specializes in these). Translations of foreign-language titles are often misleading, but the *Buenos Aires Herald* prints the original English title and translations of other foreign-language titles.

Because of devaluation, ticket prices have fallen to US$2–3 for first-run movies. Most cinemas offer half-price discounts Tuesday and Wednesday, and sometimes for the afternoon shows on other days. On Friday and Saturday nights there is usually a *trasnoche* (midnight or later) showing, but even on weeknights there may be shows beginning as late as 11 P.M.

**Abasto de Buenos Aires:** Avenida Corrientes 3200, Balvanera, tel. 4866-4800

**Alto Palermo 1–2:** Avenida Santa Fe 3251, Palermo, tel 4827-8362

**América:** Avenida Callao 1057, Barrio Norte, tel. 4811-3818

**Atlas Lavalle:** Lavalle 869, Microcentro, tel. 4322-1936

**Atlas Santa Fe 1–2:** Avenida Santa Fe 2015, Barrio Norte, tel. 4823-7878

**Belgrano Multiplex:** Obligado at Mendoza, Belgrano, tel. 4783-2186

**Cineduplex:** Avenida Rivadavia 5500, Caballito, tel. 4902-5682

**Cinemark 6 Caballito:** Avenida La Plata 96 at Avenida Rivadavia, Microcentro, tel. 4982-7117

**Cinemark 8 Puerto Madero:** Avenida Alicia Moreau de Justo 1960, Microcentro, tel. 4315-3008

**Cinemark 10 Palermo:** Beruti 3399, Palermo, tel. 4827-9500

**Complejo Cine Lorca 1–2:** Avenida Corrientes 1428, Microcentro, tel. 4371-5017

**Complejo Tita Merello:** Suipacha 442, Microcentro, tel. 4322-1195

**Electric:** Lavalle 836, Microcentro, tel. 4322-1846

**Galerías Pacífico 1–2:** Florida 753, Microcentro, tel. 6556-5357

---

The prolific Leopoldo Torre Nilsson (1924–78), who shot nearly 30 features in his relatively short lifetime, adapted Manuel Puig's novel *Boquitas Pintadas* (Painted Lips), a story of hypocrisy and petty jealousies in a small provincial town, to the screen in 1974. Torre Nilsson also filmed *La Guerra del Cerdo* (War of the Pigs, 1975); set in Palermo, it's a discomforting adaptation of Adolfo Bioy Casares's story of generational conflict and political polarization in the immediate pre-coup years. Argentine jazz legend Gato Barbieri wrote the soundtrack.

Director Héctor Olivera (born 1931) has turned two of Osvaldo Soriano's satirical novels into movies: *A Funny Dirty Little War* (1983), which depicts the comic consequences of a military coup in a provincial town (but has nothing to do, directly at least, with the dictatorship of 1976–83); and *Una Sombra Ya Pronto Serás* (Shadows, 1994), a road movie that encourages disorientation by making it impossible to tell where the movie takes place. Federico Luppi (born 1936) appeared in the former.

Starting with a bungled robbery in Buenos Aires, Marcelo Piñeyro's *Wild Horses* (1995) becomes a road romance that ends with a chase in the Patagonian province of Chubut. Héctor Alterio, who plays opposite Norma Aleandro in *Hijo de la Novia,* plays a hostage who goes along for the ride.

Gustavo Mosquera directed the innovative *Moebius* (1996), really a collaborative film school project set mostly in a Borgesian Buenos Aires subway; a disappearing train, audible but not visible, serves as a metaphor for the victims of the Dirty War. Displaying great creativity and technical proficiency on a shoestring budget, its anachronisms— antique dial telephones alongside cell phones, for

**Gaumont 1–3:** Rivadavia 1635, Microcentro, tel. 4371-3050

**General Paz 1–6:** Avenida Cabildo 2702, Belgrano, tel. 4781-1412

**Los Angeles 1–3:** Avenida Corrientes 1770, Microcentro, tel. 4372-2405

**Metro 1–3:** Cerrito 570, Microcentro, tel. 4382-4219

**Monumental 1–4:** Lavalle 780, Microcentro, tel. 4393-9008

**Normandie 1–4:** Lavalle 855, Microcentro, tel. 4322-1000

**Paseo Alcorta 1–4:** Figueroa Alcorta at Salguero, Palermo, tel. 4806-5665

**Patio Bullrich 1–6:** Avenida del Libertador 750, Barrio Norte, tel. 4816-3801

**Premier 1–3:** Avenida Corrientes 1565, Microcentro, tel. 4374-2113

**Savoy 1–4:** Avenida Cabildo 2829, Belgrano, tel. 4781-6500

**Showcase Cinemas:** Monroe 1655, Belgrano, tel. 4786-3232

**Solar de la Abadia 1–2:** Luis María Campos at Maure, Barrio Norte, tel. 4778-5181

**Village Recoleta:** Vicente López at Junín, Recoleta, tel. 4810-4446/6843

**Art Houses**

Independent films or reprises of commercial films generally show at smaller venues scattered around town. Tuesday and Wednesday discounts may be available.

A particularly welcome revival is the Cinemateca Hebráica, which was closed for several years after the terrorist bombings against the Israeli embassy and the AMIA.

**Centro Cultural Ricardo Rojas:** Avenida Corrientes 2038, Balvanera, tel. 4954-8352

**Cine Club Tea:** Aráoz 1460, Palermo, tel. 4832-2646

**Cinemateca Hebráica:** Sarmiento 2255, Balvanera, tel. 4952-5986

**Complejo del Cine Argentino Tita Merello:** Suipacha 442, Microcentro, tel. 4322-1185

**Cosmos:** Avenida Corrientes 2046, Balvanera, tel. 4953-5405

**Sala Leopoldo Lugones:** Avenida Corrientes 1530, Microcentro, tel. 0800/333-5254

instance—imply that despite modernization and the return to representative government, remnants of the old Argentina remain.

In addition to his Argentine films, Federico Luppi has appeared in two outstanding films by Mexican director Guillermo del Toro: the sci-fi thriller *Cronos* (1992) and the politically charged ghost story *The Devil's Backbone,* set during the Spanish Civil War. Luppi also played the lead role of a socially committed physician in U.S. director John Sayles's *Men with Guns* (1997), an eloquent parable on political violence in Latin America.

Norma Aleandro (born 1936), best known overseas for *The Official Story,* has won many international acting awards. She has also appeared opposite Anthony Hopkins in Sergio Toledo's *One Man's War,* a human rights drama set in Paraguay.

Cecilia Roth (born 1958), who appeared with Luppi in *A Place in the World,* has worked frequently with maverick Spanish director Pedro Almodóvar, most recently in *All About My Mother* (1999). She is married to pop musician Fito Páez.

## THEATER

*Porteños,* traditionally, are theatergoers. In the year 2000, for example, more than 300,000 attended programs at both the Teatro Colón and the Teatro General San Martín combined, and nearly 200,000 went to the Teatro Cervantes. In September 2002, in the midst of the country's worst economic crisis ever, there were 110 plays showing at 70 theaters, and three new theaters opened their doors the first weekend of that month.

Avenida Corrientes is the traditional locus of live theater, but the last few years of economic hardship have taken the luster off many of its venues and it's worth seeking out "off-Corrientes" alternatives. Ranging from vulgar burlesque with elaborate stage shows to Shakespearean and avant garde drama, the theater scene is busiest from June through August. The difference between traditional theaters and shoestring venues is not so much the quality of acting as the production budget; larger budgets allow much more elaborate sets at larger venues. The biggest productions can even move intact to the Atlantic beach resort of Mar del Plata for the summer.

The theater tradition dates from late colonial times, when creation of the Virreinato del Río de la Plata gave the city a certain legitimacy and pretensions, at least, to high culture. Over the course of the 19th century, the area's theater culture developed through institutions like the *sainete,* a humorous performance dealing with immigrant issues.

Formal theater dates from the late 19th century, thanks to the patronage of the Montevideo-born Podestá family, who built theaters in Buenos Aires and La Plata. Influential early playwrights included Montevideo-born Florencio Sánchez (1875–1910), who wrote *sainetes* but drew much of his inspiration from Ibsen; Gregorio de Laferrere (1867–1913), who wrote comic plays; and Roberto Payró (1867–1928), a novelist.

Twentieth-century European dramatists such as Federico García Lorca and Jean Cocteau found that the Buenos Aires theater scene justified the long trip across the Atlantic in the days before jets. Among Argentina's best-loved 20th-century performers are comedian Luis Sandrini (1905–1980) and Lola Membrives (1888–1969); the best-known contemporary playwright is Juan Carlos Gené. Norma Aleandro, while primarily known for her films, is active as a theater director.

## ARTS AND CRAFTS

Argentina's artisanal heritage is not so immediately evident as, say, the indigenous textile traditions of the Peruvian or Guatemalan highlands, but both the city and the countryside have characteristic crafts. The most solidly urban expression of folk art is *filete,* the elaborate rainbow signage that, in the hands of its most skilled practitioners, approaches the finest calligraphy.

Befitting their origins on the Río de la Plata (literally, River of Silver), Argentine silversmiths create truly intricate jewelry, as well as adornments such as the *facón* (knife) and *espuelas* (spurs) that accompany traditional gaucho clothing. The major center for artisanal silverwork is the Buenos Aires provincial town of San Antonio de Areco.

*Argentine silversmiths create truly intricate jewelry, as well as adornments such as the* facón *(knife) and* espuelas *(spurs) that accompany traditional gaucho clothing. The major center for artisanal silverwork is the Buenos Aires provincial town of San Antonio de Areco.*

Skilled leatherworkers produce gaucho-style clothing and horse gear such as *rastras* (belts), reins, and saddles. Both these traditions come together in the production of paraphernalia for *mate,* the herbal "Paraguayan tea" whose consumption is a cultural bellwether in the region. Traditionally, *mate* (the herb) is sipped with a silver *bombilla* (straw) from a *mate* (gourd, in a different context), which may be mounted in a leather holder.

For suggestions on places to purchase crafts, see the Shopping chapter.

# Entertainment Venues

In terms of entertainment, Buenos Aires is a 24-hour city that has as much to offer as New York or London. Argentines in general and *porteños* in particular are night people—discos and dance clubs, for instance, may not even *open* until 1 A.M. or so, and they stay open until dawn. That said, not everything of interest takes place at those hours.

All the Buenos Aires dailies have thorough event listings, especially in their end-of-the-week supplements. These include *La Nación* (Thursday); *Ambito Financiero,* the *Buenos Aires Herald's getOut!* and *Clarín* (all on Friday). *Clarín's* Friday edition includes *Sí!,* a youth-oriented pullout section. There are also listings in the German-language *Argentinisches Tageblatt* (Saturday) and

ticket line for rock star Andrés Calamaro, La Plata, Buenos Aires province

*Página 12* (Sunday). In addition, there are listings in the monthly *Viva Bue,* a freebie distributed by the national and municipal tourist offices, and in *Wipe,* a privately distibuted monthly brochure.

For tickets to events at major entertainment venues (Teatro Gran Rex, Paseo La Plaza, La Trastienda, Teatro Nacional Cervantes, Teatro Astral, Teatro Astros, Teatro Margarita Xirgú, Niceto Club, The Roxy, and Centro Cultural Borges) and to sporting events (for teams such as Boca Juniors, River Plate, and San Lorenzo), contact **Ticketek,** tel. 4323-7200, www.ticketek.com.ar. Ticketek, which adds a US$1 service charge to most tickets, has Microcentro outlets at El Ateneo, Florida 340, and at Librería Yenny in the Galerías Pacífico, San Martín 768; in Barrio Norte at Lee-Chi, Avenida Santa Fe 1670; in Retiro at Patio Bullrich, Avenida del Libertador 740; in Palermo Chico at Shopping Alto Palermo, Avenida Santa Fe 3253; at Paseo Alcorta, Jerónimo Salguero 3172, Palermo Chico; and in Belgrano at Avenida Cabildo 1978.

For discount tickets to certain events, including tango shows, cinemas, and live theater, try *carteleras,* agencies that offer last-minute specials. Among them are **Cartelera Espectáculos,** Lavalle 742, tel. 4322-1559, on the downtown pedestrian mall; **Cartelera Baires,** Avenida Corrientes 1382, Local 24, tel. 4372-5058, open 10 A.M.–10 P.M. Monday through Thursday, 10 A.M.–11 P.M. Friday, 10 A.M.–midnight Saturday, and 2–10 P.M. Sunday; and **Cartelera Vea Más**, Avenida Corrientes 1660, tel. 6320-5319, Local 2 in the Paseo La Plaza complex, open 10 A.M. to 10 P.M. daily.

## CAFÉS

No single place embodies *porteño* tradition better than Monserrat's historic **Café Tortoni,** founded in 1858, at Avenida de Mayo 825, tel. 4342-4328, www.cafetortoni.com.ar; see the separate entry in the Sights chapter. Originally facing

## THEATER IN THE CAPITAL

Despite Argentina's countless economic crises, Buenos Aires remains the theater capital of the continent. Traditionally Avenida Corrientes between Avenida 9 de Julio and Avenida Callao is the heart of the district, but many venues are showing the effects of economic hardship.

Avenida de Mayo and myriad side streets in the Microcentro are also home to important theaters, many of them historic.

Winter is the principal theater season, but events can take place at any time of year. For discount tickets, check *carteleras* or online ticket-purchasing services. All major *porteño* newspapers, including the *Ámbito Financiero,* the *Buenos Aires Herald, Clarín, La Nación* and *Página 12,* provide extensive listings and schedules.

The single most notable theater facility is the **Teatro General San Martín,** Avenida Corrientes 1530, tel. 4371-0111, teatrosanmartin@tsm.data-markets.com.ar, www.teatrosanmartin.com.ar/html/sanmatingen.html, a multipurpose complex that compensates in diversity of offerings for what it lacks in architectural merit. Covering more than 30,000 square meters, this utilitarian building (1961) has three main auditoria, a cinema, exhibition halls, and other facilities that draw up to one million visitors per year. Students with international ID cards get 50 percent discounts for most shows, and there are many free events, as well.

Other major theater venues include the following, all located in the Microcentro and vicinity unless otherwise indicated:

**Multiteatro:** Avenida Corrientes 1283, tel. 4382-9140

**Sala Pablo Neruda:** Avenida Corrientes 1660, tel. 4370-5388

**Teatro Avenida:** Avenida de Mayo 1212, Monserrat, tel. 4381-3193

**Teatro Colonial:** Avenida Paseo Colón 413, Monserrat, tel. 4342-7958

**Teatro del Pueblo:** Diagonal Norte 943, tel. 4326-3606

**Teatro La Carbonera:** Balcarce 868, San Telmo, tel. 4362-2651

**Teatro La Otra Orilla:** Tucumán 3527, Almagro, tel. 4862-7718

**Teatro Nacional Cervantes:** Libertad 815, tel. 4815-8883, www.teatrocervantes.gov.ar

---

Avenida Rivadavia, it acquired a new frontage on Avenida de Mayo as city mayor Torcuato de Alvear redeveloped the area in the 1880s. Though most tourists come for coffee and croissants, the bar serves good mixed drinks (US$5) that come accompanied by a sizable *tabla* of sliced salami, paté, cheese, olives, and other snacks that easily feeds two people; separately, drinks cost only about US$2 each.

Superannuated but hanging on, the worn-around-the-edges **Confitería Ideal,** Suipacha 384, tel. 4326-0521, is one of the Microcentro's most traditional settings for coffee and croissants. Huge pillars support oval ceilings with multiple chandeliers, but one gets the notion that when a light bulb burns out it never gets replaced; the mahogany walls are in good shape, but the upholstered chairs are coming apart at the seams, and the floor tiles are cracked, stained, and worn from a century of foot traffic. Nevertheless, the Ideal served as a set for the Madonna *Evita* film, and it also hosts tango events; see the separate entry for *milongas* later in this chapter. As of this writing, Confitería Ideal is to undergo a renovation.

By contrast, the elegant **Confitería Richmond,** Florida 468, tel. 4322-1341, looks as good as the day it opened; one of Jorge Luis Borges's favorites, it draws the *porteño* elite for both breakfast and afternoon tea, and also serves as a bar and restaurant. Its woodwork, chandeliers, tables, and upholstery are all in primo condition and, thanks to the nonsmoking section at the front, non-puffers don't have to hike through clouds of toxic gases. Prices are higher here, though, and the service can be a little lacking.

The distinguishing feature at Retiro's **Florida Garden,** Florida 889, tel. 4312-7902, is the

**Teatro Payró:** San Martín 766, tel. 4312-5922

**Teatro Presidente Alvear:** Avenida Corrientes 1659, tel. 4374-6076

There are several smaller and less conventional "off-Corrientes" venues, some of which might be called microtheaters—**Teatro El Vitral,** Rodríguez Peña 344, tel. 4371-0948 can seat only about 40 people in front of each of its three small stages. **LiberArte,** Avenida Corrientes 1555, tel. 4375-2341, is a politically and socially conscious bookstore that also offers theater programs on weekends.

The **Centro Latinoamericano de Creación e Investigación Teatral,** Bolívar 825 in San Telmo, tel. 4361-8358, correo@celcit.com.org.ar, www.celcit.org.ar, is an innovative theater and educational institution that produces plays by top Latin American dramatists.

San Telmo's **Teatro Margarita Xirgú,** Chacabuco 863/875, tel. 4300-2448, info@complejomxirgu .com.ar, www.complejomxirgu.com.ar, is the performing arts arm of the Casal de Catalunya cultural center, tel. 4300-5252. The center itself was founded by Catalán refugees from the Spanish dictatorship of Francisco Franco.

Before his death in 1977, La Boca artist and promoter Benito Quinquela Martín donated the building that serves as headquarters for the La Boca theater group **Teatro de la Ribera,** Pedro de Mendoza 1821, tel. 4302-8866. Their barrio compatriots **Teatro Catalinas Sur** have their facilities at Benito Pérez Galdós 93, tel. 4300-5707, catalinasur@arnet.com.ar, www.catalinasur.com.ar.

Some companies lack regular venues in the strictest sense—they may appear spontaneously or rent theaters to put on their productions. Less conventional groups to watch for include **Teatreros Ambulantes Las Calandracas,** California 1732, Barracas, tel. 4302-6285, loscalandracas@hotmail.com; **Teatro Callejero La Runfla; Diablomundo,** a puppet theater from the Gran Buenos Aires suburb of Temperley; and **Casita de la Selva,** La Selva 4022, Vélez Sarsfield. These groups often take it literally take to the streets, performing in parks and other public venues, but the **Grupo Teatral Escena Subterránea,** tel. 4777-8599, takes it beneath the streets, performing in Subte cars and stations.

paintings that adorn its supporting columns. Tables are uneven, and the food—the *medialunas* (croissants) in particular—is mediocre, but it has a devoted clientele. Monserrat's **London City,** Avenida de Mayo 599, is a more traditional choice for afternoon tea.

Recoleta's **La Biela,** Avenida Quintana 596/600, tel. 4804-0449, is a classic Buenos Aires breakfast spot, but even after devaluation this remains a relatively pricey place to eat. In good weather, try the patio, beneath the shade of the palm and *palo borracho* trees, and the giant *gomero* or *ombú,* which needs wooden beams to prop up its sprawling branches. It's slightly more expensive to eat outside, though, and the outdoor service can be inconsistent.

**Café de la Paix,** across the street at Avenida Quintana 595, tel. 4804-6820, gets the overflow from La Biela.

# BARS AND CLUBS

The distinction between cafés and bars is not always obvious—in fact, it's often more a continuum than a dichotomy. Some of the more stylish (or pretentious) bars often go by the English word pub, pronounced as in English, and many call themselves Irish.

## Monserrat/Catedral al Sur and Vicinity

Relocated after the demolition of its classic 25 de Mayo locale in the Microcentro, **Bar Seddon,** on the edge of San Telmo at Defensa 695, has made a successful transition to the capital's oldest neighborhood. **Viejos Tiempos,** Defensa 333, tel. 4345-0180, specializes in draft beer and closes early, around 9 P.M., and is also closed on weekends.

**@lternativa,** Hipólito Yrigoyen 851, is a dance club that charges differential admission: roughly US$1.50 for men, US$.50 for women. **Eldorado,** Hipólito Yrigoyen 947, tel. 4334-2115, features live music acts. The capital's Goths gather at **Requiem,** Avenida de Mayo 948, tel. 4331-5870, www.requiemgothic.com, on Saturday nights.

Behind its streetside restaurant, **La Trastienda,** Balcarce 460, tel. 4342-7650, has recycled a Monserrat warehouse into an attractive theater that hosts both live music and drama.

## Microcentro and Vicinity

**Downtown Matías,** Reconquista 701, tel. 4311-0327, www.matiaspub.com.ar, is the Microcentro branch of Buenos Aires's oldest Irish-style pub; drinks are mostly in the US$2–3 range, and pub lunches run about US$3. There is live music in various styles, including Celtic, depending on the night, and a 7–11 P.M. happy hour.

**La Cigale,** on the edge of Retiro at 25 de Mayo 722, tel. 4312-8275, has live music. Bar lunches cost about US$3. **La Bodeguita,** Sarmiento 1594, tel. 4375-3388, is a wine bar with live music and an international restaurant menu.

The artsy **Foro Gandhi,** in new quarters at Avenida Corrientes 1743, tel. 4374-7501, is a hybrid bookstore/coffeehouse/cultural center whose offerings include films, poetry readings, tango shows, and theater.

Note that, geographically speaking, the Microcentro pubs listed in this section are close to the Retiro line.

## San Telmo and Vicinity

**Bar Plaza Dorrego,** Defensa 1098, tel. 4361-0141, makes an ideal place to take a break from Sunday flea marketing or to enjoy a beer on its namesake plaza any other day—at least when it's not raining. Nearby **Café del Arbol,** Humberto Primo 422, serves the same purpose.

**Enoteka,** Defensa 891, tel. 4363-0011, is a wine-by-the-glass and tapas bar with a wide variety of Argentine wines but also vintages from Spain, France, Italy, Uruguay, and the United States. It's also an ideal place to take a break from the Sunday bustle at Plaza Dorrego.

**La Viga,** Cochabamba 158, tel. 4301-9983 or 4382-3282, is a bar with a small stage that, at least twice monthly, hosts **Peña La Baguala,** a folk music collective with no fixed abode.

**Espacio Ecléctico,** Humberto Primo 730, tel. 4307-1966, is a combination bar/café/art space that also offers live music on occasion. **Africa 1,** Balcarce 958, tel. 4300-6454, is a reggae venue.

**Cemento,** Estados Unidos 1234, is a cavernous warehouse that hosts *rock nacional* groups on the way up. Often threatened with closure, it somehow keeps hanging on. **Tabaco Rock,** Estados Unidos 265, is a tiny venue featuring live rock bands.

## La Boca

A restaurant by day, **El Samovar de Rasputín,** Del Valle Iberlucea 1251, tel. 4302-3190, is a lively blues-and-rock venue on weekends. On the northern edge of the barrio, opposite Parque Lezama, the **Blues Special Club,** Almirante Brown 102, tel. 4854-2338, has traditionally flown in performers from Chicago and other blues hotbeds in the States, but the economic crisis may limit that practice. It's open Friday and Saturday nights only.

## Once and the Abasto (Balvanera)

**Remember,** Corrientes 1983, tel. 4953-0638, is a multipurpose venue, but it's primarily a pub that also offers music (jazz and blues) and live theater—mostly one-person acts.

Recoleta's slick sports bars have glitz, but Buenos Aires's ultimate sports bar is **Café Bar Banderín,** Guardia Vieja 3601 in the Abasto, tel. 4862-7757. Decorated with soccer pennants dating decades back, it recalls the era when *porteños* argued about rather than gawked at soccer. There's TV now, but the mid-'50s atmosphere survives.

## Retiro

More casual than any other bar in the barrio, **Bárbaro,** Tres Sargentos 415, tel. 4311-6856, takes its punning name from a *lunfardo* term roughly translatable as "cool." And it is, but unpretentiously so.

Typical of British/Irish-style pubs is **John John,** Reconquista 924, which has good reasonably priced drinks and an "erotic happy hour" Wednesdays. Nearby, **The Kilkenny,** Marcelo T. de Alvear 399, tel. 4312-7291, is another of these putative Irish pubs, open noon–6 A.M., with a 7–9 P.M. happy hour; there are Irish beers on tap, plenty of whiskey, and live bands around midnight. Others in the same category include the **Druid Inn,** Reconquista 1040, tel. 4312-3688, which occasionally hosts live Celtic music; **The Temple Bar,** Marcelo T. de Alvear 945, tel. 4322-0474, www.thetemplebar.com.ar, and **Downtown Matías,** San Martín 979, tel. 4312-9644, www.matiaspub.com.ar.

**Milión,** bordering Barrio Norte at Paraná 1048, tel. 4815-9925, is a tapas bar occupying three stories of a magnificent 1913 mansion; minimally altered for its current use, it offers garden, patio, and interior seating. Beer costs around US$1, with mixed drinks in the US$2–3 range. There's a 6–9 P.M. happy hour for beer only on weekdays; it's open 5:30 P.M.–2 A.M. Monday–Wednesday, until 3 A.M. Thursday, and until 4 A.M. Friday, 7:30 P.M.–4 A.M. Saturday, and 7:30 P.M.–1 A.M. Sunday. Restaurant entrées cost in the US$3.50–6 range.

The nearby **Gran Bar Danzón,** Libertad 1161, tel. 4811-1108, is a sophisticated wine bar that doubles as a restaurant that offers a fine sushi special at happy hour (7–9 P.M., though the sushi chef takes Mondays off). Drinkers can lounge on the comfy chairs and sofas or at the long bar; the dining area is separate. The music could be better—it tends toward *marcha,* as Argentines call techno—but the staff is cordial and the selection of wine by the glass is impressive.

## Recoleta and Barrio Norte

Often derided as a pickup bar, the **Shamrock,** Rodríguez Peña 1220, tel. 4812-3584, is the Barrio Norte version of an Irish pub. **Buller Brewing Company,** Presidente Ramón Ortiz 1827, tel. 4808-9061, www.bullerpub.com, is a brew pub that produces seven types of beer served with tapas, seafood, and pizza.

**Locos por el Fútbol,** in the Village Recoleta complex at Vicente López 2000, has larger-than-

life-size screens for soccer matches. The **World Sports Café,** nearby at Junín 1745, tel. 4807-5444, is similar but not quite so overwhelming. **New Port,** Junín 1715, tel. 4803-3332, offers live music some nights. The Recoleta branch of the worldwide hamburger and rock 'n' roll memorabilia chain, **Hard Rock Café,** is at Avenida Pueyrredón 2501, tel. 4807-7625. It's open noon–3 A.M. daily.

**Los Porteños,** Avenida Las Heras 2100, tel. 4809-3548/0025, is a corner bar that holds only about 70 people for live blues with an exceptional house band on Friday and Saturday (Latin music) with a US$1 cover charge; drinks are reasonably priced, there's a decent bar-food menu, friendly staff, and an unpretentious crowd with a good age mix. The air quality is better than at most *porteño* bars.

**Rooster,** Anchorena 1347 in Barrio Norte, tel. 4962-5776, features diverse live music ranging from Afro-Cuban salsa to rock, punk, jazz, and metal.

## Palermo

Over the past several years, Palermo has become the focus of Buenos Aires's dining and nightlife scenes—particularly in the area around Plaza Cortázar (Plaza Serrano), popularly referred to as Palermo Soho, and in the more northerly area known as Palermo Hollywood, beyond Avenida Juan B. Justo. There's another cluster around Las Cañitas, between Avenida Luis María Campos and Avenida Libertador, and the odd venue elsewhere in the barrio.

**República de Acá,** fronting on Plaza Serrano at Serrano 1549, tel. 4581-02778, is a combination comedy club, karaoke bar, and relatively expensive Internet café. **El Taller,** Serrano 1595, tel. 4831-5501, is also a comedy club and alternative theater. Toward Plaza Italia, **Mundo Bizarro,** Guatemala 4802, tel. 4773-1967, is a self-consciously hip bar with erotic decor that attracts a youthful crowd. The trendy **El 5° Stone,** Thames and Nicaragua, tel. 4832-4961, has live and recorded rock music.

One of the most intimate entertainment venues in town, the **Club del Vino,** Cabrera 4737, tel. 4833-0048, is a restaurant, wine bar, and theater seating a maximum of about 150 people for live tango and folk music. Prices for shows vary but are generally reasonable, starting around US$3, and the air quality's not bad by *porteño* standards.

The **Krüg Bar,** Francisco Acuña de Figueroa 1437 between Honduras and Gorriti, tel. 4862-9223, krugbar@yahoo.com, has live music of inconsistent standards, an undisciplined Bohemian atmosphere, and poor air quality.

The **Niceto Club,** Niceto Vega 5510 in Palermo Hollywood, tel. 4779-6396, has become one of the area's top live music venues over the last several years; it's open Thursday, Friday, and Saturday nights. The offerings cover many styles of music.

**The Roxy,** in the misleadingly named Arcos del Sol (literally, Arches of the Sun) at Avenida Sarmiento and Avenida Casares, tel. 4899-0314, www.theroxybsas.com.ar, sits beneath a railroad bridge in Parque Tres de Febrero. Drawing performers of the caliber of Charly García, it's just what rock 'n' roll is supposed to be—rowdy and sweaty but not violent. Overhead trains shake the building and the roof leaks in heavy rain.

**Voodoo,** located in Cañitas Báez 340, tel. 4772-2453, is renowned for powerful mixed drinks. Next door, **Jackie O.,** Báez 344, tel. 4774-4844, serves a fine caipirinha and other mixed drinks.

Across the street, **Van Koning,** Báez 325, tel. 4772-9909, is a Netherlands-style pub that capitalizes on the Argentine fixation with all things Dutch (the fascination began when the country acquired its own royalty with the marriage of Máxima Zorreguieta to Crown Prince William in 2002). Dutch expatriates hold a special gathering here the first Wednesday of every month.

## Belgrano

The longtime Irish pub institution **Downtown Matías** has opened a Belgrano branch at Echeverría 3195, tel. 4545-1050, www.matiaspub.com.ar. **Mr. Floyd,** Mendoza 2350, is an interesting blend of bar and CD shop, with an emphasis on blues and rock.

## Outer Barrios

**Hangar,** Avenida Rivadavia 10921 in the far western barrio of Liniers, draws major live rock acts.

# JAZZ VENUES

**Clásica y Moderna,** Avenida Callao 892, tel. 4812-8707, is a complex hybrid of bookstore-café and live jazz venue that has occupied the same Barrio Norte location since 1938. Once frequented by writers and intellectuals like Alfonsina Storni and Leopoldo Lugones, it has since seen performances by the likes of Susana Rinaldi, Mercedes Sosa, and Liza Minelli. It's open 8 A.M.–2 A.M. daily except Friday and Saturday, when it stays open until 4 A.M.

Differing slightly in concept is the nearby **Notorious,** Avenida Callao 966, tel. 4815-8473, a combination bar, CD store, and live-music venue. It's normally open 8 A.M.–midnight daily except Sundays and holidays, when it opens at 11 A.M., but live music shows go later.

Primarily a restaurant—and a very fine one— **Splendid,** Gorriti 5099 in Palermo Viejo, tel. 4833-4477, offers live jazz Thursday and Saturday around 10 P.M. For live jazz and Balkan music(!) in Palermo Hollywood, check the schedule at **Tiempo de Gitanos,** El Salvador 5575, tel. 4776-6143, a bar/restaurant that serves an eclectic mix of Spanish and Middle Eastern dishes. Shows with dinner cost in the US$11–12 range pp.

# TANGO VENUES

Many but by no means all tango venues are in the southerly barrios of Monserrat, San Telmo, and Barracas, with a few elsewhere and in outlying barrios. Tango shows range from relatively modest and simple programs at low prices to extravagant productions at high (sometimes excessive) cost. Even the latter, though, can be a bargain when the peso sinks or discount tickets are available through *carteleras*.

sur.com.ar, is a relatively spontaneous and informal tango show venue open late every night except Sunday. The US$6 pp charge includes unlimited pizza, but drinks are additional. **La Cumparsita** Chile 302, tel. 4361-6880, is another classic tango show venue, slightly more expensive at US$7 pp.

It's a rock venue most nights, but **Mitos Argentinos,** Humberto Primo 489, tel. 4362-7810, has a Sunday afternoon tango show, 2–5 P.M., which coincides with the nearby Feria de San Telmo on the Plaza Dorrego. Both male and female tango singers are accompanied by live guitar and/or recorded music, and dancers perform to recorded music. There is no cover charge, and the food and drink are reasonably priced. Overlooking Plaza Dorrego, **El Balcón de San Telmo,** Humberto Primo 461, tel. 4362-2354, is a similar restaurant locale with tango shows.

One of San Telmo's classic tango venues, **El Viejo Almacén,** ooccupies a late-18th-century building at Balcarce and Avenida Independencia, tel. 4307-6689, valmacen@infovia.com.ar, www.viejo-almacen.com.ar. It charges US$19 pp for the show alone, US$27 pp including dinner at its restaurant directly across the street.

**La Convención,** Carlos Calvo 375, tel. 4300-9246, is a pricey Provencale venue that offers both tango classes (late Tuesday and Sunday afternoons) and tango shows (Fridays and Saturdays nights).

**Señor Tango,** Vieytes 1655 in Barracas, tel. 4303-0231, has one of the biggest floor shows in town for US$40 with dinner, which starts at 8 P.M.; without dinner the show, which starts at 10 P.M., costs US$25.

The **Centro Cultural Torquato Tasso,** Defensa 1575, tel. 4307-6506, offers tango instruction; contact them for more information.

## La Boca

**La Vitrola del Sur,** Aráoz de Lamadrid 701, tel. 4303-8331, offers daytime tango shows with fixed-price lunches.

## Once and the Abasto (Balvanera)

Literally in the shadow of the redeveloped Mercado del Abasto, part of a municipal project to sustain the legacy of the "Morocho del Abasto"

Café Tortoni and the Academia Nacional del Tango

## Monserrat/Catedral al Sur and Vicinity

The legendary **Café Tortoni,** Avenida de Mayo 825, tel. 4342-4328, www.cafetortoni.com.ar, hosts live tango song and dance shows at its Sala Alfonsina Storni, separated from the main part of the café, for around US$4 pp plus drinks and food.

Dating from 1920, **El Querandí,** Perú 302, tel. 5199-1770, querandi@querandi.com.ar, www.querandi.com.ar, is another *porteño* classic; for US$35 pp, the nightly dinner (starting at 8:30 P.M.) and show (starting at 10:30 P.M.) is toward the upper end of the price scale, but it's an elegant place.

## San Telmo and Vicinity

San Telmo's **Bar Sur,** Estados Unidos 299, tel. 4362-6086, info@bar-sur.com.ar, www.bar-in his old neighborhood, the **Esquina Carlos Gardel,** Carlos Gardel 3200, tel./fax 4867-6363, info@esquinacarlosgardel.com.ar, www.esquinacarlosgardel.com.ar, has nightly tango shows starting at US$23 (show only) and US$32 (with dinner). There are more expensive VIP boxes.

## Outer Barrios

Named for the great songwriter, the **Esquina Homero Manzi,** Avenida San Juan 3601, tel. 4957-8488, info@esquinahomeromanzi.com.ar, www.esquinahomero-manzi.com.ar, was once part of the *arrabales* (outskirts) in the barrio of Boedo. Though not quite so remote as it once was, it still holds a place as part of tango history. Dinner starts at 9 P.M. nightly; the show commences at 10 P.M.

In the southern barrio of Nueva Pompeya, **El Chino,** Beazley 3566, tel. 4911-0215, has become a tourist hangout for its rugged authenticity. Inexpensive shows and live music take place Friday and Saturday nights only; arrive well before midnight to get a table, though the music doesn't start until well after. The food is, for lack of a better description, working-class Argentine.

## MILONGAS VENUES

For those who want to dance instead of watch, or who want to learn, the best options are neighborhood *milongas,* many of which take place at cultural centers. Organized events charge in the US$2–3 range with live orchestra, less with recorded music.

For classes, a good clearinghouse is the **Academia Nacional del Tango,** directly above the Café Tortoni at Avenida de Mayo 833 in Monserrat, tel. 4345-6968, www.sectur.gov.ar/cultura/ant/ant.htm. It even offers a three-year degree in tango.

Upstairs at Confitería Ideal, the **A Toda Milonga,** Suipacha 384, tel. 4729-6390,

> *For those who want to dance instead of watch, or who want to learn, the best options are neighborhood milongas, many of which take place at cultural centers. Find out about classes from the Academia Nacional del Tango.*

osvaldo_marrapodi@yahoo.com, www.marrapoditango.unlugar.com, takes place every Thursday 3–10 P.M. Admission costs US$1.50. Instructor Osvaldo Marrapoidi also offers Tuesday lessons, 3:30–6:30 P.M. and 6:30–9:30 P.M., and individual lessons by arrangement.

Another central location is **El Sótano,** Perón 1372, tel. 4854-5647, whose orchestra-accompanied *milonga* takes place Thursday at 11 P.M. Admission costs about US$1.50.

San Telmo's highly regarded **Centro Cultural Torquato Tasso,** Defensa 1575, tel. 4307-6506, offers *milongas* Friday and Saturday night at 11 P.M. (with a live orchestra) and Sunday afternoon (with recorded music). Admission costs US$1.50 except Sunday, when it's nominal. Tango instruction is also available.

**Club Gricel,** La Rioja 1180 in the barrio of San Cristóbal, tel. 4957-7157, offers live orchestra *milongas* Friday at 11 P.M. and Saturday at 10:30 P.M. (admission US$1.50). Sunday, at 9:30 P.M., there's a cheaper event with recorded music.

## FLAMENCO VENUES

As tango partisans, Argentines may feel ambivalence toward Spanish music and dance, but several *porteño* venues offer flamenco shows and even lessons, almost always on weekends (as opposed to tango shows, which take place every night of the week). Among the options are the Puerto Madero Spanish restaurant **Dominguín,** along Dique No. 3 at Alicia Moreau de Justo 1130, tel. 4342-9863; Monserrat's **Ávila Bar,** Avenida de Mayo 1384, tel. 4383-6974; and **El Balcón de San Telmo**, Humberto Primo 461, tel 362-2354.

**Alarico,** Chile 518 in San Telmo, tel. 4300-8810, is a Spanish tapas bar that also offers flamenco shows.

# THE TANGO, THE TANGUERÍA, AND THE MILONGA

For foreigners visiting Buenos Aires, one of the city's legendary attractions is the tango, the dance that conquered European salons despite its dubious origins in the brothels and *arrabales* (outskirts) of the Argentine capital. What they usually see, in high-priced dinner-show *tanguerías*, are pairs of lithe and sexy dancers executing spectacularly intricate steps to the sounds of a professional orchestra in an elaborate setting, often a recycled historical building. It's impressive and professional, but it's not the experience of most *porteños*.

For *porteños*, dance is a participant pastime at *milongas*, informal gatherings that take place at modest neighborhood locales with not even a stage,

maybe only recorded music, and only a modest admission charge. *Milongueros,* those who frequent *milongas,* may dance tango, but that's not the only option—the term itself derives from a common style of music and dance, in 2/4 time, traditional to the Río de la Plata region. A *milonga* can also mean a spontaneous outbreak of dancing at a party.

*Tanguerías,* whatever their appeal, are for tourists. *Milongas* belong to the barrio, but tourists are welcome if they want to see—and perhaps dance—the tango as a popular art form in which couples from their teens to their *tercera edad* (retirement age) take part. The *milonga* is more than just the tango; it's a part of the *porteño* experience that transcends the stereotype of youth and beauty.

## CLASSICAL MUSIC VENUES

The classical music and opera season lasts from March through November but peaks in winter, from June through August. Unquestionably, the capital's prime classical music locale remains the **Teatro Colón,** Libertad 621, tel./fax 4378-7344, boleteria@teatrocolon.org.ar, www.teatrocolon.org.ar, though the recent economic crisis has meant increasing reliance on Argentines rather than high-profile foreigners (performers such as Luciano Pavarotti and Plácido Domingo have often graced the Colón's stage).

Among other performers that play the Colón are the Orquesta Filarmónica de Buenos Aires—often with guest conductors from elsewhere in Latin America—and the Mozarteum Argentina, tel. 4811-3448. Occasionally there is a surprise such as the rhythm-and-blues unit Memphis La Blusera, the first of its sort to take the hallowed stage, in conjunction with the Orquesta Sinfónica Nacional.

Other classical venues include the Microcentro's **Teatro Ópera,** Avenida Corrientes 860, tel. 4326-1225; Monserrat's **Teatro Avenida,** Avenida de Mayo 1212; tel. 4381-0662; Retiro's **Teatro Coliseo,** Marcelo T. de Alvear 1125, tel. 4807-1277, www.fundacioncoliseum.com.ar/teatro.htm; and

Belgrano's **Auditorio de Belgrano,** at Avenida Cabildo and Virrey Loreto, tel. 4783-1783.

**La Scala de San Telmo**, Pasaje Giuffra 371, tel. 4362-1187 or 4813-5741, scala@lascala.com.ar, www.lascala.com.ar, is an intimate high-culture performing-arts venue focused on theater and classical music, but with occasional folk indulgences. As an institution, it also trains aspiring performers.

## CULTURAL CENTERS

Buenos Aires has a multitude of municipal, national, and international cultural centers, all of which offer entertainment, events, dance and language classes, and many other activities.

The **Centro Cultural Borges,** adjacent to the Galerías Pacífico at the corner of Viamonte and San Martín, tel. 5555-5359, ccbor@tournet.com.ar, cborges@tournet.com.ar, features permanent exhibits on Argentina's most famous literary figure, as well as rotating fine arts exhibitions and performing arts events in its Auditorio Astor Piazzola. It's open 10 A.M.–9 P.M. daily except Sunday, when it opens at noon. Admission costs US$.70.

In addition to its German-language classes and library, the **Instituto Goethe,** at Avenida Corrientes 319, 1st floor, tel. 4315-3327, goethe

@buenosaires.goethe.org, www.goethe.de/hs/bue/spindex.htm, sponsors lectures, films, and concerts.

The increasingly important **Centro Cultural Ricardo Rojas,** Avenida Corrientes 2038 in Balvanera, tel. 4954-5521, rojas@rec.uba.ar, www.rojas.uba.ar, has regular theater programs as well as exhibitions, and classes and workshops in theater, dance, tango, art, language, photography, and the like.

In Monserrat, the **Centro Cultural Plaza Defensa,** Defensa 535, tel. 4342-8610, plazadefensa@buenosaires.gov.ar, is a neighborhood cultural center that hosts small-scale events. In Barracas, the **Centro Cultural del Sur** occupies a colonial-style house at Avenida Caseros 1750, tel. 4306-0301, and hosts some of the biggest events of the Festival de Tango.

The **Asociación Argentina de Cultura Inglesa,** known also as the British Arts Centre, Suipacha 1333 in Retiro, tel. 4393-6941, informes@britishartscentre.org.ar, www.aaci.org.ar, is open 3–9 P.M. weekdays, 11 A.M.–1:30 P.M. weekends except in January and February, when it's closed.

Recoleta's **Centro Cultural Ciudad de Buenos Aires,** Junín 1930, tel. 4803-1040, www.centroculturalrecoleta.org, is one of the city's outstanding cultural venues, with a museum, art exhibits, films, and concerts, many of them inexpensive or even free. It's open 2–9 P.M. Tuesday through Friday, 10 A.M.–9 P.M. weekends and holidays; there are guided visits (call tel. 4803-4057) Wednesday at 6 P.M. and Saturday at 3 and 5 P.M.

The **Fundación Cultural Japonés,** in Palermo's Parque Tres de Febrero, tel. 4804-4922, at Avenida Casares and Avenida Berro, has live theater, art exhibits, and gardening workshops.

## GAY SOCIAL VENUES

Buenos Aires has a vigorous gay scene, centered mostly around Recoleta, Barrio Norte, and Palermo Viejo, with a handful of venues scattered elsewhere. Lots of gay men hang out on Avenida Santa Fe between Callao and Pueyrredón, a good area to meet people and learn the latest.

The capital's gay venues bars and clubs are mostly tolerant and inclusive of heterosexuals.

## THE RESUSCITATION OF CARNAVAL

Carnaval is traditionally a far lesser celebration in Buenos Aires than in Brazil or even Uruguay, where Montevideo's Afro-Uruguayan communities uphold the tradition of syncopated *candombe* music. *Candombe* may still be more conspicuous on the murals of its musicians in San Telmo than in the Argentine capital's pre-Lenten celebrations, but it is making a comeback.

*Candombe* nearly disappeared after the 1870s, as overwhelming European immigration overshadowed what remained of the Afro-Argentine heritage. Elements of it survived, though, thanks to *murgas*, bands of brightly costumed dancers accompanied by drums, who adopted the music of a nearly bygone way of life. Contemporary neighborhood *murgas*, with their subtext of political protest by an underclass betrayed by its owners, display a revived urgency.

In 2002, 132 *murgas* of colorfully clad leaping dancers and pounding drummers participated in neighborhood *corsos* (parades). Bearing names like Los Amantes de La Boca (The Lovers of La Boca), La Locura de Boedo (The Madness of Boedo), Malayunta (Bad Company), Los Reyes del Movimiento (The Kings of Rhythm), Los Impacientes de Palermo (The Anxieties of Palermo), and Los Quitapenas (Sorrow Busters), they constituted, according to the daily *Clarín,* "a forceful mixture of pot-banging and ill-humor."

Nevertheless, this protest music and dance has offered a colorful outlet in hard times. Popular commercial musicians such as *rock nacional* icons Los Piojos have also gravitated to this dynamic expression of the voices of the disenfranchised.

When non-Argentine heterosexual women tire of Argentine machismo, they sometimes prefer gay bars for dancing.

**In Vitro,** Azcuénaga 1007, tel. 4824-0932, is a well-established Barrio Norte gay bar. **Angel's,** Viamonte 2168 in Balvanera/Once, is a gay bar that's open Thursday through Sunday nights.

Open Thursday to Sunday, **Bar del Este,** Bulnes 1250 in Palermo Viejo, tel. 4864-4056, bardeleste@sinectis.com.ar, is popular for danc-ing and drag shows; Saturday is the biggest night. Actively welcoming people of any sexual orien-tation, it's comfortable—it has contemporary style and lighting, and serves good strong drinks at reasonable prices.

Palermo Soho's **Bach Bar,** Cabrera 4390, is a lesbian locale that doesn't advertise the fact—there's no sign outside—but there's usually a crowd. It's open nightly except Monday begin-ning about 11 P.M.

## Holidays, Festivals, and Events

One Uruguayan said of his country that it is *"un país de feriados"* (a country of holidays). Buenos Aires could be called the same; it observes all the typical national holidays and quite a few special events on top of that. The summer months of January and February, when most *porteños* leave on vacation, are generally a quiet time; things pick up after school starts in early March.

### January
January 1 is **Año Nuevo** (New Year's Day), an of-ficial holiday.

### February/March
Dates for the pre-Lenten **Carnaval** (Carnival) vary from year to year but, in Buenos Aires, most celebrations take place on weekends rather than during the week. While unlikely ever to match the spectacle of Brazilian festivities, Carnaval is en-joying a revival, particularly with the performances of barrio *murgas* (street musicians and dancers) rather than elaborate downtown events.

### March
**Semana Santa** (Holy Week) is widely observed in Catholic Argentina, though only the days from **Viernes Santo** (Good Friday) through **Pascua** (Easter) are official holidays. Many Ar-gentines, though, use the long weekend for a mini-vacation.

**Saint Patrick's Day,** March 17, has acquired a certain fashionability in Buenos Aires, but some *porteños* seem to see it as an excuse to get roaring drunk at any of several nominally Irish pubs (Buenos Aires did see substantial Irish immigra-tion in the 20th century).

In late March, the **Exposición de Otoño de la Asociación Criadores de Caballos Criollos** is the best-of-breed showcase for the hardy horses of the sort that Aimé Tschiffely rode from Buenos Aires to Washington, D.C. in the 1920s. Spon-sored by the Asociación Criadores de Caballos Criollos (Creole Horse Breeders' Association), Larrea 670, 2nd floor, in Balvanera, tel. 4961-3387, caballocriollo@ciudad.com.ar, www.caballoscriollos.com.ar, the event normally takes place at the Predio Ferial de la Sociedad Rural Argentina, on Avenida Sarmiento (Subte: Plaza Italia).

Though it began in 1998 on Gardel's birthday of December 11, the increasingly important **Festival de Tango** now follows Brazilian Car-naval in March. Lasting several weeks, it in-cludes dance competitions and numerous free music and dance events at venues like the Cen-tro Cultural San Martín, the Centro Cultural Recoleta, and the Centro Cultural del Sur, where calendars are available; for details, contact the Festival de Tango, tel. 0800/3378-4825, www.festivaldetango.com.

### April
Buenos Aires's annual book fair, the **Feria del Libro,** has been a fixture on the *porteño* literary scene for nearly three decades. Dates vary, but it lasts three weeks and sometimes extends into May. Most but not all exhibitors are from Latin Amer-ica, but European and Asian countries also par-ticipate, and there are regular author appearances.

**ARTS & ENTERTAINMENT**

# FESTIVAL BUENOS AIRES TANGO

Despite its newness—the first event took place only in 1997—the Festival Buenos Aires Tango, tel. 0800/3378-4825, www.festivaldetango.com.ar, informacion@festivaldetango.com.ar, has become one of the city's signature special events. Lasting three weeks from mid-February to early March, this festival of music, song, and dance ranges from the very traditional and conservative to the imaginative and even the daring.

Shortly after its creation, the festival moved from December to February and March to follow Brazilian Carnaval, but it is not strictly a tourist-oriented affair; it is also widely accepted and anticipated by a demanding *porteño* public. Unlike Brazilian Carnaval, it is not a mass spectacle, but rather a decentralized series of performances at relatively small, often intimate, venues around the capital. As such, it offers opportunities to see and hear not just established artists, but also developing performers.

Most of the funding for the city-sponsored festival goes to pay the artists, and admission is either free or inexpensive; however, tickets are usually available on a first-come, first-serve basis on the day of the performance. Among the locales hosting events are the Academia Nacional del Tango, Avenida de Mayo 833, Monserrat; the Centro Cultural Plaza Defensa, Defensa 535, Monserrat; the Centro Cultural General San Martín, Avenida Corrientes 1551, Congreso; the Teatro Presidente Alvear, Avenida Corrientes 1659, Congreso; the Centro Cultural del Sur, Avenida Caseros 1750, Barracas; the Centro Cultural Recoleta, Junín 1930, Recoleta; and the Anfiteatro Juan Bautista Alberdi, at Juan Bautista Alberdi and Lisandro de la Torre, Mataderos.

It has recently moved from Recoleta to Palermo's Predio Rural, with entrances at Cerviño 4474 and Avenida Sarmiento 2704, tel. 4777-5500. It's sponsored by the Fundación El Libro, Hipólito Yrigoyen 1628, Monserrat, tel. 4374-3288, fundacion@el-libro.com.ar, www.el-libro.com.ar. Admission costs about US$1.

Toward the end of the month, the **Festival Internacional de Cine Independiente** (International Independent Film Festival) proved a success even during the economic crisis of 2002 (which marked the festival's fourth year). Featuring independent movies from every continent, it takes place at various cinemas around town.

## May

May 1 is **Día del Trabajador** (International Labor Day), an official holiday. On May 25, Argentines observe the **Revolución de Mayo** (May Revolution of 1810), when *porteños* made their first move toward independence by declaring the Viceroy illegitimate. This is not, however, the major indepedendence celebration, which takes place July 9 (see the July section).

For more than a decade now, mid-May's **Feria de Galerías Arte BA** has shown work from dozens of Buenos Aires art galleries. Like the Feria del Libro, it takes place at the Predio La Rural in Palermo.

## June

June 10 is **Día de las Malvinas** (Malvinas Day), an official holiday celebrating Argentina's claim to the British-governed Falkland (Malvinas) Islands. June 20, also an official holiday, is **Día de la Bandera** (Flag Day).

Though not an official holiday, June 24 commemorates the **Día de la Muerte de Carlos Gardel,** the anniversary of the singer's death in an aviation accident in Medellín, Colombia. Pilgrims crowd the streets of the Cementerio de la Chacarita to pay tribute, and there are also tango events.

## July

July 9, **Día de la Independencia,** celebrates the formal declaration of Argentine indepedence at the northwestern city of Tucumán in 1816. Later in the month, when school lets out, many Argentines take **Vacaciones de Invierno** (Winter Holidays), and flights and even buses out of the capital fill up fast.

During the winter holidays, the Sociedad Rural Argentina sponsors the **Exposición Internacional de Ganadería, Agricultura, y Industria Internacional,** the annual agricultural exhibition at the Predio Ferial in Palermo. For more than a century, this has been one of the capital's biggest events; for details contact the Sociedad Rural Argentina, Florida 460, tel. 4324-4700, laganadera@ogden-rural.com.ar.

## August

August 17 is **Día de San Martín,** the official observance of the death (not the birth) of Argentina's independence hero.

## September

In early September, municipal authorities block off traffic from several blocks of Avenida Corrientes, on either side of Avenida Callao, for the **Semana del Libro** (Book Week), where booksellers from around the city and the country maintain open-air stalls.

## October

October 12 is **Día de la Raza** (equivalent to U.S. Columbus Day, marking Columbus's arrival in the new world), an official holiday.

## November

November 2's **Día de los Muertos** (All Souls' Day) is the occasion for Argentines to visit the graves of their loved ones, though this is not the colorful event it is in Mexico and Guatemala.

Also in early November, the gaucho sport of *pato* holds its **Campeonato Argentino Abierto de Pato** (Argentine Open Pato Championship) at the suburban Campo de Mayo; for more information, contact the Federación Argentino de Pato, Avenida Belgrano 530, 5th floor, Monserrat, tel. 4331-0222.

From mid-November to mid-December, the **Campeonato Abierto Argentino de Polo** (Argentine Open Polo Championship) takes place at the Campo Argentino de Polo at Avenida del Libertador and Dorrego in Palermo, tel. 4774-4517. For details, contact the Asociación Argentina de Polo, Hipólito Yrigoyen 636. Monserrat, tel. 4342-8321, torneos@aapolo.com.ar, www.aapolo.com.

## December

Though the Festival de Tango has moved to March, the city still blocks off the street near the Centro Cultural San Martín for the **Milonga de Calle Corrientes,** in which partiers dance to live and recorded music on Gardel's birthday, December 11. Gardel's grave at Chacarita also draws pilgrims.

December 25 is **Navidad** (Christmas Day), an official holiday.

# Sports and Recreation

Not just a city for sightseeing, Buenos Aires also offers options for activities, ranging from the relative tranquility of a chess match to the energy of a pickup soccer game.

The main spectator sport is soccer, an Argentine passion. Befitting a country that grew up on horseback, racing and polo also draw crowds.

tomb of boxer Luis Angel Firpo, Cementerio de la Recoleta

© WAYNE BERNHARDSON

# Outdoor Activities

In the densely built Microcentro and other central barrios, there's not much open space, but hotel health clubs and private gyms are good alternatives for those who can't get out to Puerto Madero's ecological reserve, Palermo's parks, and other open spaces. Parts of these areas are closed to automobiles all week or at least on weekends.

## Protected Areas

The only member of Argentina's national park system close to Buenos Aires is the **Reserva Natural Estricta Otamendi,** a 2,600-hectare riverside reserve on the right bank of the Río Paraná between Tigre and Zárate. Just east of Puerto Madero, however, the spontaneous colonization of a former landfill by native and introduced flora and fauna created the city's **Reserva Ecológica Costanera Sur;** ironically enough, this former rubbish tip has become a favorite destination for jogging, cycling, and weekend outings by *porteños*.

## BIRD-WATCHING

Palermo has large open green spaces, but most of its parks are poor areas for bird-watching because large uncontrolled numbers of feral cats have decimated avian populations; the exception is the Jardín Japonés, which is fenced to keep felines out. The Reserva Ecológica Costanera Sur is better, but the channels of the Paraná river delta and the *estancias* of Buenos Aires province are the best nearby areas.

Argentina has about 3,000 dedicated bird-watchers, mostly affiliated with the Asociación Ornitológica del Plata, 25 de Mayo 749, 2nd floor, in the Microcentro, tel. 4312-8958, info@avesargentinas.org.ar, www.avesargentinas.org.ar. The Asociación also offers bird-watching classes and organized excursions in the vicinity of the capital.

## RUNNING

Many *porteños* have taken up running, but the largest open spaces suitable for the activity are in the northern suburbs of Palermo and Belgrano—in the more central barrios, there are only relatively small plazas. The major exception is the Reserva Ecológica Costanera Sur, the former rubbish tip reinvented as parkland near Puerto Madero.

## CYCLING AND MOUNTAIN BIKING

Buenos Aires's densely built city center, ferocious traffic, and lack of challenging terrain all make cycling at least superficially unappealing. Nevertheless, a surprising number of *porteños*—even including some policemen—get around on bicycles. There is a small but growing network of paved bicycle trails, and the car-free open spaces of Palermo's parks and the roads of suburban Buenos Aires province encourage some riders.

Bikes are for rent along Avenida de Infanta Isabel in Palermo's Parque Tres de Febrero, on both sides of the Museo Sívori. Speed riders can test themselves on the track at the Nuevo Circuito KDT, also in Parque Tres de Febrero at Jerónimo Salguero 3450 (there's another entrance on Avenida Sarmiento), tel. 4802-2619; it's open 8 A.M.–9 P.M. daily, with an admission charge of US$.50 pp. Monthly membership, however, costs only US$3 pp. The park's former Velódromo Municipal, fronting on Avenida Figueroa Alcorta, has been seemingly abandoned and is locked up.

## HORSEBACK RIDING

There are several options for riding lessons in the city proper: the Club Hípico Mediterráneo, Avenida Figueroa Alcorta 4800, Palermo, tel. 4772-3828; the Club Alemán de Equitación,

SPORTS & RECREATION

Avenida Dorrego 4045, Palermo, tel. 4778-7060; and the Club Hípico Argentino, Avenida Figueroa Alcorta 7285, Belgrano, tel. 4786-6240.

Tourist-oriented *estancias* in Buenos Aires province provide plenty of riding opportunities; the Excursions from Buenos Aires chapter provides more information.

## POLO

Argentines may have been raised on horseback, but the British influence made them mount polo ponies. The gaucho tradition has left its mark, though, as Argentine polo style is more rugged than its British antecedent.

Several places offer polo lessons, usually in the vicinity of the capital. Elitist nearly to the point of superciliousness, La Martina, Paraguay 661 in Retiro, tel. 4576-7997, fax 4311-5963, info @lamartina.com, www.lamartina.com, caters to professional polo players and celebrity aficionados. Consequently, both their gear and their lessons are at the top of the price range in a sport not known for bargains.

Recoleta's Alberto Vannucci, Avenida Callao 1773, tel. 4811-3112, info@avannuccisa.com.ar, www.avannuccisa.com.ar, specializes in blankets, saddles, and other leather goods. Logi Polo House, Cabello 3374, Palermo, tel. 4801-9631, has the best selection of mallets.

Jorge Cánaves, Avenida Libertador 6000, Belgrano, tel. 4785-3982, canaves@feedback.com.ar, is well equipped with polo gear, and may be able to organize lessons in Pilar, Buenos Aires province.

The Asociación Argentina de Polo (Argentine Polo Association) is at Hipólito Yrigoyen 636, 1° A, Monserrat, tel. 4342-8321, administracion@aapolo.com, www.aapolo.com. For information on polo as a spectator sport, see the separate Spectator Sports entry later in this chapter.

## TENNIS

Argentine professional tennis has a high international reputation, and it's a popular participant sport, though most courts are private and some require substantial membership fees. During the week, when things are not so busy, they may open to nonmembers.

Among them are the Buenos Aires Lawn Tennis Club, Olleros 1510, Palermo, tel. 4772-0983; and Salguero Tennis/Paddle/Squash, Avenida Salguero 3350, Palermo, tel. 4805-5144.

## GOLF

The Golf Club Lagos de Palermo, an 18-hole course at Avenida Tornquist 1426, tel. 4772-7261, is open 7 A.M.–5 P.M. daily except Monday. Greens fees are US$7 weekdays, US$9 weekends (when reservations are advisable).

The only other courses in town are at the private Club Ciudad de Buenos Aires, Avenida del Libertador 7501, Núñez, tel. 4703-0222 or 4703-1965; and the Golf Club José Jurado, Avenida Coronel Roca 5025 in the northwestern barrio of Villa Lugano, tel. 4605-4706.

For information on courses outside the capital, contact the Asociación Argentina de Golf, Avenida Corrientes 538, 11th floor, in the Microcentro, tel. 4325-1113, www.aag.com.ar; it has a driving range and putting greens at Avenida Costanera Rafael Obligado 1835, tel. 4802-1116. There is also a driving range at the Costa Salguero Golf Center, Avenida Costanera Rafael Obligado and Salguero, tel. 4805-4732.

## CHESS

For a chess match, tournament, or instruction, contact the Club Argentino de Ajedrez, Paraguay 1858, Barrio Norte, tel. 4811-9412, http://club-argentino.tripod.com. Nonmembers are welcome but pay more than members to participate.

## CLIMBING

A city whose highest natural elevation reaches barely 25 meters might seem an improbable place to pursue an activity like climbing, but a pair of gyms have climbing walls for town-bound *porteños* to practice before heading into the countryside. Serious rock climbing is possible in the Sierras de Tandil and the Sierra de la Ventana, both in southern Buenos Aires province, as well as in more remote areas in the Andean northwest and Patagonia.

City climbing gyms include Boulder, Arce 730, Palermo, tel. 4802-4113 (Subte: Olleros, Línea D); and Fugate, Gascón 238, Almagro, tel. 4982-0203 (Subte: Castro Barros, Línea A). Both offer climbing lessons in Buenos Aires and also organize field trips.

## WATER SPORTS

Argentines take readily to water, but the capital's beaches along the silt-laden Río de la Plata are nothing to speak of. There are better options in suburban Tigre, on the Paraná delta, and across the river in Uruguay. Boating, fishing, and even surfing are possible in some of those areas. Note that huge numbers of *porteños* spend their summers in and around Mar del Plata, on the southern coast of Buenos Aires province, but "Mardel" is many hours away except by plane.

*Two Buenos Aires gyms have climbing walls where* porteños *practice before heading into the countryside. Serious rock climbing is possible in the Sierras de Tandil and the Sierra de la Ventana in southern Buenos Aires province, as well as in more remote areas in the Andean northwest and Patagonia.*

### Swimming

For those who can't get to the beaches or afford five-star hotels, Buenos Aires has several *polideportivos* (sports clubs) with inexpensive *piletas* (public pools), but they get crowded. The most central is Polideportivo Martín Fierro, Oruro 1310 in the barrio of San Cristóbal, tel. 4941-2054 (Subte: Urquiza, Línea E). Try also Polideportivo Parque Chacabuco, Avenida Eva Perón 1410, Parque Chacabuco, tel. 4921-5576 (Subte: Emilio Mitre, Línea E).

Many private pools are open to members only, with a membership fee and monthly dues,

but others are open to the public at what, before devaluation, were high prices—as much as US$20 for day use. The weak peso, though, has made it worth looking at options like the indoor pool at Ateneo Cecchina, Mitre 1625, Congreso (Microcentro), tel. 4374-4958; Palermo's Club de Amigos, Avenida Figueroa Alcorta 3885, tel. 4801-1213 (US$1 admission weekdays, US$1.50 weekends; US$2.50 indoor pool, US$3.50 outdoor pool); the outdoor pool at Palermo's Punta Carrasco, Avenida Costanera Norte and Avenida Sarmiento, tel. 4807-1010 (US$2.50 weekdays, US$4 weekends and holidays); and the outdoor pool at Belgrano's Balneario Parque Norte, at Avenida Cantilo and Güiraldes, tel. 4787-1432 (US$2.50 weekdays, US$3 weekends, US$1 for children).

### Surfing

There's no surf to speak of anywhere in northern Buenos Aires province, but the beaches east of Punta del Este, Uruguay, get some legitimate waves—though not so good as those in Chile (Chile's Pacific Ocean beaches, though, get much colder water).

### Boating and Fishing

Boating and fishing are best in and around the intricate channels of the Río Paraná, north and east of the suburb of Tigre. City-bound folks, though, choose the Reserva Ecológica Costanera Sur and the area around the Club de Pescadores, near the Aeroparque, for casting their lines. The denizens of La Boca even take their chances in the toxic waters of the Riachuelo.

# Spectator Sports

As in most of the rest of Latin America, *fútbol* (soccer) is by far the most popular spectator sport. Rugby, however, is also popular; the national team Los Pumas has a global reputation. *Basquetbol* or *básquet* (basket) is rapidly gaining popularity and boxing may be making a comeback. Horse racing, polo, and *pato* are all equestrian sports; horse racing is the most popular, polo less so, and *pato* is a specialist interest.

## SOCCER

Argentina is a perpetual power in soccer—having won the World Cup in 1978 and 1986—and the birthplace of Diego Armando Maradona, one of the sport's legends. What its English fans like to call "the beautiful game," though, often falls short of its billing; the *Buenos Aires Herald* may have said it best with the headline "Another Boring 0-0 Tie."

Even after an ignominious first-round exit from the 2002 World Cup, the *selección nacional* (national team) rated second in the FIFA global rankings, but Argentine soccer has many other problems. One is the so-called *barras bravas,* the counterpart to British "football hooligans," who make the cheap seats and the area outside the stadiums unsafe. Often provided tickets and transportation by the clubs themselves, soccer goons have caused injuries and even deaths; anyone attending a match should take care to dress in neutral colors such as brown or gray to avoid showing an affiliation with either team.

Another problem is financial, as clubs often must trade their best players to wealthy European teams to stay solvent. Popularly known as the "Millonarios," River Plate is one of the world's best-known teams, but being a millionaire isn't what is used to be in Argentina—the club has had trouble meeting its payroll. This raised the specter of relegation to a lower division, leading *Buenos Aires Herald* sports commentator Eric Weil to remark, "This I gotta see."

Still, Buenos Aires is a soccer-mad city, with six first-division teams in the city proper and an-

other six in the suburbs of Gran Buenos Aires. The season runs from March to December; for the most current information, check the website of the Asociación de Fútbol Argentina, www.afa.org.ar, which appears in English as well as Spanish. For club contacts, see the Special Topic "Soccer Tickets."

## RUGBY

Argentine rugby is largely an amateur sport rather than a professional one, but the touring club Pumas has enjoyed great international success. In late 2002, the national team ranked fifth in the

## SOCCER TICKETS

For schedules and tickets, contact the first-division clubs below. *Entradas populares* (standing-room tickets) are the cheapest, but *plateas* (fixed seats) have better security. Again, wear neutral colors to avoid clashes with partisans of either side.

**Boca Juniors,** Brandsen 805, La Boca, tel. 4309-4700, www.bocasistemas.com.ar

**Huracán,** Avenida Amancio Alcorta 2570, Parque Patricios, tel. 4911-0757, www.cahuracan.com

**Nueva Chicago,** Avenida Justo A. Suárez 6900. Mataderos, tel. 4687-2538, www.nuevachicago .com.ar

**River Plate,** Avenida Presidente Figueroa Alcorta 7597, Núñez, tel. 4788-1200

**San Lorenzo de Almagro,** Avenida Fernández de la Cruz 2403, Nueva Pompeya, tel. 4914-2470, www.sanlorenzo.com.ar

**Vélez Sarsfield,** Avenida Juan B. Justo 9200, Liniers, tel. 4641-5663, fax 4641-5763, www.velezsarsfield.com.ar

world, behind England, Australia, New Zealand, and South Africa.

Among other locales, matches take place at the Club Atlético de San Isidro, Roque Saénz Peña 499, San Isidro, tel. 4743-4242 or 4732-2745.

## BOXING

Argentina has had an international presence in boxing ever since Luis Angel Firpo (1894–1960), the "Wild Bull of the Pampas," nearly won the world heavyweight championship from Jack Dempsey in New York in 1923. Other notable boxers have come to untimely ends: heavyweight contender Oscar "Ringo" Bonavena (1942–1976) died from a gunshot in a Reno, Nevada, brothel, and former world middleweight titlist Carlos Monzón (1942–1995) died in an automobile accident while on furlough from prison (once shot by his first wife, he was convicted of murdering his second wife in 1988).

After 2,500 *porteños* paid 50 centavos each to hear the Firpo-Dempsey fight broadcast live from New York there, Luna Park became Buenos Aires's prime boxing venue. For most of the past decade, it has hosted rock concerts rather than fights, but the winter of 2002 saw the first boxing matches in many years. Whether it will continue as a boxing site is up in the air, though the winter 2002 effort was a success. Luna Park is at Bouchard 465, tel. 4311-5100.

The organization that oversees Argentine boxing is the Federación Argentina de Box, Castro Barros 75, Almagro, tel. 4981-2965, www.fabox .com.ar, which maintains a small stadium at that address.

## TENNIS

Argentine tennis has long enjoyed an international reputation, with stars like Guillermo Vilas and Gabriela Sabatini. Most recently, in 2002, David Nalbandian of Unquillo, in Córdoba province, became the first Argentine to reach the 2002 men's finals at Wimbledon before losing to Lleyton Hewitt of Australia. Other highly ranked Argentines include Guillermo Cañas

(ranked 19th in the world as of July 2002), Gastón Gaudio (ranked 24th), and Juan Ignacio Chela (ranked 28th). Mariana Díaz Oliva is the top-ranked Argentine woman.

## BASKETBALL

Argentine basketball, for the most part, lacks a high international profile, but three Argentines have played in the NBA: Boston's Rubén Wolkowyski, Atlanta's Juan Sánchez, and San Antonio's Emanuel Ginobili. Wolkowyski and Sánchez made only brief appearances, but the 6-foot-6 (1.98-meter) Ginobili seems set for a more distinguished career: after several successful seasons in Italy, he signed a two-year, US$3 million contract with the San Antonio Spurs in 2002.

The Argentine hoopsters got a big lift when, in September 2002, the national team convincingly beat the U.S. "Dream Team" in the World Basketball Championships in Indianapolis, Indiana. This was the first U.S. loss in international basketball since National Basketball Association (NBA) players began to compete in previously amateur events, starting with the 1992 Olympics.

Buenos Aires has three teams in the first division of the Liga Nacional de Basquetbol: Boca Juniors, Arzobispo Casanova 600, La Boca, tel. 4309-4748; Ferrocarril Oeste, Avenida Avellaneda 1240, Caballito, tel. 4431-1708; and Obras Sanitarias, Avenida del Libertador 7345, Núñez, tel. 4702-4655. The season runs from early November to late March, the playoffs from late March to mid-May.

## EQUESTRIAN SPORTS

For a country that was raised on horseback, equestrian sports still have great resonance, though only the rarely played *pato* reflects the gaucho tradition.

### Horse Racing

The major racetrack in the country is the Hipódromo Argentino, Avenida del Libertador 4101, Palermo, tel. 4788-2800, www.palermo.com.ar. Races may take place any day of the week, but mostly Friday through Monday. General admission costs US$1, with minimum bets about the same.

## Polo

Argentine society has always been intricately involved with horseback riding, but the British brought polo to the country. The gaucho tradition has left its mark, though, as Argentine polo style is more rugged than its British antecedent.

First held at the suburban Hurlingham Club in 1893, the **Campeonato Abierto de la República** (Argentine Open Polo Championship) moved to Palermo's Campo Argentino de Polo in 1928; it takes place beginning in mid-November. Admission is usually free.

Many other events also take place at the Campo Argentino de Polo, at the intersection of Avenida del Libertador and Avenida Dorrego in Palermo; Arévalo 3065, tel. 4576-5600 or 4343-0972/8321. The Asociación Argentina de Polo is at

*Argentine society has always been intricately involved with horseback riding, but the British brought polo to the country. The gaucho tradition has left its mark, though, as Argentine polo style is more rugged than its British antecedent.*

Hipólito Yrigoyen 636, 1° A in Monserrat, tel. 4342-8321, administracion@aapolo.com, www .aapolo.com.

## Pato

For gauchos rather than gentlemen, *pato* is the anti-polo, a rural sport in which, originally, a live duck in a leather bag was flung into a goal from horseback. No longer so brutal, it uses a leather bag with handles, but the sport is clearly in decline even in the provinces.

Nevertheless, *pato* has not disappeared. For information on competitions, contact the Federación Argentina de Pato, Avenida Belgrano 550, 5th floor, Monserrat, tel. 4331-0222, www.fedpato.com.ar. Matches take place at the Campo Argentino de Pato, Ruta Nacional 11 and Calle Avellaneda, Km 30, Campo de Mayo, Buenos Aires province, tel. 4664-9211. The national championships take place at the Campo Argentino de Polo in Palermo.

# Shopping

Buenos Aires's main shopping areas are the Microcentro, along the Florida pedestrian mall toward Retiro; Retiro (especially around Plaza San Martín and along Avenida Santa Fe); Recoleta, in the vicinity of the cemetery; and the tree-lined streets of Palermo Viejo, where stylish shops sit between the newest restaurants and bars. Street markets take place in San Telmo, Recoleta, and Belgrano.

Since the financial meltdown of 2001–2002, fewer merchants are accepting credit cards (though many still accept debit cards). While the practice of *recargos* (surcharges) for credit card purchases has declined in recent years, some of those still accepting credit cards have reinsti-

tuted the practice. Before handing over the plastic, shoppers should verify whether the business in question intends to collect a *recargo*.

## What to Buy

### ANTIQUES

For much of the 20th century, Argentina alternated between periods of prodigious prosperity and palpable penury. During the good times, Argentines both imported and produced items of great value, but during hard times they often had to dispose of them. Over time, of course,

Antique dealers line both sides of San Telmo's Calle Defensa.

## TAXES

Argentina imposes a 21 percent *Impuesto de Valor Agregado* (IVA or Value Added Tax) on all goods and services. Tourists, however, may request IVA refunds for purchases of Argentine products valued more than 70 pesos from shops that display a "Global Refund" decal on their windows. Always double-check, however, that the decal is not out of date.

When making any such purchase, request an invoice and other appropriate forms. Then, on leaving the country, present the forms to Argentine customs; customs will authorize payment to be cashed at Banco de la Nación branches at the main international airport at Ezeiza, at Aeroparque Jorge Newbery (for flights to some neighboring countries), or at Dársena Norte (for ferry trips to Uruguay). Refunds can also be assigned to your credit card.

At smaller border crossings, however, do not expect officials to be prepared to deal with tax refunds. Some crossings do not even have separate customs officials, but rather are staffed by the Gendarmería (Border Guards), a branch of the armed forces.

once-precious items have made their way through many owners and have ended up in the hands of antique dealers.

In San Telmo in particular, antique shops form an almost unbroken line along Calle Defensa, from Avenida San Juan in the south past Plaza Dorrego to Pasaje Giuffra on the north. The variety and quality of their goods are remarkable, but dealers know what they've got—so they're resolute bargainers. Whether you're seeking that French chess set or a YPF gasoline pump, expect prices to be quoted in U.S. dollars rather than pesos, and don't expect much give.

## BOOKS

Once the center of the South American publishing industry, Buenos Aires has lost ground to other countries, but can still boast an impressive array of bookstores, from the antiquarian to the contemporary, along with specialist dealers. In addition, there are several *ferias* (outdoor stalls) throughout the city, and book-oriented events throughout the year.

## CLOTHING

*Porteños*, both male and female, are notorious fashion plates. The most stylish clothing stores are along Florida and Avenida Santa Fe, and in Recoleta and Palermo Viejo.

## CRAFTS

The most distinctively *porteño* craft is *filete*, the elaborate calligraphy that embellishes the signs of so many businesses and even used to cover city buses.

There are also regional crafts, such as textiles from the northwestern Andean provinces, often available from *casas de la provincia* (provincial government offices, all of which supply tourist information and some of which display products typical of the area).

## HOUSEHOLD GOODS

Over the past decade-plus, the quality of furnishings in Buenos Aires has improved dramatically. While many of these are large items, the recent devaluation has made them cheap enough that shipping them overseas may be worth considering.

## JEWELRY

Buenos Aires has many jewelers. The most typical materials, though, are not diamonds or gold but rather silver, transformed by skilled artisans into unique pieces often held together with *tiento* (finely braided leather). There is a concentration of prestigious silversmiths in the Buenos Aires province town of San Antonio de Areco, about 80 kilometers west of the capital. For details, see the Excursions from Buenos Aires chapter.

## LEATHER GOODS, ACCESSORIES, AND FOOTWEAR

Leather goods, an Argentine specialty, range from tightly woven *tiento* belts to shoes, jackets, coats, trousers, handbags, and many other items. Even the *pie* (base or holder) for a formal *mate* may be made of leather.

## MUSIC AND VIDEO

Compact discs and cassettes of locally produced music are readily available at bargain prices since the devaluation of 2001–2002—at US$4–6 per item, it's not so risky to try something unfamiliar. Even vinyl is available in used record stores.

Many classic Argentine films are available, but rarely with subtitles. Before buying any video, verify whether it's VHS (as used in the United States) or PAL (as used in Argentina and Europe).

## SOUVENIRS

Gaucho gear such as the sharp silver *facón* (knife), wide, silver-studded *rastra* (belt), silver *espuelas* (spurs) and *bombachas* (baggy trousers) all make worthwhile souvenirs. Before purchasing *bombachas*, though,

be sure of what you're buying—the word also means women's underwear.

*Mate* paraphernalia such as the *mate* (gourd) itself and the *bombilla* (straw) are often true works of art. The *mate* is often a simple calabash but can be an elaborate carving of exotic wood; while the modern *bombilla* is often aluminum, it is traditionally silver with intricate markings and design. In the 19th century, when wealthy households kept servants for the sole purpose of preparing *mate*, the *mate* effects were works of art, and many of them are now museum pieces.

To accompany the *mate* paraphernalia, check any supermarket for *yerba mate*, the dried leaf of *Ilex paraguayensis*, which Argentines drink in prodigious amounts.

> **Mate *paraphernalia such as the* mate *(gourd) itself and the* bombilla *(straw) are often works of art. In the 19th century, when wealthy households kept servants for the sole purpose of preparing* mate, *the* mate *effects were works of art; many of them are now museum pieces.***

## WINE

Argentine wine is underrated and was underpriced even before devaluation—in fact, it's one of few commodities that's always reasonably priced. Except for the cheapest vintages, they're rarely disappointing, but one of the treats is the fruity white *torrontés* from Cafayate, in Salta province (*torrontés* produced elsewhere may not be bad, but it usually can't match that from Cafayate).

SHOPPING

## Where to Shop

Over the past decade-plus, many older buildings have been recycled into upscale shopping centers, and several of them are good options for one-stop shopping. The most notable is the Microcentro's magnificent **Galerías Pacífico,** an architectural landmark at Florida and Córdoba, tel. 5555-5100, open 10 A.M.–9 P.M. daily except Sunday, when hours are noon–9 P.M. For a diagram of its three levels of more than 50 shops, check the street-level information booth at the Florida entrance. Shoppers who make purchases of more than about US$70 will receive a free lunch voucher for the basement-level Patio de Comidas.

Once a livestock auction house, Retiro's **Patio Bullrich,** Avenida del Libertador 750, tel. 4814-7400/7500, www.altopalermo.com.ar/s_bullrich.htm, has become a palatial 24,000-square-meter commercial space with nearly 70 shops, plus restaurants and cinemas, on four levels.

Hours are 11 A.M.–9 P.M. daily except Friday and Saturday, when it's open 10 A.M.–10 P.M.

Several other places are under the same management as Patio Bullrich. Most notably, the **Buenos Aires Design Recoleta,** Avenida Pueyrredón 2501, tel. 5777-6000, www.altopalermo.com.ar/s_bullrich.htm, is a 3,000-square-meter complex of shops and restaurants on two levels alongside the cultural center and the cemetery at Recoleta. As its name suggests, it focuses on design and interior decoration, including Oriental carpets, kitchen goods, and bedroom ware. Despite the street address, it is most easily accessible from its southeast corner, near Plaza Francia. It's open 11 A.M.–9 P.M. weekdays, 10 A.M.–9 P.M. Saturday, and noon–9 P.M. Sunday and holidays.

Three other large centers are under the same management, including the sizeable but modern and undistinguished **Alto Palermo Shopping**

Galerías Pacífico, recycled railroad offices transformed into an upscale shopping center

© WAYNE BERNHARDSON

Center, Avenida Coronel Díaz 2098, Palermo, tel. 5777-8000, and Paseo Alcorta, Jerónimo Salguero 3172, Palermo, tel. 5777-6500. The other is the recycled Abasto de Buenos Aires, at the corner of Avenida Corrientes and Anchorena, tel. 4959-3400, originally a project of U.S.-Hungarian George Soros; unfortunately, the disorientingly noisy interior detracts from the magnificence of the building itself.

It doesn't fit easily into any category, but the Primera Feria del Usado Elegante, in the Hogar de la Misericordia at Azcuénaga 1654, between Peña and Melo in Barrio Norte, sells the dregs discarded by the *porteño* elite. It's open weekends only, 10 A.M.–7 P.M.

## ANTIQUES

Sunday's outdoor Feria de San Telmo, one of the city's biggest tourist attractions (see the Sights chapter for details), fills Plaza Dorrego with antiques and bric-a-brac. There are also many antique dealers in commercial galleries with small streetside frontage, including Galería Cecil, Defensa 845; Galería French, Defensa 1070; and Galería de la Defensa, Defensa 1179. Individual San Telmo dealers include Churrinche Antigüedades, Defensa 1031, tel. 4362-7612; Loreto Antigüedades in the Galería French, tel. 4361-5071; and Arte Antica Antigüedades, Defensa 1133, tel. 4362-0861.

La Boca also has a cluster of antique dealers and second-hand shops, including Siglo XX Cambalache, Aráoz de Lamadrid 802. Half a block east, Vía Caminito, Aráoz de Lamadrid 774, specializes in pop culture collectors' items like movie posters and sheet music, along with barrio art.

## ART

Buenos Aires has a thriving modern art scene, with the most innovative galleries being in Retiro and Recoleta. Many dealers still focus on European-style works, but these will probably be of little interest to visitors, as they fail to indicate the vitality of contemporary Argentine art. The best

dealers have outstanding websites that make it possible to preview their work.

Galería Ruth Benzacar, in a subterranean structure at Florida 1000 in Retiro, tel. 4313-8480, info@ruthbenzacar.com, www.ruthbenzacar.com, showcases some of the capital's and the country's most avant-garde artists.

Galería Zurbarán is at Cerrito 1522, Retiro, tel./fax 4815-1556, cmp@zurbarangaleria.com.ar, www.zurbarangaleria.com.ar. Its website has abundant information on contemporary Argentine artists, but it's not one of the most adventurous galleries. It also has a branch called Colección Alvear de Zurbarán at Avenida Alvear 1658, Recoleta, tel. 4811-3004. Both are open 11 A.M.–9 P.M. daily, including weekends and holidays.

Galería Rubbers, Suipacha 1175, tel. 4393-6010, galeriarubbers@ciudad.com.ar, www.rubbers.com.ar, is an excellent contemporary gallery that has a branch at the Ateneo Gran Splendid, Avenida Santa Fe 1860, 2nd and 3rd floors.

Galería Vermeer, Suipacha 1168, tel./fax 4393-5102, www.galeriavermeer.com.ar, is not quite so up-to-date but it's still a good one. Others include Galería Federico Klemm, downstairs at Marcelo T. de Alvear 636, tel. 4312-2058, www.fundacionfjklemm.org; and Galería Aguilar, Suipacha 1178, tel. 4394-6900.

Christie's, the famed auction house, has a Retiro representative at Arroyo 859, tel. 4393-4222.

## BOOKS

Bookstores are where Buenos Aires shopping really shines; they are as much—or more—cultural as commercial institutions, and they take that role seriously.

Buenos Aires's signature bookstore is the Microcentro branch of El Ateneo, Florida 340, tel. 4325-6801, www.tematika.com.ar, which celebrated its 90th anniversary in 2002. It has a huge selection on Argentine history, literature, and coffee table souvenir books, plus a good selection of domestic travel titles (it is also a publishing house); unfortunately, the selection of foreign-language books has dwindled as the economic crisis has made imports expensive.

# FERIAS OF BUENOS AIRES

For sightseers and spontaneous shoppers alike, Buenos Aires's diverse *ferias* (street fairs) are one of the city's greatest pleasures. Easily the most prominent is Sunday's **Feria de San Telmo**, which fills Plaza Dorrego and the surrounding streets—authorities close Calle Defensa to vehicle traffic—with booths of antiques, *filete* paintings, and other crafts. There are professional tango musicians and dancers, and dozens of other street performers range from the embarrassingly mundane to the amazingly innovative. The *feria* lasts roughly from 10 A.M.–5 P.M. There are also many sidewalk cafés and upscale antique shops in the area.

Sunday shoppers at Feria de San Pedro Telmo, on Plaza Dorrego

So successful is the Feria de San Telmo that it's aided the increasingly thriving **Feria Parque Lezama,** a Sunday crafts fair that's gradually spread north from its namesake park up Calle Defensa and under the freeway, beyond which only the broad Avenida San Juan has been able to stop it. Parque Lezama itself now gets Sunday street performers, though not so many as Plaza Dorrego.

In La Boca, permanently docked on the improving waterfront promenade at the Vuelta de Rocha, the former ferry *Nicolás Mihainovich* holds a number of crafts stalls. Immediately across from it, at the corner of Avenida Pedro de Mendoza and Puerto de Palos, the **Feria Artesanal Plazoleta Vuelta de Rocha** takes place weekends and holidays 10 A.M.–6 P.M.; along the length of the nearby Caminito, painters, illustrators, and sculptors sell their works in the **Feria del Caminito.** open 10 A.M.–6 P.M. daily.

It's mostly *porteños* who really appreciate southern barrios like Barracas, where the **Feria de Artesanos Criollos y Aborígenes** (Creole and Indigenous Artisans' Fair) takes place at the Centro Cultural del Sur, Avenida Caseros 1750. It's open on summer weekends only, however.

After San Telmo, the most frequented tourist *feria* is probably Recoleta's **Feria Plaza Intendente Alvear,** a crafts-oriented event that's also strong on street performers. Immediately northeast of the Centro Cultural Recoleta, it's begun to stretch south along Junín; hours are 9 A.M.–7 P.M. weekends and holidays.

On weekends and holidays, crafts stalls cover most of Belgrano's main square at the easy-going **Feria Artesanal Plaza General Manuel Belgrano,** at Juramento and Cuba. Hours are 9 A.M.–7 P.M. or even later (when it's better). When it rains, the stalls are well-sheltered with tarps.

At the **Feria de Mataderos,** in the southwestern Mataderos barrio, *gauchesco* souvenirs like knives, spurs, and silver-studded belts are the key items, but for most visitors this *feria* constitutes entertainment rather than shopping.

Buenos Aires's most elegant bookstore, though, is the affiliated **El Ateneo Grand Splendid,** Avenida Santa Fe 1880, Barrio Norte, tel. 4813-6052. Opened in December 2000, it occupies a recycled and renovated cinema that deserves a visit simply to see its remarkable and apparently seamless transformation—the stage is a café, the opera-style boxes contain chairs for readers, and the curving walls of the upper stories are lined with bookshelves floor to ceiling. In addition to books, it has a good selection of quality music.

Monserrat's **Librería de Ávila** occupies a noteworthy Art Deco building at Adolfo Alsina 500, tel. 4311-8989, fax 4343-3374, libreriadeavila@servisur.com, www.libreriadeavila.servisur.com. Another classic book dealer that specializes in history, ethnology, travel literature, tango, folklore, and the like, it also hosts book presentations and even musical events, and has a café.

Even the chains carry good selections. Some of the best are the Microcentro's **Cúspide Libros,** Florida 628, tel. 4328-0973, www.cuspide.com; **Fausto,** in the Galerías Pacífico at San Martín 760, tel. 5555-5147, which has several other branches around town; and the **Boutique del Libro,** in the Jumbo Palermo shopping center, Avenida Bullrich 345, Local 1013, tel. 4778-3255.

Excellent independent stores include **Zivals,** Avenida Callao 395, Congreso, tel. 4371-7500, www.zivals.com; **LiberArte,** Avenida Corrientes 1555, tel. 4375-2341, a leftish bookstore that also offers theater programs on weekends; and **Librería ABC,** Avenida Córdoba 685, Retiro, tel. 4314-8106, which has English-language books and books about Argentina.

## Academic and Antiquarian

**Librería Platero,** Talcahuano 485, in Tribunales, tel. 4382-2215, fax 4382-3896, info@libreriaplatero.com.ar, www.libreriaplatero.com.ar, may be the city's best specialized bookstore, with an an enormous stock of new and out-of-print books (the latter ensconced in the basement stacks). It does a good trade with overseas academics and libraries.

Retiro's **Antique Book Shop,** Libertad 1236, tel. 4815-0658, breitfel@interprov.com, carries a good but expensive selection on Argentine art, literature, and travel and many books on Patagonia. Under the same management is Barrio Norte's **Librería de Antaño,** Sánchez de Bustamante 1876, tel. 4822-7178, breitfel@interprov.com, www.abebooks.com/home/breitbooks.

Named for Ernesto Sabato's *porteño* novel, **El Túnel,** Avenida de Mayo 767, Monserrat, tel. 4331-2106, is great for browsers. **Librería Huemul,** Avenida Santa Fe 2237, Barrio Norte, tel. 4825-2290, is a history specialist. Other antiquarian dealers include **Alberto Casares,** Suipacha 521 in the Microcentro, tel. 4322-6198, acasares@servisur.com, http://servisur.com/casares; **Aquilanti,** Rincón 79 in Congreso (Balvanera), tel. 4952-4546; and Retiro's **Librería L'Amateur,** Esmeralda 882, tel. 4312-7365.

## Specialist Stores

**Librerías Turísticas,** Paraguay 2457, tel. 4963-2866 or 4962-5547, turisticas@sinectis.com.ar, has an outstanding selection of Argentine maps and guidebooks, including its own guides to neighborhood cafés in the capital.

In a category of its own is the shrink's specialist **Librería Paidós,** Avenida Las Heras 3741, Local 31, Palermo, tel. 4801-2860, psicolibro@psicolibro.com, www.libreriapaidos.com; there's a Barrio Norte branch at Avenida Santa Fe 1685, tel. 4812-6685.

## Book Fairs

Several outdoor markets are book specialists. The most central *feria* takes place at the south end of **Plaza Lavalle,** between Talcahuano and Libertad, 10 A.M.–6 P.M. weekdays only. There is also a big selection at **Plazoleta Santa Fe,** on the median strip of Avenida Santa Fe (Subte: Palermo, Línea D). Caballito's **Parque Rivadavia** (Subte: Acoyte, Línea A) has a permanent weekend market with 85 stalls, and there are also stalls at the end of Línea A at **Primera Junta.**

## CLOTHING

In a jarring juxtaposition, Parisian clothier **Pierre Cardin,** Avenida Callao 220 in Congreso (Balvanera), tel. 4372-0560, shares space with the Buenos Aires chapter of the Communist party. Many of the rest of the upscale clothing outlets are in the large shopping centers, such as Galerías Pacífico and Patio Bullrich.

The most elite clothiers line the streets of Recoleta and Barrio Norte, while the edgiest are in Palermo Viejo. **Uma,** Honduras 5225, tel. 4833-4066, for instance, mixes leather and lycra in jackets, tops, and trousers.

## POLO GEAR

Unsurprisingly, the northern barrios of Retiro and Recoleta are the prime places for purchasing polo gear, at locales such as Retiro's snobbish **La Martina,** Paraguay 661, tel. 4478-9366, which also offers instruction.

**Alberto Vannucci,** Avenida Callao 1773, Recoleta, tel. 4811-3112, specializes in blankets and saddles, but is good for leather in general. A few blocks south **La Picaza,** Avenida Callao 1423, Recoleta, tel. 4801-1887, offers a broad choice of polo gear and souvenirs.

## CRAFTS

Every Argentine province and some municipalities have their own tourist information offices in Buenos Aires; the northern provinces with significant indigenous populations carry small but outstanding crafts selections. The most notable are Balvanera's **Casa del Chaco,** Avenida Callao 322, tel. 4372-5209; Retiro's **Casa de Jujuy,** Avenida Santa Fe 967, tel 4393-6096; and the nearby **Casa de Misiones,** Avenida Santa Fe 989, tel. 4322-0686.

Monserrat's nonprofit **Arte Indígena,** Balcarce 234, tel. 4343-1455, mhomps@arnet.com.ar, contains a small but representative assortment of indigenous crafts from around the country. Items on display include Quechua tapestries from the northern highlands, carved Chané masks from Salta, Toba and Guaraní basketry from the humid northeastern lowlands, and Mapuche weavings from the Patagonian provinces of the south. Hours are 9:30 A.M.–6 P.M. weekdays only.

*The nonprofit Arte Indígena sells an assortment of indigenous crafts from around the country. Items on display include Quechua tapestries from the northern highlands, carved Chané masks from Salta, basketry from the humid northeastern lowlands, and Mapuche weavings from Patagonia.*

**El Boyero,** in the Galerías Pacífico, Florida 760, tel. 5555-5307, informacion@elboyero.com, www.elboyero.com, sells items ranging from leather bags, boots, and belts to gaucho and Mapuche silverwork, *mates,* and ceramics. The **Centro de Exposiciones Caminito,** Aráoz de Lamadrid and Caminito in La Boca, is a large but standard souvenir and crafts market.

**Kelly's Regionales,** Paraguay 431, Retiro, tel. 4311-5712, houses a broad selection of crafts from around the country. **Artesanías Argentinas,** Montevideo 1386, Barrio Norte, tel. 4812-2650, www.artesaniasargentinas.org, is a well-established artisans' outlet. Nearby **Artesanías Salteñas,** Rodríguez Peña 1775, Recoleta, tel. 4814-7562, displays crafts from the northwestern province of Salta.

For readymade *filete,* check the Sunday Feria de San Telmo on Plaza Dorrego; better yet, consider hiring a *fileteador* for custom work, which starts around US$100 for a piece measuring about 20 by 30 centimeters (eight by 12 in.). Among the artisans are Adrián Clara, Avenida Entre Ríos 505, 3° B, Monserrat, tel. 4381-2676; Jorge Muscia, Carlos Calvo 370, San Telmo, tel. 4361-5942, www.muscia.com; and Martiniano Arce, Perú 1089, 1st floor, San Telmo, tel. 4362-2739, martinianoarce@sinectis.com.ar, http://webs.sinectis.com.ar/martinianoarce/.

## HOUSEHOLD GOODS

The economic boom of the 1990s, while it may have had a shaky foundation, brought sophistication and style to design and furniture in particular. Venues like **Buenos Aires Design** (see the Where to Shop section earlier in this chapter) may have set the tone, but Palermo Viejo is now the center for stylish furnishings at shops like **Urano,** Honduras 4702, tel. 4833-0977, www.uranodesign.com. The cutting-edge influence is notable even in many standard furniture shops along Avenida Belgrano, west of Avenida Entre Ríos in Congreso (Balvanera), which do not produce such unique pieces.

## LEATHER GOODS, ACCESSORIES, AND FOOTWEAR

Retiro has several leather specialists, starting with **Lionel Frenkel,** San Martín 1088, tel. 4312-9806, which sells crafts as well. Try also **Casa López,** Marcelo T. de Alvear 640/658, tel. 4311-3044, which has an additional outlet at Galerías Pacífico, Florida 760 for women's handbags and accessories in particular.

**Welcome Marroquinería,** Marcelo T. de Alvear 500, tel. 4312-8911, is one of Buenos Aires's best-established leather goods outlets. Others include **Rossi y Carusso,** Avenida Santa Fe 1601, Barrio Norte, tel. 4811-1965, which also has a Galerías Pacífico branch, and **Dalla Fontana,** Reconquista 735 in the Microcentro, tel. 4313-4354.

**López Taibo,** Avenida Alvear 1902, Recoleta, is a men's shoes specialist. For women, there's nearby **Perugia,** Avenida Alvear 1862, tel. 4804-6340, though it's threatening liquidation of its stock (this is not an unusual business tactic in Buenos Aires).

Italian immigrant Luciano Bagnasco created one of the capital's most enduring shoe stores in **Guido Mocasines, at** Rodríguez Peña 1290, Barrio Norte, tel. 4813-4095, and at Avenida

Feria de San Pedro Telmo, Plaza Dorrego

© WAYNE BERNHARDSON

Quintana 333, Recoleta, tel. 4811-4095, guidomocasines@arnet.com.ar. Another fashionable shoe store is Palermo Viejo's **Valeria Lei,** El Salvador 4702, tel. 4833-4242.

Retiro's **La Querencia,** Esmeralda 1018, tel. 4312-1879, www.laquerencia.com, produces handcrafted leather goods, gaucho gear, boots, jackets, handbags, and belts.

**Flabella,** Suipacha 263, tel. 4322-6036, works in the very specialized field of shoes for tango dancers, both male and female.

## MUSIC

In addition to their books, **El Ateneo,** Florida 340 in the Microcentro, tel. 4325-6801, and **El Ateneo Grand Splendid,** Avenida Santa Fe 1880, Barrio Norte, tel. 4813-6052, have a wide selection of quality CDs.

SHOPPING

**Musimundo,** Florida 259 in the Microcentro, tel. 4394-7203, has numerous other outlets about town, but its lowest-common-denominator stock is costing it business. **Tower Records,** Florida 770 in the Microcentro, tel. 4327-5151, carries a far wider selection at better prices.

Better than either of these chains, though, is **Zivals,** Avenida Callao 395, tel. 4371-7500, www.zivals.com, which also has a large and varied sale bin. For alternative music, try **Disquería Oid Mortales,** Avenida Corrientes 1145.

**Free Blues,** Rodríguez Peña 438, tel. 4373-2999, deals in used CDs, cassettes, and even vinyl.

## VIDEOS

Balvanera's **Arte Video,** Lavalle 1999, tel. 4372-1118, offers a selection of Argentine films ranging from classic dramas to tango films and comedies. Again, confirm that these videos are compatible with your video technology (VHS or PAL).

## POSTAGE STAMPS

Correo Argentino operates a **philatelic service** for stamp collectors in the Correo Central, Sarmiento 189, Oficina 51. The **Federación Argentina de Entidades Filatélicas** (Argentine Federation of Philatelic Entities) is at Perón 1479, 4th floor, San Nicolás (Congreso), tel. 4373-0122; it's open only Tuesday 6–8 P.M.

## WINE

San Telmo's **Enoteka,** Defensa 891, tel. 4363-0011, info@laenoteka.com, www.laenoteka .com, serves tapas as well as wine by the glass—primarily Argentine but also Spanish, French, Italian, Uruguayan, and American vintages. This is a good place to sample before purchase.

**Winery,** Avenida Leandro N. Alem 880, tel. 4311-6607, winerymail@fibertel.com.ar, sells Argentine wines by the glass and also carries a stock of imported wines. It also has a Palermo/Belgrano branch at Avenida Libertador 5100, tel. 4774-1190.

**Túnel Privado,** an outstanding wine store with well-trained personnel, has convenient branches in Retiro at Patio Bullrich, Avenida Libertador 750, Local 210, tel. 4815-3247, and at Federico Lacroze 2450, Belgrano, tel. 4771-8291.

The king of wine outlets, though, is the **Club del Vino,** Cabrera 4737, tel. 4833-0048, also one of Palermo Soho's top restaurants, bars, and entertainment venues. It publishes a monthly newsletter that covers the latest on Argentine wines, and hosts special events for its members (though it is not necessary to be a member to eat, drink, or see a show). It even has a small but beautifully presented wine museum in the basement.

# Excursions from Buenos Aires

When the pressures of city living grow too great, *porteños* escape the capital to the suburbs and countryside of Buenos Aires province, and even across the river to the neighboring republic of Uruguay. This chapter covers excursions to outlying areas in the province, such as the riverside town of Tigre and its Paraná Delta backcountry, the historic pilgrimage city of Luján, the gaucho capital of San Antonio de Areco, and the provincial capital city of La Plata, one of the country's cultural highlights.

In addition, it includes destinations along the Uruguayan side of the Río de la Plata from Carmelo in the west to the colonial heritage site of Colonia, the capital city of Montevideo, and the upper-class resort of Punta del Este, facing the open Atlantic.

In general, the excursions in this chapter cover weekend destinations that do not require air travel; for this reason, popular but more distant sites such as the southern Buenos Aires beach resort of Mar del Plata and the thunderous Iguazú Falls, on the border with Brazil, do not appear here.

© WAYNE BERNHARDSON

weekend house, Delta del Río Paraná, near Tigre, Buenos Aires province

## Tigre and the Delta

The number-one attraction in the vicinity of Buenos Aires, Tigre and the Paraná Delta are barely half an hour by train from the capital. When the capital swelters in summer heat, the delta's maze of forested channels offers shady relief, just close enough for an afternoon off, but there's plenty to do for a day trip, a weekend, or even longer. Fewer than 4,000 people inhabit the 950 square kilometers of "the islands," and they traditionally bring their produce to Tigre's Mercado de Frutos.

### TIGRE

After decades of decay, the flood-prone riverside city of Tigre seems to be experiencing a renaissance. The train stations are completely renovated, the streets clean, the houses brightly painted (and many restored), and it remains the point of departure for delta retreats and historic

© WAYNE BERNHARDSON

**Delta del Río Paraná**

Isla Martín García. In a decade, the population has zoomed from a little more than 250,000 to more than 295,500.

Tigre began as a humble colonial port for Buenos Aires-destined charcoal from the delta, languishing until the railroad connected to the capital in 1865. From the late 19th century, it became a summer sanctuary for the *porteño* elite, who built imposing mansions, some of which are still standing. Prestigious rowing clubs ran regattas on the river, but after the 1920s Tigre settled into a subtropical torpor until its recent revival.

### Orientation

Tigre is 27 kilometers north of Buenos Aires at the confluence of the north-flowing Río Tigre and the Río Luján, which drains southeast into the Río de la Plata. The delta's main channel, parallel to the Río Luján, is the Río Paraná de las Palmas.

East of the Río Tigre, the town is primarily but not exclusively commercial. West of the river, it is largely residential.

### Sights

On the right bank of the Río Tigre, along Avenida General Mitre, stand symbols of the town's bygone elegance, the **Buenos Aires Rowing Club** (1873), Mitre 226, and the **Club Canottierri Italiani** (1910), Mitre 74. Though both still function, they're not the dominant institutions they once were.

Unfortunately, Tigre's rebirth has also brought fast food franchises and the dreadful **Parque de la Costa,** Pereyra s/n, tel. 4732-6300, a cheesy theme park that's open Wednesday through Sunday, 11 A.M.–midnight. Admission, valid for all rides and games, costs US$5 pp for adults, US$3.50 for children ages 9–12.

East of the Parque de la Costa is the **Puerto de Frutos,** Sarmiento 160, tel. 4512-4493; though the docks of this port no longer buzz with products of launches from the deepest delta islands, it's home to a revitalized crafts fair that's open

11 A.M.–7 P.M. daily, but is most active on weekends. Handcrafted wicker furniture and basketry, as well as flower arrangements, are unique to the area.

Across the river, in the residential zone, the present-day **Museo de la Reconquista,** Liniers 818, tel. 4512-4496, was the Spanish Viceroy's command post while the British occupied Buenos Aires during the invasions of 1806–7. Not merely a military memorial, it also chronicles the delta, ecclesiastical history, and the golden age of Tigre from the 1880s to the 1920s. Hours are 10 A.M.–6 P.M. daily except Monday and Tuesday; admission is free.

Several blocks north, fronting on the Río Luján, the **Museo Naval de la Nación,** Paseo Victorica 602, tel. 4749-0608, occupies the former **Talleres Nacionales de Marina** (1879), a naval repair station that closed as naval ships got too large for its facilities; it now chronicles Argentine naval history from its beginnings under the Irishman Guillermo Brown to the present. It's open 8:30 A.M.–12:30 P.M. Monday through Thursday, 8 A.M.–5.30 P.M. Friday, and 10 A.M.–6:30 P.M. weekends. Admission costs US$.60.

To the west, at the confluence of the Río del la Reconquista and the Río Luján, the belle epoque **Tigre Club** (1910), Paseo Victorica 972, tel. 4749-3411, now serves as the municipal cultural center. It's all that remains of a complex that included the earlier Tigre Hotel, built in the town's heyday but demolished after upper-class *porteños* abandoned the area for Mar del Plata in the 1930s.

## Accommodations and Food

In a recycled Tigre mansion, the family-run **B&B Escauriza,** on the west side of the Río Tigre at Lavalle 557, tel. 4749-2499, fax 4749-3150, alebyb@aol.com, excau@aol.com, has four spacious rooms, attractive gardens, and a pool. Rates are US$14/20 s/d.

Standard Argentine eateries are a dime a dozen at locales like the Mercado de Frutos. For a more elaborate menu on a shady riverside terrace with good service, try **María Luján,** Paseo Victorica 611, tel. 4731-9613. Home-

made pastas cost around US$2, more elaborate dishes around US$3, and the weekday *menú ejecutivo* ("executive menu," or lunch special) around US$4.50. A full dinner including wine will cost around US$10.

## Information

The Ente Municipal de Turismo, in the Nueva Estación Fluvial at Mitre 305, tel. 4512-4497 or 0800/888-8447 toll-free, is open 9 A.M.–5 P.M. daily. There is a website, www.puertodetigre.com, which is useful but imperfect.

## Transportation

Tigre is well-connected to Buenos Aires by bus and train, but the heavy traffic on the Panamericana Norte makes the bus slow. Through the delta, there are numerous local launches and even international service to the Uruguayan ports of Carmelo and Nueva Palmira.

**Bus:** The No. 60 *colectivo* from downtown Buenos Aires runs 24 hours a day, but when traffic is heavy it can take two hours to reach Tigre.

**Train:** Tigre has two train stations. From Retiro, Trenes de Buenos Aires (TBA) operates frequent commuter trains on the Ferrocarril Mitre from the capital to **Estación Tigre;** it's also possible to board these trains in Belgrano or suburban stations. The best-maintained and best-run of any rail line into Buenos Aires province, it charges only US$.35 each way.

Also from Retiro, a separate branch of the Mitre line runs to Estación Bartolomé Mitre, where passengers transfer at Estación Maipú to the **Tren de la Costa,** a tourist train that runs through several riverside communities and shopping centers to its terminus at Tigre's **Estación Delta,** at the entrance to the Parque de la Costa. This costs about US$1 weekdays, US$1.50 weekends.

**Boat:** Catamaranes Interisleña, at the Tigre's Nueva Estación Fluvial, Mitre 319, tel. 4731-0261/0264, operates a number of *lanchas colectivas* to delta destinations. Acting like riverbound buses, they drop off and pick up passengers at docks along their route. Líneas Delta Argentino, tel. 4749-0537, www.lineasdelta.com.ar, and Jilguero, tel. 4749-0987, provide similar services. Marsili, tel. 4413-4123, Línea Azul, tel. 4401-7641, and Giacomotti, tel. 4749-1896, use smaller *lanchas taxi.*

Cacciola, Lavalle 520, tel./fax 4749-0329, info@cacciolaviajes.com, has daily launches to Carmelo, Uruguay, at 8:30 A.M. and 4:30 P.M. (US$9, three hours), with bus connections to Montevideo. The boat is pretty comfortable at one-third capacity, but when it's full the narrow seats feel cramped.

Líneas Delta Argentino also operates launches to the Uruguayan town of Nueva Palmira (three hours; US$11 plus US$2.50 port taxes), west of Carmelo. Departures are daily except Sunday at 7:30 A.M.; there is an additional Friday trip at 5 P.M.

*Rising out of the Río de la Plata, almost within swimming distance of the Uruguayan town of Carmelo, the island of Martín García boasts a lush forest habitat, a fascinating history, and an almost unmatchable tranquillity.*

## VICINITY OF TIGRE

Tigre itself may have been revitalized, but many rusting hulks still line the shore of the Paraná's inner channels. Farther from Tigre, where colonial smugglers often hid from Spanish officials, summer houses stand on *palafitos* (pilings) to prevent—not always successfully—being flooded.

Many operators at Tigre's Nueva Estación Fluvial and the Puerto de Frutos offer 40- to 90-minute excursions that are, not quite literally, enough to get your feet wet in the delta. It's also possible to use the *lanchas colectivos* to get where you want to go, including hotels and restaurants. One word of warning: *porteño* powerboaters, especially those on so-called personal watercraft, can be as reckless as motorists on the capital's roadways—don't jump in the water without looking around first.

One of the favorite excursions is the **Museo Histórico Sarmiento,** at the Río Sarmiento and Arroyo Los Reyes, tel. 4728-0570. In a house dating from 1855, built from fruit boxes and now protected by glass, President Domingo F.

Sarmiento had his summer residence; the museum preserves some of his personal effects. Open 10 A.M.–6 P.M. Wednesday through Sunday, it charges no admission; there is also a one-kilometer trail through a gallery forest typical of the delta.

### Accommodations and Food

Both accommodations and dining options are increasing in the delta. The following is just a sample of what is available.

**La Manuelita** on the Río Carapachay about 50 minutes from Tigre by Jilguero launch, tel. 4728-0248, charges US$10 pp during the week, US$12 pp on weekends. *Parrillada* runs about US$2 pp.

**Hotel I'Marangatu,** about 50 minutes from Tigre by Interisleña, on the Río San Antonio, tel. 4728-0752, charges US$12 pp including breakfast and dinner.

**Hotel Laura,** on Canal Honda off the Paraná de las Palmas, tel. 4728-1019, info@riohotellaura.com.ar, www.riohotellaura.com.ar, is about 90 minutes from Tigre by Delta Argentino launch. Rates start at US$20/26 s/d with private bath, with discounts for stays of two nights or longer.

**La Riviera,** about 25 minutes from Tigre by Interisleña launch, on the Río Tres Bocas, tel. 4728-0177, offers outdoor dining in good weather, with a wide selection of beef, fish, and pasta dishes.

### Isla Martín García

Rising out of the Río de la Plata, almost within swimming distance of the Uruguayan town of Carmelo, the island of Martín García boasts a lush forest habitat, a fascinating history, and an almost unmatchable tranquillity as a retreat from the frenzy of the Federal Capital and even the suburbs of Buenos Aires province.

**Orientation:** Only 3.5 kilometers off the Uruguayan coast but 33.5 kilometers from Tigre, 168-hectare Martín García is not part of the sedimentary delta, but rather a precambrian bedrock island rising 27 meters above sea level. Its native vegetation is a dense gallery forest, and part of it is a *zona intangible*, a provincial forest reserve.

**History:** Spanish navigator Juan Díaz de Solís was the first European to see the island, naming it for one of his crewmen who died there in 1516. In colonial times, it often changed hands before definitively coming under Spanish control in 1777; in 1814 Guillermo Brown, the Irish founder of the Argentine navy, captured it for the Provincias Unidas del Río de la Plata (United Provinces of the River Plate). For a time, mainlanders quarried its granite bedrock for building materials.

For a century, from 1870 to 1970, the navy controlled the island, and for much of that time it served as a political prison and a regular penal colony, though it was also a quarantine base for immigrants from Europe. The famous Nicaraguan poet Rubén Darío (1867–1916) lived briefly on the island in the early 1900s, while serving as Colombian consul in Buenos Aires.

Political detainees included presidents Marcelo T. de Alvear (in 1932, after his presidency), Hipólito Yrigoyen (twice in the 1930s), Juan Domingo Perón (1945, before being elected), and Arturo Frondizi (1962–63). In the early months of World War II, Argentine authorities briefly incarcerated crewmen from the German battleship *Graf Spee,* scuttled off Montevideo in December 1939.

Although the island passed to the United Provinces at independence, it was not explicitly part of Argentina until a 1973 agreement with Uruguay (which was one of the United Provinces). After the navy departed, the Buenos Aires provincial Servicio Penitenciario (Penitentiary Service) used it as a halfway house for run-of-the-mill convicts, but it was also a detention and torture site during the military dictatorship of 1976–83.

**Sights:** Uphill from the island's *muelle pasajero* (passenger pier), opposite the meticulously landscaped **Plaza Guillermo Brown,** the island's **Ofic-**

**ina de Informes** was, until recently, headquarters of the Servicio Penitenciario. It now houses provincial park rangers. Along the south shore are several *baterías* (gun emplacements).

At the upper end of the plaza stand the ruins of the onetime **cuartel** (military barracks that later became jail quarters). Clustered together nearby are the **Cine-Teatro,** the former theater, with its gold-tinted rococo details; the **Museo de la Isla** (Island Museum) and the former Casa Médicos de Lazareto, the quarantine center now occupied by the **Centro de Interpretación Ecológica** (Environmental Interpretation Center). On the opposite side of the **cuartel** is the **Panadería Rocio** (1913), a bakery that makes celebrated fruitcakes; a bit farther inland, the island's **faro** (lighthouse, 1881) rises above the trees, but is no longer in use. To the north, the graves of conscripts who died in an early-20th-century epidemic dot the isolated **Cementerio** (cemetery).

At the northwest end of the island, trees and vines grow among the crumbling structures of the so-called **Barrio Chino** (Chinatown), marking the approach to the **Puerto Viejo,** the sediment-clogged former port. Across the island, beyond the airstrip, much of the same vegetation grows in the **Zona Intangible,** which is closed to the public.

**Activities:** Though the island offers outstanding walking and bird-watching, the river is not suitable for swimming. The restaurant **Comedor El Solís,** though, has a swimming pool open to the public.

**Accommodations and Food:** Crowded in summer and on weekends, **Camping Martín García,** tel. 4728-1808, charges US$1.50 pp for tent campers, with discounts for two or more nights; it also has hostel bunks with shared bath for US$2 pp, with private bath for US$3 pp; again, there are discounts for two or more nights. Cacciola's *Hostería Martín García* charges US$32 pp for overnight packages with full board that include transportation from Tigre. Each additional night costs US$14 pp.

Cacciola's own restaurant **Fragata Hércules** is decent enough, but **Comedor El Solís** is at least as good and a bit cheaper; in winter, however, the Solís may be closed. **Panadería Rocio,** of course, is known for its fruitcakes.

**Transportation:** Cacciola, Lavalle 520 on the west bank of the Río Tigre, tel./fax 4749-0329, info@cacciolaviajes.com, offers day trips to Martín García Tuesday, Thursday, Saturday, and Sunday at 8 a.m., but get to the dock by 7:30 A.M. Arriving at the island around 11 A.M., the tour includes an aperitif on arrival, a guided visit, and lunch at Cacciola's own restaurant *Fragata Hércules.* The tour returns to Tigre by 7 P.M. There is ample time for just roaming around.

Cacciola also has a Microcentro office at Florida 520, 1st floor, Oficina 113, tel./fax 4393-6100, cacciolacentro@sinectis.com.ar. Fares for a full-day excursion are US$12 for adults, US$3 for children ages 3–10, including port charges. An overnight stay at the hostería, including transportation and full board, costs US$32 pp; additional nights cost US$14 pp.

# RESERVA NATURAL ESTRICTA OTAMENDI

In the upper delta, the Reserva Natural Estricta Otamendi comprises 3,000 hectares of riverine gallery forests, floodplain grasslands with reed-filled pools, and forested *barrancas* (natural levees) interspersed with native pastureland. The only unit of Argentina's national park system with easy access from Buenos Aires (Martín García is a provincial reserve), it's a remnant of what the pampas were like prior to the arrival of the Spaniards.

Established in 1990, the reserve is not utterly pristine. In pre-Columbian times, from about 1000 B.C. to A.D. 1500, hunter-gatherers located their temporary camps on the high ground, hunting fish, otters, and the beaver-like nutria with harpoons and bone tools. On the barrancas there are even remains of a late colonial settlement, whose ceramics suggest it came from the upper-class family of Juan de Melo or his descendants, who built the now-abandoned port of Tajíber.

## Orientation

On the right bank of the Río Paraná de las Palmas, the Reserva Natural Estricta Otamendi is about 80 kilometers northwest of Buenos Aires via RN9, an excellent paved highway.

## Flora and Fauna

Along the riverside, twisted trunks of the *ceibo* (*Erythrina cristagalli,* whose blossom is Argentina's national flower) mix with *sauces* (willows) and *canelones* (*Rapanea* spp), where the *boyero negro* (*Cacicus solitarius,* solitary black cacique) makes its distinctive hanging nests. The *choca* (*Thamnophilus ruficapillus,* rufous-capped antshrike) and the *pava de monte* (*Penelope obscura,* dusky-legged guan) are also common here.

The herbaceous floodplain, though, is the most fauna-rich area, populated with marsh deer and *carpincho* (capybara), as well as birds including the colorful *federal* (*Amblyramphus holosericeus,* scarlet-headed blackbird), *junquero* (*Phleocryptes melanops,* wren-like rushbird), *sietecolores* (*Tachuris rubrigastra,* multi-colored rush tyrant), plus the amphibious *rana criolla* (*Leptodactylus ocellatus,* creole bullfrog), and the now-rare river otter. Its permanent pools are habitat for game fish like the tasty *sábalo,* and aquatic birds like ducks and swans.

The barrancas are home to forests of *tala,* inhabited by the marsupial *comadreja overa* (*Didelphis albiventris,* white-eared opossum) and birds like the *chinchero chico* (*Lepidocolaptes angustirostris,* narrow-billed woodcreeper), and the agile *tacuarita azul* (*Polioptila dumicola,* masked gnatcatcher). Above the barranca there is a sample of native pampa grasses and some low-growing shrubs. The *misto* (*Sicalis luteola,* yellow finch) is a songbird that makes flamboyant mating displays in the spring.

## Sights and Activities

The **Sendero El Talar** is a signed one-kilometer nature trail through native pampas and *tala* forests. The **Sendero Vehicular Islas Malvinas** is a 5.5-kilometer road to the river that's also suitable for pedestrians, but the wildlife is most active at daybreak and sunset.

## Information

At the park entrance, the **Centro de Visitantes** offers advice on excursions in the park. For more information, contact Reserva Natural Otamendi, Rawson 1080, Campana, tel. 034/89-447505 y 89-432220, otamendi@deltanet1.com.ar.

## Transportation

By public transportation, the easiest route is the Ferrocarril Mitre from Retiro. Take the train toward José León Suárez and, at Villa Ballester, transfer to a Zárate-bound train; Estación Otamendi is only 400 meters from the reserve. Campana-bound buses from Retiro and Once drop passengers at the crossroads with RN9, two kilometers west of the reserve.

# The Pampa Gaucha

West of Buenos Aires is gaucho country, transformed by the herds of cattle that proliferated on the pampas after the Spanish invasion and by the horsemen who lived off those herds. Eventually, and ironically, they became the peons of the sprawling *estancias* (cattle ranches) that occupied almost every square centimeter of prime agricultural land.

Unofficially, San Antonio de Areco is Argentina's gaucho capital, and the *estancias* that surround it are some of the most historic in the country. The city of Luján, however, is equally if not more historic, with outstanding museums, and is also one of South America's major devotional centers.

## MORENO

Now a residential suburb of Gran Buenos Aires, the city of Moreno (with a population of almost 380, 000) is only 36 kilometers from the capital, but when Florencio Molina Campos lived here, it was still *tierra de gauchos* (gaucho land). Many foreigners who do not know Molina Campos by name may be familiar with his art, as he lived in the United States and exhibited his work there and in the United Kingdom, France, and Germany.

Molina Campos's former residence, built in the style of a mid-19th-century *estancia,* now contains the **Museo Florencio Molina Campos,** a museum holding about 100 of the artist's affectionate caricatures of gaucho life, as well as photographs, silverwork, and calendar reproductions

## ESTANCIA OPERATORS

Over the past decade-plus, weekending in the countryside of Buenos Aires province has become an increasingly popular option for those wishing to escape the capital. As *estancia* owners have struggled to diversify economically, some even make more income from hosting tourists than they do growing grain or raising livestock. Some *estancias* aim at daytrippers, but most of them prefer overnight guests. Some *estancias* are reasonably priced places with limited services, but others are magnificent estates with castle-like *cascos* (big houses), elaborate services including gourmet meals, and recreational activities such as horseback riding, tennis, swimming, and the like.

Affiliated with the Sociedad Rural Argentina, the **Red Argentina de Turismo Rural,** Florida 460, 4th floor, tel. 4328-0499, fax 4328-0878, www.raturestancias.com.ar, ratur@infovia.com.ar, represents *estancias* in northern and southern Buenos Aires province, as well as the in the northwestern Argentine provinces, Córdoba, and even some in Patagonia. **José de Santis,** Diagonal Roque Sáenz Peña 616, 5th floor, tel 4342-8417, fax 4343-9568, jdesantis@arnet.com.ar, www.josedesantis.com.ar, operates primarily in Buenos Aires province, with a few affiliates in Córdoba and the northeastern Mesopotamian provinces.

**Construction of the Basílica Nuestra Señora de Luján began in the 1880s.**

© WAYNE BERNHARDSON

(some of his best work was done for the Fábrica Argentina de Alpargatas, which made the linen slippers still common in Argentina today).

From a landowning family, Molina Campos (1891–1959) attributed the virtues of honor, hospitality, courage, and sacrifice to the gauchos without patronizing them. Following his first exhibition of *motivos gauchos* (gaucho motifs) in the Sociedad Rural de Palermo in 1926, he taught drawing at the Colegio Nacional Nicolás Avellaneda for 18 years; his trips around the country in the 1930s led to the calendars that made him famous, selling 18 million copies over 12 years. After traveling to the United States to study animation, he undertook similar calendar work for the Minneapolis-Moline mills; he also produced, for Walt Disney, the cartoons *Gaucho Goofy*, *El Volador Gaucho* (The Flying Gaucho), *El Gaucho Reidor* (The Laughing Gaucho) and *Saludos Amigos* (Greetings, Friends).

At Florencio Molina Campos (formerly Güemes) 348, corner of Victorica, the Museo Molina Campos is open 4–7 P.M. weekends only, but has been closed for repairs. The easiest way to get to town is by TBA's Línea Sarmiento, an electrified commuter line, from Estación Once in Buenos Aires. From the Moreno station, it's about a 15-minute walk to the museum.

## LUJÁN

History and legend blend in the Pampas city of Luján, the single most important devotional center in all of Argentina. Modern Luján, though, is a potpourri of piety and the profane, where pilgrims purchase shoddy souvenirs and, after making their obligatory visit to the landmark basilica, party until dawn.

Legend says that, in 1630, an oxcart loaded with a terra-cotta image of the Virgin Mary stuck in the mud, unable to move until gauchos removed the statue. Its devout owner, from the northwestern province of Santiago del Estero, took this as a sign that the Virgin should remain at the spot, and built a chapel for her. Apparently, though, Argentina's patron saint was not totally immovable—she has since shifted to more opulent accommodations in the French Gothic basilica, five kilometers from her original abode.

Luján (population 78,005) merits a visit for the truly devout and for those with an intellectual interest in orthodox Catholicism. It gets four million visitors per year, mostly on weekends and for religious holidays like Easter and May 8 (the Virgin's day). Also important are events like October's Peregrinación de la Juventud (Youth Pilgrimage), a 62-kilometer walk from Once that acquired a semipolitical character during the Dirty War, but has since returned to its devotional origins.

Where Luján really shines, though, is in its complex of historical museums in handsome colonial buildings—their recent improvements have turned Luján from a mildly interesting side trip into a nearly obligatory one.

### Orientation

On the right bank of its eponymous river, Luján (population 39,000) is about 65 kilometers west of Buenos Aires via RN7. Most points of interest are on and around Avenida Nuestra Señora de Luján, the broad avenue that enters town from the north, while most services are eastward toward the central Plaza Colón.

## Sights

The basilica may be Luján's most imposing site, but its museums have undergone a professional transformation that transcends the standard stuff-in-glass-cases approach of so many provincial institutions.

**Basílica Nuestra Señora de Luján:** Glazed in silver to protect her from deterioration, clothed in white and blue robes, the ceramic Virgin is a diminutive 38-centimeter image baked in Brazil. In the 1880s, on a trip to Europe, the French Lazarist missionary Jorge Salvaire created her elaborate crown; apparently deciding that was not enough, he worked tirelessly to build the Gothic basilica whose pointed spires now soar 106 meters above the pampas. Not completed until 1937, its facade has recently undergone an extensive restoration. Pope John Paul II said Mass here in 1982, only a few days before the Argentine surrender in the Falklands war.

Twice removed from the world outside, the "Virgencita" (little virgin) inhabits a separate *camarín* (chamber) behind the main altar; begging her help, pilgrims proceed at a snail's pace past plaques left by their grateful predecessors. Immediately west of the basilica, the **Museo Devocional** holds larger *ex-votos* (gifts left in thanks for her help). It's open 1–6 P.M. weekdays except Monday, 10 A.M.–6 P.M. weekends.

**Complejo Museográfico Enrique Udaondo:** On the west side of Avenida Nuestra Señora de Luján, immediately north of the basilica, the former **cabildo** (colonial town council, 1797) and the **Casa del Virrey** (1803) (House of the Viceroy) house one of the finest museum assemblages in the country. No viceroy every lived in Luján, by the way, but the Marqués de Sobremonte once spent a few hours in the house.

*Porteño* architect Martín S. Noel's 1918 restoration of the **cabildo** took some liberties with the building's original unadorned facade and a few other features. Still, the three hectares of buildings and well-kept grounds, bounded by Lezica y Torrezuri, Lavalle, San Martín, and Parque Ameghino, are distinguished for their contents as well.

Within the **cabildo** and the Casa del Virrey, the **Museo Histórico** has a thorough display on Argentine history, with a dazzling assortment of maps, portraits, and artifacts (such as caudillo Facundo Quiroga's blood-stained *vicuña* poncho) that bring that history to life. The museum box office, at the corner of Avenida Nuestra Señora de Luján and Lavalle, has a salon for special exhibits such as a remarkable display of crucifixes throughout the ages.

Immediately to the north, the **Museo de Transporte** houses an extraordinary collection of horse carriages in mint condition, including hearses, a carriage that belonged to General Mitre, and the stuffed carcasses of Gato and Mancha, the hardy Argentine *criollo* horses that A. F. Tschiffely rode from Buenos Aires to Washington, D.C. in the 1930s. There is also a Dornier seaplane cobuilt by Spaniards and Argentines, and the country's first-ever locomotive, from the Ferrocarril Oeste. The upstairs of the main showroom is devoted to an elaborate exhibit on *mate* and its ritual, from colonial times to the present.

The Complejo Museográfico, tel. 420245, is open Thursday and Friday, noon–5:30 P.M., weekends 10 A.M.–5:30 P.M. The admission charge of US$.35, paid at the corner of Avenida Nuestra Señora de Luján and Lavalle, is good for all of the museum's facilities.

## Entertainment

For most visitors to Luján, entertainment consists of spontaneous barbecues in Parque Ameghino or, when campgrounds are really crowded, on the median strip of Avenida Nuestra Señora de Luján. Alternatively, there are movies at the **Cine Nuevo Numancia 1,** San Martín 398, tel. 02323/430860, and drinking and dancing at the **Old Swan Pub,** San Martín 546, tel. 02323/433346.

## Accommodations

Many if not most pilgrims choose cheap camping;

in fact, on major religious holidays, pilgrims camp just about anywhere there's open space, including the median strip of Avenida Nuestra Señora de Luján. More formally, across the Río Luján about 10 blocks north of the basilica, shady **Camping El Triángulo,** Avenida Carlos Pellegrini (RN7) Km 69.5, tel. 0323/430116, info@lujanet.com.ar, charges US$4 for two persons, and rents tents for about US$1.50 per day.

**Hotel Royal,** across from the bus terminal at 9 de Julio 696, tel. 02323/421295, charges US$8/10 s/d for smallish but otherwise adequate rooms; it has a restaurant, but breakfast costs extra. On the east side of the basilica, the well-managed **Hotel de la Paz,** 9 de Julio 1054, tel. 02323/428742, is a dignified inn that's been around for nearly a century. Rates are US$10/12 s/d with breakfast, cable TV, and private bath; weekday rates are about 10 percent less.

**Hotel del Virrey,** the former Hotel Eros at San Martín 129, tel. 02323/420797, charges US$11/13 with private bath and breakfast. The 45-room **Hotel Hoxón,** 9 de Julio 769, tel. 02323/429970, hoxonsa@s6.coopenet.com.ar, is a step up, and the only place in town with its own pool; rates start at US$10/13 s/d with a buffet breakfast, but better rooms go for around US$12/16.

## Food

Calle 9 de Julio, just north of the basilica, consists of undistinguishably cheap *parrillas,* lined up wall-to-wall, frequented primarily by pilgrims.

For breakfast and dessert, the best choice is **Berlín,** San Martín 135, half a block east of the basilica. **Don Chiquito,** Colón 964, has a similar menu of higher quality; it's more expensive but considerably more sedate.

Befitting Luján's ecclesiastical importance, the traditional place for a more formal family lunch or dinner is the Carmelite-run **L'eau Vive,** across town at Constitución 2112, tel. 02323/421774. Fixed-price lunches or dinners, in the US$4–6 range, lean toward French specialties; they sometimes stop to observe a recorded version of *Ave Maria.* Lunch hours are noon–2:15 P.M. daily except Monday, dinner hours daily are 8:30–

10 P.M. except Sunday and Monday. The main dining room is nonsmoking.

## Information

Luján's municipal Dirección de Turismo, in Parque Ameghino's Edificio La Cúpula, at the west end of Lavalle, tel. 02323/433500, is open 9 A.M.–1 P.M. weekdays only. The newly opened Asociación Lujanina de Turismo, a block north of the basilica at 9 de Julio 922, keeps irregular hours but is most helpful.

## Transportation

Luján has good road and rail connections with Buenos Aires. The bus station is within walking distance to everything, while the train station is across town. Cheap *remises* can carry up to four passengers for a minimal fare.

**Bus:** The Estación Terminal de Ómnibus is three blocks north of the basilica, on Avenida Nuestra Señora del Rosario between Almirante Brown and Dr. Reat, tel. 02323/420044. Transporte Automotores Luján (Línea 52) runs buses to and from Plaza Miserere (Once) in Buenos Aires, while Transportes Atlántida (Línea 57), tel. 02323/420032, Interno 24, connects Luján with Plaza Italia in Palermo.

**Train:** TBA's Línea Sarmiento, at Avenida España and Belgrano, tel. 0323/421312, goes to and from the capital's Estación Once (Subte: Plaza Miserere, Línea A), but it's necessary to change trains in Moreno.

# SAN ANTONIO DE ARECO

Bidding for UNESCO World Heritage Site status, the 18th-century town of San Antonio de Areco is Argentina's unofficial gaucho capital, host to its biggest gaucho festivities, and home to a concentration of traditional craftsmen and artists difficult to match in any other place of its size. It's an irony, though, that many of those most closely associated with those gaucho traditions have Italian-immigrant surnames.

San Antonio was the home of gauchesco novelist Ricardo Güiraldes, who wrote *Don Se-*

*gundo Sombra* (1927) here. It was also the location for director Manuel Antín's 1969 movie, which featured the author's recently deceased (September 2002) nephew Adolfo Güiraldes in the title role of a dignified rustic whose practical wisdom leaves a lasting imprint on a landowner's son.

Bucking recent economic trends, San Antonio (population 17,820) emits an air of tidy prosperity even in the midst of crisis. Its biggest annual event is November's **Día de la Tradición,** celebrating the gaucho heritage, but weekends are busy all year round.

## Orientation

San Antonio de Areco is 113 kilometers west of Buenos Aires via RN8, which continues west toward San Luis, Mendoza, and the Chilean border. On the right bank of the Río Areco, it forms a mostly regular grid west of the highway; the commercial street of Alsina, leading south from the main Plaza Ruiz de Arellano, is the liveliest part of town.

## Sights

San Antonio is so pedestrian-friendly that, in a country where motorists rarely even slow down for crosswalks, townfolk often stroll in the middle of the street. That's not really recommended, but San Antonio's leisurely pace and compact core do make it attractive for walkers and cyclists.

Unlike most central plazas, San Antonio's **Plaza Ruiz de Arellano** is not the lively hub of local life, but it's an appealingly shady park surrounded by historic buildings and monuments: the **Casa de los Martínez,** site of the original *estancia* house, is at the northwest corner; the **Iglesia Parroquial** (Parish Church, 1869) is on the south side; and the **Palacio Municipal** (1885), part of which has become the Draghi family's **Taller y Museo de Platería Criolla y Civil y Salón de Arte,** a combination museum, silversmith's workshop, and art gallery, is on the plaza's north side. In the center of the plaza, the **Monumento a Vieytes** memorializes San Antonio native Juan Hipólito Vieytes (1762–1815), a participant in the 1810 revo-

lution that eventually brought Argentine independence.

Half a block north of the Plaza, the **Centro Cultural Usina Vieja** (1901), Alsina 66, is an antique power plant recycled into a fine museum and cultural center; see the specific entry for this site later in this section for more details. Three blocks northwest, facing the river at the corner of Zerboni and Moreno, the **Parque de Flora y Fauna Autóctona Carlos Merti,** tel. 2326/453783, is a small zoo open 9 A.M.–noon and 2–7 P.M. daily; admission is US$.35. Across the street, the restored **Puente Viejo** (1857) over the Río Areco may have been the country's first toll bridge; originally designed for cart traffic, it lent its atmosphere to the movie version of *Don Segundo Sombra*. It's now a horse and pedestrian shortcut to the **Parque Criollo y Museo Gauchesco Ricardo Güiraldes,** a museum memorializing the author's *gauchesco* romanticism.

It's not the only *gauchesco* institution in town, though: Luis Gasparini, son of the late painter Osvaldo Gasparini, continues to paint and operate the **Museo Gauchesco del Pintor Gasparini,** Alvear 521; see the separate entry later in this section for more detail. At the intersection of RN8 and Soldado Argentino, at the south end of San Antonio, the remains of both Ricardo Güiraldes and Segundo Ramírez (the author's model for the fictional Don Segundo Sombra) repose in the **Cementerio Municipal.**

For a day in the country without really leaving town, visit **Estancia la Cinacina,** only six blocks west of Plaza Ruiz de Arellano at Mitre 9, tel. 2326/452045, www.lacinacina.com.ar. For about US$10 pp, the visit includes snacks, a city tour, lunch, and folkoric music and dance; from Buenos Aires, with transportation, it costs about US$25 pp.

**Centro Cultural Usina Vieja:** Handsomely recycled as a museum and events center, San Antonio's onetime power plant holds permanent collections of prints by Florencio Molina Campos, massive metal *gauchesco* sculptures by José Perera, and a good sample of work by San Antonio's artisans. It's also managed impressive special exhibits that recreate overlooked everyday institutions like the simple barbershop and *botica* (apothecary), but hasn't done much in the way of historical and cultural interpretation.

The Centro Cultural Usina Vieja, Alsina 66, tel. 452021, is open 8 A.M.–3 P.M. weekdays, 11 A.M.–4:45 P.M. weekends. Admission is free.

**Museo Gauchesco del Pintor Gasparini:** Since the death of his father, Luis Gasparini continues to live in and operate this *gauchesco* art museum, which has half a dozen rooms devoted to the gaucho sculpture, silverwork, and painting (including works by Benito Quinquela Martín and Lino Spilimbergo, among others). There is also a chapel, an atelier with the family's own *gauchesco* works, and a library.

The museum, located at Alvear 521 near Plaza Gómez, tel. 453930, gaspa@arecoonline.com.ar, is open 8 A.M.–8 P.M., 365 days a year. Admission is free of charge.

**Parque Criollo y Museo Gauchesco Ricardo Güiraldes:** Set on 97 hectares of parkland, San Antonio's gaucho museum is a romantic idealization of the already romantic gauchesco literature of Ricardo Güiraldes, whose family lived on the nearby Estancia La Porteña. Created by the provincial government in the 1930s, the museum lacks the authenticity of the *estancia* itself (which is open to visits; see the Vicinity of San Antonio de Areco entry for details), but it offers genuinely ironic insights into the way Argentines—even *porteños*—have internalized the gaucho heritage.

The irony, of course, was that the landowning novelist Güiraldes, however sincere, presumed to speak for the illiterate gaucho—a defiantly independent figure who became a humble dependent laborer on the *estancias* of the oligarchy. Nowhere is this clearer than in the principal **Casa del Museo,** a 20th-century replica of an 18th century *casco* (big house): it devotes two rooms to Güiraldes himself; another to his wife Adelina del Carril; another to his painter cousin Alberto; a **Sala de los Escritores** to *gauchesco* literature including Walter Owen's English-language translation of José Hernández's epic poem *Martín*

*Fierro;* a **Sala Pieza de Estanciero** that includes the bed of tyrant landowner Juan Manuel de Rosas (who exploited gauchos ruthlessly but counted them among his most enthusiastic allies); and, finally, a **Sala del Gaucho** that stresses horse gear and *gauchesco* art, but not the gaucho's increasingly marginal status.

The Casa del Museo gives only a partial account of the gaucho; the surrounding park contains the **Pulpería La Blanqueada,** a real 19th-century roadhouse with a life-size gaucho diorama. Nearby are three other aging structures, **La Ermita de San Antonio,** an adobe chapel with an image of its patron saint; the **La Tahona** flour mill (1848); and the **Galpón y Cuarto de Sogas,** a carriage house.

Reached by the Puente Viejo shortcut, the Museo Gauchesco, Camino Ricardo Güiraldes s/n, tel. 454780, is open 11 A.M.–5 P.M. daily except Tuesday. Admission costs US$2 pp except for retired persons, who pay US$.35, and children under age 12, who get in free.

### Fiesta de la Tradición

Since 1934, November's Fiesta de la Tradición has feted San Antonio's gaucho heritage with guided visits to historic sites, lectures by top folklorists, crafts fairs, and folk music and dance—plus, of course, flamboyant displays of horsemanship. While the principal **Día de la Tradición** is theoretically November 10, the festivities normally stretch over two weekends, climaxing on the final Sunday. Reservations are critical for anyone who wants to stay in San Antonio proper rather than in the surrounding countryside or neighboring towns.

### Accommodations

Despite its tourist tradition, San Antonio proper has good but limited accommodations; the level of services has improved in recent years, as even some moderately priced hotels have features like swimming pools, air-conditioning, and the like.

During November's Fiesta de la Tradición, when reservations are imperative, visitors may lodge in communities for miles around. Prices often rise on weekends, when reservations are advisable, but bed-and-breakfast accommodations may also be available—ask at the tourist office.

At the north end of Zapiola, the **Camping Municipal** is cheap (US$2 pp) and shady, but the river floods when it rains heavily. **Hotel San Carlos,** at Zapiola and Zerboni, tel. 2326/453106, sancarlos@arecoonline.com.ar, www.hotel-sancarlos.com.ar, is an exceptional value for US$10 d double with continental breakfast, cable TV, swimming pool, and other amenities.

Modern **Hotel Los Abuelos,** immediately across the street at Zapiola and Zerboni, tel. 2326/456390, is comfortable, but what might have been a secluded central garden has instead become a driveway and parking lot. Rates for smallish rooms with private bath, high ceilings with fans, telephone, cable TV, and swimming pool are US$8/12 s/d; skip the mediocre breakfast (US$1).

Rates at **La Posada del Ceibo,** on Irigoyen between RN8 and Avenida Dr. Smith, tel. 2326/454614, elceibo@areconet.com.ar, are US$8/12 s/d with breakfast, private bath, cable TV, and pool. **Hotel Fuaz,** Avenida Dr. Smith 488, tel. 2326/452487, charges US$13 d for air-conditioned rooms with breakfast, but more spacious rooms are available for just a little more.

## Food

San Antonio has a pair of passable pizzerías, downtown's **Pizzería Dell'Olmo**, Alsina 365, tel. 452506, and **Pizza Morena,** near the river at Zerboni and Moreno, tel. 456391.

**La Costa,** at Belgrano and Zerboni, tel. 2326/452481, serves primarily *parrillada* but also pasta, with friendly service and good prices; most entrees are in the US$2.50–3.50 range. Immediately across Belgrano, **Un Alto en la Huella,** tel. 455595), has similar offerings and prices.

Brilliantly recreating the atmosphere of a traditional *pulpería,* **Puesto La Lechuza,** Alsina 188, tel. 2326/455523, serves home-cooked Argentine food—your basic *bife de chorizo* and a salad, but also appetizers of homemade salami, cheese, bread, and *empanadas.* There's usually live music on weekends; if not, ask owner Marcelo Salazar to play "Whiter Shade of Pale" on the antique Parisian organ.

The **Almacén de Ramos Generales,** Bolívar 143, tel. 2326/456376, is a *parrilla* that also sells homemade salami, cheeses, and desserts. **La Olla de Cobre,** Matheu 433, tel. 2326/453105, produces fine artisanal chocolates and other sweets. **Dulces del Pago,** Zerboni 136, tel. 454751, specializes in fruit preserves.

## Shopping

San Antonio's silversmiths are the country's finest, so don't expect to find any bargains—a silver *mate* can cost up to US$1,500, though there are of course cheaper versions. Other typical silver dress items include the long-bladed *facón* (gaucho knife), *rastra* (studded belt), and *espuelas* (spurs).

Silversmith Juan José Draghi, Alvear 345, tel. 2326/454219, draghi@arecoonline.com, has enlivened the moribund Plaza Ruiz de Arellano with the new **Taller y Museo de Platería Criolla y Civil y Salón de Arte,** on Lavalle between Alsina and Ruiz de Arellano, tel. 2326/15-511684. Other silversmiths include Raúl Horacio Draghi, Guido 391, tel. 2326/454207, who also works in leather; Gustavo Stagnaro, Arellano 59, tel. 454801; and Miguel and Martín Rigacci, Belgrano 381, tel. 2326/456049.

Sogas Areco, Moreno 280, tel. 453797, specializes in gaucho clothing and horse gear. Cristina Giordano, Sarmiento 112, tel. 2326/452829, is a weaver.

## Information

San Antonio's Dirección de Turismo, at Zerboni and Ruiz de Arellano, tel. 2326/453165, is open 8 A.M.–2 P.M. weekdays, 10 A.M.–8:30 P.M. Saturday, and 10 A.M.–6 P.M. Sunday; on weekends only, for arriving motorists, it maintains a small kiosk on Calle de los Martínez near the intersection with RN8. Their monthly *Don Segundo* is a useful commercial miniguide with a map of the town; the less-frequently published *Pregón Turismo* provides more detail on things to see and do.

## Services

Areco Online, Arellano 285-A, has reliable Internet access. Money is available through ATMs at several banks, including Banco de la Provincia, on Mitre immediately west of Plaza Ruiz de Arellano.

The Hospital Municipal Zerboni is at Moreno and Lavalle, tel. 2326/452345.

## Transportation

Chevallier, tel. 4314-5555 at Buenos Aires's Retiro bus terminal, charges US$3.50 to San Antonio (1.5 to two hours), with 12 buses daily. San Antonio's main Terminal de Omnibus is at Avenida Doctor Smith and General Paz, tel. 2326/453904, on the east side of town.

Pullman General Belgrano, next door at the Bar Parador Don Segundo, tel. 2326/15-680368, has three buses daily to Retiro.

## VICINITY OF SAN ANTONIO DE ARECO

Just off Ruta Provincial 41, northbound from San Antonio, several historic *estancias* grow soybeans and raise livestock, but tourism pays the bills. All of them take overnight guests and also offer "day in the country" excursions, including an *asado* and rural activities like horseback riding. Camping is not out of the question, at least at La Porteña.

## Estancia La Porteña

San Antonio's most emblematic *estancia*, La Porteña has belonged to the Güiraldes family since the early 19th century. Of all the farms in the area, it has the finest grounds; French landscape architect Carlos Thays, who created major public parks like Palermo's Jardín Botánico and Mendoza's Parque General San Martín, designed the plan, including the stately avenue of elm-like hackberries that leads to the main house.

The *estancia* has only a few guest rooms, so reservations are essential. Beef is the standard menu, but the kitchen will happily accommodate vegetarians with pasta and other meatless dishes, served in a dining room filled with French and British antiques. La Porteña eschews television, but there is a large swimming pool.

Estancia La Porteña, tel. 2326/453770, cellular 2325/15-684179, www.estancialaportenia.com.ar, charges US100 d per night with full board. It also has a campground, charging US$3.50 pp, but this is effectively segregated from the main grounds of the *estancia*.

## Estancia El Ombú de Areco

El Ombú de Areco, named for Argentina's wide-crowned national tree, was the *estancia* of General Pablo Ricchieri, who first forced military conscription onto the youth of Argentina. Set among four hectares of formal gardens, with a pool, on a 300-hectare property, it's the most lavish of all the area's *estancias* in terms of furnishings, facilities, and activities: satellite TV and video, telephone, horseback and bicycle riding, and games. There are six impeccable double rooms and three triples; rates for overnight accommodation start at US$70/100 s/d with full board. Vegetarians should probably verify the menu, which leans heavily toward beef.

Estancia El Ombú de Areco, tel. 2326/492080, cellular 2325/15-682598, reservas @estanciaelombu.com, www.estanciaelombu.com, also offers "day in the country" visits for US$30 pp and arranges transportation from the capital and its airports for guests. Its Gran Buenos Aires contact is at Cura Allievi 1280, Boulogne, Buenos Aires Province, tel. 11/4710-2795.

## Estancia La Bamba

Less elegant than La Porteña and less luxurious than El Ombú, Estancia La Bamba is a little rougher around the edges, but its unique personality—it began as a *posta* (way station) on the colonial Camino Real rather than as an *estancia* per se—gives it a unique ambiance. The least formal of the big three, it is perhaps the most relaxed of them all.

La Bamba, which served as a set for director María Luisa Bemberg's 19th-century drama *Camila,* can accommodate 11 persons in five rooms in the main house, another four in a cottage suitable for a family, and four more in an annex. Amenities include a swimming pool, game and video rooms, and activities including horseback riding, bird-watching, fishing, and the like. Rates range from about US$52 to US$60 pp with full board, depending on the room.

Estacia La Bamba, tel. 2326/456293, tel. 11/4732-1269 in Buenos Aires, labamba@sinectis.com.ar, www.la-bamba.com.ar, also offers a "day in the country" for about US$30 pp.

# La Plata and Vicinity

Beyond the southern boundary of the federal district, a new freeway leads to the provincial capital of La Plata, shifted here after a barely avoided civil war established the federal capital as a separate entity. About midway to La Plata, at the Berazategui exit, the site where the late *cumbia* star Rodrigo Bueno rolled his car in 2000 has become a pilgrimage site for those convinced he was a saint. Nearby Florencio Varela is the site of Los Veinticinco Ombúes, the home of naturalist/novelist William Henry Hudson.

## LA PLATA

Indignant provincial authorities, responding to the federalization of the city of Buenos Aires, expropriated six square leagues of land in the former Municipio de la Ensenada to create the new provincial capital of La Plata in 1882. Provincial Governor Dardo Rocha chose Pedro Benoit's standard grid, superimposed with diagonals like those of Washington, D.C., to be embellished with pretentious neoclassical and Francophile buildings that have, nevertheless, achieved a remarkable harmony over time. While government is its reason for existence, La Plata (population 553,002) has become one of the country's major cultural centers, with first-rate universities, theaters, concert halls, libraries, and museums.

### Orientation

La Plata is 56 kilometers southeast of Buenos Aires via the Autopista Buenos Aires–La Plata, the recently completed freeway between the two cities. The city itself consists of a rectangular grid, with regularly distributed plazas, but the connecting diagonals (which run north-south and east-west) can make the layout disorienting to pedestrians—a wrong turn can send you far out of your way.

Most public buildings are on or around Plaza Moreno, La Plata's precise geographical center, but its commercial center is near Plaza San Martín, six blocks northeast. Unlike most Argentine cities, its streets and avenues are numbered rather than named; locations are most commonly described by their intersections and cross streets rather than building numeration.

### Sights

In 1882, Governor Dardo Rocha laid La Plata's **Piedra Fundacional** (Foundation Stone) in the center of sprawling **Plaza Moreno,** which fills four square blocks bounded by Calle 12, Calle 14, Calle 50, and Calle 54. Benoit, along with architects Ernesto Meyer and Emilio Coutaret, designed the French neo-Gothic **Catedral de la Inmaculada Concepción de la Plata** at the southwest corner of Plaza Moreno, but its construction is a story in itself. Begun in 1885, the cathedral did not open officially until 1932, and its three crowning towers went unfinished until 1999. So long, in fact, did the project take that the building underwent its first restoration (1997) even before its completion! Its **Museo de la Catedral** is open 8 A.M.–noon and 2–7 P.M. daily.

Rocha himself resided in what is now the **Museo y Archivo Dardo Rocha,** fronting on Calle 50 on the northwest side of the plaza; see the separate entry later in this secion for more detail. Two blocks west, the French-style **Casa de Justicia** fills an entire block bounded by Avenida 13, Calle 47, Calle 48, and Calle 14.

On the northeast side of Plaza Moreno, fronting on Calle 12, Hannover architect Hubert Stiers built the elegant German Renaissance **Palacio Municipal** (1886), whose main **Salón Dorado** is adorned with marble staircases, imported oak floors, German stained-glass windows, and bronze chandeliers. Two blocks away, bounded by Calle 9, Calle 10, Avenida 51, and Avenida 53, the **Teatro Argentino** is a performing-arts center that has finally replaced a far more prestigious building that burned to the ground in 1977; see the Teatro Argentino entry later in this section for more detail.

Two blocks northeast, facing Plaza San Martín on Avenida 7, Hannoverian architects Gustav Heine and Georg Hagemann designed the

EXCURSIONS

provincial **Palacio de la Legislatura** in the German Renaissance style of the Palacio Municipal. Across the plaza, fronting on Calle 6, Belgian architect Julio Doral designed the Flemish Renaissance **Casa de Gobierno,** home to the provincial executive branch and a remarkable set of murals by Rodolfo Campodónico; see the sidebar "The Campodónico Murals" for details. Across Avenida 51, the **Museo de Bellas Artes Bonaerense,** Avenida 51 No. 525, tel. 221/421-8629, www.lpsat.net/museo, is a contemporary art museum open 10 A.M.–7 P.M. weekdays, 10 A.M.–1 P.M. and 3–7 P.M. weekends.

At the northwest corner of Plaza San Martín, La Plata's first railroad station is now the **Pasaje Dardo Rocha** (1887), home to several museums and other cultural institutions; see the Pasaje Dardo Rocha entry later in this section for more detail. Two blocks farther on, the **Rectorado de la Universidad Nacional** (1905), on Avenida 7 between Calle 47 and 48, now houses university offices. About three blocks east of the plaza, topped by a view tower, the **Palacio Campodónico** (1892) fills a small triangular lot bounded by Diagonal 70, Calle 5, and Calle 56. Expropriated by the provincial government in 1976, it's now a cultural center with rotating exhibitions.

Several blocks northeast, across Avenida 1, the 60-hectare **Paseo del Bosque** is a forested park that contains recreational and educational facilities including the **Anfiteatro Martín Fierro,** an outdoor theater; the extraordinary **Museo de Ciencias Naturales** (Natural Sciences Museum); the **Observatorio Astronómico** (Astronomical

## THE CAMPODÓNICO MURALS

S tretching around the grounds of the Casa de Gobierno, Rodolfo Campodónico's 28 vivid historical and thematic murals are a welcome addition to La Plata's cultural scene. The former mostly include scenes from major events in Argentine history, and the latter deal with ways of life and figures from folk culture, music, and literature.

Dating from 1999, the murals that cover the walls from Avenida 51 along Calle 5 and Avenida 53 deal with the country's history. The murals' titles and their subjects are as follows: *Primeros Habitantes,* (First Inhabitants); *Solís and el Río de la Plata,* the Spanish discovery of the Río de la Plata; *Las Fundaciones,* the early settlements of Pedro de Mendoza and Juan de Garay; *Ataque al Fuerte Sancti Spiritus, 1536,* the Querandí assault on Mendoza's settlement; *El Mestizaje,* the blending of the indigenous and European-immigrant populations; *La Virgen de Luján,* Argentina's patron saint; *Éxodo de los Indios Quilmes,* the forced deportation of the Quilmes Indians from northwestern Argentina to Buenos Aires; *Invasiones Inglesas,* the British invasions of the early 19th century; *Los Colorados del Monte,* the Federalist soldiers of the backcountry; *El Fusilamiento de Dorrego,* (The Execution of Colonel Dorrego); *Combate de Vuelta de Obligado,* a battle in the war with Paraguay; *Telégrafo, Alumbrado y Ferrocarril,* the arrival of the telegraph, barbed wire, and the railroad; *Campañas al Desierto,* the war against the Patagonian Indians; and *Los Inmigrantes,* the European immigration.

At the corner of Calle 5 and Avenida 51, the more thematic murals are as follows: *Los Isleños,* (residents of the delta); *La Construcción,* the building of urban Argentina; *Campesinos* (peasants); *Las Canteras,* (stone quarries); *Pescadores del Mar,* (maritime fishermen); *Industrio Pesada* (heavy industry); *Pescadores del Río* (river fishermen); *Homenaje al don Atahualpa Yupanqui,* an homage to the late folksinger; *Homenaje a José Hernández,* an homage to the author of the epic poem *Martín Fierro; La Doma,* on breaking wild horses; *Pulpería y Posta,* the rural stores and way stations; *Saladeros,* the 19th-century plants that salted beef and cattle hides; *Asado, Mate, Yerba,* the cultural bellwethers of the barbecue and the ritual herbal tea; and *Homenaje a Molina Campos,* an homage to *gauchesco* caricaturist Florencio Molina Campos.

Observatory); the **Jardín de la Paz** (Garden of Peace), with small pavilions for each country that has diplomatic representation in Argentina; and the **Jardín Zoológico** (Zoo).

**Museo y Archivo Dardo Rocha:** Benoit also designed the residence of La Plata's founder (1838–1921), whose varied career included stints as a journalist, soldier, diplomat, provincial legislator, national senator, and provincial governor. The museum, though, focuses on Rocha's personal effects, including furniture, art works, clothing, housewares, documents, and photographs, to the virtual exclusion of his role in the controversial shift of the provincial capital from Buenos Aires. More a homage than an analytical or interpretive institution, the Museo y Archivo Dardo Rocha, Calle 50 No. 933, tel. 221/427-5591, is open 9 A.M.–6 P.M. weekdays only.

**Teatro Argentino:** Finally rebuilt after its destruction by fire in 1977, the hideous **Teatro Argentino** reopened in October 2000 with a presentation of *Tosca*. With all the style of a multistory parking lot, this 60,000-square-meter concrete structure looks like the product of the military dictatorship that approved it—a fortified bunker that (had it been complete) might have bought the dictatorship a little more time in power after the Falklands disaster of 1982.

Still, the new Teatro Argentino looks and sounds better within than without, and remains one of the country's major performing-arts venues, with its own orchestra, chorus, ballet, and children's chorus. Its principal theater is the Sala Alberto Ginastera, which seats more than 2,000 spectators; smaller halls seat 300–700. Past performers include Arthur Rubenstein, Ana Pavlova, Andrés Segovia, and Richard Strauss.

The Teatro Argentino, on Avenida 51 between Calle 9 and Calle 10, tel. 221/429-1700, ta-relacionespublicas@ed.gba.gov.ar, www.elteatroargentino.com.ar, offers guided tours at 10:30 A.M. and 2 P.M. daily except Monday, by reservation only. These cost US$1 pp except for bilingual English-Spanish tours, which cost US$1.50 pp. There are discounts for seniors and students. For information on tickets to

performances, see the separate Entertainment section later in this chapter.

**Pasaje Dardo Rocha:** Formerly the Estación 19 de Noviembre, La Plata's first major railroad station, the French Classic–style Pasaje Dardo Rocha has undergone an adaptive reuse that has turned it into a major cultural center with several museums, plus cinemas, auditoriums, conference rooms, cafés, and other features. The municipal tourist office is also here.

Opened in 1999, the **Museo de Arte Contemporáneo Latinoamericano,** tel. 221/427-1843, www.macla.laplata.gov.ar, features works by modern Latin American artists. It's open 10 A.M.–8 P.M. Tuesday through Friday all year; weekend hours are 4–10 P.M. in spring and summer, 2–9 P.M. in fall and winter.

The **Museo Municipal de Arte,** tel. 427-1198, is a painting and sculpture museum focusing primarily on local artists. It's open 10 A.M.–8 P.M. weekdays except Monday, and 3–9 P.M. weekends. Dedicated exclusively to photography, the **Museo y Galería Fotográfica** (MUGAFO) keeps the same hours.

**Jardín Zoológico:** At the west end of the Paseo del Bosque, La Plata's Victorian-style zoo billets more than 180 native and exotic species, including giraffes, elephants, lions, monkeys, and rhinoceri, on 14 hectares. At Paseo del Bosque s/n, tel. 221/427-3925, it's open daily except Monday 9 A.M.–6 P.M. Adults pay US$.70 pp; children under 12 get in free.

**Museo de Ciencias Naturales:** Patagonian explorer Francisco Pascasio Moreno donated his personal collections of anthropological, archaeological, and paleontological artifacts to Argentina's premier natural history museum, which opened in 1888 under his own lifetime directorship. Today, more than 400,000 visitors per annum view at least some of the 2.5 million items in its 21 exhibition halls, which also deal with botany, geology, zoology, and other fields.

The four-story building is a monument to its era, its exterior a hybrid of Greek regional styles with indigenous American—Aztec and Incaic—

flourishes. Home to the university's natural sciences department, its interior also contains classrooms, libraries, offices, workshops, and storage space. That said, the museum's public displays have still not evolved far beyond taxonomy, and the 19th-century Darwinism of their creator.

The Museo de Ciencias Naturales, Paseo del Bosque 1900, tel. 221/425-7744, www.fcnym .unlp.edu.ar/museo, is open 10 A.M.–6 P.M. daily except for Mondays and New Year's Day, May Day, and Christmas Day. Admission costs US$1 pp for those over 12 years of age; there are guided tours at 2 and 4 P.M. weekdays except Monday, and hourly on weekends from 10:30 A.M.–4:30 P.M.

**Observatorio Astronómico de La Plata:** Part of the Universidad Nacional de La Plata, the local observatory has both modern telescopes and historical instruments from the 19th century. Guided tours take place every Friday at 8:30 P.M. in February and March, 8 P.M. April to September, and 8:30 P.M. October to December; for reservations, contact the Observatorio Astronómico de La Plata, Paseo del Bosque s/n, tel. 221/423-6953, www.fcaglp.unlp.edu.ar.

## Entertainment

For event tickets, one alternative is to visit Ticketek, Calle 48 No. 700, corner of Calle 9. Locutorio San Martín, on Avenida 51 between Avenida 7 and Calle 8, is also a discount ticket outlet.

**Performing Arts:** La Plata is a major theater and live music center, whose major venue is the **Centro de las Artes Teatro Argentino,** Avenida 51 between Calle 9 and Calle 10, tel. 0800/666-5151 toll-free. The box office, tel. 221/429-1733, is open 10 A.M.–8 P.M. daily except Monday. The Teatro Argentino provides free transportation from Buenos Aires for ticketholders.

Another major performing-arts locale is the **Teatro Coliseo Podestá,** Calle 10 between Calle 46 and Calle 47, tel. 221/424-8457. More intimate productions take place at spots like the **Teatro La Lechuza,** Calle 58 No. 757, tel. 221/424-6350.

**Cinema:** La Plata has two downtown movie theaters: the three-screen **Cine Ocho,** Calle 8 No. 981, between Avenidas 51 and 53, tel. 221/482-5554, and the two-screen **Cine San Martín,** Calle 7 No. 923 between Avenidas 50 and 51, tel. 221/483-9947.

## Accommodations

Frayed but friendly, no-frills **Hotel Saint James,** Avenida 60 No. 377, tel. 221/421-8089, fax 489-4291, hotelsj@lpsat.com, charges only US$7/10 s/d for rooms with private bath and telephone. For the truly budget-conscious, this may be the best choice, but it's often full.

Several decent hotels in the vicinity of the train station charge around US$8/10 s/d: **Hotel García,** Calle 2 No. 525, tel. 221/423-5369; the upgraded **Hotel Roca,** Calle 42 No. 309, tel. 221/421-4916; and **Hotel Plaza,** Avenida 44 No. 358, tel. 221/424-3109.

The **Hotel Roga,** on a quiet block at Calle 54 No. 334, tel. 221/421-9553 or 427-4070, is modern, friendly, and comfortable, for US$11/15 s/d with private bath, breakfast, and parking included. There is a five percent surcharge for credit card payments. **Hotel Cristal,** Avenida 1 No. 620, tel. 221/424-5640, hotelcristal@ciudad .com.ar, costs US$11/16 s/d.

The centrally located 70-room **Hotel La Plata,** Avenida 51 No. 783, tel./fax 221/422-9090, laplatah@cadema.com.ar, costs US$13/18 s/d including two meals, a phenomenal value for what is a very good hotel with a/c, cable TV, and similar conveniences.

**Hotel del Rey,** a 10-story tower at Plaza Paso 180 at the intersection of Avenidas 13 and 44, tel./fax 221/427-0177 or 425-9181, delrey @infovia.com.ar, has 40 well-kept midsize rooms with all modern conveniences. Rates are US$13/20 s/d with breakfast.

The star of La Plata's accommodations scene, though, is the exceptional **Hotel Benevento,** Calle 2 No. 645 at the corner of Diagonal 80, tel./fax 221/489-1078, info@hotelbenevento .com.ar, www.hotelbenevento.com.ar, a spectacularly restored 1903 building that once served as the provincial labor ministry. Modernized but with showers only rather than tubs, it charges US$14/19 s/d. It has high ceilings and attractive balconies, and is quiet despite the busy street. Rates are negotiable for two nights or more.

The utilitarian exterior at **Hotel San Marco,** Calle 54 No. 523, tel. 422-7202, info@sanmarcohotel.com.ar, disguises what is also a pretty good hotel that charges US$15/21 s/d. The four-star, 110-room highrise **Hotel Corregidor,** Calle 6 No. 1026, tel. 221/425-6800, fax 425-6805, informes@hotelcorregidor.com.ar, is a good upscale value for US$26/33 s/d, but it's not twice as good as the Benevento.

### Food

For breakfast, coffee or pastries, the best option is the tobacco-free **Confitería París** at the corner of Avenida 7 and Calle 49, tel. 482-8840.

The **Colegio de Escribanos,** on Avenida 13 between Calles 47 and 48, is a lunchtime favorite for lawyers and judges from the nearby Tribunales. Plaza Paso's **El Quijote,** at Avenida 13 and Avenida 44, tel. 221/483-3653, specializes in fine, reasonably priced seafood.

There's a pair of good Italian options with sidewalk seating: **La Trattoría,** at Calle 47 and Diagonal 74, tel. 221/422-6135, and **Prego,** Calle 11 No. 805, tel. 221/421-0854. For a more formal Italian meal, try **Abruzzese,** Calle 42 No. 457, tel. 221/421-9869.

The line between places to eat and places to drink is not always obvious in La Plata. The best blend of the two is the classic **Cervecería El Modelo,** at the corner of Calle 5 and Calle 54, tel. 221/421-1321, which prepares terrific sandwiches, plus draft beer and hard cider and free unshelled and unsalted peanuts. There is a fairly large tobacco-free area.

Another option is the **Wilkenny Irish Pub & Restaurant,** Calle 50 No. 797, tel. 221/483-1772, www.wilkenny.com.ar, a legitimately Irish-styled pub in the heart of La Plata. The food includes pub grub like lamb stew (though the bulk of the menu is Argentine and there are even a couple of Chinese dishes), plus Irish beers (Guinness, Harp, and Kilkenny) on tap by the pint and half-pint). Lunch or dinner entrees cost around US$2–4; there is a larger selection of bottle brews, plus Irish and specialty coffees. Service is excellent.

For ice cream, try **La Sorbetière,** at the corner of Calle 47 and Calle 10, or **Süss und Eis,** at the corner of Calle 47 and Calle 9.

### Information

The improved Información Turística La Plata, the municipal tourist office in the Pasaje Dardo Rocha at the corner of Calles 6 and 50, tel. 221/427-1535 or 427-3054, is open 9 A.M.–6 P.M. weekdays, 9 A.M.–1 P.M. Saturday. It distributes far-better city maps, informational brochures, and bus schedules than in the recent past, and the staff is more accommodating. There's a branch office in the Palacio Campodónico, on Diagonal 79 at Calle 8, open 9 A.M.–6 P.M. daily.

The Dirección Provincial de Turismo, on the 13th floor of the Torre Municipal at Calle 12 and Avenida 53, tel. 221/429-5553, buenosairesturismo @hotmail.com, serviciosturisticosbuenosaires @hotmail.com, is open 9 A.M.–3 P.M. weekdays only. Though sometimes bureaucratic, this provincial office can be surprisingly helpful for out-of-town sights. It also has a pair of useful websites: www.vivalaspampas.com and www.gba.gov.ar.

### Services

As a provincial capital, La Plata has a full complement of services.

**Money:** Banco de la Provincia has an ATM on Avenida 7 between Calle 46 and Calle 47, while Banco Nación has one at the corner of Avenida 7 and Calle 49. There are many others, however.

**Postal Services:** Correo Argentino is at the corner of Avenida 51 and Calle 4.

**Telephone, Fax, and Internet:** Locutorio San Martín, on Avenida 51 between Avenida 7 and Calle 8, provides long-distance phone and fax services.

Cybersonic, near Plaza Italia at the corner of Diagonal 74 and Calle 6, tel. 489-5511, is open 24 hours for Internet access.

**Travel Agency:** Asatej, Avenida 5 No. 990 at the corner of Avenida 53, tel. 0221/483-8673, laplata@asatej.com.ar, is the local branch of Argentina's student and youth-oriented travel agency.

## Transportation

**Air:** La Plata has no airport, but Manuel Tienda León, tel. 221/425-1140, provides door-to-door transportation to Buenos Aires's Ezeiza and Aeroparque.

**Bus:** La Plata's Terminal de Omnibus is at Calle 42 and Calle 4, tel. 221/421-2182; there are frequent buses to and from Retiro (US$1.20, one hour) with Costera Metropolitana, tel. 221/489-2284, and Río de la Plata, tel. 11/4305-1405.

**Train:** La Plata's century-old Estación Ferrocarril General Roca is at Avenida 1 and Avenida 44, tel. 221/423-2575. Transportes Metropolitana SA

General Roca (TMR, tel. 11/4304-0021) operates 51 weekday trains from Constitución (Buenos Aires) to La Plata (1.5 hours, US$.50); the number drops to between 35 and 40 trains on weekends and holidays. The last train returns to Constitución around 10:30 P.M., but they start up again around 3 A.M.

## VICINITY OF LA PLATA
### República de los Niños

On the grounds of what was once a golf course built for the English meat packer Swift, the provincial government built this 50-hectare children's amusement park in the northern suburb of La Plata. According to some accounts, Walt Disney took the inspiration for Disneyland and Walt Disney World from República de los Niños, but Disney visited Argentina in 1941, a decade before the Argentine park opened in 1951.

© WAYNE BERNHARDSON

República de los Niños near La Plata

Conceived by Evita, executed by 1,600 laborers under Perón loyalist governor Domingo Mercante and officially opened by Juan Perón himself, República de los Niños had a strong political content that may not be obvious today. In the context of Peronist politics, its origins as an expropriated property and a destination for underprivileged working-class children are significant.

República de los Niños displays a melange of architectural miniatures from around the world, ranging from the medieval Europe of Grimm's fairy tales to Islamic mosques and the Taj Mahal, but most notably including replicas of the Argentine presidential palace, legislature, and courts—with the obvious implication that its youthful public could aspire to office (and apparently to graft—there's also a jail). A steam train makes the rounds of the park.

República de los Niños is at Camino General Belgrano and 501, in the suburb of Manuel Gonnet, tel. 221/484-1409, www.republica.laplata.gov.ar. Hours are 10 A.M.–10 P.M. daily except Monday. Admission costs US$.35 for adults over 12, parking US$1.

From Avenida 7 in downtown La Plata, bus Nos. 518 and 273 go to República de los Niños, but not all No. 273s go all the way.

## Parque Ecológico Cultural Guillermo E. Hudson

William Henry Hudson, known to Argentines as Guillermo Enrique Hudson, was the Argentine-born son of New Englanders Daniel Hudson and Carolina Kimble, who moved to Argentina in 1836. Born in 1841, Hudson passed his youth on the farm known as Los 25 Ombúes for the *ombú* trees that once stood around the humble house in what was a very wild and remote area. Today, the 18th-century adobe house is a museum and the centerpiece of a 54-hectare forest and wetland preserve near the slum suburb of Florencio Varela.

Hudson, who left Argentina for England in 1869, left a reminiscence of his days on the pampas in his *Long Ago and Far Away* (1918), but also left memorable South American stories in *Idle Days in Patagonia* (1893) and *The Purple Land* (1885, republished in 1904). His main interest, though, was natural history, particularly birds.

Along with Hudson's birthplace, which holds his books and family documents, there still stand some of the original 25 trees for which the farm was named. The best time to see the park is after the spring rains, when the wetlands still teem with bird life—but also with mosquitos.

The Parque Ecológico Cultural Guillermo E. Hudson, tel. 11/4901-9651, is about midway between Buenos Aires and La Plata. The easiest way there is to take the train from Constitución (Buenos Aires) to Estación Florencio Varela and bus No. 324, Ramal (Terminal) 2. This will get you to within a few hundred meters of the entrance, which is up a dirt road.

# Uruguay

Uruguay shares many features with its larger neighbor, so much so that even some Uruguayans will reluctantly admit that the country might as well be an Argentine province—and it often seems like one, when Argentines pack the beaches of Punta del Este in summer. Uruguayans themselves, while their appearance and accent differ little from that of their neighbors, do not have the reputation for arrogance that other Latin Americans often attribute to Argentines.

Uruguay has many attractions not easily found in the immediate vicinity of Buenos Aires—long, sandy beaches beneath rising headlands, extensive oceanside dunes, and verdant rolling hill country. It also has an entertaining capital city in Montevideo, one of the Southern Cone's cultural treasures in the UNESCO World Heritage Site town of Colonia, and the high-powered summer resort of Punta del Este.

Still, when Argentina sneezes, Uruguay catches cold, and the Argentine political and economic collapse of 2001–2002 hit the country hard. With their currency devalued and bank accounts frozen, Argentines could not even afford to travel

## TRAVEL IN URUGUAY

**B**ecause so many travelers to the Argentine capital cross the Río de la Plata to Montevideo, Colonia, Carmelo, Punta del Este, and other important towns are covered in detail in this handbook. For the most part, conditions are similar to those in Argentina.

### Visas and Officialdom

Very few nationalities need advance visas for Uruguay, but requirements can change—if in doubt, check the consulate in Buenos Aires. Ordinarily, border officials give foreign tourists an automatic 90-day entry permit.

### Health

Uruguay requires no vaccinations for visitors entering from any country, and public health standards are among the continent's highest.

### Money and Prices

The Argentine political and economic meltdown of 2001–2002 has had severe repercussions on the Uruguayan economy. With Argentines unable to travel because of their own weak peso, Uruguayan hotel occupancy has fallen, but the Uruguayan peso has slipped much more slowly than the Argentine peso has, so Uruguayan prices remain somewhat higher than in Argentina in dollar terms. The exchange rate definitely favors the dollar.

The U.S. dollar operates as a parallel currency in Uruguay, at least in the tourist sector, where hotel and restaurant prices are often quoted in both U.S. and Uruguayan currencies. In areas away from the heavily touristed coast, this is less common.

In the short term, dollar prices are likely to continue to fall, but nobody foresees a collapse on the scale of Argentina's. Traditionally, Uruguay has the continent's most liberal banking laws; exchange houses are numerous, and bureaucracy is minimal for U.S. cash and travelers' checks.

Banks, though, keep limited hours—normally 1–5 P.M. weekdays only. ATMs are common in Montevideo, Colonia, and Punta del Este, but in smaller towns they may not work with foreign plastic. Keep a close eye on exchange rates, and avoid buying too many pesos if the rate is unstable.

Interestingly, Uruguay has phased the faces of generals and politicians out of its banknotes, which now feature artists and writers like Joaquín Torres García (Ur$5), Eduardo Acevedo Vásquez (Ur$10), Juan Zorrilla de San Martín (Ur$20), José Pedro Varela (Ur$50), Eduardo Fabini (Ur$100), and Pedro Figari (Ur$200). The one-peso coin, though, remains the stronghold of independence hero General José Gervasio Artigas.

### Communications

Uruguayan communications remain under the state monopoly Antel, despite pressures for privatization. Long-distance phone and Internet offices are fewer than in Argentina. Uruguay's country code is tel. 598; each city or town has a separate area code, ranging from one to three or even four digits. Note that while most Montevideo telephone numbers have seven digits, a handful of informational and public-service numbers have only four digits. Rural and suburban numbers can have between four and six digits.

### Getting Around

Distances in Uruguay are short and roads are good. Rental cars are readily available, but the cost of gasoline is high—in excess of US$1 per liter.

Uruguayan buses resemble Argentine ones—modern, spacious, and fast—and service is frequent on most routes. Most, though not all, towns have a main bus terminal, usually on the outskirts of town; some bus lines have separate ticket offices in more central locations.

across the river—except to fetch money from their Uruguayan accounts, which were also briefly frozen despite Uruguay's tradition of free-market banking. The Uruguayan peso also fell, though not so far as the Argentine currency, giving the Uruguayan tourist industry some breathing room by making it more competitive and attractive to Brazilians.

Montevideo and Colonia are both easily accessible by ferry and hydrofoil from downtown Buenos Aires. Montevideo is the country's transport hub, with bus services west toward Colonia and east toward Punta del Este. There are are also launches from the Argentine river port of Tigre through the Paraná delta to the Uruguayan riverside towns of Carmelo and Nueva Palmira.

# MONTEVIDEO

Although Uruguay resembles Argentina in many ways, its capital is more than just Buenos Aires in miniature. Its revived colonial quarter, the Ciudad Vieja, is a pedestrian-friendly grid of narrow streets with distinctive plazas, dotted with galleries and antique shops—though there are still *conventillos,* onetime mansions taken over by squatters. East of the Ciudad Vieja, dense sycamores line most of the streets on either side of Avenida 18 de Julio, and the avenue itself is home to a smattering of classical mansions and deco-style buildings from the early 20th century. The southeastern suburban barrios toward Palermo and Pocitos enjoy access to sandy riverside beaches—something Buenos Aires's muddy shoreline cannot match.

Montevideo is a metropolis of 1.6 million people—almost half the country's inhabitants—but nevertheless has managed to maintain a small-town ambience. Its port, superior to that of Buenos Aires for every purpose except access to the pampas, has given it an international flavor; it's also a bureaucratic city, home to Uruguay's major political institutions and the administrative headquarters for Mercosur, the shaky common market in which Argentina, Brazil, and Paraguay also participate.

## History

The determined resistance of Uruguay's aboriginal Charrúa peoples discouraged permanent European settlement until the early 18th; since then, the country's history has been that of a buffer—first between colonial Spain and Portugal, and then between republican Argentina and Brazil. Bruno Mauricio de Zabala's founding of fortified Montevideo, in 1726, was a direct response to Portuguese activity along the river, but also to Northern European smugglers and privateers. The first settlers arrived from Buenos Aires and the Canary Islands (rural Uruguayans are still known as *Canarios*).

At that time, though, it was a pretty primitive place. On the initial houses, according to one historian, "Leather made the protective roofs… . Nails being scarce, wire unheard of, rope and cord undreamed of… leather was used as cables, as chisels, in all manner of joining and riveting." By the late 18th century, though, Montevideo had acquired an air of permanence.

Montevideo spent several years under Brazilian rule in the 1820s and most of the 1840s under siege from Buenos Aires strongman Juan Manuel de Rosas before finally achieving political and economic stability in the 1850s. Most of the city's surviving colonial buildings date from the early 19th century, after which today's Centro, east of the entrance to the Ciudadela, or walled city, gradually superseded the Ciudad Vieja.

From the 1850s, Montevideo followed Buenos Aires's economic example, as British investment, particularly in the railroads, fostered European immigration and the export of produce from the countryside to the capital and overseas. For a time, this made Uruguay one of South America's most prosperous countries, with generous social welfare policies, but the economically active sector of the population was eventually unable to support a large pensioner class. Beginning in the 1960s, economic stagnation led to revolutionary political upheaval and, in reaction, a military dictatorship (1973–85) from which the country and the capital slowly but steadily recovered until recent economic setbacks.

For all this, Montevideo continues to dominate the countryside politically, economically,

Puerto de Montevideo

# MONTEVIDEO

**CIUDAD VIEJA**

Dársena
Fluvial

BUQUEBUS
(FERRY TERMINAL) ■

RBLA FRANKLIN D ROOSEVELT

CASA
MARIO ■

DIRECCIÓN
GENERAL DE
ADUANAS

★ MUSEO MUNICIPAL DE LA
CONSTRUCCIÓN TOMÁS
TORIBIO

LA PROA ■

DIRECCIÓN
NACIONAL DE
MIGRACIÓN ■

PALACIO
DEL LIBRO ■

LA PUERTA DE
LA CIUDADELA
★

BANCO DE LA
REPÚBLICA

EX-BANCO DE
LONDRES ■

BANCO LA
CAJA OBRERA
★

LINARDI Y
RISSO ■

MUSEO
TORRES
GARCÍA

MERCADO DEL
PUERTO

CASA DE
LAVALLEJA ■

HOTEL
PALACIO ■

BANKBOSTON ■

MUSEO
ROMÁNTICO ■

ANTEL ■

PLAZA
CONSTITUCIÓN

CABILDO ■

PALACIO
TARANCO ■

TEATRO EL
PICADERO ■

PANINI'S ▼

EXPRINTER
■

CASA
GARIBALDI ★

CATEDRAL
METROPOLITANA ■

CONFITERÍA
LA PASIVA ▼

HOTEL SOLÍS
■

CASA
RIVERA ■

CYBERCAFÉ
URUWAY ▼

TEATRO
SOLÍS
★

PLAZA ZABALA

MONTEVIDEO
WATERWORKS ■

CONFITERÍA DE
LA CORTE ■

SHANNON
IRISH PUB ■

CORREO
CENTRAL ■

MANOS DEL
URUGUAY ■

MERCADO
CENTRAL

IGLESIA
ANGLICANA DEL
URUGUAY ★

HOTEL NH
COLUMBIA ●

PLAZA ESPAÑA

RBLA GRAN BRETAÑA

**DETAIL**

MINISTERIO DE
TURISMO ■

COLONIA

CINE LIBERTAD/
CINE CENTRAL ■

TEATRO
CIRCULAR ■

MUSEO PEDAGÓGICO
JOSÉ PEDRO VARELA ★

CINE PLAZA ■

PLAZA
FABINI

ASATEJ ■

MERCADO DE LOS
ARTESANOS ■

PLAZA

PIZZA
BROS ▼

MUSEO DE ARTE
CONTEMPORÁNEO ★

HOTEL ARAMAYA ●

AV 18 DE JULIO

CAMBIO REGUL ■

CAGANCHA

HOTEL
LANCASTER ●

HOTEL LOS
ANGELES ●

SALA
ZITARROSA ■

CAMBIO
GALES ■

PALACIO HEBER ■

**CENTRO**

CINEMETRO ●

HOTEL
CASABLANCA ●

MANOS DEL
URUGUAY ■

EUSKAL
ERRIA ■

SAN JOSÉ

RUFFINO ▼

HOTEL
EMBAJADOR
●

EL FOGÓN ▼

ANTEL ■

BAR LOBIZÓN ▼

HOTEL LONDON
PALACE ●

OXFORD
HOTEL ●

HOTEL
WINDSOR
●

SORIANO

HOTEL
LAFAYETTE ●

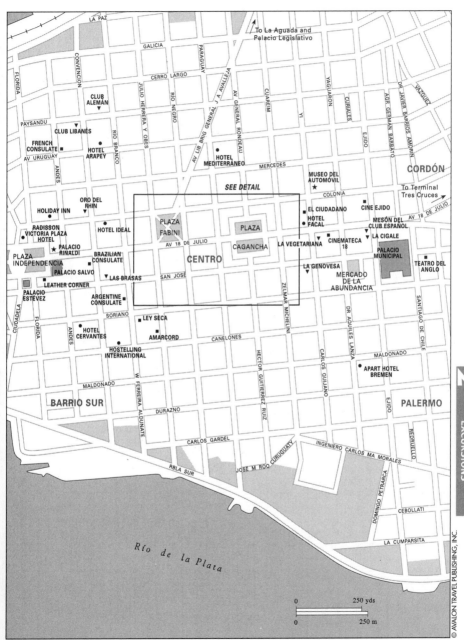

EXCURSIONS

and culturally, even more than Buenos Aires does Argentina. Still, there is a political tension between the countryside and the city, which has consistently voted the left-of-center Frente Amplio (Broad Front) into municipal power, but has been unable to elect its candidates to the presidency.

## Orientation

East of Buenos Aires, Montevideo occupies a hilly site on the left bank of the Río de la Plata. Passengers from Buenos Aires normally arrive at the Buquebus hydrofoil port on the Rambla 25 de Agosto, on the north side of the Ciudad Vieja, a slowly gentrifying colonial grid of narrow streets west of Plaza Independencia. East of Plaza Independencia lies the commercial Centro, split in half by the east-west thoroughfare Avenida 18 de Julio; businesses cluster around Plaza del Entrevero and Plaza Cagancha. South of the Centro, Barrio Sur is home to much of Montevideo's Afro-Uruguayan community; to the north, La Aguada is an improving area that's home to the national legislature and a new suburban train station. The waterfront *rambla* (street or boulevard) leads southeast to suburban barrios with large wooded parks and sandy beaches.

## Sights

Most of Montevideo's sights are concentrated in the compact Ciudad Vieja, but quite a few are also scattered around the Centro and neighboring barrios. The more northwesterly parts of the

## THE COUNTRY OF HOLIDAYS

Uruguay's political stability plus generous welfare and social policies throughout most of the 20th century earned it the nickname "the Switzerland of South America." The devastating political dictatorship of 1973–85, followed by economic changes in which a relatively small working population could no longer support a large pensioner class, undercut that reputation. One feature still survives, though: Uruguay remains the Pais de los Feriados—the country of holidays.

Uruguay celebrates all the typical holidays that Argentines and most other South Americans do—**New Year's Day** (January 1), **Labor Day** (May 1), **Día de la Raza** (Columbus Day, October 12), and **Christmas** (December 25); Uruguayan workers get those days off. They also enjoy an official holiday on **Epifanía** (Epiphany, January 6).

April 19 marks the **Desembarco de los 33,** the date in 1825 on which 33 returning exiles, with Argentine assistance, landed on the Banda Oriental to begin the campaign for independence from Brazil. May 18's **Batalla de Las Piedras** (Battle of Las Piedras) commemorates a key independence battle.

June 19 is the **Natalicio de Artigas;** unlike the Argentines with José de San Martín, Uruguayans honor their great national hero on the date of his birth rather than his death. July 18 is **Jura de la Constitución** (Constitution Day), while August 25 is **Día de la Independencia** (Independence Day).

Oddly enough for a self-proclaimed secular country, Uruguay officially acknowledges November 2 as the **Día de los Muertos** (All Souls' Day). This is particularly peculiar as it does *not* acknowledge **Semana Santa** (Holy Week) in March or April as such—rather, this time is **Semana Criolla** (Creole Week) or even **Semana de Turismo** (Tourism Week). Though this may occur only shortly after the end of the January and February summer vacations, many Uruguayans take the entire week off, rather than just Good Friday.

Uruguay's **Carnaval,** on the Monday and Tuesday before Ash Wednesday, is what Buenos Aires's must have been before the decimation of the Afro-Argentines; Montevideo's Barrio Sur still has a visible Afro-Uruguayan element that practices *candombe* (Afro-Uruguayan music and dance) ceremonies. Although these are not official holidays, they are popular ones.

As if all that were not enough, each Uruguayan is officially entitled to take the day off on his or her birthday.

Ciudad Vieja, around the port, have experienced a petty crime problem after dark.

**The Ciudad Vieja and Vicinity: Plaza Independencia,** dating from 1836 but remodeled completely in 1936, is a civic center marking the boundary between the colonial Ciudad Vieja to the west and the republican Centro to the east. The best starting point for a introduction to downtown Montevideo, its literal centerpiece is the massive equestrian statue atop the **Mausoleo de Artigas,** the subterranean crypt of independence hero José Gervasio Artigas. On the south side of the Plaza, the **Palacio Estévez** (1873) served as the presidential palace for a century-plus; it is still home to the **Museo de la Casa de Gobierno,** Plaza Independencia 776, tel. 2/1515, ext. 902, open 10 A.M.–5 P.M. weekdays, with guided tours available.

From the plaza, the late afternoon sun illuminates architect Mario Palanti's photogenic **Palacio Salvo** (1922), a 26-story baroque hotel since converted into apartments, at the foot of Avenida 18 de Julio. Palanti designed the building to be visible from its Buenos Aires doppelganger Pasaje Barolo, which he also built; from the Salvo's upper floors, in December 1939, British spies observed the German battleship *Graf Spee* taking refuge in neutral Uruguay for a few days as permitted by international law, before its captain scuttled it in the river.

Montevideo has perhaps the finest assemblage of art deco architecture in the Southern Cone countries. Immediately across the avenue from the Palacio Salvo, the **Palacio Rinaldi** (1929), an apartment building at Plaza Independencia 1356, is one of the best specimens; note the decorative relief panels on the facade.

At its creation in 1836, Plaza Independencia symbolized a break with the colonial past; the **La Puerta de la Ciudadela** (1746) at its west end is one of the last remaining fragments of the fortifications that surrounded what is now the Ciudad Vieja. Passing through the gate, the pedestrian mall Sarandí is a portion of the partly rejuvenated colonial quarter; the first major point of interest is the **Museo Torres García,** Sarandí 683, dedicated to one of Uruguay's most

notable 20th century artists. See the separate entry for the museum later in this section for more detail.

Opposite the museum, the narrow pedestrian mall Bacacay, full of restaurants, branches south to the **Teatro Solís** (1837), Buenos Aires 678, a historic performing-arts venue. See the separate entry later in this section for more detail.

Sarandí continues to **Plaza Constitución,** the colonial *plaza mayor* (1726) and predecessor to Plaza Independencia. Surrounded by colonial buildings including the landmark **Catedral Metropolitana** (1790) and the neoclassical **Cabildo** (colonial council, 1804), the sycamore-shaded plaza also features Juan Ferrari's post-colonial central fountain. The **Cabildo** contains the **Museo y Archivo Histórico Municipal,** the municipal historical museum at Juan Carlos Gómez 1362, tel. 2/915-9685, open 2:30–7 P.M. weekdays except Monday.

Two blocks south of Plaza Constitución, Montevideo merchant Samuel Fischer Lafone (founder of the Falkland Islands Company) commissioned the **Iglesia Anglicana del Uruguay** (Anglican Church of Uruguay) which, though it dates from 1845, was dismantled in the 1930s to allow construction of the Rambla Francia and then rebuilt. Four blocks north of the church, at 25 de Mayo 500, the facade of the **Banco La Caja Obrera** (1941) displays extraordinary bas-reliefs by Edmundo Prati.

Two blocks farther north, the architectural **Museo Municipal de la Construcción Tomás Toribio,** Piedras 528, is normally open 2–6 P.M. weekdays except Monday, but has been closed for repairs. Three blocks west, the monumental **Banco de la República** (1926–1938), Cerrito 351, fills an entire block bounded by Piedras, Solís, Zabala, and Cerrito.

Four blocks west of Plaza Constitución, French landscape architect Edouard André created **Plaza Zabala** (1880), named for the city's founder, on the site of the former Casa de Gobierno and an even earlier fortress. Occupying an irregular lot immediately to the north, the **Palacio Taranco,** 25 de Mayo 376, houses the **Museo de Arte Decorativo;** see the separate entry later in this chapter.

In the immediate vicinity of Plaza Zabala, several historic buildings are units of the Museo Histórico Nacional (National History Museum; see the museum's specific entry later in this chapter for more detail): the **Casa Rivera,** Rincón 437; the **Museo Romántico** (1831), 25 de Mayo 428; the **Casa de Lavalleja,** Zabala 1469; and the **Casa Garibaldi** (1830), 25 de Mayo 314.

The museums are not the only points of interest. At Rincón and Zabala, the former **Montevideo Waterworks** dates from the late 19th century. A little more than a block to the north, the neoclassical **Banco de Londres** (1890), Zabala 1480, is undergoing rehab as the **Biblioteca Americanista** (Americanist Library).

Northwest of Plaza Zabala, the **Mercado del Puerto** (1868), on the Pérez Castellano pedestrian mall, is one of the capital's top tourist destinations for its seafood restaurants and casual atmosphere; for more detail, see the Food section later in the Montevideo section for more information. The imposing building to its north, across the Rambla 25 de Agosto, is the decostyle **Dirección General de Aduanas** (1923), the customs headquarters.

**The Centro and Vicinity:** About three blocks east of Plaza Independencia, construction of **Plaza Fabini** (1964), also known as **Plaza del Entrevero** for the monument by sculptor José Belloni, opened a view down the diagonal Avenida Libertador General Lavalleja toward the barrio of La Aguada, site of the Uruguayan congress. At the southeast corner of the plaza, at Avenida 18 de Julio 998, the ornate French-style **Palacio Heber** (1894) was built as a private residence but now holds the **Museo de la Moneda y del Gaucho,** on Uruguay's financial and rural history; see the Museo de la Moneda y del Gaucho entry later in this section for detail. Across the street, the **Museo de Arte Contemporáneo,** Avenida 18 de Julio 965, 2nd floor, tel. 2/900-6662, is open 2–8 P.M. daily.

Two blocks farther east, Avenida 18 de Julio splits **Plaza Cagancha** (dating from 1836 but handsomely remodeled in 1995) in two. At its northeast corner, the **Museo Pedagógico José Pedro Varela,** Plaza Cagancha 1175, tel. 2/902-0915, www.crnti.edu.uy/museo, deals with the evolution of Uruguayan public education. Hours are 9 A.M.–7 P.M. weekdays only from mid-March to mid-December; the rest of the year, hours are 8 A.M.–noon weekdays. Admission is free.

A short distance northeast, the Automóvil Club del Uruguay's **Museo del Automóvil,** Colonia 1251, 6th floor, sports a collection of classic cars that are not seen so often on the streets of Uruguay as they once were. Hours are 5–9 P.M. weekdays except Monday, 3–9 P.M. weekends; admission is free.

To the southeast, the art nouveau **Mercado de la Abundancia** (1904–1909), San José 1312, is a national historical monument that's been recycled as a crafts outlet and cultural center. Immediately east, but fronting on Avenida 18 de Julio, the ponderous **Palacio Municipal** (1929–1930) sits atop the site of the former British cemetery—appropriately enough for a monument to bureaucracy.

From Plaza Fabini, Avenida Libertador provides an unobstructed northeast view toward the neoclassical **Palacio Legislativo** (1908), the home of Uruguay's legislature and the work of Vittorio Meano. Meano, who also contributed to Buenos Aires's Teatro Colón and the Argentine Congreso Nacional, died in a mysterious gunshot incident before the Palacio Legislativo's completion. Brightly illuminated after dark, the Palacio Legislativo, at the north end of Avenida Libertador, tel. 2/200-1334, offers guided tours in both Spanish and English, hourly from 8:30 A.M.–6:30 P.M. on weekdays.

In this neighborhood, known as La Aguada, the former **Estación de Ferrocarril General Artigas,** at Río Negro and La Paz, is undergoing restoration not as a railway station—that's moved a short distance north for the few commuter trains that serve the capital—but as part of a *plan fénix* for reinvigorating a once-bustling industrial area. Financed partly by a US$28 million loan from the Inter-American Development Bank, the former station will be the cornerstone of a cultural and commercial complex, and will include a food court, and loft housing in the vicinity.

**Museo Torres García:** Pictured on Uruguay's five-peso banknote, Joaquín Torres García (1874–1949) was a Picasso contemporary who became widely known for both abstract and figurative work. Spending much of his career in Barcelona, Paris, and New York, he also produced historical portraits of *Hombres Célebres* (famous men) which, in one instance he retitled *Hombres, Héroes y Monstruos* (Men, Heroes and Monsters), according to his interpretation of individuals such as Bach, Beethoven, Columbus, and Rabelais. The museum includes samples of the Torres García's legacy, but also works by contemporary artists.

The Museo Torres García, Sarandí 683, tel. 2/916-2663, www.torresgarcia.org.uy, is open 10 A.M.–6 P.M. weekdays, 10 A.M.–7 P.M. Saturday. Admission is free of charge, but the museum encourages donations; guided visits in Spanish and English are available. There is a museum bookshop and gift shop.

**Teatro Solís:** Montevideo's performing-arts counterpart to Buenos Aires's Teatro Colón, the neoclassical Teatro Solís (1856) has showcased performers of the caliber of Enrico Caruso, Arturo Toscanini, Vaslav Nijinsky, and Mstislav Rostropovich. Half a century older than the Colón—though Rosas's blockade delayed its completion—its facade features eight Ionic columns; the symmetrical lateral wings were a later addition. The horseshoe-shaped auditorium seats 1,600 spectators, considerably fewer than the Colón, but with outstanding acoustics.

The Teatro Solís, Buenos Aires 678, tel. 2/915-1968, normally presents a full schedule of classical music, ballet, opera, and drama, but as of writing it was undergoing a major renovation.

**Palacio Taranco (Museo de Arte Decorativo):** Occupying an irregular lot opposite Plaza Zabala, the opulent Palacio Taranco (1907–8) is the equal of French Renaissance palaces in Buenos Aires—it has antique furniture, sparkling parquet floors, and marble fireplaces in almost every room. In 1979, it saw the signing of a papal mediation that avoided war between Argentina and Chile over a territorial dispute in the southern Beagle Channel.

The Palacio Taranco is also home to the **Museo de Arte Decorativo,** with a collection of European artwork on its upper floors and a basement gallery with brightly decorated classical Greek and Roman ceramics and bronzes and early Islamic ceramics from what is now Iranian territory.

Opposite Plaza Zabala, the museum occupies an irregular lot whose entrance is at 25 de Mayo 376, tel. 2/915-6060. It's open 12:15–6 P.M. Tuesday through Saturday, 2–6 P.M. Sunday; admission is free. There are guided tours at 4:30 P.M. every day the museum is open.

**Museo Histórico Nacional:** Montevideo's national historical museum consists i of several Ciudad Vieja houses with distinct histories, contents, and perspectives. Admission to all of them is free of charge, but their hours differ.

The most broadly historical of the bunch is the **Casa Rivera,** Rincón 437, tel. 2/915-6863, www.mec.gub.uy/museum/rivera, a handsome late-colonial residence that extends for half a block; the upper floor, with wrought-iron balconies at every window, and an octagonal watchtower are late-19th-century additions. It was once the residence of General Fructuoso Rivera, the country's first president. The museum's display on pre-Hispanic Uruguay is more than just a token tribute to the country's aboriginal inhabitants (note the Charrúa Indian sculpture by Juan Luis Blanes). It's most notable, though, for the massive canvases of Uruguayan political and military figures, and of battles in the independence period. Hours are 9 A.M.–5 P.M. weekdays, 11 A.M.–4 P.M. Saturday.

Dating from 1782 but dramatically remodeled in the early 1830s, the **Casa Montero** houses the **Museo Romántico,** 25 de Mayo 428, tel. 2/915-5361, www.mec.gub.uy/museum/romantico. Also known as the *Palacio de Mármol* (Marble Palace) for its elaborate materials, its museum traces the tastes of upper-class Montevideo from independence to the early 20th century through their household artifacts; it's open noon–5 P.M. weekdays, 11 A.M.–4 P.M. Saturday.

The **Casa de Lavalleja** (1783), Zabala 1469, tel. 2/915-1028, www.mec.gub.uy, was the residence of Juan de Lavalleja, who led the "33 Orientales" whose landing in 1825 began the liberation from Brazil. The two-story building (uncommon in colonial times) served as Montevideo's first theater; it's still an impressive building, but its contents are fairly ordinary and scantier than other historical museums. Hours are noon–5 P.M. weekdays, 11 A.M.–4 P.M. Saturday.

Italian adventurer Giuseppe Garibaldi, who aided the Uruguayan resistance to Rosas in the 1840s, lived in the Spanish neoclassical **Casa Garibaldi** (1830), 25 de Mayo 314, tel. 2/915-4257, www.mec.gub.uy/museum/garibaldi. It's open by appointment only.

**Mercado del Puerto:** Originally intended as a Chilean train station, the British prefab port market—whose wrought-iron superstructure bears a strong resemblance to Santiago's historic Mercado Central—never made it out of Montevideo harbor. Erected just south of the port complex in 1868, its stalls and grills served primarily laborers for nearly a century, but several decades ago the restaurants gradually grew more sophisticated, adding sidewalk seating and turning it into a tourist attraction.

Always packed for lunch into the late afternoon (when it closes for the day), the Mercado is an informal venue whose surrounding streets teem with artisans, artists, and musicians. It's possible to eat well at the grills, where you can pick your cut off the coals while seated at the bar, but there is also table service. The interior, which features a wooden "Big Ben" clocktower, would look more appealing if authorities would remove all the illuminated plastic signs promoting an international soft drink company that needs no more publicity.

**Museo de la Moneda y del Gaucho:** French architect Alfred Massüe designed the ornate French-style Palacio Heber (1896–97) as a private residence for wealthy widow Margarita Uriarte de Heber, whose second marriage to politician Luis Alberto de Herrera took place here. Later sold to the Peirano family, then acquired by the Banco de la República, it was restored in 1985 to house two outstanding museums on Uruguayan economic history and the country's gaucho heritage.

Of the two museums, the second-floor Museo del Gaucho is the better—in fact, its assortment of gaucho artifacts, even if the presentation romanticizes the past, is as good as anything in Argentina. The items range from the usual saddles, spurs, stirrups, and belts to lances, *facones* (knives), and elaborate silver *mates* (gourds) and *chifles* (carved horns for drinking), plus paintings and sculptures by contemporary Uruguayan artists. All in all, it's the one Montevideo museum not to be missed.

The Museo de la Moneda, on the first floor, is more pedestrian but does house an impressive collection of colonial coins and medals, not to mention Uruguayan public and private banknotes that offer insights into the country's economic history. Banknotes of 500,000 pesos, for instance, recall the disastrous hyperinflation of the 1980s.

The Museo de la Moneda y del Gaucho, Avenida 18 de Julio 998, tel. 2/900-8764, is open 9:30 A.M.–noon and 1:30–7 P.M. weekdays except Monday, 4–7 P.M. weekends. Admission is free.

## Entertainment

Montevideo is not quite Buenos Aires for nightlife, but there's no shortage of places to go and things to do. Buses, however, do not run so frequently as in Buenos Aires, so it may be necessary to take a cab home.

**Bars and Pubs:** The intimate bar at **Bremen,** part of its namesake apart-hotel at Maldonado 1308, tel. 2/902-2094, occasionally hosts local tango singers (not dancers), backed by guitar, with spontaneous audience participation.

On the site of the former Café Sorocabana, **El Ciudadano,** Yí 1377, tel. 2/900-2680, 2/900-2698, www.elciudadano.com.uy, is a large but friendly bar that hosts local rock bands and high-profile musicians who come to Montevideo, mostly from Argentina; it has a well-placed stage and a fine sound system.

Ley Seca, Soriano 952, tel. 2/908-2481, has live music Thursday through Sunday. Amarcord, Julio Herrera y Obes 1231, tel. 901-9381, has live rock and pop music. The Shannon Irish Pub, in the Ciudad Vieja at Bartolomé Mitre 1381, tel. 916-9585, is a clone of its Buenos Aires counterparts.

Tango: Tango is almost as popular in Montevideo as in Buenos Aires. Fun Fun, within the Mercado Central at Ciudadela 1229, tel. 2/915-8005, is the city's classic tango venue.

Though less youthful than its name implies, Joventango, in the Mercado de la Abundancia at San José 1312, tel./fax 2/901-5561, http://canelones.chasque.net/joventango, vivaeltango @hotmail.com, does host regular tango events, including *milongas* and tango classes.

Other Performing Arts: The Sala Zitarrosa, Avenida 18 de Julio 1008, tel. 2/901-7303, hosts events of all kinds almost every night, ranging from evangelical and rock 'n' roll concerts to movies and live theater.

The Complejo Cultural Mundo Afro, upstairs in the Mercado Central, at Ciudadela 1229, tel./fax 2/915-0247, stresses Afro-Uruguayan theater and dance.

Cinema: Downtown Montevideo has several movie theaters, including the Cine Plaza, Plaza Cagancha 1129, tel. 2/901-5385; the Cine Libertad and Cine Central, both at Avenida Rondeau 1383, tel. 2/901-5384; the Cinemateca 18, Avenida 18 de Julio 1286, tel. 2/900-9056; the Cine Ejido, Ejido 1377, tel. 2/901-4242; and the Cinemetro, San José 1211, tel. 2/901-0772.

Theater: In addition to its cinemas, there are several live-theater venues, even though the landmark Teatro Solís has been closed for refurbishing. Among them are the Ciudad Vieja's Teatro El Picadero, 25 de Mayo 390, tel. 2/915-2337, and several downtown theaters: the Teatro del Centro, Plaza Cagancha 1164, tel. 2/902-8915; the Teatro Circular, Avenida Rondeau 1388, tel. 2/901-5952; and the Teatro del Anglo, San José 1426, tel. 2/902-3773.

## Accommodations

Montevideo has abundant accommodations, with several excellent values in the budget and midrange categories—especially since the recent devaluation. Choices are relatively few, however, in the Ciudad Vieja, the city's most interesting barrio.

Under US$25: The utilitarian Hotel Windsor, Zelmar Michelini 1260, tel. 2/901-5080, charges US$7/10 s/d with shared bath, US$10/13 with private bath. Hotel Arapey, Avenida Uruguay 925, tel. 2/900-7032, fax 2/600-2758, www.arapey.com, harapey@adinet.com.uy, charges US$10/15 s/d for rooms with tacky but serviceable contemporary furnishings.

Many youthful international travelers enjoy the Hostelling International affiliate, in an early 20th-century house on a tree-lined block at Canelones 935, tel. 2/908-1234. Rates range US$10–13 pp, depending on whether you're a Hostelling member or not; the hostel offers dorm-style accommodations with kitchen facilities, expansive common areas, information, and Internet access.

Rates at the well-managed Hotel Mediterráneo, Paraguay 1486, tel./fax 2/900-5090, hmediter@adinet.com.uy, range from US$12/14 s/d for standard rooms to US$18/20 s/d for more spacious "superior" rooms with a Brazilian-style buffet breakfast of croissants and fresh fruit. Streetside rooms, however, get a steady diet of noise from passing vehicles on nearby Avenida Lavalleja.

For style on a budget, try the nooks and crannies of the Ciudad Vieja's Hotel Solís, Bartolomé Mitre 1314, tel. 2/915-0279 or 916-4900, hotelsolis @starmedia.com, hotelsolis@hotmail.com, www.hotelsolis.20m.com. Rates for simple but attractive rooms with high ceilings and deco-style furnishings, in a tapering two-story structure that Uruguayan president Baltasar Brum erected for his mistress in 1901, are US$10 s with shared bath, US$22 d with private bath. There are also good restaurants and bars in the vicinity.

**Hotel Cervantes,** Soriano 868, tel. 2/900-5464, a crumbling classic that's now a historical monument, dates from 1928. Designed with direct telephone connections to Buenos Aires—a novelty in those days—it was the favorite accommodations of figures like tango singer Carlos Gardel, folksinger Atahualpa Yupanqui, and writers like Jorge Luis Borges, Adolfo Bioy Casares, and Julio Cortázar; Cortázar conceived his short story "La Puerta Condenada" in room No. 205. Rates are US$15/23 s/d.

Classic in style, the no-frills **Hotel Palacio,** Bartolomé Mitre 1364, tel. 2/916-3612, now lags behind better budget choices in the Ciudad Vieja, but it's worth consideration if you can get one of the two 6th-floor rooms with enormous balconies and expansive views of the old city. Rates are US$25 s or d.

**US$25–50:** For US$20/25 s/d **Hotel Casablanca,** San José 1039, tel. 2/901-0918, has modernized rooms in an older building, and an owner whose moods range from brusque to charmingly *simpática* (friendly). **Hotel Ideal,** Colonia 914, tel. 2/901-6389, charges US$15/25 with shared bath, US$20/30 with private bath. **Hotel Aramaya,** Avenida 18 de Julio 1103, tel. 2/908-6192, costs US$18/27 s/d with breakfast, but it's been struggling for business in the current crisis despite being a good value.

**Hotel Facal,** at Avenida 18 de Julio and Paseo Yí, tel. 2/902-8833, fax 2/902-8828, is a modernized hotel with a popular restaurant/cafeteria with sidewalk seating. Rates are US$32–34 s or d. The highly recommended **Sur Hotel,** Maldonado 1098, tel./fax 2/908-2025, is a newly rehabbed hotel with gracious management. Rates are US$23/25 s/d with private bath and breakfast except on Friday and Saturday, when they rise to US$30/35.

The best in this price category, though, is the German-run **Apart Hotel Bremen,** Maldonado 1308, tel./fax 2/903-2094, hotel@bremenmontevideo.com, www.bremenmontevideo.com. It's is a magnificently remodeled century-old building with stained-glass skylights and windows, transformed into stylish one- and two-bedroom apartments with cable

TV, fax, T-1 Internet connections, and kitchenettes. Rates start at US$45 d; the offices are half a block north, on Aquiles Lanza between Maldonado and Canelones.

**Hotel Lancaster,** Plaza Cagancha 1334, tel. 2/902-1054, fax 2/908-1117, lancaster@reduy.com, www.lancaster.reduy.com, is good value for US$35/47.

**Hotel Los Angeles,** Avenida 18 de Julio 974, tel./fax 2/902-1072, is a large (100 rooms) older (1928) hotel that retains some of its original features, such as high ceilings and common areas, but it's showing wear and tear. Rates are US$40/50 s/d with private bath, breakfast, telephone, cable TV, and room service.

**Oxford Hotel,** Paraguay 1286, tel. 2/902-0046, fax 2/902-3792, gerencia@oxford.com.uy, www.oxford.com.uy, is a well-kept 1960s hotel that's perfectly acceptable for US$41/50 s/d including breakfast, a late afternoon snack, and parking.

**US$50–100:** For US$40/52 s/d, the **Hotel London Palace,** Río Negro 1278, tel. 2/902-0024, fax 902-1633, lond@adinet.com.uy, is an excellent mid-range hotel whose immaculate and cheerful rooms more than compensate for its bland exterior. Amenities include a Brazilian-style buffet breakfast (plenty of fresh fruit), parking, a/c, cable TV, and the like.

Overlooking the river, the Spanish NH chain has rehabbed the **Hotel NH Columbia,** on the south side of the Ciudad Vieja at Rambla Gran Bretaña 473, tel. 2/916-0001, fax 2/916-0192, info@nh-columbia.com.uy, www.nh-columbia.com, which offers 138 rooms including a dozen suites, with buffet breakfast and all modern conveniences including Internet access and a fitness center. Rates start at US$65 s or d.

**Hotel Lafayette,** Soriano 1170, tel. 2/902-4646, fax 2/902-1301, lafayette@montevideo.com.uy, www.lafayette.com.uy, is a contemporary hotel with spacious rooms and breakfast for US$56/66. Tobacco-free rooms are available, and there are business facilities, a gym, and other amenities.

The highrise **Hotel Embajador,** San José 1212, tel. 2/902-0012, fax 2/902-0009, hotemb@adinet.com.uy, has 120 rooms with a/c, cable TV, a Brazilian buffet breakfast, parking, swimming pool, and the like; the rooms are spacious but not quite so good as at the London. Rates are US$66/88 s/d for standard rooms, US$88/118 for suites, but discounts are possible.

The 137-room **Holiday Inn,** Colonia 823, tel. 2/902-0001, fax 2/902-1242, hotel@holidayinn .com.uy, www.holidayinn.com.uy, charges US$70/80 s/d for standards rooms, US$84/94 s/d for superior rooms.

**Over US$100:** Also under international-chain ownership after years as a Sun Myung Moonie outpost, the **Radisson Victoria Plaza Hotel,** Plaza Independencia 759, tel. 2/902-0111, fax 2/902-1628, toll-free in the United States 800/333-3333, radisson@adinet.com.uy, www .radisson.com, has expanded to include a state-of-the-art casino. Rack rates for its 255 rooms start at US$150/170 s/d, but discount rates can be half that; there is also a 24-hour business center, a full-service spa, and many other luxuries.

### Food

It's hard to go wrong at the historic **Mercado del Puerto,** Pérez Castellano 1569. Some of its gaggle of *parrillas* (beef grills) are, according to *Buenos Aires Herald* restaurant critic Dereck Foster, "scruffy looking but they have wonderful food." By consensus, the best is the *tasca*-style **El Palenque,** tel. 2/915-4704, where hams hang from the ceiling, Galician owner Emilio Portela specializes in seafood (US$5–10 for most entrees), and there's both indoor and patio seating.

Other desirable Mercado del Puerto restaurants include **Don Tiburón,** tel. 2/915-4278, which also has indoor/outdoor seating (enjoy the pepper swordfish steak, abundant portions, and good service); and the *parrilla* **La Pradera,** where chicken costs about US$3–4, top beef cuts around US$6–7, and fish dishes like *abadejo gitana* (conger eel spiced with paprika) around US$4–7.

**La Proa,** directly opposite the Mercado at Pérez Castellano and Yacaré, tel. 2/916-2578, is a pricier seafood specialist with sidewalk seating. Downtown's **La Genovesa,** San José 1242, tel. 2/900-8729, is comparable.

**Bar Lobizón,** Zelmar Michelini 1264, tel. 2/901-1334, serves a fairly extensive pub-style menu of meat, pasta, chicken, and sandwiches with an accompaniment of rock music; it gets most of its business at night. Its namesake **Lobizón,** one block north on the opposite side of the street at Zelmar Michelini 1329, tel. 2/902-5999, is more of a lunchtime cafeteria.

For short orders, snacks, and coffee, there's a scattering of *confiterías* including the Ciudad Vieja classics **Confitería La Pasiva,** on Plaza Constitución at Juan Carlos Gómez and Sarandí, tel. 2/915-8261; and **Confitería de la Corte,** Ituzaingó 1325, tel. 2/915-6113; and downtown's **Oro del Rhin,** Convención 1403, tel. 2/902-2833.

Since Uruguayans are even more notorious carnivores than Argentines, downtown *parrillas* like **Las Brasas,** San José 909, tel. 2/900-2285, and **El Fogón,** San José 1080, tel. 2/900-0900, always draw crowds. For variety, **La Vegetariana,** Carlos Quijano 1334, tel. 2/900-7661, is one of several branches of the capital's main meatless chain.

Flashier than most Montevideo pizzerias, which tend toward the conservative, is **Pizza Bros,** Plaza Cagancha 1364, tel. 2/902-8537. **Ruffino** San José 1166, tel. 2/908-3384, is a more traditional choice. **Panini's,** Bacacay 1339 in the Ciudad Vieja, tel. 2/916-8760, is an upscale sidewalk café with an excellent, diverse Italian menu that features entrees like *ravioli neri* (black ravioli) in the US$6–10 range, plus fine desserts, Uruguayan wines, and ambiance.

Other ethnic food is primarily European, at venues like the **Mesón del Club Español,** Avenida 18 de Julio 1332, tel. 2/901-5145; the Basque **Euskal Erria,** San José 1168, tel. 2/902-3519; and the German **Club Alemán,** Paysandú 935, 4th floor, tel. 2/902-3982. The exception to the rule is the Middle Eastern **Club Libanés,** Paysandú 898, tel. 2/900-1801.

**La Cigale,** Ejido 1337, serves outstanding ice cream.

## Shopping

The **Mercado de los Artesanos,** Plaza Cagancha 1365, tel. 2/901-0158, has a wide variety of crafts. The recycled **Mercado de la Abundancia,** San José 1312, tel. 2/901-3438, has downstairs crafts stalls and upstairs *parrillas.*

For a broader crafts selection from around the country, try **Manos del Uruguay** at Reconquista 602 in the Ciudad Vieja, tel. 2/915-9522, and downtown at San José 1111, 2/900-4910.

The Ciudad Vieja is the place to look for antiques and artwork, at places like **Barboza Antigüedades,** Bartolomé Mitre 1366, tel. 2/916-3636, and **Galería Latina,** Sarandí 671, tel. 2/916-3737.

For leather, try the Ciudad Vieja's **Casa Mario,** Piedras 641, tel. 916-2356, or its **Leather Corner** branch, San José 950, tel. 2/900-7922.

**Librería Linardi y Risso,** in the Ciudad Vieja at Juan Carlos Gómez 1435, tel. 2/9157129, fax 2/915-7431, lyrbooks@linardiyrisso.com, www.linardiyrisso.com, is a specialist bookstore dealing with literature and history of Uruguay and Latin America in general. Once the studio of artist Joaquín Torres García, it has been frequented by literary figures ranging from Pablo Neruda to Mario Benedetti and Juan Carlos Onetti.

**Palacio del Libro,** 25 de Mayo 577, tel. 915-7543, is another large antiquarian bookseller.

## Information

The Ministerio de Turismo occupies spacious new street-level quarters at Colonia 1021, tel. 2/908-9105, ext. 130; it's open 9 A.M.–6:30 P.M. weekdays only. Its Aeropuerto Carrasco branch, tel. 2/601-1757, is open 8 A.M.–8 P.M. daily.

The municipal Módulo de Información al Turismo is a kiosk in front of the Intendencia de Montevideo at Avenida 18 de Julio and Ejido, tel. 2/1950, ext. 1830. Hours are 10 A.M.–7 P.M. weekdays, 11 A.M.–6 P.M. weekends.

Pérez Castellano pedestrian mall

© WAYNE BERNHARDSON

At Terminal Tres Cruces, the main bus station at Bulevar Artigas 1825, the Asociación de Hoteles y Restaurantes (AHRU), tel. 2/409-7399, maintains a particularly helpful information office. It's open 8 A.M.–9 P.M. weekdays, 9 A.M.–9 P.M. weekends.

**Immigration:** For visa or tourist-card extensions, the Dirección Nacional de Migración is at Misiones 1513 in the Ciudad Vieja, tel. 2/916-0471. Summer hours are 8:15 A.M.–1:30 P.M.; the rest of the year, it's open 12:30–7 P.M.

## Services

As the capital and only real metropolis in a small country, Montevideo has a complete range of services.

**Money:** There's a growing number of ATMs, such as BankBoston at 25 de Mayo 391 in the Ciudad Vieja. Exprinter, Sarandí 700 on the west side of Plaza Independencia, changes traveler's checks, as do exchange houses like Cambio Gales, Avenida 18 de Julio 1048, and Cambio Regul, Avenida 18 de Julio 1126.

**Consulates:** Several Latin Amerian, North American, and European countries have diplomatic representation in Montevideo, including Argentina, W.F. Aldunate 1281, tel. 2/902-8623; Brazil, Convención 1343, 6th floor, tel. 2/901-2024; Canada, Plaza Cagancha 1335, Oficina 1005, tel. 2/902-2030; France, Avenida Uruguay 853, tel. 2/902-0077; Germany, La Cumparsita 1435, tel. 2/902-5222; the United Kingdom, Marco Bruto 1073, tel. 2/622-3650; and the USA, Lauro Muller 1776, tel. 2/408-7777.

**Postal Services:** The *correo central* (main post office) is at Buenos Aires 451, in the Ciudad Vieja.

**Telephone, Fax, and Internet:** Antel, the national telephone company, has long-distance Telecentros at Rincón 501 in the Ciudad Vieja, at San José 1102, and at the Tres Cruces bus terminal. All three have Internet access for fixed amounts of time—minimum 15 minutes.

For Internet access in the Ciudad Vieja, try the Cybercafé Uruway, Ituzaingó 1333.

**Travel Agencies:** Asatej, Río Negro 1354, 2nd floor, Oficina 7, tel. 2/908-0509, fax 908-4895, uruguay@asatej.com, is the Montevideo branch of the Buenos Aires–based student and budget travel center.

Hostelling International has its central Uruguay office at Pablo de María 1583, tel. 2/400-4245, albergues@hosteluruguay.org, www .hosteluruguay.org.

## Transportation

**Air:** Montevideo's Aeropuerto Internacional de Carrasco, tel. 2/604-0330, is about 15 kilometers northeast of downtown, on the highway toward Punta del Este.

There are no nonstop flights from North America, but Montevideo is only a short hop across the Río de la Plata from Buenos Aires. American Airlines, Sarandí 699 bis, tel. 2/916-3979, and United Airlines, Plaza Independencia 831, Oficina 501, both fly from New York and Miami to B.A.; United also flies from Chicago.

Aerolíneas Argentinas, Convención 1343, 4th floor, tel. 2/901-9466, which flies from Miami, has the most frequent connections across the river from Buenos Aires. Other options from North America are via São Paulo, Brazil, with Pluna/Varig, Plaza Independencia 804, tel. 2/902-1414, www.pluna.uy; or via Santiago de Chile with LanChile, Colonia 993, 4th floor, tel. 2/902-3881.

To and from Europe, the only direct connections are with Madrid via Rio de Janeiro, with Pluna/Varig,. These flights are twice weekly.

LAPA, Plaza Cagancha 1339, tel. 2/900-8765, flies to Montevideo from Buenos Aires's Aeroparque.

**Bus:** About three kilometers northeast of Plaza Independencia, Montevideo's modern Terminal Tres Cruces, at Bulevar Artigas and Avenida Italia, tel. 401-8998, www.trescruces.com.uy, is a full-service bus terminal and shopping center with a helpful tourist information office, money

# THE VANISHING CACHILAS

Not so long ago, the finest assortment of antique automobiles south of Havana filled the streets of Colonia and Montevideo. In what was an open-air museum for vintage wheels, it wasn't unusual to see Model-A Fords, Daimlers, Studebakers, and Willys parked on the streets and rolling down Uruguay's roadways. Uruguay owed this abundance of classic cars (which they call *cachilas*) to its history of alternating good fortune and misfortune.

A prosperous country in the first half of the 20th century, Uruguay imported a wide variety of vehicles from Europe and the United States, but economic and political decline forced Uruguayans to maintain and operate what, in most other countries, would have been museum pieces. At times there were so many classic cars that the streets looked like sets for gangster movies.

This began to change when, in the 1970s, foreign collectors began to discover the abundance of *cachilas* in Uruguay. As the country's fleet of motor vehicles modernized with the renewal of automobile imports from Argentina and Brazil during the 1990s boom,

these stylish relics slowly but inexorably began disappearing.

Although not so numerous as they once were, the *cachilas* have spawned their own niche within the automotive sector. Scouts still scour the garages of provincial towns and the backroads of the interior for hidden treasures worthy of restoration and sale to collectors. This, in turn, has created a job market for artisans (sometimes elderly) who can restore and reproduce irreplaceable items such as wooden dashboards and leather upholstery. There is a market for parts as well as for entire vehicles.

Uruguayans are aware of their automotive legacy, and the law defines historic vehicles as part of the national patrimony. Except in a few high-profile cases, however, this has not restricted their sale and export, for which there is a strong incentive—cars that cost a few thousand dollars when they were built can, in restored condition, fetch nearly US$100,000. The clock is ticking for the *cachilas* that for so many decades lent their personalities to Uruguayan streets and highways roads.

*cachila* (antique automobile)

exchange and ATM, baggage storage, toilets, restaurants, public telephones, and Internet access.

Although the ferry from Buenos Aires is far faster and more convenient, there is direct bus service from Montevideo to Retiro (US$25, nine hours) four times nightly with Bus de la Carrera, tel. 402-1313, once nightly with Cauvi, tel. 401-9196; and once nightly with General Belgrano, tel. 401-4764.

Domestically, Montevideo is the hub for Uruguayan bus services, eastbound toward Mal-

donado and Punta del Este, and westbound toward Colonia and Carmelo. Companies serving Maldonado and Punta del Este (US$5, two hours) include Copsa, tel. 2/408-6668, and COT, tel. 2/409-4949; those serving Colonia (US$5, two hours), Carmelo, and other littoral destinations include COT and Chadre, tel. 2/1717, which also has a downtown office at Avenida Rondeau 1475, tel. 2/900-5661.

**Train:** This is not a very practical way of getting around much of Uruguay, but dedicated trainspotters can catch the local from the new Estación Central, just north of the old station on Río Negro, tel. 2/9290125, to the suburbs of Canelones and 25 de Agosto; the latter is about a two-hour ride (US$1.50).

**Boat:** Comfortable high-speed ferries from Buenos Aires take less than three hours to cross the Río de la Plata. The rehabbed Puerto Fluvial, on the Rambla 25 de Agosto, is convenient to the Ciudad Vieja, Montevideo's colonial core.

Buquebus has its office in the Edificio Santos, Rambla 25 de Agosto de 1825 at Yacaré, tel. 2/916-8801, fax 916-8880, www.buquebus.com. Buquebus's *Juan Patricio* takes a little less than three hours to Buenos Aires. The tourist-class seats are smallish and close together and do not recline, and the cafeteria food on board—sandwiches, empanadas, and a few other items—is pretty awful. Departures are at 11:31 A.M. weekdays and 7:01 P.M. daily; fares are US$44 pp tourist class and US$54 pp first class.

For bus-launch-bus service to Buenos Aires (US$13, eight hours) via Carmelo, Cacciola has an office at the Terminal Tres Cruces, tel. 401-9350. Departures are at 1 and 11:30 A.M. weekdays, 1 A.M. and 2:30 P.M. Saturday, and 2:30 P.M. only Sunday.

Ferryturismo, Río Negro 1400, 2/409-8198 or 901-3835, fax 901-3836, www.ferryturismo .com.uy, operates a bus-ferry combination via Colonia; departures times from Montevideo are 1:15 A.M. and 3:30 P.M. except Sunday, when there is no early bus.

**Car:** Rental agencies include Alquilato, Piedras 306 in the Ciudad Vieja, tel. 916-5195; Dollar, J. Barrios Amorín 1186, tel./fax 412-6427; and Multicar, Colonia 1227, tel. 900-5079.

# COLONIA

Only a short sail across the river from Buenos Aires, Colonia del Sacramento's picturesque 18th-century architecture has made it a UNESCO World Heritage Site and tourist town, but it's also a neighborly place whose residents sip *mate* on the sidewalk and chat across cobbled sycamore-shaded streets. Its unhurried pace—local motorists even stop for pedestrians—could not contrast more with the frenetic pace of the Argentine capital.

Traditionally, Argentines descend upon Colonia in overwhelming numbers in summer and on weekends, when hotel prices rise in accordance with demand. The town suffered dramatically, though, from the Argentine economic collapse of 2001–2002—a large majority of its annual visitors are *porteños*—and in the harsh Argentine economic times, hotel rooms have gone empty despite falling prices.

One positive consequence of the crisis may be the postponement of a megaproject—a 42-kilometer series of five bridges from Punta Lara, near the Buenos Aires provincial capital of La Plata, across the river to a point seven kilometers east of Colonia. The Argentine-Uruguayan Comisión Binacional Puente Buenos Aires Colonia (Buenos Aires Colonia Binational Bridge Commission) is promoting this environmentally suspect project for purposes of improving communications within the Mercosur common market, but its potential impact on tiny Colonia is enormous.

## History

Colonia do Sacramento (its original Portuguese name) dates to 1680, at a time when Buenos Aires was a backwater of Spain's mercantile empire and nearly all trade had to pass through the viceregal capital of Lima and then across the Andes and over the pampas. The Portuguese Manoel Lobo established the settlement directly opposite Buenos Aires on the *Banda Oriental* (Eastern Shore) of the Río de la Plata to be able to exploit the labyrinthine channels of the Paraná delta for contraband.

Colonia, then, became the focus of a continual tug-of-war between Spain and Portugal. A 1750 agreement to hand the city over to the Spanish failed when Jesuit missions, which operated with near- total autonomy until the Jesuits' expulsion from the Americas in 1767, refused to cede any of their territory on the upper Paraná. By the time the Spaniards finally established themselves in Colonia in 1777, the newly created Virreinato del

Río de la Plata had made the contraband economy nearly superfluous, as foreign imports could use the port of Buenos Aires.

Beginning in the mid-19th century, Swiss, Italian, and German immigration gave the surrounding area a dairy- and farm-based prosperity, but Montevideo's rapid growth deflected major infrastructural and industrial development toward the capital. Spared by the capital, Colonia's Barrio Histórico, its 18th-century core, remained largely intact for the evolution of the local tourist industry.

## Orientation

Colonia is less than an hour by hydrofoil or two-plus hours by ferry from Buenos Aires. It is 180 kilometers west of Montevideo via Ruta 1, a smoothly paved two-lane highway that enters town from the east and turns southwest toward the ferry port.

The town itself consists of two distinct areas: a conventional grid west of Ruta 1, centered on Plaza 25 de Agosto, and the narrow irregular streets of the Barrio Histórico west of Ituzaingó, marking the limits of the peninsular *ciudadela,* the walled colonial city. The main commercial street is east-west Avenida General Flores, which runs the length of the town on the south side of Plaza 25 de Agosto.

## Sights

Nearly all of Colonia's sights are in the Barrio Histórico, including its numerous museums, which are open 11:30 A.M.–5:45 P.M. daily except Monday. Tickets, which costs about US$.50, may be purchased at the Museo Municipal and the Museo Portugués only, but are also valid for the Archivo Regional, the Museo Indígena, the Museo Español, and the Museo de los Azulejos.

Early Colonia was a *ciudadela,* a walled fortress protected from sea and land by **bastiones** (bulwarks) like the southerly **Bastión de San Miguel,** the westerly **Bastión San Pedro** and **Bastión Santa Rita,** and the northerly **Bastión del Carmen.**

The entrance to the Barrio Histórico is the reconstructed **Portón de Campo** (1745), a gate approached by a drawbridge. To the west, several major landmarks surround the irregular quadrangle of **Plaza Mayor 25 de Mayo:** the **Museo Portugués** (Portuguese Museum, 1730), the **Casa de Lavalleja** (once the home of independence figure Juan Antonio Lavalleja), the **Museo Municipal Dr. Bautista Rebuffo** (Municipal Museum, also known as the **Casa del Almirante Brown,** though the founder of the Argentine navy never lived there), and the ruins of the 17th-century **Casa del Virrey** (also misleadingly named as no viceroy ever lived in Colonia).

At the southeast corner of the plaza, low-slung colonial houses line both sides of the sloping, roughly cobbled **Calle de los Suspiros** (Street of Sighs); one of the city's most emblematic structures (though a private residence) is the pink stucco with red tiles at the corner of Calle San Pedro.

At the southwest corner of the *plaza mayor,* ruins of the 18th-century **Convento de San Francisco** nearly surround the 19th-century **Faro de Colonia** (lighthouse), an almost pristine restoration that's open 11 A.M.–7 P.M. daily and charges admission of about US$1. Climbing its 118 steps is the best workout in town (and an enjoyable one when it's not humid); from the top, Buenos Aires, Quilmes, and even La Plata are visible in good weather. At some times of the year, the late closing hour makes it a fine place to see the sunset.

North of the plaza, at Misones de los Tapes 115, the **Archivo Regional** (1770) belongs to the simple architectural style known as *rancho portugués,* its adobe walls topped by a tile roof. The contents of the archive itself are scanty, but the building is a relic of the era when, according to Jesuit priest Martin Dobrizhoffer, Colonia thrived with contraband wealth:

> *The houses are few and low, forming a village, rather than city, yet it is far from despicable; opulent merchants, wares of every kind, gold, silver, and diamonds are concealed beneath its miserable roofs.*

To the west, on the riverfront, the **Museo de los Azulejos,** Misones de los Tapes 104, traces local architectural history through its elaborate tilework; see the Museo de los Azulejos entry later in this chapter for more detail. To the north, on Calle del Comercio, are ruins of the **Capilla Jesuítica** (Jesuit Chapel) and the modest **Museo Indígena,** which displays indigenous tools such as scrapers and *boleadoras,* plus some clippings on the pre-Colombian Charrúa and the romantic *indigenismo* of Uruguayan writer Juan Zorrilla de San Martín (1855–1931).

Northeast of the *plaza mayor,* the landmark **Iglesia Matriz** (1699) extends along the north side of the **Plaza de Armas Manoel Lobo,** but its twin-towered facade fronts on Calle Vasconcellos. Despite its early appearance, it has undergone major modifications due to combat damage, fire, and even an explosion of an arsenal during the Brazilian occupation of 1823.

On the north side of the peninsula, at San José 152, the two-story **Museo Español** (1725) was originally a private residence; see the Museo Español section later in this chapter for details on its contents. Immediately to the north is the **Puerto Viejo,** the former port. The **Teatro Bastión del Carmen,** at Virrey Ceballos and Rivadavia, integrates part of the colonial bulwarks and the Fábrica Caracciolo, a former soap factory, into the city's principal performing-arts center.

**Museo Portugués:** Built under Portuguese dominion beginning in 1730, the former **Casa de Ríos** underwent a late-18th-century reconstruction under the Spaniards. With help from the Portuguese government, its collections have improved dramatically—it has an excellent sample of maps on the Portuguese voyages of discovery (high-quality copies of the Lisbon originals), an extraordinary assortment of professionally displayed porcelain ceramics, and period clothing.

**Museo Municipal Dr. Bautista Rebuffo:** Unlike its Portuguese counterpart, Colonia's municipal museum displays more potential than accomplishment. Occupying the so-called **Casa de Almirante Brown** (1795, but rebuilt in the 1830s), it's a bit musty, both physically and in concept (or lack of it). In reality, it's pretty much a stuff-in-glass-cases affair that could benefit from a professional curator to organize and interpret its

documents and artifacts on aboriginal Uruguay, the struggle between Spain and Portugal, and Uruguay's early residents—plus a mass of deteriorating taxidermy specimens. It would also be informative to add material on Colonia's transformation of the past 20 years, and its almost total dependency on the Argentine tourist trade. Apparently, though, the elderly gentleman from whom the museum takes its name wants no tampering with the exhibits, even though some Montevideo professionals have indicated a willingness to volunteer their efforts.

**Museo de los Azulejos:** This collection of decorative tilework dates mostly from the mid-19th century—before then, beautification was a low priority in a city that was in an almost constant state of war. The stenciled artisanal tiles, many of them imported from France, vary slightly in size, shape, and design.

Sections of the floor and ceiling of the mid-18th-century building are original, others of subsequent brick. Some of the ceramic roof tiles are *tejas musleras,* so called because they were formed on the thighs of mulatto women.

**Museo Español:** The Spanish museum actually consists of two buildings, a mid-18th-century, two-story Portuguese residence and a mid-19th-century addition to the east. Its contents are mostly ordinary, though the narrative of events (in Spanish only) is thorough. What raises it above the routine are the historical portraits by contemporary Uruguayan artist and Colonia resident José Páez Vilaró, which complement the otherwise archaic materials.

## Entertainment
In a creatively readapted colonial building, **Colonia Rock,** Misiones de los Tapes 157, tel. 52/28189, serves mixed drinks and bar food. There is sidewalk seating and an interior patio, and there's live music Saturday nights. **Drugstore,** Vasconcellos 179, tel. 52/25241, has a more diverse food menu and live music some nights.

**Cine Stella,** General Flores 340, tel. 52/22169, shows current movies.

## Accommodations

The quality of accommodations in Colonia, always pretty good, has improved—even fairly modest places have a/c and cable TV. The Argentine economic crisis has depressed hotel prices.

**Less than US$10:** In a eucalyptus grove at the Real de San Carlos, five kilometers north of town, the **Camping Municipal de Colonia,** tel. 52/24444, charges US$4 pp. Public transportation is good, but in summer it can get crowded and noisy. There are also *cabañas* with private bath for rent.

**US$10–25: Hotel Colonial,** Avenida General Flores 440, tel./fax 52/30347, hostelling_colonial@hotmail.com, is the local representative of Hostelling International, charging US$8 pp plus US$2 pp for breakfast. **Hotel Español,** Manoel Lobo 377, tel. 52/22314, has also reincarnated itself as a hostel, charging US$10 pp with shared bath.

Rates at **Posada del Río,** Washington Barbot 258, tel. 52/23002, delrio@colonianet.com, www.colonianet.com/delrio, are US$10/15 s/d for rooms with start-of-the-art a/c, attractive patios, and an ample breakfast served on the terrace, but it's fallen behind some of the newer options. Service is good and friendly, however.

**US$25–50:** Appropriately enough, all the cheerful, spacious rooms are named after flowers at **Posada de la Flor,** Ituzaingó 268, tel. 52/24476, delaflor@adinet.com.uy, where rates are US$16/26 s/d with breakfast. Some but not all rooms have a/c.

**Posada de la Ciudadela,** Washington Barbot 164, tel. 52/22683, is a small, family-run hostel charging US$15 pp. **Hotel Leoncia,** Rivera 214, tel. 22369, hleoncia@adinet.com.uy, charges US$30 d with breakfast.

The classic facade at **Posada Don Antonio,** Ituzaingó 232, tel. 52/25344, atencion @posadasantonio.com, conceals a mostly modern but still appealing hotel with rates starting at US$20/30 s/d. The cheaper rooms have fans but lack a/c.

**Posada del Virrey,** in a mid-19th-century building at España 217, tel. 52/22223, tel. 598/9-4282927 from Buenos Aires, virrey@adinet.com.uy, is one of many good, stylish hotels in the Barrio Histórico; note the elaborately carved Czechoslovakian doors. The staff speaks French and some English; rooms with private bath and a/c go for US$25/35 s/d including breakfast. Some more expensive rooms come with jacuzzis.

**Hotel Italiano,** on a sycamore-shaded block at Manoel Lobo 341, tel. 52/22103, costs US$45 d with private bath and TV, breakfast included. Ask for a balcony room.

One of Colonia's old reliables, **Hotel Beltrán,** General Flores 311, tel. 52/22955, hotelbeltran@netgate.com.uy, www.colonianet.com/hbeltran, charges US$30 d including breakfast for rooms with private bath and surrounding a central courtyard. Weekend prices may rise substantially, up to US$50 d.

**Hotel Esperanza,** Avenida General Flores 237, tel. 52/22922, fax 52/24251, charges US$35 s or d during the week, US$50 on weekends. Substantially upgraded, it now includes a pool, spa, and gym, but isn't quite so stylish as most hotels in the historic district.

**US$50–100:** At **Posada Manuel de Lobo,** Ituzaingó 160, tel. 52/22463, posadamlobo @colonia.net.com, www.colonianet.com, rooms with contemporary furnishings and pleasant patios range US$30–60 d, with the higher rates on weekends.

**Hostal del Sol,** near the Bastión de San Miguel at Solís 31, tel. 52/23179, fax 52/23349, is a lovingly restored and lavishly furnished 19th-century house with high ceilings. Rates are US$50 s or d with private bath Monday through Thursday, US$60 s or d Friday through Sunday.

**Hotel Plaza Mayor,** Del Comercio 111, tel. 52/23193, fax 52/25812, plazamayor@colonianet.com, www.colonianet.com, is a spectacularly restored mansion with shady patios, lush gardens, and 16 rooms with modern conveniences including a/c and private bath with jacuzzi. Still, the rooms retain colonial style—some beds nestle in arched alcoves—and furnishings. Rates range US$55–110 s or d, but normally about 10 percent less on weekdays, including breakfast (the upper dining room has excellent river views); in the current economic situation, substantial discounts may be available.

The Spanish chain Barceló recently built the **Hotel Barceló Colonia del Sacramento,** Washington Barbot 283, tel. 52/30460, fax 52/30464, coloniadelsacramento@barcelo.com, www.barcelo.com. Rates are US$55/72 s/d.

The Barrio Histórico's traditional luxury favorite **La Posada del Gobernador,** on attractive grounds at 18 de Julio 205, tel. 52/22918, has been closed for repairs but should reopen in 2003.

## Food

For the most part, Colonia's restaurants have more style than culinary imagination, but the quality is good enough.

The standard is the *parrilla*. **El Asador,** Ituzaingó 168, tel. 52/24204, is a no-frills choice that's maintained its popularity over the years, so it must be doing something right. Other *parrillas* include **El Viejo Galeón** at 18 de Julio and Ituzaingó; **Nuevo San Cono** at 18 de Julio and Suárez; and the more upmarket **El Portón,** General Flores 333, tel. 52/25318.

**Café Colonial,** General Flores 432, tel. 52/21542, is essentially a sandwich spot, but it's good at what it does. **Casagrande,** Misiones de los Tapes 143, tel. 52/20654, prepares somewhat more elaborate short orders than most Uruguayan restaurants do.

**Pulpería de los Faroles,** Misiones de los Tapes 101, tel. 52/25399, has one of the more diverse menus in the Barrio Histórico, but prices are moderate. **Il Ristorante,** at Rivera and Rivadavia, tel. 52/25443, serves Italian cuisine.

**Almacén del Túnel,** General Flores 227, tel. 52/24666, is a traditionally good restaurant that has recently changed hands and names, so it may justify skepticism but is worth a look for its US$6 fixed-price lunch. **El Mesón,** San José 170, tel. 52/23090, serves a US$5 lunch or dinner menu, but also serves a la carte dishes ranging from fish and shellfish to pastas. Most entrees are in the US$6–10 range but some specialties, like *pulpo es-* *pañol al aceite de oliva* (octopus in olive oil) cost as much as US$15.

**Mesón de la Plaza,** Vasconcellos 153, tel. 52/24807, may be Colonia's most ambitious restaurant, with an adventurous menu that includes sturgeon, which is now being farmed in northwestern Uruguay (caviar production is also beginning). The garden has a covered patio where its possible to dine al fresco even when it rains.

**Heladería Frappé,** on General Flores between Lavalleja and Alberto Méndez, has Colonia's best ice cream.

## Shopping

The artisans' cooperative Manos del Uruguay has an outlet at the corner of San Gabriel and Misiones de los Tapes, in the Barrio Histórico. Colonia's Feria Artesanal (Crafts Fair) has a permament site at Suárez and Fosalba, two blocks north of Plaza 25 de Agosto; hours are 9:30 A.M.–7:30 P.M. daily.

## Information

The municipal Dirección de Turismo, General Flores 499, tel. 52/23700, imc.turis@adinet .com.uy, is open 7:30 A.M.–8 P.M. daily. Well-stocked with brochures, it usually has an English speaker in summer at least; there's a branch on the Plazoleta 1811, near the Puerta de Campo, tel. 52/28506.

The national Ministerio de Turismo has a ferry port branch, tel. 52/24897, open 9 A.M.–3 P.M. daily.

## Services

**Money:** Avoid changing money at the ferry port proper, where exchange rates are significantly lower than at Cambio Viaggio, just outside the port entrance at Avenida Roosevelt and Rivera. Downtown, try Cambio Colonia at General Flores and Alberto Méndez, or Cambio Dromer at General Flores 350. Banco Acac has an ATM at General Flores 299.

**Consulate:** Argentina has a consulate at General Flores 350, tel. 52/22093, open noon–5 P.M. weekdays only.

**Postal Services:** Colonia's post office is at Lavalleja 226.

**Telephone and Internet:** Antel, Rivadavia 420, has long-distance telephone service and Internet access.

**Medical:** Hospital Colonia is at 18 de Julio 462, tel. 52/22579.

**Laundry:** Lavadero Rev1án is at General Flores 90.

## Transportation

**Bus:** Colonia's Terminal de Buses, tel. 52/30288, occupies a triangular site fronting on Avenida Roosevelt, also bounded by Vicente García and Manoel Lobo. Several companies go frequently to Montevideo (US$6, two hours), including Turil, tel. 25246; COT, tel. 23121; and Chadre, tel. 24734. Chadre and Berrutti both go to Carmelo.

**Boat:** The Puerto de Colonia, the ferry port, is at the foot of Avenida Roosevelt. Ferryturismo, tel. 052/22919 or 23145, operates the high-speed ferry *Sea Cat* that travels several times daily to Buenos Aires; fares are US$24 pp for adults, US$18 for children ages 3–10. Retired individuals pay about US$1 more than children.

Buquebus's slow ferry *Eladia Isabel* sails to Buenos Aires (2.75 hours, US$10 tourist, US$15 first class) at 4:30 A.M. daily except Sunday and at 6:46 P.M. daily; the faster hydrofoil (50 minutes, US$20 tourist, US$25 first class) sails at 9:45 A.M. and 5 P.M. daily.

**Rental Cars:** Try Budget Rent A Car, Avenida General Flores 91, tel. 52/25319, or Multicar, Manoel Lobo 505, tel. 52/24893. There are other rental agencies at the ferry port. The cheapest rental cars cost around US$45 per day.

Budget and Moto Rent, on Virrey Cevallos near Avenida General Flores, both rent motor scooters for getting around town; one disincentive to this is the number of street dogs who, while not really aggressive, appear to enjoy chasing them. Scooter rates are about US$20 per day.

Budget also rents bicycles for US$10–15 per day.

# CARMELO

Rediscovered by Argentine tourists in the years before the crash of 2001–2002, the city of Carmelo (population 24,000) is a secluded river port where the Río Uruguay and the Río Paraná Guazú unite to form the Río de la Plata. Yachting and water sports are the main activities, but getting there is more than half the fun for shoestring visitors, as daily launches from the port of Tigre weave through the lush gallery forests of the Paraná delta islands en route to the Uruguayan side.

Founded in 1758 on a swampy location near the ominously named Arroyo de las Víboras (Arroyo of Vipers), Carmelo moved to the more inviting Arroyo de las Vacas (Arroyo of Cattle) in 1816, after petitioning independence hero José Gervasio Artigas.

## Orientation

In the department of Colonia, Carmelo is 75 kilometers northwest of Colonia del Sacramento via paved Ruta 21, and 235 kilometers from Montevideo via Ruta 1, Ruta 22 (which bypasses Colonia), and Ruta 21. Its recreational focus is the area around the arroyo, but most services line both sides of Calle 19 de Abril, to the north.

## Sights

Running along the north bank of the arroyo, the **Rambla de los Constituyentes** is the starting point for riverside excursions. The human-powered **Puente Giratorio** (Revolving Bridge, 1912), the first of its kind in the country, crosses the arroyo to the **Yacht Club Carmelo.**

In the town proper, the **Casa de Ignacio Barrios** (1860), 19 de Abril 246, was the residence of a major Uruguayan independence figure and is now the **Casa de la Cultura,** also housing the city's tourist office. Four blocks west, at Barrios and J.P. Varela, the **Templo Histórico del Carmen** (1830) is the focus of July 16's Festival de la Virgen del Carmen, honoring Carmelo's patron saint. The adjacent **Archivo y Museo Parroquial** (1848), originally built as a school, focuses on local and ecclesiastical history.

## Accommodations

In recent years, new hotels have opened and other have modernized; rates have risen in pesos, but devaluation has made them competitive in dollar terms.

Two campgrounds charge around US$2.50 pp: **Camping Don Mauro,** at Ignacio Barros and Arroyo de las Vacas, tel. 542/2390; and **Camping Náutico Carmelo,** on the Embarcadero, tel. 542/2058.

**Hotel La Unión,** Uruguay 368, tel. 542/2028, charges US$20 s or d with breakfast. Rates are nearly identical at **Posada El Navegante,** Rodó s/n, tel. 542/3973.

**Hotel Bertoletti** Uruguay 171, tel. 542/2030, lacks personality but is otherwise acceptable for US$25 d. **Hotel Rambla,** near the docks at Uruguay 55, tel. 542/2390, charges US$30 d with breakfast included.

**Hotel Casino Carmelo,** Rodó s/n across the Arroyo de las Vacas, charges US$30/45 s/d with breakfast; packages with two meals (US$70 d) or full board (US$100 d) are also available.

Eight kilometers north of town, the 44-room luxury **Four Seasons Resort Carmelo,** Ruta 21, Km 262, tel. 542/9000, fax 542/9999, www .fourseasons.com/carmelo, charges US$250–280 d with full board. The hotel is decorated with teakwood furniture and Asian touches like antique Buddhas and incense; all rooms also have fireplaces.

## Food

In addition to restaurants at the Four Seasons Resort and the Yacht Club, try **Perrini,** 19 de Abril 440, tel. 542/2519) and **El Refugio,** south of the bridge at Playa Seré, tel. 542/2325.

## Information

The municipal Oficina de Turismo, 19 de Abril 246, tel. 542/2001, turiscar@adinet.com.uy, occupies an office in the Casa de la Cultura, the town cultural center.

## Services

**Money:** Banco Hipotecario, 19 de Abril 249, is the best place to change money, but it lacks an ATM.

**Telephone and Internet:** Antel is at Uruguay and Ingeniero Barrios. Ciber Computer, Uruguay 372, offers Internet access.

**Medical:** Carmelo's Hospital Artigas is at Uruguay and Artigas, tel. 542/2107.

## Transportation

There are occasional flights to and from Buenos Aires via the airstrip at nearby Balneario Zagargazú. Bus and boat, though, are the primary options.

**Bus:** Carmelo has no central terminal. Berrutti, Uruguay 337, tel. 542/2504, has seven buses daily to Colonia (US$2, 1.5 hours), beginning in Nueva Palmira, and is the only company that serves this route; it also goes to Montevideo.

Sabelín/Klüver, at Roosevelt and 19 de Abril, tel. 542/3411, goes to Montevideo, as does Chadre, on 18 de Julio betweeen Uruguay and 19 de Abril, tel. 542/2987.

**Boat:** Cacciola, tel. 542/3042, sails to Tigre (US$9, three hours) at 4:30 A.M. and 3 P.M. daily except Saturday, when the afternoon departure is at 6 P.M., and Sunday, when the only departure is at 6 P.M.

**Rental Cars:** Budget, 19 de Abril 241, tel. 542/7073.

# VICINITY OF CARMELO

## La Estancia de Narbona

Near Carmelo's original site on the Arroyo de las Víboras at Km 263 of Ruta 21 toward Nueva Palmira, this crumbling 18th-century *estancia* sits atop a prominent hillock just north of the highway. Uruguay still has many *estancias,* but few can match the antiquity of Narbona's *casco* (main house), chapel, and *campana* (bell tower). It's open to the public 9 A.M.–5 P.M. Tuesday through Friday.

# PUNTA DEL ESTE AND MALDONADO

Highrise hotels soar behind sandy Atlantic beaches and elegant vessels crowd the sprawling yacht harbor at Uruguay's Punta del Este, one of South America's flashiest summer getaways—ironically enough, a place where a colonial Jesuit priest remarked that "you see nothing here but a few cabins, the abodes of misery." In January and February, the southern summer, Punta irrupts with flamboyant Argentine celebrities who make the covers and gossip columns of glossy Buenos Aires magazines, but in 1832, Charles Darwin spent 10 solitary weeks searching for natural-history specimens at a "quiet, forlorn town" that is now the jewel of the "Uruguayan Riviera."

It was in the late 1970s, as money from the corrupt Argentine military dictatorship flowed in, that Punta del Este began to grow up—literally so, as highrise hotels and flats replaced single-family homes. On the peninsula, only the southernmost sector of El Faro, whose lighthouse limits other buildings to three stories, has been spared.

Still, the compact peninsula that juts into the ocean is the place where wealthy Argentines come to play and be seen in a frenetic summer season—except when the Argentine currency collapses. Avenida Gorlero is the axis of Punta's hyperactive nightlife, but the beaches along Rambla Artigas, which rings the peninsula, are the focus of sunny summer days. Under different names, the *rambla* connects the peninsula to the riverside beaches to the west and to the ocean beaches to the east.

Maldonado, by contrast, is a business and administrative center that's been largely eclipsed by Punta's rapid growth and glitter, but still retains vestiges of its colonial origins. Founded in 1755, the fortified city fell briefly under British control during the invasion of Buenos Aires in 1806.

*Uruguay has many attractions not easily found near Buenos Aires—long, sandy beaches beneath rising headlands, extensive oceanside dunes, and verdant rolling hill country. It also has an entertaining capital city in Montevideo and the high-powered summer resort of Punta del Este.*

Darwin may have disparaged Maldonado as a place whose few residents were mostly landowners and merchants "who do all the business for nearly 50 miles around," but modern Maldonado is far better than that. In recent years, however, quite a few businesses have closed, and the city's economy is moribund compared with Punta's.

## Orientation

Punta del Este and Maldonado are about 130 kilometers east of Montevideo via Ruta I—a four-lane toll road—and Ruta 93.

Punta del Este proper occupies a compact peninsula that juts south into the Atlantic, separating the rugged surf of the Playa Brava (Wild Beach) to the east from the calmer Playa Mansa to the west. This is the point that divides the Atlantic Ocean from the Río de la Plata; in reality, Punta del Este is a much larger area that includes the departmental capital of Maldonado and a multitude of residential suburbs.

The peninsula itself divides into two separate grids: to the north, on both sides of Avenida Juan Gorlero and side streets, is the highrise hotel area with its restaurants and shopping; to the south, named for its lighthouse, the El Faro neighborhood is quieter, more residential, less pretentious, and more economical.

Punta del Este streets are commonly known by their numbers, though they also have names. Addresses below include both except in the case of Avenida Juan Gorlero, known consistently as Gorlero.

Gradually, Punta del Este and Maldonado have grown together, but the center of Maldonado is a regular colonial rectangular grid centered on Plaza San Fernando. Outside the city center, throroughfares like Avenida Roosevelt and Bulevar Artigas connect the streets of irregular suburban neighborhoods. The Rambla Claudio Williman follows the riverside beaches to the west, while the Rambla Lorenzo Batlle

Pacheco tracks along the ocean beaches. Buses along each *rambla* pick up and drop off passengers at numbered stops, known as *paradas*.

## Sights

Punta del Este is the place to go and to people-watch, but Maldonado has more historic sites.

**Punta del Este:** Avenida Juan Gorlero is Punta del Este's throbbing heart, open for business all night in summer and on weekends, but at other times it can seem positively sedate. Lively **Plaza Artigas,** fronting on Gorlero between Arrecifes (25) and El Corral (23) is the site of the a perennial crafts fair, the Feria de los Artesanos, open 6 P.M.–1 A.M. daily in summer, 11 A.M.–5 P.M. weekends only the rest of the year.

It's almost always sedate in the vicinity of the **Faro de Punta del Este** (1860), a 43-meter lighthouse built by Tomás Libarena with a crystal prism brought from France. A spiral staircase of 150 steps, not open to the public, leads to the top.

On the Playa Mansa side of the peninsula, the sheltered **Puerto Nuestra Señora de la Candelaria** has 400 slips for visiting yachts. On the Atlantic side, **Playa El Emir** is Punta's most popular surfing beach; to the north, note the **Mano de la Playa** (Hand on the Beach) by Chilean sculptor Mario Irarrázaval, who built a similar but much larger piece in the Atacama Desert.

Calmer riverside beaches stretch west along the Rambla Williman toward and beyond Punta Ballena. To the east, the Rambla Lorenzo Batlle Pacheco passes a series of beaches facing the open Atlantic. All of these have *paradores,* simple restaurants with beach service.

**Maldonado:** Remodeled in 1975 and planted with dawn redwoods, Maldonado's **Plaza San Fernando** features a statue of independence hero José Gervasio Artigas, a fountain, and a stage for musical events.

On the west side of the plaza, the neoclassical **Catedral San Fernando de Maldonado** (1895) took nearly a century to complete; Antonio Veiga sculpted its altar, while the image of the Virgen de Santander came from the steamer *Ciudad del Santander,* which sank near Isla de Lobos in 1829.

At the southwest corner of the plaza, the Spaniard Bartolomé Howel designed the **Cuartel de Dragones y de Blandengues,** a masonry military barracks with impressive iron gates, whose grounds fill an entire block bounded by 25 de Mayo, 18 de Julio, Pérez del Puerto, and Dodera. Built between 1771 and 1797, it includes the **Museo Didáctico Artiguista,** tel. 42/225378, dedicated to Uruguay's independence hero, and the fine arts **Museo Nicolás García Uriburu.** It's open 8 A.M.–6:30 P.M. daily except Monday; admission is free of charge.

Two blocks east, the **Museo San Fernando de Maldonado,** at the corner of Sarandí and Pérez del Puerto, tel. 42/231786, served as the colonial customs house and prison; it now houses a fine arts facility with rotating exhibitions, and a permanent collection of puppets from Uruguay and around the world. Hours are 1–7 P.M. daily except Monday; admission is free.

Two blocks west of the Cuartel de Dragones y de Blandengues, the **Plaza Torre del Vigía** (1800) surrounds a colonial tower built high enough to allow sentries to sight passing boats on the river.

A block north of Plaza San Fernando, better organized than in the past, the eclectic **Museo Regional R. Francisco Mazzoni,** Ituzaingó 789, tel. 42/221107, occupies an 18th-century house filled with colonial-style furnishings and natural history items. It has also added a modern art gallery in a rehabbed outbuilding. Hours are 1–6 P.M. daily except Monday; admission is free.

## Entertainment

Punta del Este has a good selection of cinemas, including the **Cine Casino 1&2,** at Gorlero and Inzaurraga (31), tel. 441908; the **Cine Fragata,** Gorlero 798, tel. 42/440002; the **Cine Gorlero,** in the Galería Libertador at Avenida Gorlero and Calle 27 (Los Muergos), tel. 42/444437; the **Cine Libertador,** in the Galería Libertador at Avenida Gorlero and Calle 25 (Los Arrecifes), tel. 42/444437; and the five-screen **Cines Lido,** at the corner of Calle 20 (El Remanso) and Calle 31 (Inzaurraga), tel. 42/440911.

**Bars: Moby Dick,** on Rambla Artigas between Virazón (12) and 2 de Febrero (10), near the yacht harbor.

## Accommodations

Accommodations are far fewer but generally cheaper in Maldonado than in Punta del Este proper; unless otherwise indicated, the lodgings below are in Punta. Rates are seasonal—January and February are the peak months—but when times are hard, prices are negotiable.

**Under US$25:** Maldonado's best bargain is **Hotel Isla de Gorriti,** Zelmar Michelini 884, tel. 42/225223, US$10 pp with shared bath.

Hostelling International has a Punta del Este affiliate at **Hostal El Castillo,** on Calle 31 (Inzaurraga) between Calle 20 (El Remanso) and Calle 18 (Baupres), tel. 09/440-9799, hostalelcastillo@hotmail.com, which charges US$10 pp for dorm-style accommodations with shared bath. Breakfast is additional.

**US$25–50:** Maldonado's new and central **Hotel Catedral,** Florida 823, tel. 42/242513, hotel_catedral@yahoo.com, charges US$20 pp for rooms with private bath, plain furnishings, heat, and ceiling fans but no a/c.

Open in summer only, **Hotel Península,** Avenida Gorlero 761, tel. 441533, fax 441813, hotpenin@adinet.com.uy, charges US$25/40 s/d.

On the north side of Plaza San Fernando in Maldonado, **Hotel Le Petit,** at the corner of Florida and Sarandí, tel. 42/223044, charges US$50 d in summer, but just US$15 pp the rest of the year.

**Hotel Marbella,** Inzaurraga (31) No. 615, tel. 42/441814, fax 442039, is a respectable middle-class hotel with reasonable comforts except for the breakfast room, which can be uncomfortably crowded even when the hotel isn't all that full. Rates are US$50 d with private bath and breakfast in the high season, but only US$15 pp off-season.

**US$50–100:** Near the lighthouse, the **Petit Hotel,** Calle 9 (La Salina) No. 717, tel. 42/441412, hotelpetit@multi.com.uy, is a budget

gem—a small, cheerful, family-run hostel with quiet, attractive gardens and other common areas. Rates start at US$35/50 s/d for good standard rooms, and rise to US$40/60 for superior rooms nearer the garden. It's an outstanding value with continental breakfast, cable TV, and telephone.

Also near the lighthouse, the architecturally utilitarian but very friendly **Atlántico Hotel,** at the corner of Calle 7 (Capitán) and Calle 10 (Dos de Febrero), tel. 42/440229, fax 42/444934, hatlanti@adinet.com.uy, charges US$30 d in the low season and US$52 d in the high season. Rates include cable TV, telephone, swimming pool, and a buffet breakfast.

The central **Hotel San Diego,** Calle 18 (Baupres) No. 919, tel. 42/440718, fax 42/440760, sandiegopuntadeleste@hotmail.com, www.visit-uruguay.com/sandiego.htm, charges US$38/55 s/d in the peak season, but US$25/40 the rest of the year, with discounts possible.

Larger than it appears from its modest streetside entrance, the **Palace Hotel,** Avenida Gorlero at the corner of Calle 11 (Solís), tel. 42/441919, fax 444695, palacepunta@hotmail.com, charges from US$35 pp with breakfast in summer, but off-season rates are only half that. Most rooms look onto the lush secluded grounds.

Surprisingly simple but attractively furnished rooms at **Hotel Champagne,** Gorlero 828, tel. 42/445276, fax 42/445278, hotelchampagne@i.com.uy, cost US$80 d in the high season.

One of the peninsula's oldest hotels, dating from 1911 but modernized in the 1980s, the **Gran Hotel España,** La Salina (9) 660, tel. 440228, fax 442054, ghespana@adinet.com.uy, www.hotelespana.com, enjoys a fine location near the lighthouse. Rates start at US$70/85 s/d.

**US$100–150:** Rates at the modern, multistory **Hotel Tanger,** on Inzaurraga (31) between Baupres (18) and El Remanso (20), tel. 42/440601, fax 42/440918, range from US$50–60 d in the low season to US$85–105 d in the high season, including breakfast. It has a pool and solarium, and the pricier suites have jacuzzis.

**Hotel San Fernando,** a modern hotel with a rooftop terrace at Las Focas (30) No. 691 between Baupres (18) and El Remanso (20), tel. 42/440720, fax 42/440721, hotelsanfernando@hotmail.com, charges US$110 d. Each of the 60 rooms has a/c, a strongbox, and other standard conveniences.

**Over US$150:** On the peninsula, the bright new **Punta del Este Golden Beach Resort & Spa,** El Mesana (24) No. 34, tel./fax 42/441314, informacion@golden-beach.com, www.golden-beach.com, is a luxury spa facility where rates start at US$157 d in summer, but off-season prices can go as low as US$70 d.

The 800-pound gorrilla of Punta del Este accommodations is **Hotel Conrad,** Rambla Williman and Avenida Chiverta, tel. 42/491111, fax 42/489999, reservations@conrad.com.uy, www.conrad.com.uy, a 302-room megahotel-casino just north of the peninsula. High-season rates start at US$300 s or d, but fall to US$220 s or d in spring and fall, and US$180 s or d in winter.

## Food

Punta del Este has a larger and more fashionable selection of restaurants than Maldonado does, but Maldonado has some excellent values.

**Punta del Este: Sumo,** on Gorlero between El Corral (23) and La Galerna (21), has Punta's finest cheap *chivitos* and other short orders. The popular *parrilla* **Martín Fierro,** at Rambla Artigas and El Foque (14), tel. 42/447100, is open in summer only. **La Pasiva,** at Gorlero and Los Meros (28), tel. 42/441843, is an inexpensive local pizzería. The reliable Argentine chain **Pizza Cero,** at La Salina (9) and 2 de Febrero (10), tel. 42/445954, is open only in summer.

**El Pobre Marino,** at Solís (11) and Virazón (12), tel. 42/443306, is a relatively inexpensive seafood choice. Other seafood choices include moderately priced **La Fragata,** Gorlero 800 at Los Muergos (27), tel. 42/440001; the Basque-style **Gure Etxe,** at Virazón (12) and La Salina (9), tel. 42/446858; the pricier **El Viejo Marino,** at Solís (11) and El Foque (14), tel. 42/443565; and the equally expensive **Mariskonea,** Resalsero (26) 650, tel. 42/440408.

**Il Baretto,** on La Salina (9) between El Trinquete (8) and 2 de Febrero (10), tel. 447243, is a moderately priced Italian restaurant with wonderful ambience, plus live jazz and other music. **La Stampa,** on El Foque (14) between Juan Díaz de Solís (11) and La Salina (9), tel. 447243, is a more upscale Italian venue.

**Blue Cheese,** at Rambla Artigas and El Corral (23), tel. 42/440354, is a well-established mid-range French restaurant. **Bungalow Suizo,** on Rambla Batlle Pacheco at Parada 8, near Avenida Roosevelt, tel. 42/482358, is a local favorite specializing in fondue at mid-range prices.

Between the peninsula and Maldonado, **La Bourgogne,** tel. 42/482007, at Pedragosa Sierra and Avenida del Mar, is a highly regarded (and expensive) French restaurant that flavors its entrées with herbs from its own gardens (the herbs themselves are also for sale here).

**Lo de Tere,** at the corner of Rambla Artigas and Calle 21 (La Galerna), tel. 42/440492, lodetere@adinet.com.uy, www.lodetere.com, is one of Punta's top international/Italian restaurants, famous for its *taglierini neri* (black pasta) with seafood. Entrées are expensive, in the US$8–10 range. So are the desserts, but don't miss the *maracuyá* (passion fruit) parfait. The budget-conscious should note that the first four parties that arrive for lunch before 1 P.M. or dinner before 9 P.M. get a 40 percent discount; all others before those hours get a 20 percent discount. There is a good tobacco-free area and outdoor seating for sunny days and warm evenings.

The Argentine ice creamery **Freddo** has a branch at Gorlero (22) and Los Muergos (27). The best in town, though, is the local outlet **Arlecchino,** on Gorlero between La Galerna (21) and Comodoro Gorlero (19).

**Maldonado: Al Paso,** 18 de Julio 888, tel.42/222881, is a well-established, reliable *parrilla,* with most entrées in the US$3–4 range except for fish dishes, which are slightly more expensive.

**Pizzería El Oasis,** Sarandí 1105, tel. 42/234794, is also popular for its *parrillada.* **Pizzería Carlitos,** Sarandí 834, tel. 42/221727, is a run-of-the-mill pizzería; **Pizza y Pasta,** Sarandí 642, is more expensive but superior in quality, diversity, and ambience, set among the pleasant gardens of the Circolo Italiano.

Try **El Grillo,** at Ituzaingó and Sarandí, for *chivitos* (steak sandwiches) and other short orders. The **Círculo Policial de Maldonado,** Pérez del Puerto 780, tel. 42/225311, has inexpensive lunch and dinner specials.

**Tasca Made in Spain,** at Ituzaingó and Dodera, tel. 42/251592, is a mostly Catalonian restaurant run by Uruguayans who spent 12 years in Catalonia and in the Canary Islands. Open for lunch and dinner, it has tasty stuffed ñoquis for US$4, fish dinners for US$6–8, and *natillas* (Spanish custard) for about US$1.50.

The relatively expensive **Mesón del Centro Español,** 18 de Julio 708, tel. 42/224107, specializes in Spanish seafood.

## Shopping

Manos del Uruguay has a leather shop on Gorlero (22) between Inzaurraga (31) and Las Focas (30) in Punta del Este. Uruguayan artists display their work at La Ciudadela, at the corner of Mareantes (13) and Virazón (12). Local artist Ignacio Zuluaga has an atelier open to the public at Capitán Miranda (7) No. 676, near the lighthouse, tel. 42/446192.

Los Patos, Sarandí 643 in Maldonado, stocks Uruguayan crafts.

## Information

Punta del Este and Maldonado each have separate tourist representatives.

**Punta del Este:** The municipal Dirección de Turismo, in the Liga de Fomento building at the corner of Baupres (18) and Inzaurraga (31), tel. 42/446510, is open 9 A.M.–9 P.M. weekdays, 9 A.M.–3 P.M. weekends. The private Liga de Fomento, tel. 42/440514, is open 8 A.M.–6 P.M. weekdays, 8 A.M.–3 P.M. weekends.

The national Ministerio de Turismo, Gorlero 942, tel. 42/441218, is open 9 A.M.–6 P.M. daily. The private Centro de Hoteles y Restoranes, on Plaza Artigas, tel. 42/440512, is open 10 A.M.–8 P.M. all year.

At the western approach to town, there's an Oficina de Informes, on Rambla Williman at Parada 24 (Las Delicias), open 8 A.M.–midnight in January and February; it closes at 8 P.M. until mid-April and at 6 P.M. the rest of the year.

The free weekly *Siempre Punta de Bolsillo* is a guide to what's going on in town, at least among the self-anointed beautiful people who dominate Punta's social scene.

**Maldonado:** For most purposes, the municipal Oficina de Información Turística, 25 de Mayo 761, tel. 42/250490, on the south side of Plaza San Fernando, is the most convenient source of information. There's also an Oficina de Informes in the Campus Municipal at Sarandí and Burnett, tel. 42/225929, comunicaciones@maldonado .com.uy, www.maldonado.gub.uy.

**Bookstore:** Punta del Este's Librería del Sol, on Las Focas (30) between Gorlero (22) and El Remanso (20) sells English-language books and magazines.

**Immigration:** The Dirección Nacional de Migraciones, in Maldonado on Ventura Alegre between Sarandí and Román Guerra, tel. 42/237624, is open 12:30–7 P.M. weekdays.

**Consulate:** Argentina operates a Punta del Este consulate at Los Arrecifes (25) No. 544, tel. 42/441632 or 440694 from mid-December to mid-March and July 2 to August 5 only. Hours are 2–9 P.M. weekdays.

**Warning:** The tap water in Punta del Este and Maldonado is truly foul-tasting. There's no evidence that it's toxic, but sticking to bottled water is a good idea.

## Services

Punta del Este and Maldonado have similar but not identical services.

**Money:** In Punta del Este, BankBoston has an ATM on Gorlero (22) between La Galerna (21) and Comodoro Gorlero (19), but there are several others. In Maldonado, Banco BBVA has an ATM on Florida, on the north side of Plaza San Fernando.

Maldonado has several exchange houses in the vicinity of Plaza San Fernando, including Cambio Porto at Florida 764, and Cambio Dominus at 25 de Mayo and 18 de Julio.

**Postal Services:** There's a Punta del Este post office on Gorlero between Izaurraga (31) and La Angostura (32). In Maldonado, the post office is on Ituzaingó between Sarandí and Román Guerra.

**Telephone and Internet:** In Punta del Este, Antel is at Arrecifes (25) and El Mesana (24). Cyber Max del Uruguay, at Gorlero (22) and Los Muergos (27), has good Internet access.

In Maldonado, Antel is at the corner of Joaquín de Viana and Florida.

**Medical:** The Hospital de Maldonado is at Ventura Alegre s/n, about eight blocks northwest of Plaza San Fernando, tel. 42/225889.

**Laundry:** In Punta del Este, Mr. Lav, on El Mesana (24) between Las Focas (30) and Las Gaviotas (29), is open 10 A.M.–6 P.M. daily.

In Maldonado, Espumas del Virrey is at Zelmar Michelini 1081, tel. 42/220582.

## Transportation

Punta del Este and Maldonado have air connections with Buenos Aires, land links with Montevideo, and bus-boat combinations as well.

**Air:** Aeropuerto Internacional Laguna del Sauce, tel. 42/559389, is about 15 kilometers west of Maldonado. There are regular shuttles to the airport from Punta del Este's bus terminal.

Aerolíneas Argentinas, in the Edificio Santos Dumont on Gorlero between Inzaurraga (31) and Las Focas (30), tel. 42/444343, flies frequently to Buenos Aires's Aeroparque. LAPA, at the same address, tel. 42/444669, also flies to Aeroparque Friday through Monday only.

Pluna, at Avenida Roosevelt and Parada 9, tel. 42/490101, flies to Aeroparque and, in summer, to several Brazilian cities.

**Bus:** Most services into Punta del Este stop over at Maldonado. Terminal Maldonado is at Avenida Roosevelt s/n, tel. 42/225701, and Terminal Punta del Este is at Playa Brava, tel. 42/488380, near the isthmus.

Several companies travel to and from Montevideo, including COT, tel. 42/225026, 42/486810; Plata, tel. 42/234733; and Copsa, tel. 42/489205.

To get around town, Maldonado Turismo, at Gorlero and Las Focas (30), (tel. 437181), links Punta del Este with the easterly suburbs of La Barra and Manantiales. Its buses leave from La Angostura behind the bus terminal.

**Boat:** Ferrytur, in the Galería Sagasti, alongside the Casino at Avenida Gorlero and Izaurraga (31), tel. 42/442820, fax 42/445312, makes bus-boat connections to Argentina.

**Rental Cars:** Rental agencies include Avis, on Inzaurraga (31) between Gorlero (22) and El Mesana (24), tel. 42/442020; Budget, Muergos (27) No. 578, tel. 42/446363; Hertz, on Inzaurraga (31) between Gorlero (22) and El Remanso (20), tel. 42/489778; and Multicar, Gorlero 860, tel. 42/443143.

# VICINITY OF PUNTA DEL ESTE AND MALDONADO

Besides water sports and sunbathing in the day and partying at night, there are a number of worthwhile sights in the vicinity of Punta del Este and Maldonado.

## Isla Gorriti

From the yacht harbor, frequent launches cross to and from Isla Gorriti, immediately west of the peninsula. In addition to its beaches and *parador* restaurants, it holds the remains of the **Baterías de Santa Ana,** a colonial Spanish fortress.

## Isla de Lobos

About eight kilometers southeast of Punta del Este, in the open Atlantic, the nearly barren 41-hectare Isla de Lobos is home to breeding colony of about 200,000 southern sea lions (*Otaria byronia*).

It was once home to the southern elephant seal (*Mirounga leonina*), but uncontrolled hunting for its blubber eliminated the species here.

Now topped by a lighthouse (1906), the rocky islet has been a tourist destination since 1920. Rising 43 meters above the ocean, the structure boasts the most powerful sea-level light in South America, with a range of 22.5 nautical miles.

Isla de Lobos played a grim historic role during the British invasion of 1806, as the British marooned Spanish prisoners here without food or water. Many died attempting to swim to the mainland.

To arrange trips to Isla de Lobos, contact Punta del Este's Unión de Lanchas, tel. 42/442594, at the harbor on the Rambla Artigas.

## Casapueblo

Punta del Este's most exceptional sight is Uruguayan painter Carlos Páez Vilaró's contemporary Casapueblo, a whimsical Mediterranean-style villa on a sloping headland at Punta Ballena, 10 kilometers to the west of Punta del Este. Lacking right angles and so blindingly white that you need sunglasses to approach it, it resembles the rounded mud nest of the *rufous hornero* (ovenbird).

A showcase for unconventional art, Casapueblo has grown over the years to include a hotel, a restaurant, and a bar. Parts are open to the public for a small charge, others to members only. Hours are 10 A.M.–6 P.M. daily.

Accommodations at **Club Hotel Casapueblo,** tel. 42/579386, fax 42/578485, www.clubhotel.com, cost US$40 pp Monday through Thursday, US$45 pp weekends and holidays, from mid-March through mid-December. Summer prices are about US$65 pp Monday through Thursday, US$73 pp weekends except between Christmas and New Year's, when they're even higher.

## La Barra de Maldonado

Until the 1940s, when the construction of summer houses began apace, La Barra de Maldonado was a modest fishing village. The undulating **Puente Leonel Viera** (1965), a bridge crossing the Arroyo de Maldonado, opened up the

Casapueblo, Punta Ballena

© WAYNE BERNHARDSON

EXCURSIONS

area east of Punta del Este to beachside development.

Conspicuous because of the kitschy great white shark at its entrance, Barra's **Museo del Mar,** just across the bridge in Barrio El Tesoro, tel. 42/771817, elmar@adinet.com.uy, http://vivapunta.com/museomar, houses an impressive collection of shells and corals. It also covers historical material on Punta del Este, including photography and information on individuals such as Juan Gorlero, the former Maldonado mayor and tourism promoter for whom Punta's main avenue is named. Hours are 10 A.M.–8:30 P.M. daily in summer, 10 A.M.–6 P.M. weekends and holidays only the rest of the year. Admission costs US$3 for adults, US$.50 for children.

The 28-room beachfront **La Posta del Cangrejo,** tel. 42/770021, fax 770173, laposta@adinet .com.uy, www.netgate.com.uy/laposta, has hosted the rich and powerful since the 1960s, when it housed Kennedy-administration officials for a legendary meeting of the Organization of American States, during which the Argentine-born Cuban delegate, Che Guevara, tweaked the officials' noses (figuratively speaking, that is). U.S. president George H. W. Bush experienced the Mediterranean elegance of La Posta del Cangrejo's suites in 1990. Rates are US$70–150 d in winter, US$200–360 d in summer. Its restaurant comes highly recommended.

## José Ignacio

Beyond La Barra, about 30 kilometers east of Punta del Este, the former fishing village of José Ignacio has become a magnet for those—like plutocrat Argentine cement heiress Amalia de Fortabat—who'd rather not advertise their presence on the Uruguayan Riviera. Fishing boats still sell the day's catch on the beach, and the most conspicuous landmark is the 32.5-meter **Faro José Ignacio** (1877), a lighthouse with a visibility of 16.5 nautical miles and a light visible for nine nautical miles.

Since 1973, the fourth-generation family-run **Santa Teresita,** Las Calandrinas s/n, tel. 486/2004, has become famous for its "gourmet home-cooking." Known as the home of the seaweed omelette, it also offers specialty appetizers such as ceviche with a dozen different dips, and entrées like *pescado a mi manera* (literally, fish my way) in the US$7–10 range, plus desserts like lemon mousse ice cream. It's open for lunch and dinner in summer, lunch only the rest of the year, and has both indoor and outdoor seating.

Repeat patrons swear that Santa Teresita is even better than celebrity restaurateur Francis Mallman's nearby and more highly publicized (and more highly priced) **Los Negros,** which uses fresh ocean fish and whose dining rooms all have ocean views.

# Resources

# Glossary

**aduana**—customs

**aduana paralela**—"parallel customs," corrupt customs officials

**albergue juvenil**—youth hostel

**albergue transitorio**—a by-the-hour-hotel, frequently used by young and not-so-young couples in search of privacy

**anexo**—telephone extension

**arbolito**—street changer, so called because they are planted in one spot

**arrabales**—geographically and socially peripheral parts of the city, identified with immigrants and the rise of the tango

**asambleas populares**—neighborhood assemblies of protestors and activists frustrated with Argentine institutions

**avenida**—avenue

**balneario**—bathing or beach resort

**baño compartido**—shared bath (in a hotel or other accommodations)

**baño general**—shared or general bath (in a hotel or other accommodations)

**baño privado**—private bath

**barras bravas**—"soccer hooligans," violent gangs affiliated with soccer teams

**barrancas**—high ground on the original banks of the Río de Plata, now far inland in San Telmo, Belgrano, and other parts of Buenos Aires because of continual landfill

**barrio**—neighborhood

**boleadoras**—rounded stones tied together with a leather thong and used for hunting by Indians of La Pampa

**bono**—bond, a provincial letter of credit serving as a parallel currency equivalent to the peso

**bronca**—a singularly *porteño* combination of aggravation and frustration; there is no precise English equivalent; the closest meaning is "wrath" or, in Britain, "aggro" (the latter according to *Buenos Aires Herald* editor Andrew Graham-Yooll)

**cabildo**—colonial governing council

**cajero automático**—automatic teller machine (ATM)

**calle**—street

**camioneta**—pickup truck

**candombe**—music and dance of Afro-Argentine *porteños,* of whom few remain

**característica**—telephone area code

**carne**—beef; other kinds of meat are *carne blanca* (literally, "white meat")

**carretera**—highway

**cartelera**—discount ticket agency

**casa chorizo**—"sausage house," a narrow residence on a deep lot

**casa de cambio**—money-exchange facility, often just "cambio"

**casco**—"big house" of an *estancia*

**casilla**—post office box

**caudillo**—in early independence times, a provincial warlord, though the term is often used for any populist leader, such as Juan Domingo Perón

**cerro**—hill

**chamamé**—accordion-based folk music of the northeastern Argentine littoral

**chopp**—draft beer

**ciruja**—literally "surgeon," a scavenger who picks recyclables from the garbage on Buenos Aires streets; synonymous with *cartonero*

**cobro revertido**—collect or reverse-charge telephone call

**cocoliche**—pidgin blend of Italian and Spanish spoken by Mediterranean European immigrants

**coima**—bribe

**colectivo**—a city bus

**comedor**—simple eatery or dining room

**confitería**—a restaurant/café with a menu of *minutas* (short orders)

**conventillo**—tenement, often an abandoned mansion taken over by squatters

**corralito**—unpopular banking restriction imposed by the Argentine government during the debt default and devaluation of 2001–2002

**costanera**—any road along a seashore, lakeshore, or riverside

**criollo**—in colonial times, an Argentine-born Spaniard; in the present, normally a descriptive term meaning "traditionally" Argentine

**desaparecido**—"disappeared one," victim of the military dictatorship of 1976–83

**descamisados**—"shirtless ones," working-class followers of Juan and Evita Perón

**dique**—deep-water basin dredged in the harbor of Buenos Aires

**doble tracción**—four-wheel drive, also known as *cuatro por cuatro* (the latter written as "4X4")

**edificio**—building

**escrache**—public demonstration, originally identifying human-rights violators at their residences, but since extended to perceived corrupt officials and institutions

**estancia**—cattle or sheep ranch controlling large expanses of land, often with an absentee owner, a dominant manager, and resident employees

**estatuas vivas**—"living statues," mimes in touristed areas of Buenos Aires

**estero**—estuary

**feria**—artisans' market

**farmacia de turno**—pharmacy remaining open all night for emergencies, on a rotating basis

**feria**—outdoor crafts or antiques fair; alternately, an outdoor bookstall

**fichas**—tokens, formerly used on the Buenos Aires subway

**filete**—traditional art of *porteño* sign painters, in a calligraphic style

**fileteador**—*filete* artist

**gasoil**—diesel fuel

**gauchesco**—adjective describing romantic art or literature about (not by) gauchos

**golfo**—gulf

**golpe de estado**—coup d'etat

**hipódromo**—horserace track

**hospedaje**—family-run lodging

**indígena**—indigenous person

**indigenista**—adjective describing romantically pro-indigenous literature, music, and art

**infracción**—traffic violation

**isla**—island

**islote**—islet

**istmo**—isthmus

**IVA**—*impuesto de valor agregado,* or value added tax (VAT)

**lago**—lake

**laguna**—lagoon

**latifundio**—large landholding, usually an *estancia*

**local**—numbered office or locale, at a given street address

**locutorio**—telephone call center

**lunfardo**—*porteño* street slang that developed in working-class immigrant barrios like La Boca but is now more widely used in Argentine Spanish, though not in formal situations

**machista**—male chauvinist

**malevo**—street bully

**media pensión**—half board (rates include breakfast and either lunch or dinner), at a hotel or guesthouse

**menú**—menu; also, a fixed-price meal

**mestizo**—individual of mixed indigenous and Spanish ancestry

**milonga**—informal neighborhood dance club, which often includes tango as a participatory rather than spectator activity

**minuta**—a short order meal such as pasta

**mirador**—overlook or viewpoint

**museo**—museum

**ñoqui**—"ghost employee," collecting a state salary despite performing little or no work; literally, "gnocchi"

**palacete**—mansion

**pampa**—broad, flat expanse in and around Buenos Aires

**pampero**—southwesterly cold front

**parada**—bus stop

**parque nacional**—national park

**paseaperros**—professional dog walker

**partido**—administrative subdivision of an Argentine province, equivalent to a county

**payador**—spontaneous gaucho singer

**peaje**—toll booth

**peatonal**—pedestrian mall

**pensión**—family-run accommodation

**pensión completa**—full board, at a hotel or guesthouse

**picante**—spicy-hot; the Argentine tolerance for spicy food is very low, however, and most visitors may find foods labeled *picante* to be relatively bland

**piquete**—protestors' roadblock

**piropo**—sexist remark, ranging from humorous and innocuous to truly vulgar; also, on *filete,* an aphorism

**playa**—beach

**polideportivo**—sports club

**porteño**—native or resident of Buenos Aires

**propina**—tip, as at a restaurant

**puente**—bridge

**puerto**—port

**Pullman**—first-class bus, with reclining seats and luggage storage underneath

**pulpería**—general store, usually in a rural area

**quinta**—country estate

**radiotaxi**—a taxi that is available by appointment rather than hailed on the street

**recargo**—surcharge on credit card purchases

**remis**—meterless *radiotaxi* charging a fixed rate within a given zone

**residencial**—permanent budget accommodations, often also called hotel

**río**—river

**rotisería**—delicatessen

**ruta**—route or highway

**saladero**—meat-salting plant of late colonial and early republican times

**s/n**—*sin número,* a street address without a number

**sudestada**—cold wind out of the southeast

**tango canción**—"tango song," with music and lyrics expressing nostalgia

**tanguero**—tango dancer

**tarifa mostrador**—hotel rack rate

**tenedor libre**—literally "free fork," all-you-can-eat restaurant

**toldo**—tent of animal skins, inhabited by mobile Indians of the pampas in pre-Columbian times

**turco**—Argentine of Middle Eastern descent (literally, "Turk")

**trasnoche**—late-night cinema showing

**trucho**—bogus

**villa miseria**—urban shantytown

**viveza criolla**—"artful deception," ranging from small-scale cheating to audacious chutzpah

# Spanish Phrasebook

Spanish is Argentina's official language, but the stereotypical *porteño* intonation—equivalent to a Bronx accent in New York—is unmistakably different from any other Spanish accent. Argentine Spanish in general is distinctive, often Italian-inflected, most notable for pronouncing the "ll" diphthong and the "y" as "zh." *Llegar* (to arrive), for example, is pronounced "zhe-gar," while *yo* (I) is pronounced "zho."

Another distinguishing feature is the use of the familiar pronoun *vos* instead of *tú*. Verb forms of the *voseo* (use of *vos*) differ from those of the *tuteo* (use of *tú*), although Argentines will always understand speakers who use *tú*.

At tourist offices, airlines, travel agencies, and upscale hotels, English is often spoken. In the provinces, it's less common, though its use is spreading, especially in the travel and tourism sector.

Visitors (especially students and business people) who spend any length of time in Buenos Aires should look for Tino Rodríguez's *Primer Diccionario de Sinónimos del Lunfardo* (Buenos Aires: Editorial Atlántida, 1987), which defines *porteño* street slang—some of its usage requires *great* caution for those unaware of the words' every meaning.

## Pronunciation Guide

Spanish is a more phonetic language than English, but there are still occasional variations in pronunciation, especially in Argentina.

### Consonants

**c**—like the *c* in "cat" when before an *a, o,* or *u*; like *s* when before *e* or *i*

**d**—as *d* in "dog," except between vowels, then like *th* in "that"

**g**—before *e* or *i,* like the *ch* in Scottish "loch"; elsewhere like *g* in "get"

**h**—always silent

**j**—like the English *h* in "hotel," but stronger

**ll**—like the *z* in "azure"

**ñ**—like the *ni* in "onion"

**r**—always pronounced as strong *r*

**rr**—trilled *r*

**v**—similar to the *b* in "boy" (not as English *v*)

**y**—like *ll,* it sounds like the *z* in "azure." When standing alone, it's pronounced like the *e* in "me."

**z**—like *s* in "same"

**b, f, k, l, m, n, p, q, s, t, w, x**—as in English

### Vowels

**a**—as in "father," but shorter

**e**—as in "hen"

**i**—as in "machine"

**o**—as in "phone"

**u**—usually as in "rule"; when it follows a *q* the *u is silent; when it follows an h* or *g,* it's pronounced like *w,* except when it comes between *g* and *e* or *i,* when it's also silent (unless it has an umlaut, when it again is pronounced as English *w*).

Native English speakers frequently make errors of pronunciation by ignoring stress—all Spanish vowels (a, e, i, o, and u) may carry accents that determine which syllable of a word gets emphasis. Often, stress seems unnatural to nonnative speakers—the surname Chávez, for instance, is stressed on the first syllable—but failure to observe this rule may mean that native speakers do not understand you.

## Numbers

0—cero

1—uno (masculine)

1—una (feminine)

2—dos

3—tres

4—cuatro

5—cinco

6—seis

7—siete

8—ocho

9—nueve

10—diez
11—once
12—doce
13—trece
14—catorce
15—quince
16—diez y seis
17—diez y siete
18—diez y ocho
19—diez y nueve
20—veinte
21—veinte y uno
30—treinta
40—cuarenta
50—cincuenta
60—sesenta
70—setenta
80—ochenta
90—noventa
100—cien
101—ciento y uno
200—doscientos
1,000—mil
10,000—diez mil
1,000,000—un millón

## Days of the Week

Sunday—domingo
Monday—lunes
Tuesday—martes
Wednesday—miércoles
Thursday—jueves
Friday—viernes
Saturday—sábado

## Time

Argentines normally use the 12-hour clock (A.M. and P.M.), but they sometimes use the 24-hour clock, especially for plane and bus schedules. Under the 24-hour clock, *las diez de la noche* (10 P.M.) would be *las 22 horas* (2100 hours).

What time is it?—¿Qué hora es?
It's one o'clock.—Es la una.
It's two o'clock.—Son las dos.
At two o'clock.—A las dos.
It's ten minutes to three.—Son tres menos diez.

It's ten minutes past three.—Son tres y diez.
It's 3:15 (or a quarter after three).—Son las tres y cuarto.
It's 2:30.—Son las dos y media.
It's 2:45 (or a quarter 'til three).—Son las tres menos cuarto.
It's six A.M.—Son las seis de la mañana.
It's six P.M.—Son las seis de la tarde.
It's ten P.M.—Son las diez de la noche.
Today—hoy
Tomorrow—mañana
Morning—la mañana
Tomorrow morning—mañana por la mañana
Yesterday—ayer
Week—la semana
Month—mes
Year—año
Last night—anoche
The next day—el día siguiente

## Useful Words and Phrases

Argentines and other Spanish-speaking people consider formalities important. Whenever approaching anyone to ask information or for some other reason, use the appropriate salutation—good morning, good evening, etc. Standing alone, the greeting *hola* (hello) can sound brusque.

Note that most of the words below are fairly standard, common to all Spanish-speaking countries. Many, however, have a more idiomatic Argentine equivalent; refer to the glossary for these.

Hello.—Hola.
Good morning.—Buenos días.
Good afternoon.—Buenas tardes.
Good evening.—Buenas noches.
How are you?—¿Cómo está?
Fine.—Muy bien.
And you?—¿Y usted?
So-so.—Más o menos.
Thank you.—Gracias.
Thank you very much.—Muchas gracias.
You're very kind.—Muy amable.
You're welcome.—De nada (literally, "It's nothing").
Yes—sí

No—no
I don't know.—No sé.
It's fine; okay—Está bien.
Good; okay—Bueno.
Please—por favor
Pleased to meet you.—Mucho gusto.
Excuse me (physical)—Perdóneme.
Excuse me (speech)—Discúlpeme.
I'm sorry.—Lo siento.
Goodbye—adiós
See you later—hasta luego (literally, "until later")
More—más
Less—menos
Better—mejor
Much; a lot—mucho
A little—un poco
Large—grande
Small—pequeño; chico
Quick; fast—rápido
Slow—despacio
Bad—malo
Difficult—difícil
Easy—fácil
He/She/It is gone (as in "She left" and
    "He's gone").—Ya se fue.
I don't speak Spanish well.—No hablo bien el
    español.
I don't understand.—No entiendo.
How do you say . . . in Spanish?—
    ¿Cómo se dice . . . en español?
Do you understand English?—
    ¿Entiende el inglés?
Is English spoken here? (Does anyone here
    speak English?)—¿Se habla inglés aquí?

## Terms of Address

When in doubt, use the formal *usted* (you) as a
form of address. If you wish to dispense with
formality and feel that the desire is mutual, you
can say *Me podés tutear* (you can call me "tú")
even though Argentines use the slightly different
verb forms that correlate with the familiar pronoun *vos.*

I—yo
You (formal)—usted
you (familiar)—vos; tú

He/him—él
She/her—ella
We/us—nosotros
You (plural)—ustedes
They/them (all males or mixed gender)—ellos
They/them (all females)—ellas
Mr.; sir—señor
Mrs.; madam—señora
Miss; young lady—señorita
Wife—esposa
Husband—marido or esposo
Friend—amigo (male); amiga (female)
Sweetheart—novio (male); novia (female)
Son; daughter—hijo; hija
Brother; sister—hermano; hermana
Father; mother—padre; madre
Grandfather; grandmother—abuelo; abuela

## Getting Around

Where is . . . ?—¿Dónde está . . . ?
How far is it to . . . ?—¿A cuanto está . . . ?
from . . . to . . .—de . . . a . . .
Highway—la carretera
Road—el camino
Street—la calle
Block—la cuadra
Kilometer—kilómetro
North—norte
South—sur
West—oeste; poniente
East—este; oriente
Straight ahead—al derecho; adelante
To the right—a la derecha
To the left—a la izquierda

## Accommodations

Is there a room?—¿Hay habitación?
May I (we) see it?—¿Puedo (podemos) verla?
What is the rate?—¿Cuál es el precio?
Is that your best rate?—¿Es su mejor precio?
Is there something less expensive?—¿Hay algo
más económico?
Single room—un sencillo
Double room—un doble
Room for a couple—matrimonial
Key—llave
With private bath—con baño privado

With shared bath—con baño general; con baño compartido
Hot water—agua caliente
Cold water—agua fría
Shower—ducha
Electric shower—Ducha eléctrica
Towel—toalla
Soap—jabón
Toilet paper—papel higiénico
Air-conditioning—aire acondicionado
Heating—calefacción
Fan—ventilador
Blanket—frazada; manta
Sheets—sábanas

## Public Transport

Bus—el autobús
Bus stop—la parada
Bus terminal—terminal de buses
Airport—el aeropuerto
Launch—lancha
Dock—muelle
I want a ticket to . . .—Quiero un pasaje a . . .
I want to get off at . . .—Quiero bajar en . . .
Here, please.—Aquí, por favor.
Where is this bus going?—¿Adónde va este autobús?
Roundtrip—ida y vuelta
What do I owe?—¿Cuánto le debo?

## Food

Food—comida
Menu—la carta; el menú
Glass—taza
Fork—tenedor
Knife—cuchillo
Spoon—cuchara
Napkin—servilleta
Soft drink—gaseosa
Coffee—café
Cream—crema
Tea—té
Sugar—azúcar
Drinking water—agua pura, agua potable
Bottled carbonated water—agua mineral con gas
Bottled uncarbonated water—agua sin gas

Beer—cerveza
Wine—vino
Milk—leche
Juice—jugo
Eggs—huevos
Bread—pan
Watermelon—sandía
Banana—banana
Apple—manzana
Orange—naranja
Peach—durazno
Pineapple—ananá
Meat (without)—carne (sin)
Beef—carne de res
Chicken—pollo; gallina
Fish—pescado
Shellfish—mariscos
Shrimp—camarones
Fried—frito
Roasted—asado
Barbecued—a la parrilla
Breakfast—desayuno
Lunch—almuerzo
Dinner; a late-night snack—cena
The check or bill—la cuenta

## Making Purchases

I need . . .—Necesito . . .
I want . . .—Deseo . . . or Quiero . . .
I would like . . . (more polite)—Quisiera . . .
How much does it cost?—¿Cuánto cuesta?
What's the exchange rate?—¿Cuál es el tipo de cambio?
May I see . . . ?—¿Puedo ver . . . ?
This one—ésta/ésto
Expensive—caro
Inexpensive—barato
More inexpensive—más barato
Too much—demasiado

## Health

Help me, please.—Ayúdeme, por favor.
I am ill.—Estoy enfermo.
It hurts.—Me duele.
Pain—dolor
Fever—fiebre

Stomach ache—dolor de estómago
Vomiting—vomitar
Diarrhea—diarrea
Drugstore—farmacia

Medicine—medicina
Pill; tablet—pastilla
Birth-control pills—pastillas anticonceptivas
Condom—condón; preservativo

# Suggested Reading

## ARCHAEOLOGY, ETHNOGRAPHY, AND ETHNOHISTORY

Schávelzon, Daniel. *Historia del Comer y del Beber en Buenos Aires.* Buenos Aires: Aguilar, 2000. Urban archaeologist Schávelzon chronicles the evolution of the *porteño* diet through salvage excavations in the city, finding among other surprises, that beef consumption was not always so great as some have assumed.

## GUIDEBOOKS AND TRAVELOGUES

Darwin, Charles. *Voyage of the Beagle* (many editions). Perhaps the greatest travel book ever written, Darwin's narrative of his 19th-century journey is filled with insights on the people, places, and even politics he saw while collecting the plants and animals that led to his revolutionary theories. The great scientist observed the city of Buenos Aires, the surrounding pampas and parts of neighboring Uruguay, and met key figures in the country's history, including the dictator Rosas.

France, Miranda. *Bad Times in Buenos Aires.* Hopewell, NJ: Ecco Press, 1998. A timeless title, perhaps, but it refers to the author's sardonic analysis of her experiences of the early 1990s.

Green, Toby. *Saddled with Darwin.* London: Phoenix, 1999. An audacious if uneven account by a young, talented writer of his attempt to retrace the hoofprints—not the footsteps—of Darwin's travels through Uruguay, Argentina, and Chile. Self-effacing but still serious, the author manages to compare Darwin's experience with his own, reflect on contemporary distortions of the great

scientist's theories, and stay almost completely off the gringo trail.

Guevara, Ernesto. *The Motorcycle Diaries: A Journey around South America.* New York and London: Verso, 1995. Translated by Ann Wright, this is an account of an Argentine drifter's progress from Buenos Aires across the Andes and up the Chilean coast by motorcycle and, when it broke down, by any means necessary. The author is better known by his nickname "Che," a common Argentine interjection.

Head, Francis Bond. *Journeys across the Pampas & among the Andes.* Carbondale, IL: Southern Illinois University Press, 1967. Nearly a decade before Darwin, "Galloping Head" rode across the Argentine plains and over the Andes into Chile in the early years of Argentine independence. Originally published in 1826, some of Head's observations on the gaucho's abilities and adaptability resemble Darwin's, but Head detested Buenos Aires itself.

Naipaul, V.S. *The Return of Eva Perón.* New York: Knopf, 1980. The great but controversial British Nobel Prize–winning author's acerbic observations on Argentine society, in the context of his visit during the vicious dictatorship of 1976–83.

Petrina, Alberto, ed. *Buenos Aires: Guía de Arquitectura.* Buenos Aires and Seville: Municipalidad de la Ciudad de Buenos Aires and Junta de Andalucía, 1994. An outstanding architectural guide with eight walking tours of the city, embellished with architectural sketches and photographs.

Symmes, Patrick. *Chasing Che: A Motorcycle Journey in Search of the Guevara Legend.* New York: Vintage, 2000. Symmes follows the tire marks of Che's legendary trip from Buenos Aires through Argentina and Chile in the early 1950s.

## HISTORY

Andrews, George Reid. *The Afro-Argentines of Buenos Aires, 1800–1900.* Madison: University of Wisconsin Press, 1980. Groundbreaking research on the supposed disappearance of the capital's Afro-Argentine community, which once comprised nearly a third of its total population.

Crow, John A. *The Epic of Latin America,* 3rd ed. Berkeley: University of California Press, 1980. A comprehensive history of the region, told more through narrative than analysis, in an immensely readable manner. Several chapters deal with Argentina.

Cutolo, Vicente Osvaldo. *Buenos Aires: Historia de las Calles y Sus Nombres.* Buenos Aires: Editorial Elche, 1988. This weighty two-volume set details the history not just of nearly every street in the city, but also the stories behind the street names.

Dujovne Ortiz, Alicia. *Eva Perón.* New York: St. Martin's Press, 1996. Filled with controversial assertions, this nevertheless absorbing biography is at its most eloquent in describing the transformation of a poor provincial girl into a powerful international figure through a relentless and bitterly ruthless ambition blended with a genuine concern for the truly destitute. Shawn Fields's translation to English, unfortunately, is awkward.

Goñi, Uki. *The Real Odessa.* New York and London: Granta, 2002. Remarkable account of the controversial links between the Juan Perón government and the shadowy organization that spirited Nazi war criminals from Europe to Argentina. Employing a variety of archival sources on a topic that most often relies on rumor, Goñi implicates the Vatican and its Argentine branch as go-betweens in negotiations with the remains of the Nazi regime.

Guy, Donna J. *Sex and Danger in Buenos Aires.* Lincoln: University of Nebraska Press, 1991. An academic account of the seamier side of immigration, relating it to sexual imbalance in the population, homosexuality, prostitution, the rise of the tango, and even Peronism.

Lynch, John. *Spanish-American Revolutions, 1808–1826,* 2nd ed. New York: W. W. Norton, 1986. Comprehensive account of the independence movements in Spanish America.

Moya, José C. *Cousins and Strangers: Spanish Immigrants in Buenos Aires, 1850–1930.* Berkeley: University of California Press, 1998. An account of the capital's and the country's ambivalent relationship with immigrants often disparaged as *Gallegos* (Galicians).

Parry, J. H. *The Discovery of South America.* London: Paul Elek, 1979. Well-illustrated history of early voyages and overland explorations on the continent.

Rock, David. *Argentina 1516–1987: From Spanish Colonization to the Falklands War and Alfonsín.* London: I.B. Taurus, 1987. Comprehensive narrative and analysis of Argentine history prior to the presidency of Carlos Menem.

Rock, David. *Authoritarian Argentina: The Nationalist Movement, Its History and Its Impact.* Berkeley: University of California Press, 1993. Building on the author's earlier work, Rock examines the durability of right-wing nationalism that led to the 1976–83 "Dirty War," even as comparable nationalist governments were failing in Spain, Portugal, Mexico, and other countries.

Scobie, James R. *Buenos Aires: From Plaza to Suburb, 1870–1910.* New York: Oxford University Press, 1974. Classic account of the city's explosive growth of the late 19th century, and the transition from "Gran Aldea" to "Paris of the South."

Shumway, Norman. *The Invention of Argentina.* Berkeley: University of California Press, 1991. An intellectual history of Argentina's founding myths, and the degree to which elitist debate excluded entire sectors of society from participation and resulted in frequent ungovernability.

Slatta, Richard. *Cowboys of the Americas.* New Haven and London: Yale University Press, 1990. Spectacularly illustrated comparative account of New World horsemen, including both Argentine gauchos and Chilean *huasos*.

Vidal, Emeric Essex. *Buenos Aires and Montevideo in a Series of Picturesque Illustrations Taken on the Spot.* Buenos Aires: Mitchell's English Book-Store, 1944. Originally published in London in 1820, this British naval officer's remarkable travelogue literally paints a picture—with full-color illustrations to complement his text descriptions—of Buenos Aires in the early independence years.

## GOVERNMENT AND POLITICS

Castañeda, Jorge G. *Utopia Unarmed: The Latin American Left After the Cold War.* New York: Knopf, 1993. A former academic, now Mexico's foreign minister, makes Argentina the starting point in his analysis of the democratization of Latin America's revolutionary left, with a particularly good analysis of the Montoneros urban guerrilla movement.

Caviedes, César. *The Southern Cone: Realities of the Authoritarian State.* Totowa, NJ: Rowman & Allanheld, 1984. Comparative study of the military dictatorships of Chile, Argentina, Uruguay, and Brazil of the 1970s and 1980s.

Verbitsky, Horacio. *The Flight: Confessions of an Argentine Dirty Warrior.* New York: The New

Press, 1996. Account of the worst excesses of the military dictatorship of 1976–83, based on interviews with Francisco Scilingo, a self-confessed torturer and murderer who shoved political prisoners out of airplanes over the South Atlantic. Scilingo was the first Argentine military officer to break the silence over human-rights violations.

## LITERATURE AND LITERARY CRITICISM

For more suggestions on Argentine literature, see the Literature section in the Arts and Entertainment chapter.

Martínez, Tomás Eloy. *The Perón Novel.* New York: Pantheon Books, 1988. Based on the author's own lengthy interviews with the exiled caudillo, for which fiction seemed the appropriate outlet. According to Jorge Castañeda, "Whether Perón ever actually uttered these words is in the last analysis irrelevant: he could have, he would have, and he probably did."

Martínez, Tomás Eloy. *Santa Evita.* New York: Knopf, 1996. One of Argentina's leading contemporary writers tackles the Evita myth in a fictional version of her post-mortem odyssey from Argentina to Italy, Spain, and back to Buenos Aires.

Meyer, Doris. *Victoria Ocampo: Against the Wind and the Tide.* Austin: University of Texas Press, 1990. Biography of the woman who led the Argentine equivalent of Britain's Bloomsbury Group, through her literary magazine *Sur* and friendships with Jorge Luis Borges, Adolfo Bioy Casares (married to her sister Silvina, also a writer), and international figures such as Andre Malraux, José Ortega y Gasset, and Rabindranath Tagore. The volume includes 15 of Victoria's own essays.

Wilson, Jason. *Buenos Aires: A Cultural and Literary Companion.* New York: Interlink, 2000.

Part of the Cities of the Imagination series, this is a breathlessly thorough summary of what *porteño* authors as well as other Argentine and foreign authors have written about the Argentine capital. It's particularly good at providing a sense of what untranslated Argentine authors have written about the city.

Wilson, Jason. *Traveller's Literary Companion: South & Central America, Including Mexico.* Lincolnwood, IL: Passport Books, 1995. An edited collection of excerpts from literature—including fiction, poetry, and essays—that illuminates aspects of the countries from the Río Grande to the tip of Tierra del Fuego, including Argentina (Buenos Aires in particular) and Uruguay.

Woodall, James. *Borges: A Life.* New York: Basic Books, 1997. An analytical—in the Freudian sense—biography of Argentina's most prominent literary figure. Originally appeared in Britain under the title *The Man in the Mirror of the Book* (London: Hodder & Stoughton, 1996).

## ENVIRONMENT AND NATURAL HISTORY

Hudson, William Henry. *The Bird Biographies of W.H. Hudson.* Santa Barbara, CA: Capra Press, 1988. A partial reprint of the romantic naturalist's detailed description of the birds he knew growing up in Buenos Aires province, with illustrations.

# Internet Resources

The following list of general-interest sites does not include private tour operators (which are covered in the Travel Basics chapter), museums (covered in detail in the Sights chapter), or services like hotels and restaurants (covered in the Accommodations and Food and Drink chapters).

**Aerolíneas Argentinas**
**www.aerolineas.com.ar**
This is the homepage for Argentina's struggling flagship airline.

**Aeropuertos Argentinos 2000**
**www.aa2000.com.ar**
The site for the private concessionaire operating most of Argentina's international and domestic airports, including Buenos Aires' Ezeiza and Aeroparque. In English and Spanish.

**Ambitoweb**
**www.ambitoweb.com**
Online version of *porteño* financial daily *Ambito Financiero.*

**AmeriSpan**
**www.amerispan.com**
Information on language instruction throughout the Americas, including Argentina.

**Apertura**
**www.apertura.com**
Business-oriented Buenos Aires magazine.

**Argentina Business**
**www.invertir.com/index.html**
Guide to business and investment in Argentina.

**Argentina Travel Net**
**www.argentinatravelnet.com**
Portal for Argentine travel sites, though not nearly all of the links are closely related to travel. In Spanish and English.

**Asociación Argentina de Albergues de la Juventud (AAAJ)**
**www.hostelling-aaaj.org.ar**
Argentine hostelling organization, with a limited number of facilities throughout the country.

**Asociación de Alberguistas del Uruguay**
**www.internet.com.uy/aau/esp/aau00m1.htm**
Uruguayan Hostelling International affiliate, with a wide network of hostels around the country.

**Asociación de Fútbol Argentina**
**www.afa.org.ar**
Argentina's professional soccer league. In English and Spanish.

**Asociación Ornitológica del Plata**
**www.avesargentinas.org.ar**
Buenos Aires–based bird-watching and conservation organization.

**Automóvil Club Argentino (ACA)**
**www.aca.org.ar**
Argentine automobile association, useful for information and up-to-date road maps. Offers discounts for members of affiliated clubs, such as AAA in the United States and the AA in Britain.

**B y T Argentina**
**www.bytargentina.com/ecentro.htm**
Short-term apartment rentals and other information on Buenos Aires, in English and Spanish.

**Buenos Aires Herald**
**www.buenosairesherald.com**
Abbreviated version of the capital's venerable English-language daily, recently relaunched and improved.

## Caballito
**http://caballitoenlinea.com.ar**

Portal website to an interesting but little-touristed residential barrio.

## Centers for Disease Control
**www.cdc.gov**

U.S. government page with travel health advisories.

## CIA Factbook
**www.odci.gov/cia/publications/factbook /geos/ar.html**

The world's most notorious organization of spooks offers a handy public service in its annual encyclopedia of the world's countries, which appears in its entirety online.

## Ciudad Autónoma de Buenos Aires
**www.buenosaires.gov.ar**

Comprehensive city-government site, which includes tourist information, in Spanish only.

## Clarín
**www.clarin.com**

Outstanding online version of the capital's tabloid daily, the largest circulation newspaper in the Spanish-speaking world.

## Country Commercial Guide
**www.usatrade.gov/website/CCG.nsf**

U.S. State Department detailed summary of business climate and possibilities in Argentina and other foreign countries.

## Currency Converter
**www.oanda.com**

Present and historic exchange-rate information.

## Department of Health
**www.doh.gov.uk/traveladvice/index.htm**

British government agency with country-by-country health advice.

## Department of State
**www.travel.state.gov**

Travel information and advisories from the U.S. government; its warnings err on the side of extreme caution.

## Dirección General de Patrimonio
**www.dgpatrimonio.buenosaires.gov.ar**

Within the city-government site, this separate page is a comprehensive guide to historical resources, both archaeological and contemporary.

## Dirección Provincial de Turismo
**www.vivalaspampas.com**

Buenos Aires provincial tourism office, based in the capital city of La Plata.

## Feria del Libro
**www.el-libro.com/index.html**

Buenos Aires's heavily attended annual book fair.

## Festival del Tango
**www.festivaldeltango.com**

Information on the capital's increasingly popular series of autumn (March through April) tango events.

## Fondo Nacional de las Artes
**www.fnartes.gov.ar**

Official federal government site with information on performing arts, architecture, cinema, and related fields.

## Gay in Buenos Aires
**www.gayinbuenosaires.com.ar**

Portal to articles and services of interest to homosexual residents and visitors.

## Grippo
**www.grippo.com.ar**

Argentine-oriented Internet directory, with a large assortment of links.

## Hostelling International Argentina
**www.hostels.org.ar**

Argentine Hostelling International affiliate, with information on travel and activities throughout the country.

**Instituto Geográfico Militar**
www.igm.gov.ar
Military geographical institute, preparing and selling maps of the country.

**Instituto Nacional de Estadísticas y Censos (INDEC)**
www.indec.mecon.ar
Home page for federal government statistical agency.

**La Maga**
www.lamaga.com.ar
Website of the arts- and literature-oriented magazine.

**La Nación**
www.lanacion.com.ar
Major *porteño* daily, with an excellent Sunday cultural section.

**La Plata**
www.laplata.gov.ar/index.htm
Portal website of the capital city of Buenos Aires province.

**Latin American Network Information Center (LANIC)**
http://lanic.utexas.edu
Organized by the University of Texas, this site has a huge collection of quality links to Argentina and other Latin American countries.

**Lujanet**
www.lujanet.com.ar
Portal for Luján, the historical and pilgrimage center of Buenos Aires province.

**Mercado**
www.mercado.com.ar
Business-oriented Buenos Aires weekly magazine.

**Mercopress News Agency**
www.falkland-malvinas.com
Montevideo-based Internet news agency covering politics and business in the Mercosur common market countries of Argentina, Brazil, Uruguay, and Paraguay, as well as Chile and the Falkland/Malvinas Islands. In English and Spanish.

**Metrovías**
www.metrovias.com.ar
Details on Buenos Aires's subway system.

**Ministerio de Relaciones Exteriores**
www.mrecic.gov.ar/consulares/pagcon.html
Argentine foreign ministry, with information on visas and consulates, in English and Spanish.

**Negocios**
www.negocios.com.ar
Business-oriented Buenos Aires magazine.

**Páginas Amarillas**
www.paginasamarillas.com.ar
Yellow Pages for the entire country.

**Página 12**
www.pagina12.com
Outspoken left-of-center daily which has shifted away from reporting and toward opinion, but features some of the country's best writers.

**PalermOnline**
www.palermonline.com.ar
Portal to sights and services in one of the city's liveliest barrios, Palermo.

**Puerto de Tigre**
www.puertodetigre.com
The suburban gateway to the popular Paraná delta.

**San Antonio de Areco**
www.arecoturismo.com.ar
The country's symbolic gaucho capital, in Buenos Aires province.

**Secretaría Nacional de Turismo**
www.turismo.gov.ar
National tourism authority, with information in Spanish and English.

**Trespuntos**

**www.3puntos.com/index.php3**

Investigative weekly newsmagazine.

**UkiNet**

**www.ukinet.com**

Freelance writer Uki Goñi's human-rights-oriented website, with an archive of his best work from Britain's *Guardian* and other sources.

## Usenet Discussion Groups

**Soc.culture.argentina**

No-holds-barred discussion group that touches on many issues besides travel.

**Rec.travel.latin-america**

Regional discussion group dealing with all Latin American countries, with a steady number of postings on Argentina.

# Index

Index

M
Index

Index

Index

# U.S.~Metric Conversion

1 inch = 2.54 centimeters (cm)
1 foot = .304 meters (m)
1 yard = 0.914 meters
1 mile = 1.6093 kilometers (km)
1 km = .6214 miles
1 fathom = 1.8288 m
1 chain = 20.1168 m
1 furlong = 201.168 m
1 acre = .4047 hectares
1 sq km = 100 hectares
1 sq mile = 2.59 square km
1 ounce = 28.35 grams
1 pound = .4536 kilograms
1 short ton = .90718 metric ton
1 short ton = 2000 pounds
1 long ton = 1.016 metric tons
1 long ton = 2240 pounds
1 metric ton = 1000 kilograms
1 quart = .94635 liters
1 US gallon = 3.7854 liters
1 Imperial gallon = 4.5459 liters
1 nautical mile = 1.852 km

To compute Celsius temperatures, subtract 32 from Fahrenheit and divide by 1.8. To go the other way, multiply Celsius by 1.8 and add 32.

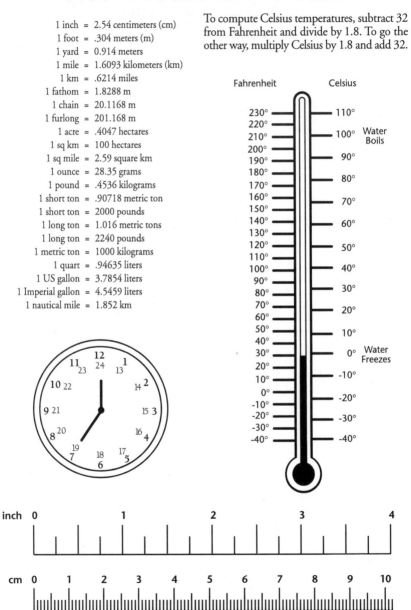

# Acknowledgments

Similar to my efforts in writing about Guatemala and Chile, this book owes its existence in its present form to numerous individuals in North America, Argentina, and elsewhere. Once again, the highest praise to Bill Newlin and his Emeryville staff at Avalon Travel Publishing for continuing to offer author-friendly contracts to writers even as other guidebook publishers are ruthlessly eliminating them.

In the course of more than 20 years' experience in Argentina and Buenos Aires, nearly half that as a guidebook writer, I owe enormous unpayable debts to friends, acquaintances, and officials throughout the country. My apologies to anyone I may have overlooked or perhaps omitted because of an errant keystroke.

In Buenos Aires and vicinity, thanks to Diego Allolio; Joaquín Allolio; Mario Banchik of Librerías Turísticas; Mirta S. Capurro of the municipal Subsecretaría de Turismo; Diego Curubeto; Juan Carlos Dasque; Jorge Helft, and Marion Eppinger for keeping me up-to-date on Argentine art; Alberto Fernández Basavilbaso of the Ministerio de Relaciones Exteriores; Pablo Fisch, Silvina Garay, and Martín Chaves of Asatej; Rafael Amadeo Gentili; Josh Goodman; Andrew Graham-Yooll and Derek Foster of the *Buenos Aires Herald;* Harry S. Ingham; Juan Massolo; Manuel Massolo; Dori Lieberman; Pablo Blay and Mariana Travacio; Ernesto Semán; Marta S. Tejedor; and Cristián Soler of Tigre.

In Montevideo, special mention to Fernando Assunçao of the Museo del Gaucho y de la Moneda; Hugo García Robles; Manuel Pérez Bravo of Hotel Mediterráneo; Andrés Linardi of Librería Linardi y Risso; and José García Briones of Hotel Solís.

Stateside, thanks to Leandro Fernández Suárez of the Argentine consulate in Los Angeles; Patricio Rubalcaba and Misty Pinson of LanChile, Miami; Pete Gold of American Airlines in San Francisco; and Cristina Castro of American Airlines in Dallas. A special mention goes to Diana Page, now at the U.S. Embassy in Mexico City.

And finally, thanks to my wife María Laura Massolo; my daughter Clio Bernhardson-Massolo; my Alaskan Malamute Gardel, who slept at my feet through most of the process of writing this up, while patiently awaiting his next walk around the neighborhood; and Gardel's adopted Akita brother Sandro, who reminds me when I need to take a nap.

PERU

ECUADOR

CHILE

BOLIVIA

BRAZIL

ARGENTINA

# EXPLORING THE *South* OF THE WORLD

### INTRODUCING LANCHILE VACATIONS
*Uniquely Customized Land Adventures*

LanChile now offers **LanChile Vacations**, an array of customized packages for a complete travel experience. You can create a vacation tailored exactly to your clients' specifications, whether they are traveling alone or in a small group, and whether they choose from the modules outlined in our programs, or create a unique itinerary crafted around their individual interests and desire for adventure. So while your clients enjoy unforgettable cultural and natural adventures, you can relax knowing they will experience travel in its most perfect form. LanChile's 72 years of travel expertise will stand behind your clients every step of the way. Enjoy the complete experience of travel with **LanChile Vacations**.

*All LanChile Vacations are commissionable.*

For reservations and information, please call LanChile Vacations
at 1-877-219-0345 or visit us at www.lanchilevacations.com